ISBN 978-0-282-00897-0
PIBN 10840254

1 MONTH OF
FREE
READING

at

www.ForgottenBooks.com

By purchasing this book you are eligible for one month membership to ForgottenBooks.com, giving you unlimited access to our entire collection of over 1,000,000 titles via our web site and mobile apps.

To claim your free month visit:

www.forgottenbooks.com/free840254

English
Français
Deutsche
Italiano
Español
Português

www.forgottenbooks.com

Mythology Photography **Fiction**
Fishing Christianity **Art** Cooking
Essays Buddhism Freemasonry
Medicine **Biology** Music **Ancient**
Egypt Evolution Carpentry Physics
Dance Geology **Mathematics** Fitness
Shakespeare **Folklore** Yoga Marketing
Confidence Immortality Biographies
Poetry **Psychology** Witchcraft
Electronics Chemistry History **Law**
Accounting **Philosophy** Anthropology
Alchemy Drama Quantum Mechanics
Atheism Sexual Health **Ancient History**
Entrepreneurship Languages Sport
Paleontology Needlework Islam
Metaphysics Investment Archaeology
Parenting Statistics Criminology
Motivational

THEATRICAL BIOGRAPHY:

OR,

THE LIFE OF

AN ACTOR AND MANAGER.

INTERSPERSED WITH SKETCHES, ANECDOTES, AND
OPINIONS OF THE PROFESSIONAL MERITS OF
THE MOST CELEBRATED ACTORS AND
ACTRESSES OF OUR DAY.

BY

FRANCIS COURTNEY WEMYSS.

———

" Vanitas vanitatis, et omnia, vanitas !"

———

GLASGOW:

PUBLISHED BY R. GRIFFIN & Co.

———

MDCCCXLVIII.

PREFACE.

HAVING been frequently asked to commit to paper the varied scenes of an Actor's Life, in which I have been engaged, I have commenced, partly from memoranda made at various periods, the present journal. If any amusement may be derived from such a source, reader, it is at your service; but should the frequent occurrence of the personal *I*, disgust you, lay down the book. If you travel through it — spare its faults — under the assurance of its veracity. Wherever a change of opinion has taken place it is faithfully chronicled, without reference to the first impression, which remains as it first struck the author, thus endeavouring to do full justice to my professional brethren.

THE AUTHOR.

LIFE OF

AN ACTOR AND MANAGER.

CHAPTER I.

Birth. Parentage. Education. High School of Edinburgh. Early Pursuits. Private Theatricals. First Appearance in Public. Strolling Actors. Wise Reflections. Theory *versus* Practice.

THUS to commence, then. Know all men, that I, Francis Courtney Wemyss, late Manager of the Chesnut Street Theatre, Walnut Street Theatre, Arch Street Theatre, Philadelphia; Holiday Street and Front Street Theatres, Baltimore; Pittsburgh Theatre, *et cetera, et cetera*, first drew the breath of life in Finch Lane, Cornhill, London, on the 13th of May, 1797. My father was an officer in the British Navy, descended from one of the proudest of the proud families of North Britain, who lost his life in the service of his country, and lies buried in the Island of Malta. My mother was born in Boston, Massachusetts, while that State was a colony of Great Britain. Of my boyhood, I can say but little, more than, that I was for a short period on board the Utrecht, with my father, who intended that I should follow his own profession. After his death, I was placed under the care of his brother, Otho H. Wemyss, Esq., Advocate, Edinburgh, was sent to the High School, where I remained three years under the tuition of Mr. Carson, the present Rector of the far-famed school. While there, Dr. Addams, who had for fifty years presided as Rector, died, and was honoured by the Lord Provost and Baillies of the city, with a public funeral, of which the boys, to the number of seven hundred, formed one of the most interesting parts of the procession. He is well known to the literary world as the author of Roman Antiquities, a Latin Dictionary, and a Latin and English Grammar on a superior principle, including all the best rules of Rudiman, and many valuable literary works. No praise from a pen of mine can add the smallest lustre to a name which will ever be held dear while science and learning

deserve a niche in the temple of fame.   He was succeeded in
the Rectorship by a Mr. Pillans, a very learned gentleman,
whose English pronunciation of Latin words had nearly caused
a revolution in the School, which Mr. Taws assisted in reducing
to obedience, to the no small annoyance of the refractory boys'
fingers.

The first bias my mind received towards the stage was thus
early given in acting the part of Lady Randolph, in the tragedy of Douglas, at the house of a schoolfellow named Miller,
in which I elicited much *undeserved* approbation.   Private
Theatricals are, at the best, ludicrous, and have a dangerous
tendency on any young mind imbued with romance.   Although
I had not at this time the most distant idea of the possibility
of ever becoming an actor, the applause I received on this
occasion acted on my imagination at a later period in life, and
kindled a flame which nothing could extinguish.

After going through the usual number of Latin and Greek
verbs, and being rather an apt scholar, bearing off several
primia at the public examinations, I was one morning called
into my uncle's study, and a communication laid before me
from Mr. Thomas Courtney, jun., my mother's brother, offering
to take charge of my future welfare if I should think proper
to change my views in life, (having been up to this time
intended for a surgeon in the navy).   To this proposition I
gave a willing assent, and my whole pursuits were at once
altered : instead of ardently pursuing a liberal profession, I
was to be tranformed into a plain, plodding man of business.
Messrs. Courtney and Sons, having introduced into Scotland
the manufacture of raven duck, since dignified by the name
of linen drilling, established a house in Dundee, where the
junior partner was to reside, and to whose care my future
destiny was now entrusted.

Never did boy enter upon life with brighter prospects, or
never did boy exert himself more successfully in the outset.
My attention and assiduity gained me the entire confidence
and approbation of my uncle, and at the early age of sixteen,
I was entrusted with the superintendence of a business, which
in the various departments of flax-dressing, spinning, bleaching, warping, winding, weaving, lapping and packing, employed
nearly two-thirds of the manufacturing population of Kirkaldy, Dysart, East and West Wemyss, Perth, Dundee, Forfar,
Arbroath, Brechin, Montrose, and Aberdeen,—all furnishing
their quota of labour, and all passing for inspection through
my hands.   The government contract, held by the house of
Courtney and Sons, requiring the weekly delivery of at least
two hundred pieces of cloth, not less than seventy-nine yards
each in length, and as much more as could be furnished ;
nay, at the age of fifteen I had actually signed policies of

insurance and chéques upon the bank, as the authorised agent of Thomas Courtney, jun., when business required his presence in London. What, then, it may well be asked, could induce me to throw away such advantages?

TOO MUCH INDULGENCE AND TOO MUCH MONEY.

My lamented uncle has been for years numbered with the dead; the only fault I can lay to *his* charge, was *too much kindness in general, and only one act of harsh severity.* Picture a headstrong, high-spirited boy of sixteen, placed on a par with men, associating with men, entrusted with business, and transacting business like a man, money at his command, and no control exercised over his actions, his word a law to those around him. Thus situated, is it to be wondered at, if assailed in all quarters by temptation, I sometimes exceeded the bounds of prudence. Accustomed to associate with men, I forgot I was a boy, and gambling, the most seductive of vices, became the source of difference between my uncle and myself. Not contented with the card parties, at which, in his company, I was a frequent visitor, I enrolled myself as a member of clubs, composed of clerks and young tradesmen, who met at an hotel once or twice a week. My visits to these places were communicated with much exaggeration to Mr. Courtney, who, at once, peremptorily forbade me to touch a card except in his presence.

To break up these associations, he signified his intention of taking me with him to London, on a visit to my mother; and little did I think, when joyfully preparing for this trip of pleasure, it would be the last time I should ever see my dear mother more. She died ten days after my arrival. Thus the loss of my surviving parent turned a visit of intended enjoyment into one of mournful condolence, and hastened my return to Dundee.

I had a brother two years older than myself, who, from sudden fright, had been labouring under temporary insanity. He was just recovering; and his friends, fearful the shock of his mother's death might occasion a relapse, his uncle invited him to follow us to Dundee, hoping, by change of scene, to obliterate all traces of recent sorrow. He accepted the invitation, and from the moment of his arrival in Baines' Square, the demon of discord appeared. A coolness, without any apparent cause, took place in Mr. Courtney's treatment towards me : he was distant and reserved; while I have frequently heard him lavish praise upon my brother for work which had been actually performed by me; nor did he ever, owing to my stubborn disposition, become sensible of his mistake, until I had finally left

A 5

the factory, and William was found incapable of doing what
had been previously supposed to be his, but was now discovered to be the labour of Master Frank. Poor fellow, he was
not accountable for his actions, and I verily believe, would
have laid down his life to serve him, of whom he was uncon-
sciously the worst foe. He died at Kirkaldy shortly after I
entered my professional career.

About this time, Mr. Henry Johnston, accompanied by
Bartley, and James Wallack, then a boy, arrived in Dundee,
and announced a medley performance at the theatre. Before
the commencement of the entertainment, a change of scene
placed Mr. Johnston within the walls of a prison, on suspicion
of debt : having suddenly left Ireland, and taken leave of his
creditors, who, following close at his heels, surprised him in
the North of Scotland. Thus, my first acquaintance with
the man, who was destined to be the means of my embracing
the stage as a profession, commenced within the walls of the
Dundee gaol. Sympathy for a man of talent in distress, first
induced me to visit him; when, finding his situation almost
destitute, I used every effort in my power to alleviate his distress, furnishing him with every luxury which my uncle's
house could afford, frequently spending my evenings in his
society, until I imbibed from his conversation a romantic
veneration for the drama, and its humblest professor, ending
in an attempt to establish a private theatre in Bains' Square,
in which I acted once a fortnight before all the fashionables of
Dundee. Here it was, I acquired a reputation among my
companions for dramatic talent, which fixed the stake upon
which I was to hazard all,

Mr. Johnston having been released from prison under the
act of " cessio bonorum," became manager of a company of
comedians in Paisley, afterwards obtaining the Montrose and
Aberdeen Theatre. In the latter cities I visited him by invitation, to be present at the first masquerade ever given so
far north in the land of steady habits. The fortnight I
remained in Aberdeen was spent chiefly in the society of the
officers of the 42d Highlanders, then stationed there, whom I
had known in Dundee : poor fellows, how many of them
shortly afterwards found a bloody, but a glorious grave at
Waterloo.

On my return home, a crisis approached little dreamt of,
and which, in the space of a few short hours, changed my
future position in society. I had been engaged during the
day, superintending and stowing in the warehouse, a cargo of
Riga T. R. flax, which had arrived from London. The subscription assembly was to take place at the Town Hall in the
evening, to which my uncle, my brother, and myself, were
going; I was much fatigued, and not being very fond of

dancing, would willingly have foregone the ball. My brother William, busily engaged in adorning his person, had neglected to copy a letter of some importance to Mr. Willis, of Kirkaldy, which my uncle, much displeased at the neglect, desired me to copy, at once. I told him I was very tired, and that William had better be called down. He said rather harshly, "No, sir, do it yourself." This I refused. What followed, I never can forget. He deliberately rose from his seat, reached the letter-book, placed it open on his desk, lighted the candles, placed a chair before the desk, and then addressed me thus—"Young man, I give you five minutes to determine. If you do not begin to copy this letter at the expiration of that time, by the God above us, we shall see whether you or I are master here, for I begin to doubt it." He laid his watch upon the table, and pacing up and down the room, became each moment more excited. When the time expired, he again asked me if I intended to copy that letter. The monosyllable *no* was scarcely uttered, when I found myself prostrated by a blow—*that blow made me an actor.* I rose, took the pen, copied the letter, and left the house, with a firm determination never to enter it again. That evening, Mr. Courtney and my brother, the cause of all the mischief, visited the ball, while I paraded the streets, scarcely knowing, from passion and mortification, what I was doing, and caring still less. With my mind in this feverish state, Henry Johnston, and the idea of becoming an actor, first presented itself.

I addressed a letter to Mr. Johnston, telling him I had resolved to leave Dundee for ever, requesting his instruction and support, as I wished to make the stage my profession. In the morning, I informed Mr. Courtney of what I had done.—He laughed at the idea, but finding me seriously bent upon it, he used his utmost endeavour to combat it. As an amusement, he said, he had no objection to it, but to make it the only dependence, whereby to live, he never could consent, adding—"Your own headstrong and ungovernable temper led to a collision, which I most sincerely regret, and could wish obliterated from your memory." I replied, "You have degraded me, sir, by a blow, and I feel I never can be comfortable again under your roof; on your return from London, you will not find me here." And thus we parted.

Henry Johnston, in a few days after this interview, passed through the town of Dundee, with his company, on the way to Montrose. He also urged me most strenuously to abandon my intention; but finding me fixed in my resolve, promised to aid my views to the utmost of his power, as a poor requital for the kindness, he was pleased to say, I had heaped upon him. It was decided I should hold myself in readiness to obey his summons, and he would write to me as early as he could to make arrangements for my reception. At the end of three weeks I received the following letter from him :—

"DEAR FRANK,   "Montrose, July, 1814.
    "Suppose you muster your Dundee friends for a trial here in Zanga, on Friday next, if you are still bent upon ruin; but remember the hints and predictions of one who has no other motive at heart than your welfare, in return for kindness, when placed in a most unhappy situation. Spencer has agreed to support you as Carlos. Respects to all. Yours sincerely,
          (Signed,)   "HENRY ERSKINE JOHNSTON."

On receipt of this, I started the following evening for Montrose, where I arrived early on Friday morning. I breakfasted at Mr. Hunter's, The Montrose Arms, and asked with a palpitating heart for a play-bill, which, to my astonishment, announced the Tragedy of Douglas as the play for this ominous Friday. Enquiring of Mr. Johnston the reason of the change, I learnt that Mr. Spencer, who was to have played Carlos, was confined with a fit of gout, and the Revenge could not be acted. But, said he, "You have played Norval; do it to-night; it will give me an opportunity of judging, and in case of failure, which we will not anticipate, your secret will be confined to your own breast." I, therefore, acted Young Norval, with his name in the play-bill for the part, and this should, in strict justice, be considered my first appearance on a public stage; but no record of it being in existence, I date my theatrical career from my opening in Glasgow, as Selim, in the Tragedy of Barbarossa, two months later. Douglas was thus cast on the occasion—Young Norval, Wemyss; Glenalvon, Scott; Lord Randolph, Emley; Old Norval, H. Johnston; Lady Randolph, Mrs. St. Leger; and Anna, Miss Charlotte O'Keefe. Thus was the decisive step taken. I returned to Dundee, with the perfect understanding that I was to meet Mr. Johnston in Glasgow, on the opening of the theatre there, of which he had become the lessee.

On a fine summer morning I crossed the Tay, with the determination of walking to Kinghorn, and so crossing the Frith of Forth to Leith, proceed to Edinburgh; the distance to be accomplished, about thirty-six miles. This, to a young man, who had never walked ten miles at any one time, was a serious undertaking; however, I arrived at the "lang town" of Kirkaldy, where I made a halt, sleeping at the factory of Messrs. Courtney and Son, there; received five pounds from Mr. Jamieson, their agent, telling him I was on my way to Glasgow, but not divulging the secret of my journey. Crossing to Leith the following morning, I secured a place in the Glasgow mail, from the Bull's Head, in Leith Walk, and resolved to spend the day with my uncle and Aunt Wemyss— the last I ever passed in their company. Mr. Otho Wemyss accompanied me to the coach, little dreaming, when he bade God bless me, and send me safely to my journey's end, on what errand I was bound. The guard's horn blew, the words "all right" pronounced, and I was fairly started. We arrived in Glasgow at two o'clock on Monday morning, when I retired to bed to dream of success, and a prosperous career.

After a hearty breakfast at the Tontine Coffee-House, I walked to the theatre, where I found the play announced for the opening was Hamlet, in which Mr. and Mrs. Charles Kemble were to play Hamlet and Ophelia; H. Johnston, the Ghost; Mrs. St. Leger, the Queen; Emley, Laertes; Berry, (the best comedian in Scotland,) Polonius; and Spencer, the King. This was the best acted play I had seen. The impression made upon my mind was one of unqualified delight: such language delivered by such artists is not often heard out of London. I can, at a distance of twenty-six years, recall almost every action of·every player engaged on that night.

My reception by Mr. Johnston was, as Baillie Nichol Jarvie says, " the north side of friendly"—coolness is scarcely a sufficient name—it was actually rudeness. He called me into the manager's room, and addressed me thus—"Well, young man, here you are, I see. Have you your uncle's consent for this folly?" (He knew I had not, as I had distinctly explained to him my situation in Montrose, when he pledged himself to do every thing in his power to advance my interest in the profession I had chosen.) I of course answered, " No." " *Then I do not suffer you to act until I have his written consent.*" And, without another word, he walked out of the room, leaving me perfectly astonished at the change in his behaviour, heretofore so kind and courteous. Had he, when the subject was first broached between us, acted thus, although I might have felt hurt at his conduct, my judgment, knowing myself to be a minor, and a runaway boy, might have pronounced it right; but I was at this moment in Glasgow, on his express invitation, with the full knowledge of every thing that had transpired between my uncle and myself, and the positive assurance, not only of his protection, but assistance. From what has since occurred, I may say, with justice, had Mr. Johnston at this time devoted a small portion of his leisure to my instruction, he would have repaid himself handsomely, from my future exertions, and deserved the gratitude of one, to whom he had acknowledged himself under many personal favours. He chose the course already mentioned, and converted a warm friend and devoted enthusiast into a bitter foe.

My situation at the close of this interview was any thing but agreeable. I had left my home, without money, offended my friends, depending upon the word of a man who had suddenly apprised me that I had nothing to hope from him. Thus foiled, prudence should have dictated an immediate return; but my pride was wounded, and the fear of ridicule prevented an acknowledgment of error, which would have immediately reinstated me in the affection of my uncle. I therefore boldly resolved to make an application to a strolling manager, named Moss, well known in the theatrical world, and not unknown to fame, in a metropolitan theatre. He was at this time with his company at Falkirk. Thither I proceeded in the canal boat, and waited upon him, dressed for the occasion—when, after an interview of nearly an hour, it was agreed I should open on the following Thursday, as Young Norval, and be rated on the books for a *share*. Well pleased with this arrangement, all present difficulty seemed overcome, and I was already, in my opinion, the future hero of the company. Here, again, I was doomed to meet a bitter mortification. I was punctual, according to promise, at the theatre for rehearsal; but, oh! *"what a check to proud ambition"*—this theatre, the object of my hope, and my desire, was a *barn*, fitted up in the rudest style; but I consoled myself with the knowledge that John Kemble had acted in a barn; therefore, it could be no disparagement to me, and there was something romantic in the idea of thus entering the profession at the lowest round of the ladder. But when the ladies and gentlemen assembled to rehearse, Falstaff's ragged regiment in apparel were princes to them—with the solitary exception of the manager, there was not a decently-dressed individual. As to a whole coat, that appeared to be a luxury totally unknown; yet, there was a shabby genteel appearance among them, which spoke of better days, and a certain strut, by which the strolling player is readily detected by the eye of a professional brother. As each actor was introduced, I could scarce repress a smile—but my courage failed; I resolved not to make one of their number. Approaching Mr. Moss, I requested a few moment's conversation; related to him as much of my history as it was necessary he should know; told him I had decided on returning home, and wished to decline acting altogether. To his credit be it spoken, although he had a prospect of a well-filled house, he approved my resolution, offering to lend me the means, if necessary, of putting, as he said, my praiseworthy intention into practice. This was my second and last interview with Moss. Poor fellow, he is dead; but this generous act of his would shame many of those who are continually railing at the immorality of the stage, yet would not stretch forth their hand to prevent a youth from plunging headlong into such a vortex of vice and dissipation, as they describe it. *Verbum sat,* which, being rendered into plain American, means —"nuff sed."

CHAPTER II.

Effects of Badinage. Reflections and Regrets. Stage Fright. Gratitude of a Manager. A Lawyer's Opinion of the Stage as a Profession. Two Letters. Look on this Picture and on that.

IF I could believe in the doctrine of predestination, I should say it was my fate to become an actor; for I solemnly declare, at the moment I placed my foot in the Glasgow mail coach, as it passed through Falkirk, to return home, I had firmly resolved to abandon, for ever, my foolish project, and by strenuously devoting myself to business, make all the atonement in my power for the loss of time and trouble I had occasioned to my relations. One unfortunate occurrence again altered all my well formed resolutions. On my arrival in Dundee, on the 20th of June, 1814, Mr. Courtney was entertaining a party of gentlemen at dinner. The officiousness of a servant, in announcing my arrival, produced a message requesting my presence in the dining-room. This summons I readily obeyed; but no sooner had I opened the door, and stood fairly over the threshold, than one universal roar of laughter burst from the crowded table, accompanied with expressions like the following: "Make room for Roscius"— "Here comes the proud representative of Shakspeare's heroes" —"Right welcome back to Denmark"—"A frog he would a wooing go," &c. &c. &c.

This ill-timed badinage sealed my fate. Smarting under the lash of jests, the truth of which I could not but inwardly acknowledge, I replied to my uncle's question of—"Are you cured of your folly, and determined for the future to attend closely to business." · "No, sir, I am off again to-morrow morning." Not another word was uttered upon the subject; but from that moment, I used all my endeavours to obtain his consent to my becoming an actor. Instead of candidly acknowledging myself disgusted with scenes I had witnessed, I uttered the first untruth that ever passed my lips to Mr. Courtney, stating my return was only for the purpose of obtaining from him a written acknowledgment of his approbation of the course I was pursuing, without which Mr. Johnston would not permit me to act; that my mind was firmly fixed upon the subject; that his refusal would have the effect of driving me into the society of the first strolling company who would receive me, instead of commencing my career in a respectable theatre, with every prospect of success.

Thus urged, his kindness and indulgence got the better of his judgment. He furnished me with the necessary document, generously adding a monthly allowance of ten pounds sterling, which was afterwards reduced to five, and finally to three; which sum he continued to allow me to the hour of his death. Thus, the folly of friends, in a moment of hilarity, prevented by an ill-timed jest, the return of a headstrong lad of seventeen, to the path which interest and duty pointed clearly to be right.

The die being now cast, before I proceed, let me do justice to one whose memory I revere, whose kindness I abused, to whom I was indebted for more than parental indulgence. His liberality in not withdrawing from me his countenance and support, but granting me pecuniary aid, with the hope that I should repent my folly, will be so strongly contrasted with the conduct of my father's family, that, had Mr. Courtney followed their advice, I should, in all probability, have become the worthless vagabond they feared. Many a time has the monthly allowance, which arrived punctually to the hour, been the support not only of myself, but others in the same distressed situation. Those only who have experienced the vicissitudes of a strolling player's life, can know or feel the joy with which such a windfall as three pounds would be hailed in what is termed *a bad town*, where, probably, all were in debt, many without a penny in their pockets, and none with a dinner to supply their wants. Through his bounty was I enabled to avoid the shifts and tricks of my professional associates, although I have felt, and keenly too, the bitter smart of poverty. I can proudly say, in reviewing this part of my career, that no dishonourable act stains its progress, never having quitted a town, as a strolling actor, in which I did not faithfully discharge every claim against me.

The character of Mr. Thomas Courtney, junior, may be thus summed up. He possessed a soul of honour, a heart at all times open to a tale of distress, and a hand ever ready to relieve it; he was the orphan's friend, the poor man's hope, and the rich man's example. To him may be truly applied Shakspeare's language—

> " He was a man, take him for all in all,
> Eyes shall not look upon his like again."

Death closed his career at the early age of twenty-eight; but he lives in the recollection of his numerous acts of kindness, and may my children, while they drop a tear to the memory of their father's benefactor, learn to imitate his virtues, and avoid their father's failings.

With what different feelings did I now leave the town of Dundee for Glasgow—reconciled to my uncle, furnished with a supply of cash, amounting to fifty pounds, and the written approval of my course—to present myself before Mr. Johnston, convinced that every difficulty was surmounted. When I met him, he seemed at a loss how to receive me. Being informed I had procured my uncle's approbation, he desired me to meet him in the green-room on the following morning. Here I was introduced to Mr. Charles Kemble, who drew anything but a flattering picture of the life of an actor, giving himself as an instance of the precarious tenure of their engagements, enjoying the favour of the public in the highest degree; but from the caprice of the management, excluded at that time from both the London theatres, of which he was one of the brightest ornaments, and strongly recommending me to abandon all thoughts of the stage.

It was now arranged that I should make my first appearance as Selim, in the play of Barbarossa, which part was selected by Mr. Johnston on account of my youth. I committed the words to memory, expecting to receive from the manager those instructions in the business of the stage he was so capable of imparting; but to my astonishment, Mr. Johnston did not even attend my first and only rehearsal.

The awful night, pregnant with my fate, arrived. I entered on my theatrical career on the first night of the Glasgow fair, July 14th, 1814: never shall I forget the dreadful sensation I experienced, as I heard the prompter's bell ring to begin the play. My mouth became perfectly parched, my tongue refused its office, and, dressed as I was, one word would have prevented my attempt. *Stage fright*—I will not attempt to describe thee—actors know too well what it is; and auditors, who see no difficulty in acting, should be placed but once before the lamps, in a crowded theatre, to make them silent critics for ever.

Like William the Conqueror, I made a stumbling entrance to my future throne. Wishing to appear erect, and not to lose an inch of my height, I was carrying my head with martial precision, when my toe caught in the stage carpet, bringing me to a kneeling position before the mighty Barbarossa, not in the most graceful manner. This added to my fright, and induced a facetious member of the company to declare, at the end of the performance, if I wanted my voice again, it would be found in the folds of the green curtain, beyond which not a sound had penetrated. Yet, I was loudly applauded by the audience, and perfectly satisfied with my reception; so much so, that I ventured to ask Mr. Johnston what emolument I was to receive for my future exertions. Here is his reply.

(COPY.)

SIR,—It is my opinion you will never make an actor, and the sooner you

return home again, the better. When you resume your late respectable
situation in society, I shall be proud and happy to renew our late friendship.
"Yours, &c.

(Signed)   HENRY ERSKINE JOHNSTON."

And thus ended all the promises of support, so liberally
made on his part, and so foolishly depended upon on mine.
We separated, to meet again in Philadelphia, in the year
1838, when he applied to me for an engagement at the Walnut Street Theatre. What strange events daily occur in this
world. Who could have supposed that the Glasgow manager,
who so summarily dismissed a boy of seventeen, in 1814,
should in 1838, have applied to that boy for permission to act
in a Philadelphia theatre, of which he had become the manager, and he refused, for want of talent, having become perfectly superannuated.

Thus repulsed, Mr. Emley, an excellent actor, and my constant companion, advised me to make an application to an old
friend of his, a Mr. Neville, who had the management of a
small itinerant company, then playing in Port Glasgow. I
accordingly addressed a letter to him, and received a most
flattering answer, offering me a fair trial, stating he had been
introduced to me, by Dr. Horsley, in Dundee, when a member
of the Edinburgh company of comedians, under the management of Mr. Henry Siddons, and had a favourable idea of my
talent if properly cultivated; requested me to proceed without delay, to Port Glasgow, and all minor points could be
settled between us when we met. On the 4th day of September, 1814, I departed from Glasgow, in the Clyde steamboat,
and on the following Monday, played Young Norval, at Port
Glasgow.   The manager being pleased with the performance,
engaged me as a member of his company, the same evening,
at the enormous sum of fifteen shillings, (not quite 3 dollars
50 cents) per week, with a promise of increase, as I should
improve, or appear worthy; which promise he faithfully kept.
I paid eight shillings per week for board and lodging.   But
never having, heretofore, known the want of money, I have
frequently, in one afternoon, spent double the amount of my
weekly stipend; until finding myself in debt, from which I
had no other means of extricating myself, than by pawning
my watch and chain, on which I borrowed ten pounds sterling,
which I was unable to redeem for as many months. This was
a salutary warning, teaching me the necessity of living according to the rules of economy, and may be called my first
lesson in adversity.

On the 22nd of September, my salary was raised to one
pound sterling, for studying the words of Captain Absolute,
in the Rivals, at six hours notice, and presenting myself before the public, perfect to a monosyllable. I was not aware

that I had performed anything like a miracle, until on the following Saturday, a very flattering note informed me of the increase of remuneration, and conveyed to me the thanks of Mr. Neville and his partner Mr. Shaw, for my kindness on the occasion.

The company consisted at this period of Messrs. Neville and Shaw, (the managers,) Mr. and Mrs. Ryder, Mr. Mullender, Mr. Hart, (known as old Joe Hart,) Mr. M'Cann, Mr. Martin, Mr. Mitchel, Mr. Wemyss, Mrs. Mills, Mrs. Shaw, Mrs. Neville, and Mrs. Hart. Many pleasant hours have I passed in the society of the Ryders. To Mrs. Ryder, I am indebted for my first instruction in the business of the stage: to her alone, I attribute the rapid improvement I made during the first six months of my career. When she left the company, my good genius departed with her. The Port Glasgow company occupies a place in my memory, associated with the most unalloyed pleasure I ever experienced in my profession. The managers were most friendly to me; each actor seemed to take pride in affording me every information in his power. Pleased with these attentions, I looked upon the life of an actor, as one of uninterrupted felicity. The difficulty I had experienced in enrolling my name among them, adding to my satisfaction at the result.

Thus pleased with myself and with every one around me, I received the following letter from my uncle Courtney. My refusing to listen to the proposal therein contained proves the entire ascendancy which the stage at this time possessed over my mind.

(COPY.)

DEAR FRANK,

I have but just returned from Edinburgh, where I found your Uncle and Aunt Wemyss in the greatest mental distress, on account of the line of life you have thought proper to adopt. At their instigation I am induced to repeat the offer already made, provided you will abandon your present folly, of allowing you the choice of any profession you may name, for the prosecution of which, I will provide you with a suitable maintenance, until you shall be enabled to live by the profits of your occupation. Weigh this well in your mind, and after due consideration, let me know the result of your determination; at all events, write a few lines to your uncle in Edinburgh.

Yours most affectionately,

(Signed) THOS. COURTNEY, JUNR.

Bain's Square, Dundee, Sept., 1814.

On the day I received this letter, my first Benefit was to take place.* The play fixed upon was George Barnwell, the afterpiece The Lying Valet. My name was announced in

* This produced me, after paying the charges of the managers, the enormous profit of three shillings and sixpence.

large letters for George Barnwell—first time. Thinking this a good opportunity of conveying to my friends the idea that I was making rapid strides in my new profession, I enclosed a bill of the play to each of my uncles—one to Mr. Courtney at Dundee, the other to Mr. Wemyss at Edinburgh. I should scarcely have recorded this circumstance, but that my uncle Wemyss alludes to it hereafter in a most bitter manner.

Looking at my past life as I *now* do, I am astonished that any infatuation (and such I admit a passion for the stage to be) could have induced me to have rejected the offer contained in the above letter, yet such was the case; and had a fortune beyond my wildest hopes been tendered to me at that time, coupled with the positive injunction of never again appearing upon the stage, I should have rejected it without the slightest regret : my only wonder is, that Mr. Courtney continued his kind allowance, urged as he was by Mr. Wemyss to abandon me to my fate, and even reproached by him as encouraging me in my headstrong disobedience.

A few days brought me an answer to both my letters, the contents of which were as follows :—

(COPY FROM O. H. WEMYSS.)

"Dublin St., Edinburgh, Sep., 1814.

Your unexpected epistle, so well calculated to call forth all the angry passions on a subject requiring peculiar care and circumspection, now lies before me.

" The infatuation must indeed be irresistible, that can induce any human being, blessed with an ordinary share of intellect, voluntarily to prefer the society of the profligate and lowest dregs of the community, together with a life of contempt, penury, and wretchedness of every description, and not unfrequently attended with ulterior consequences of a still more alarming nature, to the countenance and esteem of a numerous circle of friends and relations, and to those habits of industry, which must infallibly have led, in a few years, to a useful, creditable, independent situation in society.

" Such, however, is your resolution, not taken under the impulse of passion, arising from any grievance, real or pretended, or from any distaste to the line of life which your friends had, with your own approbation, destined you, but deliberately taken, and wilfully adhered to, in face of repeated remonstrances, and of offers so generous and liberal, as were perhaps never before made to any young man in similar circumstances. Woeful experience will teach you, too late, the real value of these advantages you have thus unaccountably neglected. I say, *too late*—for you deceive yourself miserably if you imagine you can at any time relinquish your present disgraceful career, and resume your proper sphere in society : your best friends may not always be willing to receive even a returning penitent. Habits of idleness inimical to all manly exertions, will insensibly be formed, while every hour of lost time, by preventing the necessary previous tuition, will infallibly obstruct any attempt to establish you in a more useful, creditable situation in society.

" I am not so presumptuous as to expect to succeed, where others, entitled to equal respect with myself, have already failed; but I feel it an imperious call of duty to make the attempt. Let me then conjure you in the most forcible manner, again to peruse your Uncle Courtney's letter, offering you the option of any profession you may desire, *which shall be prosecuted at his expense*. *Should you, then*, be inclined to avail yourself of this uncommonly generous offer, I shall indeed feel a proud satisfaction in conveying to him your sentiments, procuring a total obliteration of the past, and forwarding your views, as far as consistent with reason and propriety—*but this resolution must be immediate*. Should you still persist in your present ruinous and disgraceful career, your refusal can add nothing to the poignancy of that distress, which I, in common with all your friends, have felt from your misconduct; but supported by the proud consciousness of having performed my duty to you, from the earliest hour up to the present moment, I shall attempt the painful task of forgetting for ever that such a being exists, as was once the object of my fondest care, and unremitting solicitude, and from whom I had every reasonable prospect of much better things. You cannot have forgotten how, in earnest conversation, I once told you I would rather see you a *common hangman* than a *player*; since the one, though unquestionably the lowest, was still a *useful* member of society; while the other, in my opinion, was something worse than *useless*. These opinions would remain unaltered, even if you, by a miracle, should become a perfect paragon, exceeding any thing ever dreamt of, not to say, actually seen or heard, of theatrical excellence, instead of gaining, with a set of miserable strollers, a pittance less than the wages of a common porter, or daily labourer.

" To me it is now perfectly immaterial under what name* you play the fool, or whether your fooleries shall be successful or not; however, the practical bull of enclosing your play-bill might have been spared: but the piece was certainly well chosen. In Barnwell, if I mistake not, there is an affectionate, ill-used uncle, suffering the extreme of misery, from the profligate habits of an infatuated and misled nephew. If the similarity of situation was felt by the actor, the character must have been portrayed with much natural effect.

" Having thus put it once more within your power to extricate yourself with honour from the ruinous and disgraceful career in which you have so imprudently embarked, my paper permits me to add three words only—

PAUSE—REFLECT—DECIDE:

and on your decision it rests, whether this shall or shall not be, the last letter you ever receive from your justly offended, but still affectionate uncle, (Signed) OTHO HERMAN WEMYSS."

This letter would probably have had a greater effect, had the language been less strong. I acknowledge nothing could be more felicitous than the hit at my playbill; but to use my uncle's own expression, nothing could be so well calculated to call forth all the angry expressions. Comparing a player to a hangman, and giving the latter the preference in society,

* My uncle had previously requested that I would cease to dishonour my father's memory, by using his name as the designation of a mountebank.

is a very pretty idea, but most galling to the feelings of a romantic noviciate, desirous only of obtaining fame in the theatrical world. I had been habituated to admire, from my birth, his talent as an advocate, and this letter is the offspring of no common mind. Notwithstanding his bigoted hostility to the stage, I should hail with satisfaction the hour of our reconciliation, which I hope is not far distant.

I will now proceed with Mr. Courtney's letter, written in a very different spirit; and although he would freely have given thousands to have recalled me from my foolish career, offering every thing that man could offer, to induce me to adopt some other mode of obtaining a living; yet finding me determined to persevere, he used his utmost endeavour to make the thorny path as smooth as possible, aiding me by advice, which his own acute observation on mankind rendered him so capable of affording,—that no old actor ever placed a better set of general rules before a pupil for his instruction, than Mr. C., without any green-room knowledge of the profession, here penned for my guidance.

(COPY FROM THOMAS COURTNEY, JUNR.)

"DEAR FRANK,—   *   *   *   *   *
  *   *   *   *   *   *   *   *
  *   *   * Now that you are embarked in your profession, and feel so certain of doing well, I trust you will spare no pains to make yourself as respectable as you can; and of all things, as a player, avoid ever looking at your audience, but always at the person who addresses you on the stage, and whom you have in your turn to address. I consider this fault the greatest a man can be guilty of, and we find is only practised by vain, weak-minded men, who fancy that their persons and their attitudes are alone the source from which they are to derive applause, instead of learning that it is the style of delivery, added to the feeling, that the player portrays, in his wish to impress his audience with the meaning of his author: that alone gives delight. You will be sure to discover this if you pay strict attention to good performers, such as John Kemble, Charles Young, &c., &c.; and as you have had an excellent education, and are supposed not to want ability, I hope we shall find that you excel in whatever you undertake; for a man must never think of half measures—his very soul must be full of what he engages himself in, whether it be in acting, or whether it be in amusement; whether in the counting-room or behind the counter; whether as a sportsman in the field, or as a private gentleman, enjoying the social conversation of his friends, it is alike in all; and the man who succeeds best is he who is never absent, and only taken up with what he has immediately before him. I hope you will also see, that it is impossible to please, without first studying and well understanding your author: therefore, before you play any new part, you ought to make a point of reading over the whole play with studious attention, at least three times, before you attempt to commit to memory your own part, for you will

often find points that ought to fix your attention, in a second or third reading, which would have been overlooked in a first perusal, which should be considered only as a cursory review. Think particularly of this, and always bear in mind, that you are playing for reputation, which will prompt you to act as well, before half a dozen people, as before a crowded audience. The actors with whom you are playing, are sure to give a right estimation to the line of conduct which is pursued in this way, and must acknowledge it to proceed from a superior mind. Try also to improve yourself in your temper; for it often occurs on the stage, in cases of unruly displeasure on the part of an audience, without the cause being in the actor, that a man who wants moderation and sense, is apt to show spleen towards the company present, which must spoil his style, if he be ever so good a player.

" These little remarks, I hope, you will attend to, as far as you think and feel them to be correct, and I suppose it will not surprise you, now you have regularly embarked in this profession, to have your Uncle Otho, Mr. Sinclair Weymss, and myself, among your audience: but you may be sure, we shall take care not to see you, before we see you on the stage, that we may form our opinion of your usual method of playing.

" With regard to the reduction of your income, what I wrote to you in my last is my fixed determination upon it: I will give you no more than five pounds per month, beginning on the first day of September. Your cousin, Sinclair Wemyss, was surprised I should allow you anything. I shall consider that I do more than my duty, in granting you an allowance of sixty pounds sterling, per annum, which is a livelihood of itself; and your profession must pay its own expenses, and keep you besides, or it will be but a poor one; however, whether it does or not, cannot now be helped, it is your own choice, and you must be satisfied with it. I expect to hear from you regularly, and am always,

" Your affectionate uncle,
"Dundee, Sept., 1814."   (Signed,) " THOS. COURTNEY, JUNR."

I shall not pause to decide which of these letters was the most judicious : I am certain they were both written in the same spirit—*anxiety for my welfare.* The former closed the doors against me for ever, unless its terms were complied with instantly, while the other was intent, upon preventing, if possible the evils feared by both; but which happily for me have not been realised.

CHAPTER III.

Rather too long a Walk for Pleasure. Great Benefit. Shaw, the Singer. Whiskey Punch and Burns' Cottage. Theatrical Row. M'Alpine and M'Cann. Tricks of Strolling. Effects of the first "hiss" upon the nerves of a Novice. Berry, the Edinburgh Comedian.

IN a few days after the receipt of these letters, the season closed at Port Glasgow. I spent a few days at Greenock, where the Glasgow company were then performing, and proceeded on the summons of Messrs. Neville and Shaw, to commence in company of Mr. and Mrs. Ryder, my first strolling journey. The next town at which we were to perform, was Irvine : and with three shillings and sixpence in my pocket, the proceeds of my benefit, I started to walk this journey.

Mr. and Mrs. Ryder's family, consisted of three children, two young girls and an infant boy, the last, rather a tax upon travellers, as he had to be carried the whole distance. In order to relieve the lady as much as possible, I volunteered to carry him, mile and mile, with his father ; but before we reached Kilwinning, I was scarcely able to carry myself. Mrs. Ryder proved the best pedestrian of the party, and I have ever gratefully remembered the care and attention she heaped upon me after our arrival in Irvine, when the blistered state of my feet rendered me unable to walk for two or three days. She is dead—but a kinder heart never beat in woman's bosom—yet withal, she possessed a most violent temper. Many a time has my presence averted the storm from poor Ryder ; but with all her faults, when she died, he lost, in truth, his better half, for she was a most excellent and thrifty housewife.

Irvine is a very pretty little town, surrounded by a variety of diversified walks. Our theatre was the Town Hall which Neville had fitted up with much taste, and more tact, than commonly falls to the lot of an actor descending from the stilts of a royal theatre, to be the humble manager of a company of strolling players.

Our company was here reinforced, by the addition of Mr. Berriman and Miss Laing. The Irvine folks appeared delighted with our efforts; the pieces were really well acted, the tact of the manager refusing to attempt whatever he deemed beyond the talent of those under his control, and selecting such pieces, as he was enabled to present, with every part filled with ability. With all the knowledge I subsequently acquired of patented theatres, few, if any out of London, could have filled their " *dramatis personæ*" as well as this little company.

Of the good people of Irvine, I, at least, am bound to speak with gratitude, the hall upon my benefit night being literally crammed. As I was fortunate enough, thus, to eclipse all the better actors, it is but fair I should assign the reason. A gentleman of the town had written a trifling drama on the subject of Burns' Tam O'Shanter, which was produced for Ryder's benefit, in which I was cast the part of " Cutty Sark." With the tuition of Ryder, the witches' scene, in the interior of Alloa Kirk, so well described by the immortal poet, was placed upon the stage, with all the effect which paint, canvass, and dress could give it. The business of the scene was capitally arranged; and with such spirit was it kept up, that when I obtained the tail of Tam's mare, on the middle of the Brig of Doon, one universal shout of "Well done, Cutty Sark," followed the descent of the curtain, each night of performance. The little urchins in the street would salute me as I passed, with "Well done, Cutty Sark," and when my name was announced for a benefit, every body was determined to be there; an overflowing house was the consequence, but Cutty Sark had nearly become a professional nickname, of which I was not at all ambitious, although it had put several pounds sterling in my pocket.

This season was very successful, and I left the little town, with regret, to proceed to Kilmarnock, a brisk manufacturing town not far distant; here my old friend Emley and his wife, (late Miss Fanny O'Keefe,) joined the company, which the managers were gradually recruiting for the winter season, which was to be passed at Ayr.

While in Kilmarnock, I received another pleasant fling, at the respectability of my profession, in reply to a request made, that my uncle would remember me to all inquiring friends—here it is—" * * * * * * * * *

You request to be remembered to all friends—WHO ARE NONE—for ever since it was known you had taken to the stage, you have been looked upon as a lost character, and no one thinks it worth their while to mention your name. I fear your Edinburgh friends have cut you for life. * * * * * * * *

This only served to increase the romantic attachment I had formed to the theatrical profession, while the daily encouragement I received, to renewed exertion, was the approbation bestowed upon my efforts by the managers. Mr. Neville was pleased to compliment me highly on my evident improvement, and his partner, Shaw, took every opportunity to sound my praise.

He was an *original*—well known as a singer of merit in Edinburgh, and having also received the approbation of a London audience, his boast, that I was a credit to any company, and should be in London in three years, if I continued to pay the same studious attention to the profession, fell like music upon my ears, inspiring me to study long parts, with almost inconceivable rapidity. The season at Kilmarnock was brought to an abrupt termination, by a sudden ebullition of passion upon his part. He had played a concerto admirably upon the violin, between the play and farce, and afterwards sung "Tak your auld cloak about ye;" when, as he left the stage, an auditor, whose soul was not attuned to sweet sounds, took the liberty of saluting him with "a hiss." The curtain had reached the stage, and Shaw would not even take time to

B

open the stage door, but thrusting his head under the curtain, hissed furiously back again, uttering some of the most blasphemous expressions ever heard by man. The effect produced was a dead silence, followed by an immediate outcry for an apology, which he refused to make, until riot and confusion prevailed to such a height, that, fearful of his personal safety, he suddenly rushed before the curtain, asking if they wished to see his bl—y brains. Fortunately for Shaw, some wag called out "that's too good—a fiddler's brains, where can he find them." This sally turned the feeling of anger into one of laughter and contempt. He escaped the consequence of his folly; but the company was compelled to beat a sudden retreat, not being suffered to play longer than the end of the week. This was a source of mortification to all, and shortly after, caused the separation of the managers. Shaw, I have never seen since.

From Kilmarnock we bent our course to Ayr, where we passed the winter. Here I became a favourite with the public, and for the first time, began to feel myself of some importance to the theatre. I was worked hard, and not very well paid; but the romantic enthusiasm with which I pursued my now favourite occupation, allowed me little time to think of hardships, which were made the food of mirth, rather than complaint. My leisure hours were chiefly spent at Mrs. M'Culloch's, whose house I strongly recommend to any of my readers who may visit Ayr, vouching for the goodness of her table, and moderation of her charges. Many a happy hour have I spent under her roof, and many a hearty supper have I enjoyed, in good fellowship, after a trip to Burns' cottage, in the early part of the day, had laid the foundation for an evening of mirth and joviality. I would fain draw a veil over the scenes of dissipation in which I indulged during my four months' residence in Ayr. My society was courted both by high and low, and I was in real danger of becoming a confirmed drunkard. I never knew what it was to retire to bed perfectly sober,—it is true I was not drunk, but the whiskey-punch (and excellently well did my lady hostess brew it,) had always made strong innovations on sobriety,—merry is the best term; for a set of merry dogs we were. Lucky is it for me I am able to record I had strength of mind sufficient to shake off an evil and a growing habit, which confirmed me in my future sober resolutions; and as experience, if not too dearly bought, is cheaply purchased, so my frolics in Ayr were attended with ultimate beneficial results. Having once escaped an abyss, which has swallowed up so many actors, I never again ventured to sport on the edge of it. Poor M'Alpine, had you but followed my advice and example, you would have been at this moment an ornament to your profession. Poor fellow, he was another victim to the duplicity and hollow friendship of Mr. Henry Johnston. Enjoying the esteem of a numerous circle of friends in Glasgow, possessing the qualities of a convivial companion, in a greater degree than usually falls to the lot of a private individual, being decidedly one of the best comic singers I ever heard—in an evil hour, he was persuaded to make a trial of his powers on the stage; his success was complete, but unfortunately for him, it interfered with the views of the manager, who, after a few nights, the profits of which were his only object, refused him an opportunity of acting, even gratuitously. Being a native of the town of Ayr, and the éclât of his Glasgow performance having reached the ears of Mr. Neville, he started to Glasgow for the purpose of engaging him. He made his first appearance in his native city as Octavian, in the Mountaineers, in which I played Count Virolet. He next appeared as Romeo, and such was the anxiety to witness his performance in a character which he had never before studied, that he agreed to play Durimel in the Point of Honour. Finding more difficulty than he had anticipated, in committing the words to memory, and that he had overtasked himself, he foolishly neglected it altogether, passed the preceding night in dissipation, and recklessly refused to act the part at all. Public excitement was raised to the highest pitch by his previous excellent performances, so that not a seat remained untaken in the boxes. The whole house was filled to overflowing, at least half an hour previous to the usual time of commencing. Every argument was used in vain to induce him to appear before the audience and apologize; he steadily refused, but offered to repeat the part of Octavian, if the audience could be reconciled to the change. In this dilemma, Mr. Neville requested me to make an apology to the following effect:

"Ladies and gentlemen,—I am deputed by the managers to inform you, that in consequence of a most untoward and unforeseen event, it will be utterly impossible for Mr. M'Alpine to appear before you in the character of Durimel, as announced this evening. The prompt book of the play having been mislaid or lost, the managers throw themselves upon your indulgence, and request to be allowed the favour of substituting the play of the Mountaineers, in which Mr. M'Alpine will support the part of Octavian."

The apology, the first I had ever been called upon to utter, was well received by the audience, until some young man in the pit, who had provided himself with a book of the Point of Honour, offered it to the managers. A deputation with the book was sent behind the scenes, but Neville, like a good general, had secured a retreat, and was nowhere to be found, well knowing the utter impossibility of performing the play.

Foiled, however, in the attempt to see the manager, the opinion quickly gained ground that the managers were averse to Mr. M'Alpine's attempting the part, so that when the curtain rose, on the first scene of the Mountaineers, and Mr. Emley and myself were discovered as Kilmallock and Count Virolet, we were saluted with cries of—" Off !" " off !" " Point of Honour or no play "—" M'Alpine." We continued to speak for some time without the possibility of being heard, until the top of one of the benches, hurled with violence on the stage, made us both depart in double quick time.

The stage once vacated, the uproar continued, while the cries for the manager became so loud and long, that Neville at last made his appearance in company with M'Alpine, entering into an explanation, very wide of the truth, (a practice too common in theatres when a discontended audience have to be suddenly appeased,) pacifying the audience by a promise on the part of M'Alpine to sing the comic song of the Mail Coach after the play of the Mountaineers. Thus terminated a row, which at one time threatened the destruction of the interior of the theatre.

This was the last time I ever saw M'Alpine play. He continued to improve in his profession with astonishing rapidity, and was pronounced by many excellent judges, a young man of uncommon talent, who would shortly arrive at eminence. Alas! that "man should put an enemy into his mouth to steal away his brains." All his bright prospects have been crushed by his own folly, and the conviviality of his temper proved his ruin. The last I heard of him was as the hero of a strolling company in Cartmel, near Ulverston, Lancashire; his performance only tolerated from the recollection of what he had been, and in all probability, he has sunk into an early grave, another victim to intemperance.

It was in Ayr I first formed the resolution of providing myself with my own theatrical wardrobe. Having received a present from London of two very handsome tunics, I resolved to lay by a certain portion of my weekly receipts to purchase whatever might be necessary for correctly dressing the parts entrusted to me. How well I accomplished my object, those who have ever seen me on the stage are the best judges. It soon acquired for me the reputation of being one of the most attentive actors to costume, and one of the best dressers in the country : this aided me very materially in my future provincial engagements.

I know that actors of the old school have exclaimed loudly against the practice; and that managers have taken most unwarrantable liberties with the public, in consequence of many performers choosing to find their own wardrobe, cannot be denied. If an actor now refuses to find his own dresses, he will frequently be compelled to appear in rags and filth; yet the comfort may be obtained at so slight a sacrifice on the part of any actor, that the reputation he is sure to obtain from his audience will amply overpay him for the attempt. Yet would I endeavour to persuade the public to prevent managers from encroaching too often on their good nature, where actors either will not, or cannot find their own dresses, by loudly hissing, not the actor, but the manager, boldly explaining the cause of disapprobation. A few lessons of this description would speedily correct the evil.

Whenever a new piece is advertised with the additional flourish of new scenery and dresses, unless they are new, it is an imposition, which should be treated as such by the spectators. How frequently does a play-bill trumpet forth the expense and labour bestowed upon a new, when in the third or fourth scene, on comes an old acquaintance of the audience not even touched by the brush of the artist, while the performers, with the exception of two or three principal characters, appear in the old standing dresses, worn nightly; whereas a few pounds judiciously expended, would have rendered them new in appearance, and produced every requisite effect. This parsimony, when theatricals are well supported, should not be tolerated an instant; and even in the degraded state to which I have see the drama reduced, is unjustifiable, and only tends to make bad, worse.

Every line in a play-bill should be strictly true; but to such a height has the pernicious system of puffing been carried, that it is a common saying, "that the greatest liar in world except a newspaper, is a play-bill." The consequence of thus frequently disappointing the public, has produced an apathy towards the theatre, which it will take years to destroy.

My first participation in a trick too frequently resorted to by strolling players, occurred the night previous to my departure from Ayr. Harry M'Cann, (Paddy M'Cann—glorious Paddy, who, when engaged to carry a torch in a procession, provoked the laughter of every one connected with the theatre, by declaring to Kean he was improving in his profession, for he was acting the light business at the Cobourg every night,) a worthy little fellow, and at this time my constant companion, having failed in his attempt at a benefit, and instead of realizing a profit, finding himself indebted four pounds to the manager, (not an unfrequent case on such occasions,*) was placed under stoppage of five shillings per week,

---

* Here let me observe, that the public labour under an erroneous impression with regard to actors' benefits. It is usually supposed that actors

which had so crippled his finances, he was unable to discharge
a debt of two guineas at his lodgings; for which sum, all his
wearing apparel, together with his stock of wigs, red stock-
ings, and other properties most needful to a low comedian.
He was allowed to take each evening at the theatre what he
wanted for that night's performance, provided it did not exceed in bulk the size of a common pocket handkerchief,
which was to be regularly brought home after the performance. He therefore extracted the most necessary articles, re-
placing their bulk by small pieces of painted canvas or other
useless articles which abound in all theatres. These things
were deposited in the trunks of his brother actors, who were
more fortunately situated than himself, while the bundle of
rubbish was regularly deposited at the bottom of the trunk.
To me he applied on the last occasion to place in my trunk
two or three wigs and a pair of russet boots, the possession of
which was a matter of great importance to him. I confess I
felt a few qualms of conscience as I gave my reluctant consent, on receiving the pledge of his honour that the money
should be faithfully paid, which was done in my presence two
weeks afterwards. Never shall I forget the alarm of his land-
lady when the trunk was opened in her presence to see that
the things were safe. She was under the impression that
they had been abstracted by some one about her house, not
thinking it possible a strolling actor could have honour
enough to pay a debt after having abstracted piece-meal the
only security she thought herself possessed of. She actually
offered him the two guineas to say nothing about the matter,
as it might injure the reputation of her house. This was too
much for our risible faculties : he confessed himself the offender; and with a hearty shake of the hand and an extorted
promise to prove kind to the next unhappy actor who might
be placed in difficulty, we left her, with her opinion of the
honesty of the play-actors much improved, and an anecdote
which she repeated to every company of actors who visited
Ayr for many years afterwards.

The season at Ayr having terminated, Neville and Shaw
dissolved their partnership, Neville retaining the management, Shaw leaving the company, and taking with him Mrs.

play gratuitously for each other on these occasions. On thr contrary, the
expenses are fixed at a certain sum by the manager, which, if not received at the doors, the unfortunate actor is placed under stoppages until
the deficiency is paid into the treasury; although in many instances, if it
had not been for the exertions of the actor whose name is placed at the
head of the play-bills, the manager would not probably have received
half of the amount taken on the occasion without including the deficiency
which the actor has to make good.

Shaw, and his sister, Mrs. Mills. Mr. and Mrs. Ryder and family also left us, to commence management on their own account, at Port Glasgow; a speculation in which they strongly urged me to embark as a partner. In short, this may be termed the breaking up of our snug and happy party. In a short time afterwards, we were scattered in all directions, many of us never to meet again.

Neville's first effort on his own account was at Mauchline, where he decidedly failed, our force being inefficient. He was advised to try his fortune for a few nights, at Catherine Mills, a large manufacturing village, but a few miles distant. Having obtained permission from the resident proprietor, Mr. Buchanan, to perform for twelve nights, a barn was fitted up for the purpose; and here it was, I for the first time, numbered myself among the barn-door fowl of the profession, without which my strolling adventures would have been incomplete. The houses for the first four nights were excellent; after which, we could scarcely muster money enough to pay for candles. With some difficulty, the manager contrived to pay his actors; but for his other debts, I doubt much whether they are paid to this hour.

To me, our visit to Mauchline was marked by an incident. It was here for the first time that I was hissed—the part, *Fainwould*, in *Raising the Wind*. I suppose I deserved it, but it was the admirable acting of Emley, in Jeremy Diddler, that caused the offence. He made me laugh so heartily at the breakfast table, that I could not speak for laughing, until the audience tried to change my tune. I went off the stage laughing, while the audience were hissing, but I did not return that night: I ran out of the (theatre,) barn, home. How the farce was finished, I never exactly heard. I received a long lecture from the manager the following morning, upon the folly of my course, concluding with what I then thought a remarkable expression, but which experience has taught me was correct, that no actor, however high 'his station, ever passed through his career, without at some period encountering the displeasure of an audience; that I must make up my mind to such scenes, if I intended to remain upon the stage, and that nothing but my inexperience prevented him from discharging me forthwith.

M'Cann and myself lodged in the same house, and most excellent quarters we had, passing a pleasant fortnight, notwithstanding the bad business. Not so the manager: his troubles were beginning, as we thought ours ending. Being in arrears for rent, his goods and chattels were arrested " in transitu," as a lawyer would express himself. So well had the landlord taken his measures, and with such secrecy, that he not only secured the scenery, wardrobe, dresses and properties of the manager, but the trunks containing the wearing apparel of the actors, and whatever little private property they possessed—all was in possession of the Philistines.

Unconscious of what had happened, M'Cann, Emley, Mrs. Emley, her children, and myself, were on our road to Cumnock, as merry as larks, little dreaming of the mishap which was shortly to overtake us, only thinking what sort of a house we should open to on the following evening, none of us overburdened with money, but all in high spirits. We reached our destination, ordered dinner, which, while we were in the act of enjoying, Neville presented himself, with a face full of sorrow, to recount the sad tale of our undoing. To me it was of awful import. Every thing I possessed, except the clothes in which I was seated, appeared lost, without the possibility of recovery. But actors, like other human beings, seem to be most merry when they have most cause for sorrow. The bad puns, which passed by wholesale, elevated my spirits, and the first expressions of regret past, I never spent a more pleasant evening.

A council of war was assembled, when the ladies retired, and the course we proposed to pursue being marked out and determined upon, matters were left to take their chance, and not permitted to interrupt our hilarity. It was now my knowledge of business was to be turned to account. Being able to talk sensibly of warp and weft, winding, heckling, spinning, bleaching, &c., I resolved to wait upon Mr. Buchanan, inform him who I was, and trust to his generosity to release us all from our present dilemma. I started early in the morning for the mills, procured an interview with the foreman, Mr. B. being unfortunately absent. After a well told tale, I succeeded in releasing all the things, promising in the name of Mr. Neville, that the landlord should be paid out of our first receipts, and returned in triumph to my companions, bringing the captured ammunition into port, free from all charge for conveyance to Cumnock. This very act, so adroitly managed on my part, caused my separation from Neville. Once in possession of the scenery, &c., he did not feel disposed to comply with the terms on which they had been released. On this I peremptorily insisted, and went so far as to threaten I would return to Catharine Mills and inform Mr. Buchanan of the breach of faith contemplated. I carried my point, obtaining the money, but I lost my situation, and shortly after bade adieu to Scotland, which I have never visited since.

It was in Cumnock I heard of the death of poor Berry, one of my first theatrical acquaintance, once the idol of the the Edinburgh audiences, and, beyond doubt, the best low comedian of this day. Liston, Matthews, and Emery, combined, would not have formed a better actor than Jack Berry; but dissipation and repeated acts of neglect of his profession, through dissipation, at length so exhausted the kindness and patience of Mr. Henry Siddons, that he was reluctantly compelled to abandon him; and, in leaving the Edinburgh theatre, the last restraint upon his unhappy failing, was lost in Dumbarton, where he and his wife had been giving an entertainment of a theatrical nature. He fell in a state of intoxication against a glass door, lacerating his arm in so dreadful a manner as to produce lockjaw, from which, by the care and attention of his physician, he recovered, but was never the same man again. He became a member of a travelling company, performing in the open air, at fairs: and thus the man whose talents had delighted the most enlightened audience in the British empire, was converted into the low buffoon of a mountebank's caravan. He died in abject misery, almost shunned by his pot-house companions. Let his example be a warning to others, who, while they breathe a sigh to the memory of lost talent, will avoid that dangerous of all seductions to an actor—convivial meetings, and free and easy societies—where your company is valued only by the song you may be able to sing, or the amusing anecdote you are expected to relate—where many who court your society within the walls of a tavern, would refuse to acknowledge an actor's salute in the open day, in the broad highway. To all such be your motto—

Nemo me impune lacesset.

CHAPTER IV.

Parting of old Friends. Grave of Burns. Gretna Green. Alnwick. Kendal. New Acquaintance. Journey Across the Mountain. Harrogate Springs. Mr. Booth and Mrs. Renaud, (late Mrs. Powell,) Theatre Royal, York. Captivity of Bonaparte. Edmund Kean. Canterbury and Rochester.

THE separation from Neville being finally determined upon, I saw the landlord at Mauchline paid in full, and passed on to pay a farewell visit to my numerous friends in Ayr; having once more tasted the good cheer of Mrs. M'Culloch's table, I turned my course towards England, resolved if possible, to procure a situation in Mrs. Butler's company, then performing at Kendal, Westmoreland; or, failing there, to proceed to Newcastle-on-Tyne, and offer my services to Mr. Macready, for any sum he might think proper to offer; hoping, under his excellent tuition, to rise rapidly in the profession. Full of these resolutions, I arrived in Cumnock, where I booked my name for an outside seat in the coach for Carlisle, which was to start the following day—the last evening I spent in the society of those who remained of my first theatrical companions, with whom I expected to have passed a much longer period of my life. It was a merry and a sad parting. I was aware I carried with me the good wishes of the whole fraternity, and I know I parted from them with regret. Emley and M'Cann were the only two I was ever destined to meet again. With the latter I corresponded regularly, until within a few months of his death; previous to which I lost sight of him, and have learned he was confined in the King's Bench Prison for debt. False pride prevented him from making known his situation. If I could not have paid his debts, I could, at least, have administered to his wants, and would willingly have shared the last guinea in my possession with him. We have stood, shoulder to shoulder, in many a scrape, and a braver little fellow never left the land of St. Patrick. —Peace be to his ashes.

The ceremony of shaking hands—and, in this instance, hearts went with them—being over, I received and exchanged several small presents, as tokens of remembrance, mounted the coach-box with the driver, and, as the guard gave the signal for departure, waved a last adieu to the assembled company. My reflections, for the first ten miles, were by no means pleasant. Old associations had rendered the Port Glasgow company dear to my feelings. The kindness I experienced from one and all, the ready manner in which many of them had instructed me in the profession, were all presented to my memory; and, in justice, I must add, I never met a company of players so totally devoid of those little feelings of envy and jealousy which frequently render the lives of actors unpleasant, destroying that harmony which ought to exist, where people, from their avocation, are compelled to pass a greater portion of their time in each other's society.

I arrived at Dumfries about 12 o'clock, where I slept; and, early in the morning, visited the grave of Burns. Having passed many a joyful hour in the cottage where he was born, I could not lose the opportunity of viewing his last resting place on earth. At six o'clock in the morning, I again mounted the coach-box and proceeded rapidly to that famous spot in English history, *Gretna Green*, "where runaway couples cross the boundary of their native kingdom to visit a Scotch blacksmith, whose fetters having been tightly rivetted, most of them wish in vain to unrivet again, before the end of twelve months." This place was, of course, an object of curiosity to most of the passengers, and the driver indulged us with five minutes' delay; after which we proceeded at a

sharp pace to the inn, where we changed horses, and which
is the last possessing the same accommodation in leaving
Scotland.

After an absence of seven years, I entered England, widely
metamorphosed. When I departed, as a boy, with spirits full
of youthful hope, for the roof of my uncle in Edinburgh, my
prospects in life were of the brightest nature. My own actions
had altered the position of affairs. I was now out of employment, travelling only upon the chance of finding an engagement. The beautiful town of Alnwick, the first stopping-
place upon my route, awakened a train of feeling, which
forced me to acknowledge, I had embarked in a Quixotic expedition, which would, in all probability, plunge me into the
depth of wretchedness before I could expect to reap the
slightest remuneration, beyond a mere subsistence. My
thoughts reverted to Dundee, and to those friends whose
offers had been so repeatedly rejected, and I wished, from the
bottom of my heart, I had never deserted my home. In this
state of mind I reached Carlisle, where I had to remain nearly
a day, and where I replenished my exchequer by the sale of
my watch-chain, bade adieu to melancholy recollections, and
started onward in the mail for Penrith, passing through Shap,
and over the mountains of Westmoreland, to Kendal, at which
place I arrived at two o'clock on the morning of the 12th of
April, 1815.

At the Crown Inn I enjoyed an excellent night's rest, and
breakfast over, my first inquiry of Mr. Riggs, the worthy
landlord, was whether the company of comedians had left the
place. To my great joy, he answered in the negative, immediately furnishing me with a play-bill, for the following evening. It announced, The School of Reform, and We Fly by
Night, for the benefit of Mr. Meadows (now of Covent-Garden
Theatre.) I waited upon Mrs. Butler, stating my views and
wishes, when she informed me Mr. Thomas Mercer was on
the point of leaving the company; but, being a total stranger
to my talent, she must require a specimen of my abilities,
before she could make me an offer of any description. It was
therefore agreed, that I should play Henry, in Speed the
Plough, for Mr. Hallam's benefit, on Wednesday evening. At
the theatre, I was introduced to her brother, Mr. George
Jefferson; it was a neat building, regularly built, and capable
of holding from sixty to seventy pounds. I was much pleased
with the manner in which the business was conducted. Meadows played Tyke, with a feeling and talent rarely seen in a
country theatre, and the whole performance was such as to
make me anxious to become a member of the company. On
Wednesday, I appeared in Henry, to a house fortunately well
filled. The actor being a favourite, the *debut* was pronounced

so promising, that I was offered fifteen shillings per week, the highest salary given, which I cheerfully accepted, really happy to think I had obtained a situation. The following ladies and gentlemen composed the company:—Mr. G. Jefferson, stage manager; Mr. Brewer, Mr. Meadows, Mr. Mercer, Mr. Hallam, Mr. George, Mr. Martin, Mr. Bristow, Mr. J. O'Conner, Master Samuel Butler, Mr. Stoker, Mrs. Butler, Mrs. Murray, Mrs. Mercer, Miss Craven, Miss Stoker, Miss Butler, Mrs. Martin; to which list I have now to add, Mr. Wemyss. In Mrs. Butler's company I remained three years. A very laughable adventure took place, arising from the custom of closing all the licensed theatres during the Passion Week. The actors, on these occasions, generally divide themselves into small parties of four and five, and visit the villages in the neighbourhood, where dramatic amusements are seldom seen, and never for a longer period than three or four nights. A party of this description, consisting of Mr. Mercer, Mr. Meadows, Mr. J. O'Conner, Mrs. Murray, and Miss Craven, having announced George Barnwell for representation, at Kirby Longsdale, found themselves deficient in numbers to complete the cast; and, as the leader of our orchestra, Mr. William Mercer, had accompanied them, they persuaded him to make his first appearance on any stage, as the Uncle, in George Barnwell. As he had frequently boasted, that the young lads (as he used to call them, although he was but twenty-five years of age himself) knew nothing of acting, he would do it, if only to show them what it was. Therefore, having diligently perfected himself in the words of the author, (which, at rehearsal, he spoke very well, but with a broad Yorkshire dialect,) he prepared to give the lads a lesson, which was to be of service to them during their natural lives. But when the time arrived, stage fright deprived this boaster of his courage—he could scarcely utter a word. The stage being cleared for his entrance, he commenced thus—

"If I were superstitious now."——(A dead pause.)

"I say, if I was superstitious."—(Another pause.)

"If I was superstitious, I should say." (Aside)—"Tom, why don't you stick me?"

But Tom, who played George Barnwell, did not intend to let him off so easily, but remained in his retirement, convulsed with laughter. So the Uncle was compelled to proceed, which he did, thus—

"Oh, religion is a blessed thing."——(A pause.)

"Religion is much"——(Another pause.)

"Religion is——Oh, Tom, I say, do stick me." (Aside.)

To this Tom replied, in the words of the Author—"Oh, it is impossible." This line produced such a ludicrous effect upon the audience, who had become aware of the matter, that the only thing to restore gravity was to despatch the Uncle as quick as possible: but this was not to be so easily done. Mr. William Mercer's memory had, by this time, returned—he suddenly exclaimed, "Stop, Tom, I know it now—I can repeat every word of it." And he began—"If I were superstitious now, I should say"—dingle, dingle, went the prompter's bell, and down came the curtain, amid the uproarious laughter of the audience; and so ended the third act of the tragedy of George Barnwell, and the last attempt of Mr. Mercer to give practical lessons in acting.

The season at Kendal being concluded, we next proceeded to Northallerton, in Yorkshire. This distance is something over sixty miles, which, on a fine summer morning, in company with O'Conner, Meadows, William Mercer, and Mr. Kelly, I started to walk. We allowed ourselves two days to accomplish the task, walking twenty miles before breakfast the first day, fourteen to dinner, and fourteen after dinner; thus accomplishing forty-eight miles the first day, over a mountainous country, and leisurely walking fifteen miles on the following day. So accustomed had I become to fatigue of this description, that a walk of thirty miles was no common occurrence, for a day's amusement, when we had no act at night.

In Northallerton we remained six weeks, when we repaired to the races at Beverley, and from thence to Harrogate Springs, for the summer. Here it was I first met

BOOTH,

the most eccentric of all mad tragedians. He was the first London star I ever acted with, and at that time in the height of his popularity. Who could have supposed that the "Wilford," who trembled with fear before this little tragedian, at Harrogate, in 1815, should, years afterwards, have paid him thousands of dollars as the manager of an American theatre? His performance of Bertram, at this time, was terrifically grand. His mind was in its full vigour, and a well cultivated soil it was. A more delightful companion, "*when not in his mood,*" it would be difficult to find. Gifted with powers of conversation the most agreeable, master of several languages, Lucius Junius Booth was born to control those over whom he wished to cast a spell of fascination. He was the only actor who had dared to measure strength with Kean—failing only through his own imprudence—trifling with his reputation—and at the same time with the public, who were desirous of fostering talent, which had suddenly burst upon them in a blaze of excellence. He first played at Covent Garden, then

c

at Drury Lane, then back to Covent Garden, until he was finally driven from the London stage, stamped with fame and character, to realise a fortune in the provincial theatres.

He was accused of being a servile imitator of Kean, which being reiterated by the London Press, became a received opinion, but a very erroneous one. It was only necessary to see the two actors on the stage together, to dispel it at once.— Booth felt and acted, when on the stage with Kean, as if conscious of his inferiority, which he candidly acknowledged; but, when separated, there are many of Kean's warmest admirers who do not hesitate to pronounce his performance of Richard equal, and his Hamlet superior, to Kean's representation of the same characters.

As I shall frequently have to mention Mr. Booth again, I shall only observe that he played three nights at Harrogate, and three nights at Ripon, in the same week, and left us all delighted with his acting, and equally well pleased with him off the stage.

Here, also, I met Mrs. Powel, of Drury Lane, (Mrs. Renaud,) the rival of the great Mrs. Siddons, who, when young, must have been a beautiful woman. Her acting spoke more to the heart than that of any lady I ever saw before or since, identifying herself with the character she was performing, until you forgot the woman in the actress. The first part I acted with her was Jaffier, in Venice Preserved. I had requested her indulgence in the morning at rehearsal, on two accounts—the first, the short time I had allowed for preparation, and the second, the consciousness of my inability to support her properly—but that I would do the best I could with a part far beyond my ability, and of which I knew nothing but the words. In the kindest manner, she repeated the part to me, impressing upon my mind those portions of the dialogue usually producing the greatest effect upon an audience. To her tuition I owed the success of my performance; and as we left the stage, at the end of the first act, her expression of "*Very well, indeed, sir—excellent,*" enabled me to proceed with that confidence which, in an actor, is the sure forerunner of success. The press complimented me highly on this performance, and even the manager condescended to thank me in the green-room. For years afterwards, I used to consider Jaffier my best part, and felt a desire to act it, long after I had ceased to appear in tragedy. Mrs. Renaud remained with us one year, playing a few nights in each town, and left us in Kendal, in 1817, to join the Edinburgh company, where she remained until her death. Her performance of Elvira, in Pizarro, and Alicia, in Jane Shore, was the perfection of the dramatic art; while her Lady Macbeth, although not so powerful, was second only to Mrs. Siddons. How they could spare such an actress from the London boards, was a question asked very often, but not readily answered. Oh, these Managers! these Managers!!

The eventful year of 1815 was made memorable by another remarkable occurrence. In company with Mr. George and Mr. O'Connor, I had paid a visit to the city of York, where the theatre was then under the management of Mr. Fitzgerald.— The play was the Fortune of War, the afterpiece the Wandering Boys, in which Mansel, famous for a well-written Defence of the Stage, was acting Count de Croissy, when a gentleman in the dress circle of boxes suddenly placed his feet upon the cushion of the hand-rail, and holding himself in that position by the pillar of the boxes, with scarcely breath enough to make himself distinctly heard, demanded that the performance should cease, until he addressed the audience.— This was met by hisses, and cries of "turn him out," until, amid the uproar, the name of Bonaparte was heard, followed by a cry of "hear him, hear him." He proceeded nearly thus, his agitation choking his utterance :— "Gentlemen, I have the pleasure—to inform you—Napoleon Bonaparte—has surrendered himself a prisoner of war—(dead silence, every one intent upon catching the next word)—to Captain Maitland, of his Majesty's ship Bellerophon." The whole audience rose—cheer followed cheer—the men waved their hats, the ladies their handkerchiefs—God save the King was called for—the whole company, male and female, appeared upon the stage, sang the national anthem, the audience joining in the chorus. At the conclusion, three cheers were given—Rule Britannia was played by the band, and three-fourths of the audience immediately left the theatre, to talk of the wonderful news, and to ask each other if it could be true. Thus ended my first visit to the York theatre. My readers will agree with me, that it was not easily to be forgotten.

From Harrogate we proceeded to Richmond, in Yorkshire, crossed to Northallerton, for the race week, returning to Richmond; and, at the close of the season, taking our departure for Whitby, where we remained during the winter, and opened the spring campaign at Ripon; from thence to Beverley; back to Harrogate and Richmond; then, over the mountains, to Ulverstone, in Lancashire, and Kendal, in Westmoreland—thus performing my first tour of a regular provincial circuit, occupying two years, from my first joining the company at Kendal; during which time Mr. Meadows, Mr. Hallam, Mr. and Mrs. Mercer, Mr. Brewer, Mr. Bristow, and Miss Craven, left us, their places being supplied by Mr. Calvert, then playing under the name of Young, but now known by his contest with the Rev. Mr. Best, and his admirable answer to that gentleman's attack upon the stage and its professors,) Mr. O'Conner, Mr. Francis O'Conner, Miss O'Conner, and Miss Stannard.

It was during my stay in Mrs. Butler's company, I had the misfortune to lose the friend and protector of my youth, Mr. Thomas Courtney, jun. He died in London, during the month of October, 1817; but he lives in my heart, and will continue there until that heart ceases to beat. Those only who knew his worth could appreciate his loss.

Requiescat in pace.

In Mrs. Butler's company I remained nearly three years, during which time an attachment had taken place between Miss Butler and myself, which was the cause of my departure. No objection was offered to our marriage by the friends of either party, but our extreme youth. I was scarcely twenty years of age, and the young lady not more than seventeen. It was agreed by all parties, that we should separate for twelve months, at the expiration of which time, if we remained steadfast in our affections, we were to be united, with the perfect approbation of our friends. Under this arrangement we parted, breathing vows of eternal constancy, *never to meet again.*

Mr. Munden, of Drury Lane theatre, procured me a situation with Mr. Dowton, in Canterbury, at a salary of twenty-five shillings per week, where I arrived in January, 1818, making my first appearance as Rover, in O'Keefe's play of Wild Oats. The company consisted of Mr. Hamerton, (the stage manager,) Mr. W. Dowton, Mr. H. Dowton, Mr. Wharton, Mr. Owen, Mr. John Sloman,) Mr. Marshall, Mr. Hamerton, jun., Mr. Jeffries, Mr. Hubbard, Mr. Wemyss; and, shortly afterwards, Mr. Calcraft, Miss Barry, Mrs. H. Dowton, (afterwards Mrs. J. Sloman, Mrs. Owen, Miss Leigh, Miss Kennedy, Mrs Hamerton, jun. A company of handsomer women I never saw collected within the walls of a theatre.

The four months I passed in Canterbury was really a round of delight. Miss Barry led the way, with a social party, which was repeated by the ladies alternately, every non-play night; while each Wednesday night we played in Feversham, starting in coaches provided for that purpose, after dinner, and returning after the play to Canterbury, forming a trip of pleasure occasionally made uncomfortable by a rainy day; but so full of fun and good humour, that we were like so many school-boys let loose for a holiday.

From Canterbury we proceeded to Rochester. In this city I first became familiar with the faces of the London actors, every week bringing down some star to grace our little theatre. Notwithstanding all which attraction, and the garrison at Chatham, Rochester is the worst theatrical town I ever acted in, in England. Here I was first introduced to that bright luminary of the stage,

EDMUND KEAN.

How shall I attempt to describe "the star" of the British stage the man, who, without a single friend, overcame obstacles almost insurmountable ; and, by one bold effort, swept the cold and polished school of Kemble from the stage, astonishing the English metropolis by his bold and natural conception of character, which he executed in such a style of excellence, that "no one but himself could be his parallel."

Treated with marked indifference, amounting almost to insult, by the actors and actresses who filled the " dramatis personæ," on the night of his first appearance at the Theatre Royal, Drury Lane ; and finding, before the end of the season, those same dignified ladies and gentlemen, who would scarcely return with civility the salute of an obscure country actor, among his most servile flatterers—filling the theatre nightly to overflowing—rejecting the society of the noble and learned —seeking his companions among those actors whom he had known in adversity, and to whom he ever proved a kind friend —he moved like a comet, to be wondered at, but not approached. Throughout his triumphal career,—raising the prostrate fortunes of the theatre to which he was attached— reigning sole monarch, without a rival, in the estimation of the public,—and yielding up, at last, a broken spirit, in one great effort to sustain his fame.

Whatever may have been the faults of his private life, his public career was a triumph of genius over prejudice; and the name of Edmund Kean, like that of Garrick, will descend to posterity, as "the actor" of his age.

The first time I ever saw him act, I played Wellborn, to his Sir Giles Overreach, in Massinger's Play of A New Way to Pay Old Debts. With the exception of my first appearance at Glasgow, I never suffered so much from stage fright; but his known kindness and affability, to actors of every grade, soon relieved me from my embarrassment. I supped with him after the performance, and, from that hour, he became my friend. Many years afterwards, in Baltimore, I had the good fortune to extricate him from a most unpleasant and dangerous situation. But, of this, hereafter,—if, good reader, you can travel with me across the Atlantic.

Mrs. Glover paid us a flying visit, during which I acted, for the first time, the part of Frank Heartall, in Cherry's comedy of the Soldier's Daughter. Charles Woodley should have been my character on the occasion, but Calcraft being absent, I was compelled to assume the light comedy hero. There is

an expression of the author's frequently used in this character
during the dialogue of, "In for it again," which proved a
source of much annoyance to me on this occasion, but is too
good a joke not to be recorded. A gentleman in the boxes,
who did not appear to relish my acting, and who must have
been something of a wit, having his patience worn out, repeated the words of " In for it again," after me thus, " Yes,
by heaven you are IN for it only, for I will be hanged if you
can play it. I wish you good night," and immediately left
the boxes. This produced a roar of laughter, not only from
the audience but from the actors, which must have ruined the
whole play, had I not goodnaturedly added at the first pause,
" Well, NOW I AM IN for it, sure enough," which was received
by a round of applause, and the play passed off without further interruption.

It was in the city of Rochester I found my name was
travelling beyond the company I was immediately attached
to. Mr. Thomas Robertson, the manager of the Lincoln circuit, unsolicited, made me an offer of one guinea and a half
per week, to lead the light comedy and juvenile tragedy in
his company. Here, then, was the offer of a regular line of
business, and an increase of six per cent to my income. This
offer I accepted, and in six weeks from this time I finished
my career with Mr. Dowton, leaving the society of Mr.
Calcraft, Mr. Marshall, and Mr. Sloman, with regret.

Thus, in four years I had doubled my income, as derived
from my professional exertions. The last part I played in
Rochester was Don Lodowick, in the Jew of Malta, for Mr.
Hamerton's benefit. I passed two days in London, with my
family, and then proceeded " en route" to Peterborough,
Northamptonshire.

CHAPTER V.

Peterborough. Joe Cowell. Wilkinson and Meadows. Singular Loss
of Memory. Shameful Breach of Decorum. Out, out, Damned Spot.
A Just Manager, and an Honest Man. Mr. Thomas Robertson. Offers
of New Engagements. Damnation of Mr. Buck's Tragedy of the
Italians, at Drury Lane Theatre.

I ARRIVED in Peterborough on the 10th of June, 1818, making
my first appearance, in Mr. Robertson's company, as Richmond, in "Richard the Third," following it by Rover, in
" Wild Oats," which had become quite a favourite character
with me. The company consisted of Mr. and Mrs. T.
Robertson, Mr. Fortescue, Mr. Henry, Mr. Collins, Mr.
Frederick Robertson, Mr. Cooke, Mr. J. O'Connor, Mr. Red-

ward, Mr. Beresford, Mr. Perry, Mr. Stanhope, Mr. and Mrs. Brooke, Miss Danby, Miss S. Danby, Miss R. Stannard, Mrs. Norris, Mr. Cowell and Mr. Wemyss.

The manager was pleased to express to me his satisfaction at my success, and during the time I remained a member of his company, which was nearly two years, I enjoyed as much felicity as ever falls to the lot of a country actor. Respected by the manager, one of the few members of the company admitted to his private parties, held in estimation by the audience, my pockets well filled, my theatrical wardrobe increased until it had become an object of envy to many of my brother performers, I had nothing left to wish for—but—a London engagement. Could I have divested myself of ambition, I could have terminated my theatrical career in the Lincoln circuit, possessed of a handsome competence. We visited Peterborough, Spalding, Boston, Lincoln, Newark-upon-Trent, Grantham, Wisbeach, Whittlesea, and Huntingdon, in each of which towns I had the fourth part of a benefit; that is to say, the names of two performers were announced at the head of the bills, and they shared the amount of the house with the manager, after eight pounds. This is decidedly the most equitable mode of giving benefits—the actor risking nothing but his personal exertions, in case of failure; if successful, the manager received a portion of the gain, to bear the loss of a less profitable night—by which means every actor was certain of obtaining some little emolument from the night intended for his benefit. My finances were never in such a flourishing state, although I have received ten times the amount of weekly salary.

A country actor, of rising reputation, looks forward with feverish anxiety to the moment that will allow him the opportunity of trying his powers before a metropolitan audience—that test of merit which proves fatal to so many, and from which there is no appeal. Let an actor, on his first appearance in London, be rejected, and his prospects are blighted for ever. He returns to the country a ruined man, (professionally,) managers rarely feeling disposed to offer engagements under such circumstances, and the public ready to pronounce his failure a just retribution for his presumption. But let success crown his efforts, and the theatres in which he has previously played will be scarcely large enough to admit the audience which will nightly flock to witness his performance, each town claiming the merit of having been the first to discover and foster his talent.

Formerly, a London engagement was the *ne plus ultra* of an actor's wishes. Once successful there, he was fixed for life, or during good behaviour. Not so now. A London engagement is the most precarious; caprice of managers, desire of new faces on the part of the public, with a hundred other minor causes, render the London actor (unless on the topmost round of the ladder) the most dependent of his tribe. He is not sure of his engagement from season to season. Thus, country actors have lost half those ardent feelings of romance, which determine to stop at nothing short of the accomplishment of their desires. The ultimate reward of their poverty and professional toil has faded from their view, the spirit of emulation slumbers if it be not entirely destroyed, and without a vigorous effort to reform existing abuses, the drama, which has withstood for ages the attacks of bigots, will fall a victim to the suicidal acts of its own professors.

In September, 1818, Mr. Cowell left us, in the city of Lincoln, to try his fortune at Drury Lane. He appeared there on the 8th of October, being fully successful. We all felt pride at his having established himself with the London public: he was extremely popular with us, both before and behind the curtain. His loss was supplied by Mr. Meadows, of Bath, whom I had not seen since he left Butler's company, and from whom I learned I was indebted to him for my recommendation to the situation I now held. Our acquaintance was renewed, and ripened into a friendship which remains firm to this day. He is one of those members of the profession of whose friendship I feel proud, and whose conduct does honour to the stage. He spent the summer season with us, and returned in the winter to Bath, where he was held in high estimation.

He was succeeded by another equally worthy, but quite an original, Wilkinson, of the English Opera House, London, whose admirable performance of Geoffrey Muffincap, in Peake's farce of "Amateurs and Actors," stamped his fame as one of the best low comedians of the day. He passed the winter with us in Boston, and returned to London in the spring. He is another who may be held up as an example of what actors ought to be—upright, honest and honourable in all his dealings, a warm friend, and an excellent husband and father.

During the race week at Huntingdon, in the autumn of 1819, while acting the part of Charles Surface, in the "School for Scandal," my memory suddenly abandoned me on the stage, notwithstanding the word was freely given, not only by the prompter, but by the actors on the stage. I could not recollect one single sentence, but was forced to retire up the stage, and seat myself. The audience, knowing I was generally correct in the words of my author, loudly applauded, while I remained at least a minute, unconscious of any thing around me; when, bowing to the audience, I resumed the part as fluently as if no interruption had taken place. How to account for this singular event, I am at a loss, even now, twenty years after its occurrence. I had played the part before, was perfect to a monosyllable, yet could not think of a single word, and exhibited a degree of childish sensitiveness whenever the subject was alluded to. Never afterwards did I appear on the stage in this character without a feeling of doubt and fear, and an anxiety to finish the second speech in the fourth act as rapidly as possible.

From Huntingdon we went to Whittlesea in the Isle of Ely, where, for the first and only time in my theatrical career, I appeared upon the stage in a state of intoxication. Being holiday time, I was induced to taste some old English ale, brewed expressly for this festival, kept by all the substantial farmers in the neighbourhood, who vie with each other as to the age and strength of their malt liquor, freely disbursed among their friends. Although I did not drink more than one glass, so powerful was the effect, that I soon became aware I was " *non compos :*" however, to the theatre I hied. Whether the glare of the Float aided the fumes of the liquor, I know not, but well do I remember, that no answer did I return, but a laugh, to all Rob Roy's flaming speeches—not one word of the part of Rashleigh Osbaldistone did I utter during the whole performance. I laughed, and the audience laughed with me, or at me ; had they hissed me it would have been more to their credit, and what I richly merited. The crime carried along with it the punishment—a sick headache —and long did I remember the feeling of shame with which I encountered my manager on the following morning ; he said not a word, but he looked—what he thought he ought to say. According to the rules of the theatre, I had forfeited all claim to my salary, and wishing to avoid a lecture, I did not go near the treasury until sent for, when Mr. Robertson addressed me nearly thus :—" Young man, your own sense of right and wrong, and the deep contrition you have shown for your impropriety of conduct, will make a more lasting impression than any harshness I can inflict—there is your money—your only reproach will be never to mention the subject again."

This well-timed lenity had its effect ; but Mr. Robertson always knew how to make himself respected, even when compelled to censure. The collected profession could not have surprised me off my guard on any occasion after this, when I had my duty to perform at the theatre in the evening ; but such was the just manner in which the Lincoln manager conducted all the affairs of his company ; it was a rule with him, that all forfeiture of salary, for neglect, belonged to the actors, and should, on no occasion, be allowed to find its way into the manager's pocket ; the forfeits, therefore, were cheerfully paid, whenever incurred, and a fund created, from which actors in distress were occasionally relieved, and from which the mem-

bers of the company derived a source of gratification and
social intercourse—a supper or dinner being given regularly
once a year.   If the forfeits amounted to a sufficient sum, they
were appropriated to defray the expense.   If the calls upon
this fund had been too frequent, or no forfeitures had been
incurred, the manager cheerfully made good the difference,
with a complimentary speech on the good behaviour of the
company for the preceding year.   Mr. Robertson was regarded
more like the father of a family, than the director of a theatre;
and were I asked to point out a strictly just and honest man,
Mr. Thomas Robertson, the Lincoln manager, *would be that
man.*   Health, happiness, and prosperity to him and his, is my
fervent wish.   We parted the best of friends; and, should
fate ordain we meet again, the hearty shake of the hand, that
genuine mark of friendship, would be cordially reciprocated.

Of Mrs. T. Robertson, it is unnecessary to say more than
she has been an excellent actress; and although somewhat
impaired by age, there are few of the younger ladies in the
profession who possess her flow of animal spirits, added to
which she is an authoress of some merit, and a woman possessing a strong, well cultivated mind.

In the month of August, 1819, I received an offer from Mr.
Macready, lessee of the Theatre Royal, Bristol, of two pounds
per week, and the clear half of the receipts of a benefit.   Before accepting this offer, I laid it before Mr. Robertson, asking
his advice, which he gave in the most friendly manner, adding,
" I shall be sorry to lose you, but I think your reputation will
be increased, and I would make the trial; but I exact from
you a promise, if you find yourself uncomfortable, that you
accept no other situation without first writing to me."   I
therefore closed with Macready, in the full hope that my appearance in Bristol would be the stepping-stone to a London
engagement.

The Bristol Theatre was to open on Monday evening, the
15th of November; and the last time I played in the Lincoln
company, was on the 18th of October, 1819, on which occasion
Mr. Rayner, now of Covent Garden Theatre, made his first
appearance as Tyke, in the " School of Reform."   I played
Mr. Ferment; and how a London audience could tolerate Mr.
Rayner's Tyke, with Emery's performance of the same part
vivid in their recollection, is a theatrical paradox which not
unfrequently occurs.   Without any disparagement to Mr.
Rayner's talents, Mr. Meadows was as far superior to him, in
Tyke, as Mr. John Kemble ever was to Mr. Barrymore, in
Hamlet.

Before bidding a final adieu to Lincoln, I ought to mention,
that in a trip of pleasure to London, to spend the Passion
Week, I saw on Easter Monday, Mr. Buck's tragedy of " The

Italians," *damned* at Drury Lane Theatre. It was the first time I had ever witnessed any thing of the kind, and it had at least the charm of novelty to recommended it. The pit, to a man, indulged in the motion formerly known as the "O. P. dance;" this, with the discordant yells of the gallery, the hissing and clapping of hands in the boxes, laid in a reasonable stock of headache for a week. The first signal of decided hostility was shown to Mr. H. Kemble, who played one of the heroes; "Kemble, do your duty," from an auditor in the pit, was the signal for a general attack. Had Mr. Buck's friends been less noisy, the play might have escaped. but the display of a placard, prepared for the purpose, reading thus—" Will a British public suffer an insolent actor (alluding to Kean) and his pot companions, to trample on deserving merit?" sealed the fate of the play. Mr. Rae and Mr. Hamblin were the only two individuals who obtained any thing like a hearing, while the ladies, Mrs Glover in particular, came in for a full share of censure. Mr. Stephen Kemble at length came forward, and commencing an address, with, "Ladies and gentlemen, I assure you I was called out of town"——a wag in the gallery, asked in the same tone of voice, " Why the devil did you not take the ' Italians' with you ?"

This was followed by a roar of laughter, and the manager could no longer succeed in obtaining a hearing. The noise and tumult became louder every moment, until a placard was displayed, in the front of the stage, with the words, "' *The Italians, is withdrawn.*"

Three cheers followed the annnuciation, and in a short time the house was empty, leaving the actors to enjoy the Castle of Wonders by themselves.

———

CHAPTER VI.

Theatre Royal Bristol. First Night of the Season. Darkness Made Visible. Success in Rover. Macready the Manager, and Macready the Tragedian, Father and Son. Bath Theatre. Domestic Afflictions. Infringement of Managerial Discipline. Departure for Exeter. Royal Deaths. Fire. Actors' Losses. Kindness of the People at Exeter Oppression of Managers. Open Rebellion. First Attempt at Management.

I left Lincoln on Wednesday, the 20th of October, 1819; spent a fortnight in London, during which time I visited the theatres every night, and arriving in Bristol on Saturday morning, the 13th of November, found my name announced for Rover, in " Wild Oats," for Monday evening. I waited upon Mr. Macready, to report my arrival, and securing lodgings in King's street, a few doors from the theatre, prepared to open the campaign, which the manager himself had announced in the following manner :—

"MR. MACREADY most respectfully acquaints the ladies and gentlemen of Bristol, and its vicinity, that during the vacation every possible exertion has been made to complete the decorations and embellishments of this theatre, in a style worthy the inhabitants of a city second only to the metropolis of the nation. In this undertaking, the gratification and accommodation of the public in general, have superseded every other consideration. The first mechanics have been employed, and without any comment on the actors' abilities, their efforts will be submitted to the *opinion, judgment, decision,* and support of the Bristol audience."

On entering the theatre on Monday morning, I was rejoiced to find Miss Leigh, whom I had formerly known in Canterbury, was engaged as the first comedy actress; this was an agreeable meeting to both parties, for of all the annoyance to which an actor is subjected, there is none so horrible as a first rehearsal in a new company. The nods, the winks, the observations, made sufficiently loud to be overheard, and the strictures passed upon the new comers, have shaken the nerves of some of the oldest stagers.

However, time, which waits for no man, brought on the hour to commence the performance. During the day I had felt more than unusually nervous; the thought of playing Rover on those boards, where Lewis, Elliston, and Stanley, had in turn been the favourites of the audience, in the same character, which was to prove the touchstone of my own abilities, had rendered me doubtful of success.

On my first appearance I was most cordially received by an excellent house; the first scene passed off smoothly, but in the middle of my second scene, the *gas* was suddenly extinguished, and the whole house left for several minutes in complete darkness. This was an awkward occurrence, but it put the audience in good humour, and the play proceeded with much spirit. As I left the stage, at the end of the fourth act, I received two distinct rounds of applause, the most cheering sounds to me I ever heard within the walls of a theatre. I was again warmly applauded in the scene in Banks' cottage, and was flattering myself with a triumph, all but won, when the unfortunate gas was again extinguished, and all efforts to rekindle the flame proved abortive. We had to finish the play by the aid of a dozen tallow candles, hastily caught up from all quarters of the theatre. Thus ended my first appearance in Bristol. The press, the following day, was loud in my praise, and I was convinced I had made a most favourable impression on my audience,

My second appearance was in Doricourt, in the "Belle's Stratagem;" my third, as Sir George Airy, in the Busy Body;" then Dick Dowlas, in the "Heir at Law," &c. &c.

I was never better received by any audience before whom I have had the honour of playing, than by the citizens of Bristol. Congratulated upon my success from all quarters, I looked forward to a pleasant winter season, but my sojourn with Mr. Macready was destined to prove of short duration.

I received a letter from London, dated December 3d, 1819, informing me of the death of my beloved grandmother. This blow, although long expected, was a painful bereavement. Brought up under her eye, born under her roof, and accustomed to regard her with even more reverence than my own parents, it was but natural I should be anxious to pay the last mournful office of respect by being present at her funeral. I requested Mr. Macready's permission, which he had the brutality to withhold. I resolved at all hazards to go to London, and communicated to him my resolution; his answer was in keeping with his previous refusal. He told me "to go at my peril." *I did go*, and the breach of my engagement was the consequence.

I left Bristol on Thursday evening, and returned in the night coach on Saturday, ready to play Colonel Mannering on the Monday, for which I found myself announced. He refused to pay me a single shilling for the past week, and when I expressed myself perfectly willing to leave the theatre, and abandon my engagement, which was for the season, he insisted upon my giving him six weeks' notice. This I complied with, and immediately wrote to Messrs. Bennet & Hughes, of Exeter, from whom I received an offer of engagement, by the return of mail. No sooner was Macready acqainted with this fact, than he expressed a desire to retain me. At the expiration of the six weeks he insisted upon my remaining one week longer, to make up the time I had devoted to my domestic troubles, and for which he had already deprived me of a week's income. This it was impossible to comply with, and he retained a balance of five pounds sterling which he owed me, and which I never received, although, after my departure, feeling somewhat ashamed of his conduct, he asserted publicly in the green-room that he had sent the money after me. It might have been so, for I believe he was an honest man, but if such a letter was ever forwarded to Exeter it never came to hand.

Notwithstanding the great cause I have to complain of Mr. Macready's conduct toward me, yet I learned more during my short stay in his company, of the practical part of my profession, than any two years of past experience had afforded me. He was a strict disciplinarian—one of the best instructors of

acting I ever met, but a perfect oddity in his manner of imparting *that* instruction. Billy Lascelles, of whom many
singular anecdotes are related, was the only man who knew
completely how to manage him. Many a pound note, in addition to his regular salary, has he received for obligations
conferred, by acting parts at short notice, when a sudden discharge of some member of the company, for real or supposed
offence, had created a vacuum in the dramatis personæ of the
play of the evening.

One anecdote I will relate, before I bid him adieu, which
will serve to illustrate his general character, and manner of
transacting business. Mr. Darley and Mr. Garthwaite, sustaining two characters in a play, in which it was necessary for
both to wear their hats, Mr. Darley had neglected to take his
on the stage, for which he forfeited both the actors, alleging
that Mr. Darley had transgressed the rules of the theatre
by appearing on the stage improperly dressed, and that
Garthwaite deserved to be forfeited, for not laying his hat
aside, and thus exposing to the audience the fault of his
companion. To this act of injustice Garthwaite refused to
submit, and actually left the theatre. He was engaged from
the York Theatre some time afterwards, but refused to treat
with Macready until he consented to return the forfeit, and
acknowledge himself in error; not a very difficult matter to
effect, for once convinced he was wrong, he was ever willing
to make reparation.

While in Bristol I first met

Mr. WILLIAM MACREADY,

a gentleman who deservedly ranks high, as one of the most
finished actors of the English stage. Indebted to nature for
no personal requisite, but by laborious study, and love of his
profession, attaining eminence. He is a polished scholar and
a gentleman, although an irascible one. In the study of his
profession, he possessed advantages, in the tuition of his
father, which must have made an actor of any young man
possessing one-tenth of Macready's ability. No wonder, then,
he rose so rapidly to fame, aided by such parts for originals as
Gambia, Pescara, Amurath, and Ludovico, and surrounded
by such actors as Young, Charles Kemble, and Miss O'Neil,
to call forth all the powers of a cultivated mind. To Mr.
Shiel's tragedies he owes his present position; and well did
he repay the author for confiding to his hands the daring vil-
lains of his creation.

On his first appearance at Covent Garden Theatre, it
wanted but one laugh to have turned all the laboured efforts
of the actor into ridicule. Had the tittering which com-

menced on the first bench of the pit, extended a little further,
this gentleman, who justly prides himself on having placed
the plays of Shakspeare before his countrymen in their proper
garb, would have returned to the country a broken-hearted
and rejected actor ! few men, like Vandenhoff, possessing iron
nerve sufficient to encounter two failures, yet finally make
good his position on the London stage.

He acted with us but two nights, "Coriolanus" and
"Richard the Third." By a singular chance, Kean played
the same part at Bath on the same night, which, as I had
seen Macready play the part at Covent Garden, I took the
opportunity of paying a visit to my friend Meadows, for the
purpose of witnessing. At Bath I was introduced to Mr.
Woulds, Mr. Rowbotham, Mr. Conway and Mr. Paul Bedford,
and many pleasant hours we spent together.

In the month of January, 1820, I started from Bristol, in a
snow storm, on my journey to Exeter, where I arrived in
safety, and found myself underlined for Rover, on Wednesday
evening; but I found the whole city in a state of commotion,
in consequence of the death of the Duke of Kent, (the father
of Queen Victoria,) for whose reception a box had been splen-
didly fitted up at the theatre, which he was to have visited
on Monday evening. By the advice of the mayor, the theatre
was closed for one week, as a mark of respect to the memory
of the royal duke. Thus, the managers not only lost the
profits of an overflowing house, but the actors lost their
week's salary; this was the first stumbling block in this most
unlucky of unlucky seasons.

On the following Monday I opened in Rover. The company
consisted of Mr. Bennett and Mr. Hughes, (the managers,)
Mr. Harvey, Mr. W. H. Bennett, Mr. Dawson, Mr. J. Dawson,
Mr. Butler, Mr. J. Salter, Mr. Libby, Mr. Harris, Mr. Southey,
(brother to the poet laureate of England,) Mrs. Hughes, Mrs.
Bennett, Mrs. Dawson, Mrs. Harvey, and, shortly afterwards,
Miss Leigh. My first appearance was pronounced most satisfactory, both to the audience and the managers; but fortune
treated us most scurvily. Scarcely had I played one week
before the death of the King, (George the Third,) again closed
the theatre, during a general mourning of three weeks.

The managers devoted this forced vacation to the production of the burletta of "Rochester," which had been so successful in London, at the Olympic Theatre, under the direction
of Mr. Elliston. This piece was furnished with new and appropriate scenery, dresses and properties, was well rehearsed,
and placed before the audience in a style of perfection not
often witnessed in a provincial theatre. The house was
crowded on the first representation, and the success perfect.
After the second performance, about one o'clock in the morn-

ing, I was aroused by a violent knocking at my bed-room door, and a request from Mr. Bennett, who was much afflicted with asthma, for God's sake to take the key and run as fast as possible to the theatre—*which was on fire.* I was the first actor who reached the spot, just in time to see the roof fall in : all hope of rescuing any thing from the theatre, was at an end. By great exertions the flames were prevented from spreading devastation all around. The morning dawned on a heap of smouldering ruins, and a company of actors out of employment. This was the first theatre I ever had the misfortune to belong to which was destroyed by fire, although conflagrations, during my career, have been very numerous.

The people of Exeter, with a praiseworthy spirit, set on foot a subscription for the relief of the actors, and in less than forty-eight hours a sum amounting to one hundred and seventy pounds was received, which was distributed among those actors who had lost their theatrical property by this fatal occurrence.

The directors of the New Assembly buildings, leading on to the Northernay, at that time only roofed in, granted the use of the building to Messrs. Bennet and Hughes, and by almost magical rapidity, we played in an entire new theatre on the following Monday. The scenery was brought from the Dock (now Devonport) Theatre—the dresses for " Rochester," made up by the assistance of countless volunteers. We opened to a splendid house, and " Rochester" had a most successful run. This misfortune occurred on the 5th of March, 1820.

The managers were not insured, and consequently were heavy losers; but by exertions of the most indefatigable nature, they succeeded in having their theatre rebuilt, and opened on the 10th of January, in the following year, 1821. It is without exception the most beautiful theatre out of London. How the old building was destroyed must ever be matter of surmise, but it was generally attributed to the introduction of the gas. An immense chandelier was suspended from the centre of the dome, from which the audience part of the theatre was solely lighted ; the continued heat in so confined a space, was supposed to have produced spontaneous combustion ; the fire originated in the roof, and cannot reasonably be attributed to any other source.

This season was a most disastrous one to the actors, who lost six weeks' salary in four months. It is true the managers, also, had been great sufferers, but they possessed many resources—they had a theatre in Plymouth, another in Dock, besides Weymouth and Totness, and a theatre in the Isle of Guernsey ; to any one of which they could have repaired, with an assurance of success. They preferred availing themselves of the sympathy of the public of Exeter, warmly awakened in their behalf, and had no cause to complain of the result, their receipts having exceeded their most sanguine expectations. It was with feelings of surprise, therefore, we saw a notice posted in the green-room, that the salaries would be reduced during the ensuing season at Plymouth.

This proposition, under the circumstances, was illiberal and unjust. The actors had borne patiently the deprivations of the season, which had curtailed more than one-third of their income—they had, one and all, strenuously contributed to the completion of the temporary theatre, so fortunately thrown in their way—the managers had reaped a rich harvest from those exertions, and the reward of the actor was to be a permanent reduction of his salary during the whole season, at Plymouth, and Dock, (Devonport,)—a most ungenerous and ill-timed parsimony, which I, for one, determined not to submit to.

A meeting of the company was called, to take into consideration this proposition of the managers, at which I offered a resolution, that rather than submit to the terms offered, we should form a strolling expedition, on our own account, or take the Plymouth Theatre on our own responsibility, as a commonwealth, paying the managers such a rent for the use of their property as might be agreed on between us. This last proposition was rejected by Messrs. Bennet and Hughes, and the alternative presented, to accept their terms or close the theatre altogether, until the summer season at Weymouth.

I now offered to advance forty pounds sterling, without any consideration but the re-payment of the money at the first moment the treasury should contain as much over the current expenses, for the strolling expedition. This plan was organized by myself, Mr. Dawson, Mr. J. Dawson, and Mr. Butler, who seceded from the theatre, taking with us Mr. and Mrs. Southey, Miss Leigh, Mrs. Dawson, Mr. Harris, and Mr. Libby, adding Miss L. Leigh, and Mr. and Mrs. Osbaldistone. I am sure the latter gentleman then never dreamt of being the lessee of the Theatre Royal, Covent Garden, London, or F. C. Wemyss of being manager of the Chesnut street Theatre, Philadelphia, when we entered our first managerial speculation, into which we were driven more by necessity than choice.

CHAPTER VII.

Rural Wanderings. Castle of Launceston. Great Torrington. Liskeard. Plymouth. Letter from an Aged Relative. Booth and Clara Fisher. First Offer of a London Engagement. Robert Gore Elliston, the Napoleon of the Drama. All at Coventry. Actors in Durance. Pageant of the Coronation. Politics Interrupting Pleasure. Wigan. American Engagement all but Abandoned. First Starring Expedition. Preparations for a Long Voyage.

WE commenced our new arrangement at Great Torrington, in Devonshire, a very pretty romantic little town, about thirty miles from Exeter. Our plan was to pay one pound sterling per week to each individual, the overplus to be appropriated to a general fund, to provide against reverses. Mr. Wemyss, Mr. Butler, Mr. Osbaldistone, and Mr. J. Dawson, were appointed managers—one of the four to have sole and undivided control of the affairs of the company, alternately, in each town we might visit. We cast lots for precedency, and it fell to my lot to commence; consequently, I had all the trouble of organizing our new scheme. The scenery was really handsome; we hired a tolerable wardrobe from Mr. Libby, and started, at the close of the Exeter season, well equipped.

In Great Torrington, I first wielded the theatrical sceptre, over a small but very merry and contented set of subjects. We remained in Torrington three months, at the expiration of which, we had neither added to nor diminished our funds: we paid our way, and no more. Having secured the waggons to transport our baggage to Liskeard, in Cornwall, according to agreement, I surrendered the power into the hands of Mr. James Dawson, who was to be our next governor, as the actors facetiously termed us.

J. Dawson, Butler, and myself, started to walk to Launceston, where we intended to sleep, and proceed leisurely the next day to Liskeard, the Cornish mountains and scenery rendering this mode of travelling preferable to riding; but it was so long since I had indulged my walking propensities that I soon regretted the cross-road we were travelling. Before I had proceeded two-thirds of the distance, I found myself unequal to the task, and was glad to avail myself of a conveyance, for a few miles, in a lime cart, which overtook us, in which I enjoyed two hours as sound sleep as ever fell to the lot of a tired mortal. Dearly, however, did I pay for this luxury; a drizzling rain, denominated a Scotch mist, had been falling during a portion of the time, which, saturating my coat with unslacked lime, literally burnt it off my back, and left me, on my arrival at Launceston, *minus* that precious garment, falling to pieces wherever it was touched. This misfortune was soon replaced, although it caused many a laugh at my expense, in Liskeard.

Whether it was that I was tired with our expedition, and thought the goal reached, gave me a favourable impression of the town, I am not prepared to say, but I think Launceston, with its old fashioned and ruined castle, the most beautiful and picturesque place I ever saw, surpassing Richmond, in Yorkshire, for beauty of situation. Tired as we were, we rambled about for three or four hours, and were really loth to leave the place, which we did, having fully determined to visit it professionally at the first opportunity.

While in Liskeard, in answer to a letter wherein I had recapitulated the sad mishap of my wearing apparel, I received the following from my grandfather; so characteristic of the sprightly humour of an old gentleman in his seventieth year, that I must give it an honourable place in these recollections.

(COPY.)

LONDON, August 22d, 1820.

" DEAR FRANK:

" The best answer to your melancholy letter is the enclosed 10*l.* bank post bill. You shall not be lost while I have a shot in the locker for 10*l.*, and you shall still have the 20*l.* in October, when you write for it; for how the devil can the service, if we withhold the supplies, go on; and I should be very loth to let my lord duke go to bed supperless.

" These little, and sometimes greater disasters too, oft happen to gentlemen of the sock and buskin.

" Mr. and Mrs. Abbot are well, but at the country house—will not see your letter until evening, and I was loth you should wait another day for the needful. Uncle George joins in love, and I remain,

" Your affectionate grandfather,

(Signed) THOMAS COURTNEY."

MR. FRANCIS COURTNEY WEMYSS.

In Liskeard we remained five weeks, under the management of Mr. J. Dawson, and added a few pounds to our common stock: we then made an arrangement with Bennett and Hughes for the Plymouth and Dock Theatres, where we passed the winter of 1820. Butler was the manager here, but was too lazy and indolent to attend to the duties of his position. He requested me to officiate for him, for which he was to give me as handsome a suit of clothes as I chose to order.

In Plymouth I met Mr. Booth and Miss Clara Fisher, (then a child of seven years of age, and a most extraordinary instance of precocious dramatic talent,) to both of whom I was under obligations for their liberal conduct, particularly the former, whom I had met previously at Harrogate.

Plymouth and Dock, although only two miles distant, have

each their own peculiar audience. The Plymouth Theatre enjoys the privilege of a patent, is elegantly built, and as capacious as Drury Lane, or Covent Garden, being capable of containing, at country prices of admission, from three to four hundred pounds sterling, yet rarely yielding in its nightly receipts more than thirty pounds, and not unfrequently falling below five pounds. From its size and beauty, and being so seldom filled, it had, at the time I speak of, acquired the significant title of the *Theatre of splendid misery*. The Dock Theatre, on the other hand, is one of the most inconvenient in England; but for the fact of possessing a regularly built stage, and an excellent stock of good scenery, it is a more like a country barn furnished up for theatrical representation, than a theatre situated in a large and flourishing town. When full, it will hold about eighty pounds sterling; but throughout a long season you can calculate upon an average of twenty, the inhabitants being partial to theatrical amusement, and having the garrison and dock-yards to assist in filling the house.

Here both Mr. Booth and Clara Fisher played to good houses in comparison to their receipts at Plymouth, and by a strange perversion of taste, the inhabitants of Plymouth would ride over to this inconvenient theatre to see a play, when their own palace, with the same attraction, would be utterly deserted.

In Plymouth and Dock we passed four months very agreeably, Osbaldistone alone contriving to make himself and others as uncomfortable as possible. Fortunately, his power to do injury was very limited, and finally fell entirely upon his own shoulders.

It was in Plymouth I received the first offer of a London engagement, from no less a personage than

Mr. ROBERT ELLISTON,

the Napoleon of the drama, of whom it has been justly said, if thrown overboard, in rags, from one side of a ship, he would appear before his tormentors could turn round, upon the other side of the deck dressed as a gentleman, ready to begin the world again; who, as the manager of a minor theatre, led the town captive, daily infringing the rights of the patentees of the Royal theatre, with impunity, and who as the lessee of a patented theatre, forthwith brought civil actions against the minor theatres for infringing *his rights;* the favourite of the public by whom he was spoiled; honoured by the smiles of royalty, until on one occasion at least, he actually imagined himself a king—in representing the character of George the Fourth, in the pageant of the coronation respond-

ing to the applause of his audience by the emphatic phrase of
" *Bless you, my people.*"

One of the best actors on the London stage, decidedly in
talent, the most versatile of those by whom he was surrounded,
crowning the play of the Iron Chest with that success, which
has made it keep possession of the stage, by his excellent acting
in a part in which John Kemble, with all his popularity, had
failed, although written expressly for him by Colman the
younger—whose merry laugh and quizzical expression of countenance in comedy, would force a stone to laugh with him;
whose known powers of guiding the unruly passions of the
most offended audience, has never been equalled by manager
or actor; to whom no man could talk without being persuaded,
against his reason and his will, that he was wrong. The well
authenticated anecdotes of Elliston would fill a volume, from
the perusal of which no one would rise fatigued.

An offer from such a man, for which I was indebted to Mr.
Munden was not to be slighted, or an opening at Drury Lane
Theatre, of which he was lessee, thrown aside without due de-
liberation. The great desideratum of my hopes and fears was
within my reach; once lost, the opportunity might not readily
occur again; I therefore resigned into the hands of the Messrs
Dawson all my right and title to the occupation of the theatres
in Plymouth, Dock, Liskeard, Bodmin, Penzance, Truro, and
Falmouth, laid down the managerial truncheon, and departed
for London full of anticipated honours. On my arrival I found
the situation for which my services were required, so many
degrees below the object my ambition aimed at, that I at once
declined it, and not even the wishes of Mr. Munden, that I
should play any character of my own selection for his benefit,
which was shortly to take place, could induce me to abide such
a result. I concluded an engagement with Mr. Elliston as a
member of his country theatres at Coventry, Leamington, Spa,
Northampton, &c., &c., where I spent a delightful summer.

Previous to my departure I acted Sponge, in the burletta
of Where Shall I Dine, at the Adelphi theatre, for my friend
Wilkinson's benefit, in fulfilment of a promise, made when we
were together in Lincoln, from which I could not recede, so
that I made my first bow before a London audience on Monday, April 2nd, 1821. I was loudly applauded thoughout the
whole of this performance, receiving no less than three different offers of engagements before I left the theatre that
evening, all of which I refused, having suddenly taken up a
whim to visit the United States of America.

At Coventry, where I first played under Elliston's banner, I
met my old friend Meadows. Mr. S. Penley, of Drury Lane,
was the manager, and a more gentlemanly young man, or one
more calculated to conciliate the good will of a company of

actors, it would be difficult to find. The company consisted
of Mr. S. Penley, Mr. Meadows. Mr. Wemyss, Mr. Farrell,
(the late manager of the Pavilion theatre, White-chapel) Mr.
Montague Penley, Mr. Lawrence, Mr. Julian, Mr. Manford,
Mr. Kent, Mr. Shakspeare, (this gentleman was the last remaining descendant of the immortal poet, consequently a
great lion,) Mr. Cleaver, Mr. Hughes, Mrs. Edwin, (of Drury
Lane,) Miss Turner, Mrs. Taylor, Mrs. Hughes, Miss Davis,
and Miss Brown.

Meadows and myself lived in the same house, and were
companions on all occasions. The summer of 1821 was a
series of delightful jaunts to Warwick, Birmingham, Northampton, Weadon, &c., &c. During the season at Leamington
Spa, we acted every Wednesday night at Coventry, on which
occasion the manager provided vehicles for our conveyance,
then well known at Spa as pleasure cars: six were generally
crammed into each, and we returned after the play to Leamington. During these excursions, we usually disturbed the
good people of the village of Kenilworth about one o'clock in
the morning, by singing God save the King, in full chorus, in
honour, as we were pleased to say, of the revels of the Earl
of Leicester to Queen Elizabeth.

Everybody acquainted with English theatricals is aware,
that by law, actors and actresses playing without a licence,
are liable to be apprehended as sturdy vagrants and vagabonds,
and as such, committed to the house of correction. Some
squabbling having taken place between Mr. Elliston and the
magistrates of Coventry, in which the latter felt themselves
insulted by the dignified patentee of the Theatre Royal,
Drury Lane, they resolved upon avenging their wrongs upon
the unconscious actors. And on our arrival from Leamington,
while dressing for the play of Venice Preserved, a gentleman
with a red collar and cuffs to his coat, usually known as a police officer, walked into the room, and informed us in the most
polite manner, that we were his prisoners; that none of us
must leave the building, until the return of Mr. Penley,
who was forthwith summoned before the mayor. We enjoyed
this joke highly, feeling really disappointed, when Penley returned, after an absence of an hour and a half, and informed
us everything was amicably arranged. Had we have been
committed to prison, as threatened, it would have created a
sensation in the profession throughout the country, and in all
probability have made the fortune of more than one of our
community, who, whatever might have been the opinion of
the public as to their merit as players, were universally respected for their deportment off the stage.

The curtain rose about half past nine o'clock to a much
better house than we should have had, if no excitement had

existed. I played Jaffier in the play, and Carwin in Therese, afterwards.

This dilemma arose out of the question of the termination of the license, the manager construing his right to play sixty nights, when and how he pleased, during one calendar year, while the magistrates insisted that the sixty nights, to which the license extended, must be played consecutively, excluding only the Sabbath-day, which they contended was the meaning of the act of Parliament, and in accordance with this decision we closed the Theatre.

The first time I acted with Mr. Elliston was in Coventry, the part of Ennui in the Dramatist, on which occasion he was pleased to compliment me very highly, and renewed the old offer to play the following season at Drury Lane. However, I could not forget that he had tried to persuade me at our first interview, that Willoughby in this same play was an appropriate part to make a debût before a London audience. What a difference between the Mr. Elliston, manager of a country theatre, and the same gentleman, lessee of the Theatre Royal, Drury Lane. In the former character he was a delightful companion, promoting fun and frolic, joining in it heart and soul, the merriest among the merry, idolized by the actors, who, accustomed to this familiarity, on a visit to London, ventured sometimes to address him as an old companion, but were sure to meet the cold and haughty shoulder, which plainly said, "I am astonished at your impertinence: do you know to whom you are speaking? keep your distance—here; I know you not."

During the summer of 1821, took place the coronation of George the Fourth, as King of England, a spectacle which brought together the rich, the noble, and the talented, from every quarter of the globe; an event which had not occurred for better than half a century before, which was celebrated in a style of gorgeous splendour, recalling the days of chivalry and tournament, the nobility of England vying with the representatives of royalty throughout Europe, and eclipsing many of them in extravagant display of unbounded wealth.

This august ceremony was afterwards given in mimic display by Elliston, at the Theatre Royal, Drury Lane. The "fac simile" of the original received the approbation of the citizens of London and Westminster, the King himself condescending to visit the theatre, during the representation, of course stamping it with fashion. It was, in fact, as perfect as such a representation could possibly be.

The manager having reaped a golden harvest in London, wisely resolved, at the close of the season, to represent this magnificent scene throughout the provincial theatres, commencing in Northampton, to which place we were summoned,

where, under the direction of Mr. Lee, formerly the stage
manager of the Adelphi Theatre, (under Rodwell and Jones,)
—who has immortalised his name in the annals of theatricals,
by his exquisite performance of Muddle, in the burletta of
Rochester. It was produced, with all the requisite properties
and dresses, Mr. S. Penley personating the King; Mr.
Montague Penley, Prince Leopold; Mr. Wemyss, Lord
Castlereagh; the two last named dressed in the full order of
the Garter. Every gentleman in the theatre was required to
personate not only one, but, in some instances, half a dozen
characters. I have only particularised those who, speaking
theatrically, could not double, the costliness of their costume,
which required at least half an hour to adjust properly, preventing the possibility of a rapid change of dress. The
procession, in passing, occupied at least three quarters of an
hour.

In Northampton, everything passed off with great eclât, and
is remembered by those who witnessed it, as the most delightful
theatrical representation ever seen. The champion and the
procession accompanying the King into the body of the
cathedral, passing through the very centre of the audience,
had a magical and grand appearance.

From Northampton we proceeded to Coventry, decidedly at
that time one of the most radical towns in England. Here
the actors had to endure the groans and hisses of the audience,
as the representatives of those persons politically offensive to
the spectators. The procession was a scene of tumult, each
character being received with tumultuous applause, or with
hisses, cat-calls, and other deafening noise. I, as Lord
Castlereagh, was the first obnoxious person who made his
appearance. From the moment I placed my foot upon the
stage, until the last page supporting my train disappeared, it
was one cry of "Shame! shame!" "Off! off!" "Queen!"
"Queen!" "Who sold his country?" "Ha!" "Off!" "Go
along!" mingled with hisses and groans. This ceremony generally occupied about two minutes. The Duke of York
followed me, and the change from hissing and hooting, to
applauding and huzzaing, was wonderful. The next who
incurred their displeasure were the King's Attorney-General
and the Judges. Prince Leopold was favourably received; but
for his Majesty, it was reserved to try the strength of the parties. Here the row generally terminated in a fight between
his Majesty's loyal subjects and the admirers of the Queen,
which lasted until the scene changed to the banquetting-hall.
This was repeated on every representation; and when the last
night arrived, I felt relieved from the most disagreeable task I
ever had imposed upon me during my theatrical career.

We returned to Northampton for the season, and here

Meadows left us, to make his first appearance at Covent Garden Theatre, as Scrub, in the Beaux's Stratagem.

In Northampton, I received a letter from Mr. Miller, the agent of Messrs. Warren and Wood, of Philadelphia, so unsatisfactory, that I abandoned all thoughts of pursuing the application in that quarter any further, notwithstanding I had refused London offers, in order to meet the wishes of my friends Hughes and Wilkinson, whose strong recommendations in my favour had opened the correspondence.

The Leamington company was now disbanded, the London actors returning to their winter engagements in the metropolis, and the others wandering, no one knew whither. Among many good fellows this happy season introduced me to, I must not forget the leader of our orchestra, Paddy Day. Many a tedious hour was relieved by his good fellowship.

Mr. Howard, the manager of the Lancaster circuit, offered me an engagement, at a guinea and a half per week, to join him at Wigan, which I accepted, and once more turned my face towards the north. I opened with him in Tangent, in The Way to Get Married.

My stay with Howard was unusually short. However, the cause of separation was so truly laughable, it deserves to be recorded. Having to act Kenmure, in the Falls of Clyde —as that time a very popular piece in every country theatre —in the duel scene, in which Kenmure's being wounded, and supposed to be dead, turns the rest of the plot of the drama; the pistols missed fire, and were again cocked with no better success. Another pair of pistols was furnished by the property man; this only added to our difficulty, as mine exploded; but not all the efforts of my adversary could induce his pistol to go off. Now, as I was to be killed and not him, the only option left was to fall without cause, or to lower the curtain and begin the scene again. We adopted the latter course; for which, the manager in anger, made use of expressions both harsh and unnecessary. At last I cut the argument short by saying, "If you please, Mr. Howard, you will accept my six weeks' notice and we will part." "Certainly, sir. You have only been rather too quick for me. I should have proposed the same thing at the close of the performance, for your airs of grandeur are only fit for Covent Garden or Drury Lane, and won't do for my theatre."

During my six weeks' expiation, for an unintentional error, with Howard, I received the following letter from Mr. Miller, which again directed my views to the United States of America:

D

(COPY.)

" London, Feb. 25, 1822.

" DEAR SIR :—

"I am fully authorised to conclude an engagement with you, and I am inclined to think it would answer both yours and the managers' purpose. Our friends, Mr. Wilkinson and Mr. Hughes, speak in high terms of your abilities, and I am satisfied that their report is correct. Still, if it si likely I can have the pleasure of seeing you play in or near London within the next few weeks, I should be glad to do so. This, however, shall not stand in the way of an arrangement. Will you be good enough to say what you think of the terms offered to you in September last? If I recollect rightly, I made you a distinct and detailed offer. I cannot just now turn to Mr. Wood's letter, though I have it on my file, and he does not in his last letter recapitulate them. The new theatre opens on the first of December, so that we have plenty of time. I hope, and indeed feel assured, that you will make it extremely well worth your purpose. Hoping to hear from you shortly, I remain, dear sir,   Yours truly,

"69, Fleet Street.   (Signed)   " JOHN MILLER."

Before the receipt of this letter, I had engaged to play six nights at Kirkham, with the manager of the Kendal theatre, (Mr. Cooper,) at the close of the season in Wigan. It was from Kirkham, therefore, on the 4th of April, 1822, that I finally agreed to the terms offered by the American managers, and began to prepare for my departure. In Chorley, I again met my old friend Jack Emley, reduced to a mere shadow of his former self, surrounded by a house full of noisy children, the complete picture of a strolling actor rapidly sinking into oblivion. I could scarcely believe that any man, possessing superior talent in the profession of his own choice, could have suffered himself to recede so far in the estimation of the public for want of energy—the highest object of his ambition, being a pipe of tobacco and a pot of porter. So long as he could command these without much trouble, he seemed perfectly indifferent to every thing around him; laughing as merrily, as if his pockets were lined with guineas, and he had not a care in this world. He accompanied me as far as Preston, where he shook hands, and parted to meet no more. "Good bye, Jack." "God bless you, Frank, my boy, and send you safe across the herring pond," were the last words we exchanged. He returned to Chorley, and I made the best of my way to Kirkham.

Here I met Mr. Cooper, who was anxiously expecting my arrival. I opened in Vapid, in the Dramatist. Being announced as the star of the company, I was of course received well by the audience. The company was by no means a bad one, consisting of Mr. Cooper, (the manager,) Mr. Robson, Mr. Lardner, Mr. Lardner, jr., Mr. Egerton, Mr. Hall, Mr. Hutchinson, Mr. Goddard, Master Stanley, Mrs. Cooper, Mrs.

Lardner, Mrs. Robson, Mrs. Lardner, jr., and Mrs. Aldis, (formerly Mrs. Stanley, of the New York Theatre).

From Kirkham, I proceeded direct to London, to make the requisite preparations for the voyage, which was to commence a new era in my theatrical life. In the year 1822, it was a difficult matter to induce an actor to cross the Atlantic; and even Mr. Miller, the agent of Warren and Wood, told me he could scarcely calculate upon my departure until he saw me on board of the packet, although I assured him, that having pledged my word, no offer on this side of the Atlantic could induce me to stay, although they might expedite my return. Offer upon offer was made, and many urged even to rudeness, but without being able to shake my resolution—until it became a standing joke among those actors with whom I was upon terms of friendship, to ask whenever they met me, "Well, Wemyss, when do you retire into banishment?"

CHAPTER VIII.

Expectations of America. Windsor Theatre. Last Engagement in England. Captain Sherburne, and the Ship Robert Edwards. Departure from England. Arrival at New York. Yellow Fever. Park Theatre. Journey to Philadelphia. First Impressions of the Quaker City. The New Theatre in Chesnut Street. Introduction to Messrs. Warren and Wood.

HAVING determined to cross the Atlantic, my first care was to provide myself with a new stage wardrobe, determined, if I failed in the United States of America, that it should not be for want of exertion on my own part. I expended on my outfit, three hundred pounds sterling, adding such of the dresses I then possessed, which I deemed sufficiently handsome. A better wardrobe, or of more general utility, no actor ever commenced an engagement with. Yet I was not buoyed up with any extravagant ideas of brilliant success; my plain calculation was, having been considered a respectable actor in my own country, surrounded by competitors of every grade, I have a right to expect I may be considered something more than respectable in America, where numbers prevail not; and such aid as external ornament could bestow, I was resolved to have.

What could induce Mr. Wood to send to England for a light comedian, while he was himself sustaining all the principal parts, and in high estimation as an actor, with the public, I am at a loss to conjecture. Had I been in possession of that secret before my departure, never should I have left England on such a Quixotic expedition. Expecting to find a clear field for exertion, which I was promised, I was willing to make the attempt; but to sail three thousand miles to oppose an established favourite, was an idea that never entered into my calculation, and for which, I certainly never would have abandoned my prospects in England, which appeared most favourable, during my American negociation.

Fate ordained it otherwise; and many a bitter hour of regret I experienced during the first year of my engagement, of which I shall speak in its proper place.

Surrounded by offers on all sides, I accepted an engagement for six weeks, from Mr. Smith, the manager of the Windsor Theatre, where I could superintend my preparations, and attend to my theatrical duties at the same time. This was the last theatre I acted in, in England.

During the season at Windsor I met with an accident, which had nearly kept me in England against my will, and in face of all my declarations. In acting Corinthian Tom, in the Burletta of Tom and Jerry, I had one of my knees so twisted, as to render it doubtful whether I should be able to act for months; however, I was determined it should be no trifle which should prevent the fulfilment of my engagement, which I subjoin.

"DEAR SIR,

"I am favoured with your letter, dated 1st of May, and agree, without hesitation, on the part of the proprietors of the Philadelphia Theatre, (Messrs. Warren and Wood,) to secure to you an engagement for three years, at a salary of six guineas per week, with the accustomed benefits and advantages, on your engaging to play the light comedy of the theatre, and being with Messrs. Wood and Warren by the first of December, 1822, the time fixed for opening their new theatre. Should you require a more formal and detailed agreement previous to your sailing, I engage to have it prepared and witnessed.

"I am, dear Sir, yours truly,
(Signed) "JOHN MILLAR,
(Agent to the Theatre.)

"69, Fleet-street, London, May 22d, 1822."

Every thing being ready for my departure, I secured a passage in the ship Robert Edwards, from London to New York, there being no vessel in port whose destination was Philadelphia. My baggage was placed on board, and I started for Portsmouth, to join the ship on her arrival at the Isle of Wight.

On the 26th of September, 1822, I placed my foot upon her deck, where Captain Sherburne welcomed me on board, and on the following day, with a fair wind, we tripped our anchor, and I bade adieu to my native land.

We had an agreeable, although a very long passage, arriving in New York on Saturday, the 16th of November. On reaching Sandy Hook, the first intelligence we received from the Pilot was very flattering to a foreigner; it was simply this—" Gentlemen, I think you had better not venture up to the city, the yellow fever rages there very badly."

What a delightful reception, after a long voyage; however, we *did* go up to the city, and without any evil effects, although the populous city of New York looked like a deserted village. The gloomy impression made on my first approach has never been totally obliterated; the words "infected district" will occur whenever I think of my arrival. I slept the first night at the Courtland House; but by the recommendation of Capt. Sherburne, removed the following morning to Niblo's Hotel, corner of William and —— street, where I remained until my departure for Philadelphia.

On Saturday evening, myself and fellow passengers visited the Park Theatre, to see Matthews play Dr. Ollapod, in the Poor Gentleman. The house was not crowded, and the play very indifferently acted, giving me a most unfavourable impression of the actors. It was certainly the worst company I had ever seen in a metropolitan theatre.

After the performance, I met my old friend Joe Cowell, who was attached to the theatre, having arrived in America only a few months before me. He afterwards became very popular, both in New York and Philadelphia.

In his company I wandered through the streets of New York, visiting such places as he pointed out to me, and feeling as only those *can* feel who, in a foreign country, meet a friend whom they know takes some interest in their welfare, relieving the horrible knowledge of being *alone* among multitudes.

On Saturday, the 23rd of November, 1822, I took my departure from New York for Philadelphia, and by some unaccountable mistake got on board the wrong steamboat, so that, instead of proceeding to New Brunswick, I found myself with all my heavy baggage landed at Elizabethtown Point, with the prospect of remaining until Monday, or proceeding by a private conveyance to Trenton by land, and so endeavour to reach the boat before her departure from that place. I therefore hired a dearborn to convey me thither. At New Brunswick, the negro who drove informed me that one of his horses was so lame, it would be impossible to proceed before the morning. I ordered him to hire another, with which we proceeded to Kingston, where I arrived at two o'clock on Sunday morning; and finding it impossible to reach Trenton in time for the boat, I resolved to remain. This was the first country inn I had seen in America; it is on the top of a hill, on the left hand side of the road coming from New York—by whom kept I am ignorant to this day—but never was wayfaring passenger better treated; everything was as clean and comfortable as it was possible to be. I have seen a great many inns in my time, good, bad, and indifferent, but never enjoyed myself more than on the present occasion.

I slept soundly until ten o'clock, when I ordered breakfast, and an excellent one it was; despatched the black man home, who had driven me from Elizabethtown; concluded a bargain with the landlord, to convey me and my baggage to Philadelphia that day, in an extra stage—so that I may say, I arrived in my carriage and four in that city, on Sunday evening, the 24th of November,—this journey from New York having cost me nearly sixty dollars.

At Judd's Hotel, in Third street, (now Congress Hall) where I alighted, quite an animated scene met my view; the house was crowded in every part, travellers flocking from all quarters to witness the great race at Washington City, between Sir Charles and Eclipse, which ended in disappointment. This scene, from its novelty, was most agreeable to a stranger; and although I had travelled over some very bad roads—that is, bad by comparison, for our English roads being so good, made the contrast more forcible; I had reached my destination in time for the fulfilment of all my engagements.

My first impressions of Philadelphia were most favourable. There was something in the bustle of the hotel, which pleased me; the rush to the dinner table on the sound of the bell; the rapidity with which the ample provision disappeared from the table, really amused me. During my first dinner at Judd's Hotel, I shall record a circumstance at which I have laughed at least a hundred times, in presence of the gentleman who caused my surprise. A high-minded and honourable young man, from the State of Georgia, having indulged in potations deep of champagne, (which, bye-the-bye, at American tables flows as freely as water,) was involved in some wordy quarrel at the upper end of the table, which he suddenly terminated by rolling an apple with some force the full length of the table, exclaiming at the same time, if anybody wanted to fight, he has only to bring me that apple. There must have been from forty to fifty people seated in different knots, of four and five in each party, who only laughed at the sudden ebullition of feeling; nor would I have noted the occurrence, but to shame the host of travellers who, passing through America with railroad speed, retail these anecdotes as illustrative of the general character of the Americans; although in what they term the polite and polished circles of Paris and London, isolated cases, far more disgraceful than the present, occur daily without producing any remarks, excepting from the party where the breach of good manners occurs.

I came to America with all the prejudices of an English-

man,—have involved myself in many scrapes in defence of
England, which I never hear assailed without defending; but
I have lived for upwards of twenty years among the Americans, and I do not think any inducement could prevail upon
me, permanently to take up my abode in my native country;
yet it does not follow that I should sit quietly by and hear
England reviled for those very qualities which form the boast
of a native American—namely : love for the land of their
birth. And never do I hear an Englishman loudly denouncing
his native land, that I do not quickly repeat the lines of the
poet :

" ——— For be it understood,
He left his country for his country's good."—AHEM !

But to return to Philadelphia—the cleanliness of its streets,
their uniformity, the hurry of business at this time decidedly
in her favour, as compared to the lengthened visages of the
citizens of New York just emerging from the scourge of the
yellow fever, formed a pleasing contrast, reviving my spirits.

The most striking object was the Bank of the United States,
built in a prominent situation in Chesnut street, and in a
very chaste style of architecture; the State House, from
whose halls issued that declaration which severed from the
English Crown, the brightest gem in her colonial possessions;
the Museum, in the same building; the Academy of Fine
Arts—all in Chesnut street—and last, not least, the New
Theatre then building in the same street, were viewed with
different feelings of interest.

The language spoken by all around me, the nasal twang
with which it was pronounced, alone revealing the secret that
I was not in England, but making me feel a stranger in what
I might otherwise have conceived to be the land of my fathers,
spoke to the feelings of the heart, pronouncing *me* to be *the
foreigner*.

I waited upon Mr. Warren at his house in Sansom street,
leaving my card and a letter from his agent, Mr. Miller. He
called at the hotel in the course of the day, and appointed the
following morning, (Tuesday, the 26th of November,) to meet
him at the theatre, where he would introduce me to his
partner, Mr. Wood, to whom he wished me to talk about
matters of business, and most hospitably invited me to spend
the evening in his society.

I was very much pleased with the appearance of the Chesnut Street Theatre, then nearly completed; its only eyesore
in my estimation, being the chandelier suspended from the
dome, which by others, was considered its greatest beauty;
but the fate of the Exeter Theatre immediately occurred to
my mind; and another objection to this mode of lighting the

theatre, is; that it exposes to view that very portion which
should be kept as much as possible in the shade, and which
has contributed more to the downfall of the drama, than all
the other causes put together; I allude to the third tier of
boxes, where licentiousness prevails in its worst form.

I was introduced to Mr. Wood, with whose urbanity and
apparent kindness I was more than pleased, and distinctly
remember saying, among other foolish things in his praise,
that he was the most perfect gentleman I had ever met in the
profession. As regards outward appearance, I have had no
reason to alter my opinion; but if his conduct towards me,
stripped of his specious manners, are to form his claim to that
character, he must not choose me as his biographer; yet I
may well afford to forgive all his transgressions, in that he
provided me with a wife. Had he kept me engaged in professional duty, in all probability I should never have thought
of marrying; and in this important event of a man's life, I, at
least, never can regret my visit to America.

CHAPTER IX.

Opening of the New Theatre.   List of the Company.   Mr. Cooper.
First Appearance in America.   Reception.   Newspaper Criticisms.
James Wallack.   His Address to the Baltimore Audience.   Booth in
America.   Mathews.   Convivial Parties.   Marriage.   Tom and
Jerry.   Stephen Price.   First Appearance in Baltimore.   Washington
City.   Return to Philadelphia.   Season of 1823 and 1824.

THE theatre opened on Monday, the 2d of December, 1822,
with a neat address, written, as the play-bills informed me, by
Mr. Sprague, of Boston, and very well delivered by Mr. Wood.
The play was, The School for Scandal, which was admirably
acted—*Warren* playing Sir Peter Teazle; *Wood*, Charles
Surface; *H. Wallack*, Joseph Surface; *Jefferson*, Crabtree:
Francis, Sir Oliver Surface; *T. Jefferson*, Sir Benjamin Back-
bite; *Hathwell*, Rowley; *Burke*, Moses; *Darley*, Careless; *John
Jefferson*, Trip; *Green*, Snake; *Mrs. Wood*, Lady Teazle; *Mrs.
La Folle*, Lady Sneerwell; *Mrs. Francis*, Mrs. Candour; and
Mrs. H. Wallack, Maria.

Mrs. Wood was the only person in the play with whom I
was not perfectly satisfied; although I afterwards became one
of that lady's warmest admirers. As an actress, in smooth,
level speaking, she had no equal on the American stage; but
she must forgive me for saying, I think her sister, Mrs.
Darley, would have been a much better representative of
Lady Teazle.

This comedy was followed by the melo-drama of the Wan-

dering Boys, which was also very well performed, but did not
~~~~~~~~ an exalted opinion of the talent of the artists, the
)eing decidedly bad, and entirely out of keeping.
'nanner in which these pieces were acted, convinced
J a harder task before me, to insure success, than I
aerto suffered myself to suppose. The members of the
lphia company were veteran actors, who understood
rofession, and whose exertions were duly appreciated
discriminating audience. They consisted of—Messrs.
n and Wood, the managers; Mr. Henry Wallack, Mr.
on, Mr. Burke, Mr. Francis, Mr. Wilson, Mr. T. Jeffer-
{r. J. Jefferson, Mr. D. Johnston, Mr. Barclay, Mr.
Mr. Wheatley, Mr. Hathwell, Mr. Parker, Mr. Bignall,
urray, Mr. Andes, Mr. Scrivener, and Mr. Lopez, the
)ter; Mrs. Wood, Mrs. Darley, Mrs. Entwistle, Mrs. H.
.ck, Mrs. La Folle, Mrs. Burke, Mrs. Francis, Mrs. Jef-
.son, Mrs. Anderson, Mrs. Simpson, Mrs. Green, Mrs. Mur-
.y, Miss Hathwell, Miss Parker, Miss L. Hathwell, Miss H.
Hathwell; to whom was now to be added, Mr. Wemyss, and
before the end of the season, Mr. and Mrs. Mestayer and their
family.

With such an array of talent, every part was filled by an
actor fully competent to sustain the reputation of the theatre;
and the unfavourable opinion I had formed of the state of the
Drama, from the first play I witnessed in the city of New
York, was converted into a feeling of gratification, at the
regular manner in which the business of this theatre was
conducted.

It was agreed upon by Mr. Wood and myself, that I should
make my first appearance as Vapid, in the Dramatist; to be
followed by Marplot, in the Busy Body; and Rover, in Wild
Oats, but no night was fixed upon. I had stipulated for three
parts, at the opening of my engagement, to ensure a fair
hearing, and avail myself of the opportunity to make, if
possible, a favourable impression upon the audience. Had I
supposed the first part would have been the touchstone, I
should have selected Marplot, which was decidedly at that time
my best effort, and which I purposely reserved, either to
to follow up a successful *debut*, or to retrieve lost ground,
which I knew it would do, in case of failure. But my
manager had determined I should not succeed, before I
placed my foot upon the American stage—that is, if he could,
by any means, prevent it.

The first object of curiosity to me in the theatre was the
announcement of

MR. THOMAS COOPER,

a name bright in the annals of theatrical fame—at one time
the pride and boast of the American stage—who has received
more money from the public, and drawn more into the treasury of the theatre, than any actor of the present day—whose
name, at the head of the play-bills, was the assurance of a
well-filled house—whose style of declamation was held up as
worthy of imitation, both by the pulpit and the bar—who
has, in most inclement weather, travelled a hundred miles a
day, over roads almost impassable—playing on alternate
nights, in the cities of New York and Philadelphia, to delighted
audiences, until he was denominated " the flying actor"—
whose haughty demeanour and rudeness, amounting almost to
insult to his brother actors, rendered him an object of fear
instead of admiration.

As an actor in the vigour of his fame, he must have been
one of the best of the Kemble school. It was not my good
fortune to see him until he was in the wane; but even then,
his performance of Damon, in Damon and Pythias, was a
masterpiece of art, which all who now perform the part on
the American stage—from Mr. E. Forrest to those of humble
pretensions, have imitated as closely as possible. Carrying his
energy almost to the verge of caricature, who, that has seen
Mr. Cooper in this part, can forget the manner in which he
receives from Lucullus the intimation of the death of his
horse, upon whose swiftness of foot depended the life of his
dear friend, perilled by this act; the perfect stupor which for
an instant overcomes his whole frame, suddenly roused to
frenzy by the ideal picture of the blood of Pythias flowing for
him; his stern resolution to sacrifice on the instant both himself and the slave, who, from affection for his master, had
wrought the ruin of his honour. Nothing on the stage—not
even the third act of Othello, by Kean—ever surpassed this.
It was painfully true to nature, equalled only by his delirious
joy when he arrives just in time to save his friend, and falls
exhausted by his efforts at the foot of the scaffold,—receiving,
instead of tumultuous applause, the tears of the audience.—
This was the conception of a master-mind. For my own part,
after witnessing it, I always wished to leave the theatre, that
nothing might break the charm for the evening.

What a pity it is that great actors should remain upon the
stage after they have outlived their reputation; yet how few
retire until old age has so impaired their faculties, that respect
for what they have been, alone restrains an audience from open
insult. Of all professions, the player contemned and despised,
as he frequently is, possesses no means of recording to posterity

the triumph of his art; therefore, the recollection of his taste and beauty should be at least preserved intact by the generation in which he flourishes.

And here let me ask, why an actor should not receive from society the honours due to talent? The physician, the barrister, the clergyman, the soldier, are all received with the honour due to their occupation. The player, whose toil is equal, and whose task to gain eminence is more severe, is only received as a clever buffoon, tolerated, but not accepted in the bosom of society. It is true, the Kemble family form an exception to this general rule of exclusion; but even they hold their position upon suffrance, not upon right.

On the 6th of December, I first saw Mr. Cooper act Virginius, which, in my humble opinion, was a failure. The play was so mutilated, that with difficulty I could recognise Knowles' Tragedy—a liberty no manager or actor should take, unless to remove indecent language or allusion, which must mar any work. It matters not who the author may be; the more celebrated the name, the more disgraceful the outrage: but for caprice, to mangle the work of an absent author, is, to say the least of it, a most unfair proceeding.

It was not until I saw Mr. Cooper play Damon that I would admit his claim to rank as an actor of the highest merit, notwithstanding his popularity; but after that performance, it required but little rhetoric to persuade me he was capable of any effort which could be required from a man of genius, feeling that the reputation he enjoyed was justly merited.

On Wednesday, the 11th of December, I made my first appearance in America, as Vapid, in the dramatist. I was ever a fortunate fellow, on the first night before a strange audience, and on this occasion, the most important to me in my theatrical life, Dame Fortune was not inclined to let me off without some freak to annoy and disturb me.

In the first scene of the second act, the house was suddenly filled with smoke, inducing a belief that the theatre was on fire, which caused a simultaneous movement of alarm towards the doors, until Mr. Wood stepped forward and explained from whence the smoke proceeded. This satisfied the audience, who resumed their seats; but such an incident in a first appearance in a foreign country, of whose manners I was totally ignorant, was calculated to shake firmer nerves than mine.

However, all progressed smoothly enough, and the scene between Lord Scratch, Lady Waitford, and Vapid, behind the sofa, was received with both applause and genuine laughter, which Mr. Warren's excellent acting as Lord Scratch, aided very much in producing, and I left the stage with the applause of the audience ringing most gratefully in my ears.

But it was in the fourth act that the approbation of the audience became so decided, that by the advice of Mr. Warren, and elated by my own feelings, I agreed to speak the Epilogue, which I had declined in the morning. I had cause to regret this conclusion, as, passing through the ordeal of a five after-act play, a gentleman in the boxes, favoured me with a smart hiss, (for pronouncing, as he said, the word *girl* like *gal*.) It was instantly drowned in applause; but it gave to Mr. Wood the plea, of which he took such ungenerous advantage, to declare to Mr. Miller that I was obnoxious to the audience. *The fact*, I have no wish to conceal; it was the first and last hiss ever directed at me on the Philadelphia stage for years. Of the next, I shall have occasion to speak more in detail; the circumstance is well known to every frequenter of the theatre, and the uproar it created had nearly been productive of serious consequence to others beside myself.

I had no reason to complain of my reception. Mr. Warren congratulated me upon my success, and Francis who had witnessed the whole performance, assured me it was satisfactory to the audience. One thing is certain, whatever may have been the opinion of the public on the present occasion, I was a better actor when I first played in Philadelphia, than I ever esteemed myself at a later period of my life, when established as an acknowledged favourite in the Chesnut Street Theatre. That the performance of Vapid could not have been very bad, the proof is, that unknown to a single individual out of the theatre, it should have been received with sufficient approbation to call forth the congratulations of one of the managers who had sustained a principal part in the play. I will dwell no further upon it than to add the opinion of the press on the same character, on the 11th of December, 1822; and on the 12th of April, 1826, during the whole of which period I was a member of the theatre, containing the best stock company ever assembled within its walls.

From the Philadelphia Gazette, Dec. 12, 1822.

"New Theatre.—The house was very respectably attended last evening, to witness the revival of ' The Dramatist, or Stop him who Can.' The only novelty presented in the *dramatis personæ* consisted of a Mr. Wemyss, who made his first appearance in the character of Vapid. Report had spoken in golden terms of his theatrical acquirements. That he possesses a great degree of merit as a young performer, will not be denied; but it is equally manifest, from his last night's representation, that study, experience and practice, are to be superadded to his natural accomplishments, before he can expect to tread the stage with great credit to himself.

"He appears to possess a great flow of fine feeling, and an elasticity of spirits, which, prudently martingaled, may in a few years render him respectable in the light and fashionable walks of the stage.

" His voice did not appear to have attained its proper pitch. This may be obviated when he becomes more familiar with the house. Upon the whole, with a suitable degree of application, we consider he may become an acquisition of no inconsiderable value to our theatre.

From the United States Gazette, April 12, 1826.

" * * * *. Vapid the Dramatist, was written for Lewis, as indeed, also, the principal character in each of his (Reynolds') comedies ; and it is said, the author, in drawing the portrait, sat for himself. Supported as it was by Mr. Wemyss, Mr. Reynolds could not have wished for a better representative; if we are not mistaken, this gentleman made his first appearance in this city in the same part. We well remember, however, of witnessing his enaction of Vapid about four years ago ; but the gratification we then experienced was considerably augmented by the improvement we discovered in the performance of it this evening. Whatever might have been the execution of Mr. Lewis, we feel convinced that Mr. Wemyss could not lose by comparison with him, were he now alive : he may be allowed to plume himself upon and consider it as a chief d'œuvre. * * * * We cannot forbear mentioning the two scenes where Mr. Wemyss showed to so much advantange, that no one who saw him could refrain from expressing their approbation of his excellence. The first and second scene in the second act, when starting from his concealment behind the sofa, he exclaimed—"Prologue or Epilogue !"—"I'm the man ?"—" I'll write you both." To describe the expression of his countenance, his situation, the amazement, not unmixed with horror of Lord Scratch, and the confusion of Lady Waitfort, would be a subject fit for Hogarth, and the last scene of the fourth act. There were other parts where he was admirable; but we may not stop to enumerate them, dismissing him by observing it was a finished performance."

These two opinions were written, the *first* when I was perfectly unknown, and the *last* when I was surrounded by friends and needed not the encomium of the press to designate my position with the audience. It is scarcely possible, taking into consideration I was an actor of eight years' standing and repute before I came to the United States, that in four years after my arrival, there should have been so marked a difference in the performance of the same part, as to entitle me to such lavish praise, unless I had deserved a little more than I received at the hands of the first critic, considering also that I did not act the part more than four or five times between the first and last representation.

From the 11th of December until the 18th, my name was not mentioned in the play bills. On the following Wednesday, I was announced for Rover, in " Wild Oats," Mr. Cooper having played on all the intervening nights. This was giving a stranger a fair field with a vengeance ; and I had discovered the secret,—a most disagreeable one to me,—that no light comedian was wanted; but a walking gentleman was the only

department in which this excellent company was deficient,
and which I determined should never be filled by me.

Although my third appearance should have been in the
play of the Busy Body, as Marplot, I found myself announced
on the 21st of December, for Doucourt, and I heard no more
of the play of the Busy Body, for many months, when I agreed
to act Sir George Airy, to Mr. Wood's Marplot, which I found
to be a favourite character of the manager.

Of all the characters in the varied round of the drama,
which a light comedian may be called upon to assume, Doricourt, in the Belles Stratagem, is decidedly the most difficult.
Until an actor is firmly rooted in the good opinion of his audience, the necessity of extravagance in the assumed mad
scene, and the fear of carrying that extravagance too far, in a
case where the actor and his audience are strangers to each
other, places the former in a most delicate situation; yet this
was selected by Mr. Wood for my third appearance. Fortunately, the excellent tuition of Mr. Macready, in Bristol, had
made me perfectly conversant with the business of the play,
and enabled me to escape on this occasion the censure of the
audience, and even to carry off no small share of approbation.

On the 23rd, I again appeared as Colonel Freelove, in the
Day after the Wedding, to the Lady Elizabeth of Mrs. Tatnall,
an actress of some little repute, but by no means equal either
to Mrs. Wood, Mrs. Darley, or Mrs. Entwistle; but it was on the
28th I had to perform the most difficult task yet placed before
me. A stranger in the city of Philadelphia, in the fifth part
I played was one entirely new to me, the words of which I had
to commit to memory, and to appear before the public, in one
of Mr. Wood's most popular characters, without the audience
being apprised of the fact that it was a first attempt. This
was Prince Hal, in Shakspeare's play of Henry the Fourth.
Cooper played Hotspur, and Warren, Falstaff. I endeavoured
to avoid this, in vain; Mr. Wood was peremptory, and it was
my business to obey. I can at least say, I was perfect in the
language, but it was a *most execrable exhibition,* and the applause
I received was most undeserved.

On the 1st of July, 1823, I played Hans Gayvelt, in Colman's
play of the Law of Java, which, although well got up, was a
failure, being played twice, and consigned to the "Tomb of
the Capulets," notwithstanding it had the aid of Henry Wallock, Jefferson, and Warren, in the principal characters, and
the music very well sung, led by Mrs. Burke, at that time the
principal female vocalist in the United States, and an universal
favourite, aided by the other ladies and gentlemen of the
theatre.

On the 17th of January, Mr. James Wallock made his first
appearance in the new theatre as Rolla, in Pizarro, a character

so decidedly his own, that competition was sure defeat: he was at that time very popular, or I should rather say, attractive. His popularity was never diminished, but his attraction wore out from frequent repetition of the same characters. As a manager, he was the best qualified who ever assumed the reins of an American theatre, and the termination of his career, by the burning of the National Theatre in New York, was a retrograde movement, of twenty years at least, to the just taste for theatrical amusement, which his judicious arrangements in every department was fostering.

He was not only popular as an actor, but as a man; and his address to the audience at the Holiday Street Theatre, in Baltimore, in the year 1835, was a just and manly rebuke, to that ridiculous custom of calling for a favourite performer at the close of every engagement, to return thanks for patronage received, even in a failing engagement. I give it as copied in the "Vade Mecum," of the 17th of October, from the Baltimore papers.

"LADIES AND GENTLEMEN,—I appear before you at your call. I am unaccustomed to extemporaneous speaking; but however reluctant I may usually be to address a public audience, I am free to confess, that I never felt more embarrassment than on the present occasion. I am but a plain man, and speak the words of truth, notwithstanding my profession leads me to assume the garb of fiction. If I were to tell you that I leave Baltimore gratified, I should tell you a lie—for, of the ten nights I have played in this city, this is the only audience I have had the pleasure of witnessing, and you have my sincere thanks for honouring my name by your appearance this evening. I am aware of the duties—of far more importance to you than my poor services—that have prevented your honouring me with your attendance, which, otherwise, if I may be allowed to judge by the audience I have received in other cities, would, I doubt not, have been more general. I therefore repeat, that I thank you most kindly for doing me the honour you have, by appearing here to-night; and, with the hope that when I may come among you again, I shall at least occasionally see such an audience as the one before me, I bid you farewell."

Mr. Wallack acted six nights by himself, and afterwards appeared with Mr. Cooper, in Venice Preserved, Douglas, Othello, Julius Cæsar, King John, and Rule a Wife and Have a Wife, when he took his departure for the season, and shortly after returned to England.

On the 15th of February, I had the pleasure of shaking hands with Mr. Booth, who was announced to appear as Richard the Third, on the 17th. Always eccentric in his movements, he suddenly left England, without the place of his destination being known, and made his first appearance in America, in Richmond, Virginia—thus losing the aid of the press, in the eastern cities, in promulgating his arrival and preparing the audience for the reception of a really great actor. Where he passed his time, previous to Kean's first visit, is unknown; but he lost the opportunity of first impression, by his delay, and had again, in the New World, to combat the charge of imitation—whereas, by using common prudence, he might have turned the similarity of size and style of acting between Mr. Kean and himself to such advantage, before an American audience, (by securing that judgment in his favour which he subsequently obtained,) as to have made him a formidable rival to the great master of his art, on his first appearance in the United States.

Unheralded as he was, with the recollection of Kean fresh on the minds of the audience, his first appearance in Philadelphia was a failure. The house was indifferently attended. Although the judgment of the few was in his favour, the million could not, at that time, be persuaded to see him. After a few nights' performance, the engagement was postponed until after the appearance of

Mr. CHARLES MATTHEWS.

A more honourable or honoured name is not to be found in the catalogue of dramatic worth than the eccentric individual here named. A man, of whom the stage may justly feel proud—irreproachable in his private character, a giant in professional talent, Atlas-like, supporting, on his own shoulders, the burden of entertaining an audience throughout the evening—it will scarcely be credited, that he was permitted to retire from the Theatre Royal, Covent Garden, because his talents were considered too limited, being esteemed only as a mimic, not an actor. But, if his Sir Fretful Plagiary, in the Critic, and Morbleu, in Monsieur Tonson, be not considered acting of the highest grade, I have yet to learn what acting consists of.

His assumption of character in his monopologue, proved to the managers, when too late, the treasure they had lost.

By his own exertions he succeeded in filling the English opera house, night after night, with the elité of London; acquiring independence, and being perfectly independent of managers or actors, although always " At Home."

A more nervous, irritable, fretful creature, never trod the stage. Inattention or loud talking by the audience would at any time overthrow his best exertions, and render him not only uncomfortable but really unhappy.

In social intercourse he was a delightful companion, inspiring all around him with his own hilarity; the life and spirit of any party of which he was a member. Those who have been amused by his droll caricatures upon the stage may form a slight idea of his power to add to the pleasure of a convivial party. ' But even here he would brook no rival: " *aut Cæsar, aut nullus*," appears to have been his motto both on and off the stage. If any one attempted to share with him the task of moving the risible faculties of his guests or companions, Matthews would yield at once the contest and become a silent observer.

In derision, it has been said, he was after all only a *mimic*. Now, in what does acting consist but the *power* of mimicry? The rapid changes of face, of voice, of manner, which Matthews possessed in a pre-eminent degree, are the very claims of a *comic* actor to public favour, without which he can never hope to succeed. Then shame upon such slander, which had its origin in professional pique. Mr. Matthews was one of the best comedians belonging to the British stage—gainsay it who may.

He made his first appearance on the Philadelphia stage, in the characters of Goldfinch and Morbleau, on the 24th of February, 1823, playing a round of dramatic characters to the delight of crowded houses, before he favoured the audience with his " Trip to Paris," " Country Cousins," " Mail Coach Adventure," and his " Youthful Days." His benefit was the most crowded house I ever witnessed in the Chesnut-street Theatre.

A misrepresentation on the part of Mr. Wood to Mr. Price, manager of the Park Theatre, New York, respecting the character of Tom King, procured me an introduction to the private circle of Mr. Matthews' friends, which rendered me his most intimate acquaintance during his residence in Philadelphia; Mr. Warren, Mr. Burke and myself, being the only actors present at the delightful dinner parties which took place at Mr. Head's, in Washington Square.

I afterwards partook of his hospitality at his cottage, near London, when he appeared much annoyed and hurt at the manner in which his " Trip to America" had been spoken of on this side of the Atlantic, declaring his resolution to visit the United States again, for the purpose of presenting it to the American public. This he carried into effect; and the ungenerous reception he met, although partially healed by acts of subsequent kindness, sunk deeply into his heart, and hurried him into the grave, lamented by all his brother actors.

Booth returned to finish his engagement after the departure of Mr. Matthews; but the result was the same. The reason assigned for not visiting the theatre when he acted before was, every body was waiting to see Matthews. Now, every body had spent the money appropriated to amusement, and were tired of the theatre; Matthews had gone, and the theatre was no longer a place of fashionable resort.

It was not until Booth played Hamlet, for the benefit of the Greek Fund, when he appeared before a large and fashionable audience, that he began to be appreciated, and steadily increased in popularity, until he became the greatest favourite in certain characters belonging to the American stage. He purchased a farm in Maryland, near Baltimore, between which and his profession he was steadily employed—during the day selling produce in the market, and at night performing the hero of one of Shakspeare's tragedies at the Holiday-street Theatre.

Mr. Wood having quietly disposed of my pretensions, by good-naturedly placing me upon the shelf—a term my theatrical readers will perfectly understand—to be used when and how he pleased, I had so much time upon my hands, that for want of better employment I began to make love, remembering that a celebrated author had said, "whenever doubts or fears perplex a man, the form of woman strikes upon his troubled spirit, like the rainbow stealing from the clouds, the type of beauty and the sign of hope." Like Rolando, in the Honey Moon, I resolved to marry; and on the 10th of April, 1823, I was united to Miss Strembeck, the youngest daughter of the late worthy Sheriff of the city and county of Philadelphia. "How dost thou, Benedict, the married Man."

Tom and Jerry, or Life in London, was produced in Philadelphia, on the 25th of April; and to the success of that compound of flash and folly, which turned for a time the heads of the play-going community, both in England and America, am I indebted for the favour with which I was henceforward received by the public. Corinthian Tom was the first part in which I had an opportunity of displaying my extensive wardrobe, of which I availed myself to the fullest extent. From the complete success which crowned our efforts in this piece, I nightly gained ground; and ultimately, notwithstanding all obstacles, I reached the object of my wishes, the unqualified approbation of a Philadelphia audience.

The season closed on the 30th of April, with a new play, and Tom and Jerry. What induced the managers to cut short a piece which was crowding the house nightly is a mystery, known only to themselves; however, the proprietors of the Circus, in Walnut-street, were indebted to them, for Cowell instantly produced it there, and played it without intermission to the close of his season; so that Warren and Wood created a desire to see Tom and Jerry, for the benefit, not of themselves, but of Messrs. Price and Simpson, who reaped a golden harvest, while we were playing to miserable houses in the city of Baltimore.

Before bidding adieu to my first season in Philadelphia, Mr. Price made me an offer for New York, which my engagement with Warren and Wood did not permit me to accept.

At what time

STEPHEN PRICE

became connected with the stage, I am utterly ignorant; but it was in the year 1823 that the success of Matthews' engagement induced him to form, and carry into execution, the bold idea of *farming*, if I may be allowed the expression, the talent of those actors belonging to the London stage, which he thought might be made available in the United States, thus making Philadelphia, Boston, and Baltimore pay for the amusement offered to the public in New York; acquiring for himself in England the title of " Star Giver General to the United States," and for the Park Theatre, the reputation of being the first in the country—which, until this period had been claimed, and (judging from the talent of the actors engaged at the two establishments), justly so by the Chesnut-street Theatre of Philadelphia, the critical acumen of whose audience was the severest ordeal the English stars had to encounter.

To Mr. Price's exertions the Americans are indebted for the opportunity of witnessing the performance of Mr. Kean, Mr. Matthews, Mr. Macready, Mr. Conway, Mr. Charles Kemble, Mr. Power, Mr. Wood, Mrs. Wood, Miss Fanny Kemble, Miss Clara Fisher, Madame Vestris, and Miss Ellen Tree, with a host of talented artists of minor importance.

He was a *bon vivant*, a glorious companion over a bottle of champagne, an excellent friend, a good manager, in business a man of honour, although a strict disciplinarian.

After directing for years with profit and success the destiny of the theatres in the New World, he carried the war into Africa; and boldly seized the helm of Drury Lane for one season, sustaining himself in London against all the odds that could be brought to bear upon him. But the speculation was eventually ruinous to his fortune, but not his credit: the honourable manner in which he paid the demands of his creditors, with a legal discharge in his pocket, ought to have secured him a better reception from his fellow-citizens than he received in New York, upon his return to his native country.

On the 3rd of May, 1823, I left Philadelphia, accompanied by my wife, for the city of Baltimore; and on the Monday following, (the 5th of May,) opened as Vapid, in the Dramatist, at the Holiday-street Theatre. The season was a bad one; no uncommon occurrence in the city of monuments and churches. Notwithstanding the excitement of Tom and Jerry, which was excellently produced, the managers were unable to pay their salaries; and although the actors agreed to receive two-thirds of their nominal amount as payment in full, the managers were unable to keep the theatre open, and we repaired to the city of Washington, where we remained nearly four months, during which time I received but six dollars per week; yet I may say I was perfectly happy. In Baltimore and Washington I spent the early days of a married life—generally the brightest of man's career—therefore, the annoyance of the theatre was forgotten in the comforts of home.

We returned to Baltimore in September; and here it was, while smarting under breach of contract in a foreign country, I received a letter from England, containing the intelligence that Mr. Wood had written a most unfavourable account of my reception in America, condoling with me on the event, and strongly urging my immediate return at any sacrifice.

This led to an angry interview; and a correspondence, which terminated in a sort of compromise, in which the position I was to hold in the theatre was fully defined. I agreed to play many second rate characters, which, by the nature of my contract, I might have refused, but retained the power to reject any which I might deem derogatory.

Here, let me do justice to Mr. Warren, who throughout this early contention, not only openly expressed his dissent to the course Mr. Wood was pursuing, but by his kindness endeavoured to soothe the wounded feelings of professional pride by acts of private hospitality; and to his introduction am I indebted for the acquaintance of many of my best and warmest friends, both in Philadelphia and Baltimore.

The company returned to Philadelphia, after a very unprofitable season in Baltimore, and opened in the former city with the play of Henry the Fourth—Duff sustaining the part of Hotspur, and the Three Singles; Mrs. Battersby, from the Park Theatre, New York, was also added to the company. On the first of January, 1824, the Bride of Abydos was produced, —Mr. Cooper sustaining the part of Selim, and Mrs. Duff the heroine. On the 7th of January, took place the benefit in aid of the Greek Fund; on which occasion Booth played Hamlet before a very crowded audience, who, for the first time, appreciated his talents as an actor. He returned to the city on the 16th of February, to fulfil an engagement which proved profitable to himself and the managers; and from that period he rapidly assumed the position of the best actor belonging to the American stage.

On the 21st of January, Pearman made his first appearance as Count Belino, in the Devil's Bridge; but it was not until he played Jocoso, in Howard Payne's drama of Clari, that the audience gave him credit for even mediocrity of talent; consequently the houses were not well filled.

De Camp also made his first bow in Philadelphia in the month of January, as Monsieur Morbleu; but the recollection of Matthews was too fresh in the minds of the audience to allow a leaf of the bays, which this part entwined around his brow, to wither, and consequently De Camp was not received with much favour—he was used by the manager as a support to Pearman, but with indifferent success.

On the 12th of March, a tragedy from the pen of James N. Barker, Esq., of Philadelphia, was produced, entitled, Superstition. As this may be termed my first really *original* part, I will give the cast of the dramatis personæ: Sir Reginald Egerton, Warren; George Egerton, Wemyss; Ravenworth, Darley; Walford, Wheatley; Charles, Wood; the Unknown, Duff; Judge, Greene; Villagers, Hathwell, Jones, Bignall; Officers, Johnston, Murray, J. Westmayer; Isabella, Mrs. Wood; Mary, Mrs. Duff; Alice, Mrs. Durang; Lucy, Mrs. Greene. This play was well acted and well received. But Mrs. Duff so far *out acted* Mrs. Wood, that the manager was careless about repeating a piece which added to the reputation of the former lady, at the expense of his wife, who, although a great favourite, did not happen to "*hit*" the part of Isabella, while Mrs. Duff made an impression on the audience which rendered her the heroine of the play. It was repeated a few nights afterwards, and then thrown among the MSS. of the library, to be forgotten. I have been surprised, that no manager ever rescued so good a play from oblivion.

On the 30th of March I essayed my first benefit, choosing for the performance the melo-drama of Kenilworth, and the farce of A Roland for an Oliver. I lost by this night about thirty dollars; but many a thirty I afterwards received from the same source to balance the account.

On the 24th of April, a star of no common magnitude appeared in the person of

Mr. CONWAY,

a gentleman possessing every personal requisite for an actor, whose unfortunate stature rendered him a victim to the press; and although the cowardly assassin who was *known* to have stabbed his fame saved his person from the consequences of his baseness by falsehood, disavowing publicly in the green room the authorship of his own writings, yet the high-minded gentleman and scholar, whose wounded feelings could obtain no redress, retired in disgust from the pursuit of the profession

E 5

to which he did honour, and assumed the humble station of prompter, to avoid—what—tell it not in Gath—publish it not in the streets of Ascalon—the ribaldry of a newspaper whose columns were notorious for want of decency, and whose circulation was upheld only by that love for reading scandal against our neighbours inherent in the human race, but from which we shrink intuitively when levelled at ourselves.

Theodore Hook drove Mr. Conway from the stage, by his savage attacks in the John Bull. Mr. Price endeavoured to restore him to the position he felt he ought to hold ; but even in America the poisoned shaft had reached him. Although those who witnessed his performance, appreciated his talent ; yet he failed to attract anything like a numerous audience, finally burying himself and his sorrows under the waves of the Atlantic, by jumping overboard, on his passage from New York to Charleston, having evidently meditated this suicide, when he put his foot upon the steamboat, which he had resolved should never bear him to the shore. His fate met universal commiseration from those who knew him best, and could appreciate the noble qualities of his nature.

He made his appearance in Philadelphia, as Hamlet; played an engagement of six nights by himself, and then in conjunction with Mr. Cooper. The theatre closed on the 19th of May, with his benefit; Cooper playing Brutus, in Julius Cæsar, and Conway, Marc Antony, in the play, and Frank Poppleton, in the farce of Too late for Dinner.

During the season of 1823 and 1824, nothing occurred to disturb the harmony of the compromise commenced in Baltimore. I was fortunate enough to obtain Mr. Bromley, in Simpson and Co., as an original part, and a lucky one it proved to me, paving the way for the situation I was shortly destined to hold in the good graces of the audience; and so ended my second season in Philadelphia.

CHAPTER X.

Building of the Chatham Theatre, New York. Sudden close of the Chesnut Street Theatre. Offer from New York. First appearance in that City. Enterprise of Barrere. Henry Placide. The Actor a Broker.

IT was during the spring of 1824 that Barrere commenced building the Chatham Garden Theatre, in New York, the first of a host that followed, prostrating the drama by the rapid increase of theatres, without audiences to support them; yet I must not be understood as casting censure on the enterprise of Mr. Barrere. What he undertook, he carried through with judgment; collecting a company, worthy of the best days of the drama in the United States, which he placed under the direction of Mr. Kilner, the manager of the Federal Street Theatre, in Boston. Among others, he engaged from the Philadelphia Theatre, Mr. and Mrs. H. Wallack, Mr. and Mrs. Burke, and Mr. John Jefferson, thus breaking into the summer arrangements of our Theatre; and by withdrawing much of the talent of the company, compelling the managers to announce their determination of abandoning the season at Baltimore, altogether. Thus I found myself out of employment, without the power of obtaining it, unsanctioned by Messrs. Warren and Wood.

The rules of the theatre would not admit of my acting elsewhere during my engagement, which was for three years, from the 1st of December, 1822; but was likely to be reduced one half, by the continued closing of seasons, without any urgent necessity for such a course.

A diplomatic correspondence, if I may be allowed the use of such a term, commenced on the 8th of July, between Mr. Wood and myself, (to enable me to accept an offer, made by Messrs. Fisher and Jones, to act a few nights at Vauxhall Gardens, for which they offered me ten dollars a night,) the cautious style of which might serve as a model to any prime minister. All I wanted was his permission to act elsewhere, without infringing existing engagements, which, having obtained, I felt once more at my own disposal.

While fulfilling my engagement with Fisher and Jones, I unexpectedly received an offer from Mr. Barrere, to play in the Chatham Theatre, New York, now in the full tide of success. He offered me the same amount of salary paid to Mr. George Barrett, (whose place he wished me to supply,) and a benefit before I left, by which he insured me to make not less than fifty dollars. This proposition I accepted, and made my first appearance in New York city on the 20th day of September, 1824, as Marplot, in the "Busy Body." My reception was beyond my most sanguine expectations, and the Theatrical Register thus spoke of it:—"Mrs. Centlivre's comedy of the 'Busy Body,' introduced to a New York audience Mr. Wemyss (formerly of the Philadelphia Theatre,) in the character of Marplot. He sustained the part well throughout; and if we may judge from the applause which he received, gave general satisfaction. He appeared to have realized the author's idea of a good-natured, silly, and officious person, having no business of his own, and anxious to be acquainted with that of every body. Mr. Burke personated the part of Sir Francis Gripe with great effect, and exhibited a true picture of the avaricious and amorous old dupe. He was particularly excellent in the last scene, when he found he had been fooled, and the audience testified their approbation by repeated rounds of applause.   The parts of Sir George Airy, by Mr. Wallack, and Miranda, by Mrs. Hughes, were all we could wish."

The result of this performance was an offer from Mr. Barrere of a permanent engagement, which my unlucky contract with the Philadelphia managers prevented the possibility of my accepting, much to the annoyance of Barrere, to whom I admitted I was not comfortably situated in the Philadelphia Theatre, and who could not understand why I should prefer, under such circumstances, to return, when he offered me terms more advantageous than I could have ventured to propose.

No theatre could be conducted with more spirit and enterprise than the Chatham Garden, during its first season. Notwithstanding the strength and talent of the regular company, there was not an actor or actress of talent in the United States, whose services could be procured, who were not engaged to give occasional aid.   The plays were excellently acted ; and I must acknowledge I left New York with regret, to return to Baltimore, in obedience to the summons of Mr. Wood.

The Baltimore season was commenced and terminated without an occurrence to render it worthy of a passing notice.

We commenced the season in Philadelphia, on the 4th day of December, 1824. And now, chance, for the first time, opened the fair field to me, promised in England, and which I expected to have found on my arrival.

Mr. H. Wallack visited Charleston on a starring excursion ; Mr. Duff was confined with gout ; Mr. Wood laid up with quincy ; and Mr. Wemyss, nightly placed before the audience in the most favourable position, rapidly rose in their estimation.

Misfortunes they say never come singly, so with equal truth may it be observed, one lucky adventure is generally followed by another. While I was becoming hourly a favourite in my profession, I received from home between thirteen and fourteen hundred dollars, the proceeds of about three hundred pounds I had left invested in the British funds ; but which the uncertain payment of Messrs. Warren and Wood rendered desirable I should have placed nearer my disposal.

I had formed a friendship with Mr. W. C. Conine, the lottery and exchange broker of Baltimore, who had now visited Philadelphia for the purpose of extending his business, by opening an office in this city. The party with whom he was to have associated himself, not making his appearance agreeable to promise, he requested me to superintend the fitting up of the office, promising to return before the drawing of the

Union Canal Lottery. So well pleased was he with the arrangements I had made on his behalf, that he acceded to a proposition made by me. We commenced business in Third street, trading under the name of W. C. Conine.

Prosperity seemed now to flow in upon me from all quarters. The favourable impression which I had made upon Mr. Kilner during my short stay in New York, induced him to offer me a situation in Boston, at the old Federal Street Theatre, of which he was the manager; Finn, his partner, wishing me to name my own terms and expectations.

Being now really serviceable to Warren and Wood, and established with a rising reputation, in favour with my audience, Mr. Wood urged me to renew our business relations, and bury the recollection of past grievances. A proposition was made, agreeable to all parties, which I accepted, and stated to Mr. Finn my regret that I could not at present accept his offer, having formed a further engagement in Philadelphia.

My original engagement would have expired by limitation, on the 30th of November, 1825. But I was now, in a pecuniary point of view, independent of the managers; my business yielding me a greater income than I received from the treasury of the theatre. The mutual assistance we were enabled, each to render the other, was now the only bond which continued our connection.

The first star of the season was Booth, who played Richard the Third, on the 6th of December, followed by Cooper. Conway also paid us a short visit, playing to miserable houses. On the 8th of February, 1825, "Cherry and Fair Star," with its looking-glass bower, and innumerable reflected representations of dancing cupids, was produced with great success, not only attracting crowded houses, but giving general satisfaction to the audience.

CHAPTER XI.

Brilliant Prospects of the New Season. Kean, Miss L. Kelly, and Forrest. Row Extraordinary. The Acting American Theatre. Neagle, the Artist. The Author in Trouble. National Prejudices. Foolish Quarrels.

THE season which commenced in Philadelphia, on the 21st of November, 1825, with the "West Indian," and "Love, Law and Physic," was one, rendered memorable by the second visit of Kean, the first appearance of Miss L. Kelly; and last, although by no means least, the introduction of Mr. E. Forrest, as a *star*, in his native city—three events, of themselves sufciently important to make an "*epoch*" in the history of the drama.

Cooper was the first star of the season, as usual, attracting good houses, although his Richard the Third was an execrable performance. Strange as it may appear, he was not even perfect in the text, for which he was justly handled by the able critic of the United States Gazette, who wrote under the signature of "Jacques."

Watkins Burroughs also played an engagement, in the early part of the season, and had an excellent benefit—but, "cetera desunt."

Mr. Kean arrived in New York during the fall of 1825 : of his reception no one is ignorant. The insult said to have been offered to the citizens of Boston, during his first visit to the United States, by refusing to act, because the house was not sufficiently filled, was felt and resented by every city in the Union. In New York, after the first and second night, the storm was hushed, and peace restored between the actor and his audience; but in Boston, the only city who could plead justification, and in whom resentment was praiseworthy, he was not permitted to act,—flight alone preserved his personal safety. He had entered into an engagement with Messrs. Warren and Wood, to play in Philadelphia; but after his reception in New York and Boston, Mr. Wood became alarmed, and wrote to Kean that while the present excitement continued, if he came to Philadelphia in fulfilment of his contract, he could not be answerable for the consequences.

The manager having thus expressed his fears, it naturally followed that Mr. Kean should decline a contest so unequal—*a whole nation in arms against a single individual, and that individual a foreigner and an actor !*

In New York, he published the following Card in the Courier and Enquirer :—

" MR. EDITOR :—Sir—With oppressed feelings, heart rending to my friends, and triumphant to my enemies, I make an appeal to that country famed for hospitality to the stranger, and mercy to the conquered. Allow me to say, sir, whatever are my offences, I disclaim all intention of offering anything in the shape of disrespect towards the inhabitants of New York. They received me from the first with an enthusiasm, grateful, in those hours, to my pride—in the present, to my memory. I cannot recall to my mind any act or thought that did not prompt me to an unfeigned acknowledgment of their favours as a public, and profound admiration of the private worth of those circles in which I had the honour of moving.

" That I have committed an error appears too evident, from the all-decisive voice of the public; but surely it is but justice to the delinquent, whatever may be his enormities, to be allowed to make reparation where the offences were committed. My misunderstanding took place in Boston —to Boston I shall assuredly go to apologise for my indiscretions. I visit this country now under different feelings and auspices than on a former occasion. Then I was an ambitious man, and the proud representative of Shakspeare's heroes. The spark of ambition is extinct, and I merely ask a shelter in which to close my professional and mortal career. I give the weapon into the hands of my enemies; if they are brave they will not turn it against the defenceless.

(Signed,)   EDMUND KEAN."

On the evening of the 9th of January, in answer to a call from the audience, Mr. Wood, after what had passed, had the temerity to inform them that it was his wish, as well as his interest, to gratify the audience; but he had no power to drag Mr. Kean before them. If he declined fulfilling his engagement, Mr. Wood had no power to compel his appearance.

Knowing what had taken place, I could not suffer a friend, to whom I was indebted for many acts of kindness, to labour under a charge which was adding fuel to fire. I stated to several gentlemen, who felt an interest in his cause, that Kean would willingly visit the city, if assured of personal safety; that Mr. Wood had written to him that his life might be endangered by the fulfilment of an engagement he had openly this night accused him of violating.

The result is known. Mr. Mortimer was despatched to New York to inquire into the truth of all the statements; the theatre was closed for two nights; and on Wednesday, the 18th of January, Kean appeared as "Richard the Third." The row which followed was a serious affair—the outrages perpetrated disgraceful to a civilized community. Rotten eggs, children's bullet-buttons, and other small missiles, were thrown upon the stage in countless numbers; long before the opening of the doors, the approaches to the theatre were blocked up by a dense mass of human beings, eager to obtain admission. The appearance of Kean was the signal of assault. In vain he attempted to make himself heard amid the din and uproar. In pantomime, he proceeded; leaving the stage, to be greeted in a similar manner upon his re-appearance. His was a situation in which his worst enemy might have pitied him. At length, wearied by their own exertions, the noise partially ceased, and afforded him an opportunity of addressing a few words to the audience:—"Friends of the drama, this is your quarrel—not mine." From that moment he was suffered to proceed with less interruption—the curtain falling amid hisses and applause so nearly equal, as to render it doubtful which party obtained a triumph. Many there were, who, having shown their disapprobation of his conduct, by saluting him with a sharp hiss on his first appearance, became warm advocates for his engagement to progress without further insult. A vast crowd assembled round the stage door in Carpenter Street, to witness his departure from the theatre.

As he entered the carriage, a gentleman on the steps proposed three cheers for Kean, which were given with hearty good will, and in those cheers, his pardon, so far as Philadelphia was concerned, was pronounced. He had erred—he had been punished—and the attempt to renew the scene, when he appeared as Othello, had been suppressed promptly. The offenders being so small a minority, were ejected from the theatre, and his engagement brought to a prosperous conclusion, on the 2nd of February, 1826, during which he played Richard the Third, Othello, King Lear, Sir Giles Overreach, Sir E. Mortimer, Reuben Glenroy, Macbeth, Brutus, and Hamlet. The theatre, on the night of his benefit, when he repeated Richard the Third, was crowded from the pit to the gallery. When the curtain fell he was loudly called for, and addressed the audience in nearly the following words:— "Ladies and gentlemen—my life has been a chequered one—at one time reaching the pinnacle of ambition—at another sunk in the lowest ebb of misfortune. I appeared before you at the commencement of the present engagement, sick and dejected by the gloom which the malignity of enemies had thrown around me, anxious and willing to resign the contest; but the kindness of a Philadelphia audience has dispelled these visions of despair, and I hope I shall have the honour, early next season, of appearing before this kind auditory."— He retired amid the cheering of the audience, which lasted several seconds after he left the stage, Mr. Wood appearing and promising he would perform Hamlet on the following evening, the only night he had at his disposal.

What a compound of generosity, talent, and folly, was Edmund Kean; he never forgot an act of kindness, and was sure to repay it tenfold : but the following anecdote will prove that he was also tenacious, and unforgiving of wrong.

When, in the height of popularity, while performing at Portsmouth, England, he was requested by the manager, and two or three of his friends, to accompany them after rehearsal to the Inn, and take a glass of Madeira; the landlord being apprised that Mr. Kean was of the party, ushered them into an elegant room, where he thanked the *actor* for the honour that he did him, and overwhelmed him with civilities. Kean, fixing his eyes upon the landlord, and looking only as he could look, said : "Mr. ———, I came into your house at the request of these gentlemen, to partake of some refreshment, not to be pestered with your civilities, which, to me, are so many insults. Look at me, sir—well—do you recollect me?— I see you *do* not—but you *know* that I am Mr. Kean—Edmund Kean, sir—that same man that I was fifteen years ago, when you kept a small inn, and I was a member of a strolling company of players, who acted at your fair. I remember well that I went one day into the bar of your house, and called for half a pint of porter, which, after I had waited your pleasure patiently, was given to me by you with one hand, while the other was extended to receive the money. Never can I forget your insolent demeanour, or the acuteness of my mortified feelings. Look at me again, sir. What alteration beyond that of dress do you discover in me? Am I a better man than I was then? What is there in me now, that you should over-whelm me with your compliments? Keep your wine, sir—it would choke me. Come, gentlemen, let us leave his house;" and the actor walked away from the mortified and abashed landlord. This was related to me by an eye-witness, and was I believe, published in the London Theatrical Observer, some years ago.

In consequence of the active part I had taken in bringing the engagement of Mr. Kean before the public, Mr. Wood looked upon me with no very favourable eye; all the old prejudices between us were revived, and he was not long in finding, as he supposed, an opportunity to make me feel his power. To this cause I attribute the fracas which took place some time afterwards, in the play of "Columbus," of which I shall have occasion to speak more at large in its proper place.

In the month of January of the present year, (1826,) in conjunction with Mr. Lopez, the prompter of the theatre, I commenced the publication of a work entitled "The Acting American Theatre, embellished with portraits of the actors belonging to the American stage, intended as a companion to "Oxberry's English Drama." This work, although a losing concern to me, deserves a kind remembrance, for having placed conspicuously before the public a most deserving young artist, who now stands acknowledged as one of the first portrait painters in the United States; I allude to a Mr. Neagle, whose picture of Patrick Lyon has procured for him a well-merited reputation. He painted for me for this work the portraits of Mr. and Mrs. Francis, Mr. and Mrs. Duff, Mr. Wood, Mr. Warren, Mr. Hilson, Mrs. Hilson, Mr. Cowel, Mr. and Mrs. Barnes, Mr. E. Forrest, Mr. Macready, Mr. Wemyss, Mr. Booth, Mr. Kean, Mr. Jefferson, Mr. Foote, Mr. Lee, Miss Kelly, Mrs. Waring, Mrs. Burke, Mr. Thayer, and Mr. Roberts.

Mr. Durand, of New York, and Mr. Longacre, of Philadelphia, then considered the best artists in the United States, were engaged to engrave these portraits; but after issuing sixteen numbers, I found my subscription list daily languishing. The work was unfortunate from the commencement; Mr. Poole, the publisher, failed, involving the accounts in a maze of difficulty. I found it impossible to extricate them. Murden, the theatrical publisher of New York, the agent for the work, also failed, making no return of sales.

The only parties to whom I was indebted for attention, and prompt remittances, are my old friend Boole, of. Baltimore, and Mr. Bourne, of New York.

Tuesday, the 3d of February, 1826, introduced to Philadelphia one of the greatest favourites who had trod their boards for years, in the person of

MISS LYDIA KELLY.

Perhaps I am scarcely justified in recording Miss Kelly's name as a *star* of foreign growth—her popularity being purely American. Mr. Stephen Price engaged her in London, in consequence of Miss Jones having refused to cross the Atlantic, the popularity of her sister, Miss Fanny Kelly, the melodramatic heroine of the British stage, lending a charm to her, name, of which the American manager judiciously availed himself.

No opportunity ever offered more favourable to the views of a young and fashionable girl to take the town by storm. The Philadelphia audience were tired of the faces of the ladies belonging to the theatre: although Miss Kelly's features were too masculine to be considered handsome, yet the dashing figure and lively spirit of her acting at once carried the feelings of her audience captive. She made her curtsey in the character of Letitia Hardy, in the "Belle's Stratagem," with triumphant success. Engagement following engagement in rapid succession; she must have remained at least two months during her first visit, leaving the theatre with a reputation established as a leading star in the theatrical hemisphere.

Everything seemed to operate in her favour. The ladies having been prevented from visiting the theatre during Kean's engagement, on his departure, appeared to claim exclusive right to occupy the dress-boxes. So strongly did they turn out in Miss Kelly's favour, that a gentleman might consider himself highly favoured if he could obtain a seat. She was the reigning goddess of comedy: and the excellent manner in which they were acted was a constant theme of praise—their continued attraction, a proof of the gratification received by the audience. We had Wood, Warren, Jefferson, Duff, Wemyss, Francis, Burke, and occasionally Cooper and Burroughs; while in the female department, no theatre in America could approach us in talent, Mrs. Wood, Mrs. Duff. Mrs. Darley, Mrs. Anderson, and Mrs. Francis, all ranging throughout the dramatis personæ.

Philadelphia has contributed largely to that fortune which Miss Kelly boasts she has acquired, without receiving from a manager a single dollar until all his expenses were fully paid, sharing the profits only, and entailing no extra expenses upon the management—an example all stars ought to follow.

Although thus generous, she was rigid in exacting her rights. On one occasion, during the management of Lamb and Coyle, she refused to proceed with the fifth act of "Know your Own Mind," until the money due her was forthcoming. It was ridiculous enough to see Lady Bell, sitting on the stage, receiving in her lap the roleaus of silver, handing them to her Irish waiting-woman to count, who bore them off in triumph before the eyes of the poor actors, who knew too well the consequence of this drain upon the treasury. *No salaries for them.*

She was a termagant, but an agreeable one: quarrelling with you to-day, and to-morrow willing to make any reasonable concession to reinstate herself in your good opinion, it was impossible to be angry with her for any length of time. She had a difficult task to "*manage managers,*" but she was fully equal to it.

As an actress she will be remembered with pleasure, as one whose popularity remained undiminished to the last hour of her appearance; retiring from the stage with her fame in its meridian, she played Letitia Hardy, Beatrice, Lady Teazle, Rosalind, Miss Hardcastle, Mrs. Oakley, Lady Bell, Violante, Juliana, Juliet, Emily Tempest, Lydia Languish, Portia, Miss Dorrllon—and had likewise considerable pretensions as a vocalist. She left us on the 25th of March, playing a longer consecutive engagement than any star within my recollection.

I now approach a period of my theatrical career which had almost terminated it abruptly. The play of "Columbus," having been revived, I was cast the part of Harry Herbert, an English adventurer. During the first rehearsal I had carelessly neglected to bring my written part of the character to the theatre, and was reading the following passage from the prompt-book :—

" Will you, great sir, condescend to indulge the last wish of vanity, and when you have nothing else to do, write to England the story of my fate, that when my fortunes shall be inquired after, my friends, with joy sparkling through a tear, may say, ' Herbert stuck to his commander to the last, and died as every Englishman should.' "

Mr. Wood interrupted me by exclaiming, " You must *not* say *that*, sir: say ' brave man,' *not* 'Englishman.' " Not perceiving any reason for such an alteration of the language of the author, I merely asked the necessity for such a change —the answer was, " The necessity is *my will and pleasure.*" This led to "*a scene,*" not very creditable to either party. If I failed in the respect due to my manager, he certainly did not adopt the course best suited to convince me of the impropriety of openly violating the established rules of the theatre. Threats were exchanged, which rendered it impossible for me, without loss of self-respect, to withdraw from the position in which I found myself most unexpectedly placed.

I was officially informed by the prompter that if I persisted in speaking the sentence, as printed, the manager had instructed him to forfeit me my week's salary. And here the matter should have rested, until the overt act, which rendered me liable to the penalty, had been committed: but a second communication produced a result in which the feelings of both parties were totally disregarded; nor will I insult my readers by transcribing the gross language which took place between us.

On the afternoon of the 17th of April, a friend called at my lottery office, in Chesnut street, to inquire whether there was any truth in the report that Mr. Wood and myself had had a serious quarrel. When answered in the affirmative, he told me there was a party formed to hiss me, during the performance, which was to take place in the evening. I was inclined to laugh at this, deeming it improbable that any audience would trouble themselves about the disputes of managers and actors, where their own amusement was not interrupted; but I found that he was correct, and that I must be prepared to meet the result. As the play progressed, the actors began to think I should yield the point; however, at the proper time I delivered the obnoxious speech, exactly as I found it in the prompt-book. Two or three slight hisses followed, and I was congratulating myself that this tempest in a tea-pot had subsided. In this I was deceived; when I next appeared I was saluted by such a general hiss as is seldom heard within the walls of a theatre.

I immediately dropped my assumed character, and addressed the audience :—

"LADIES AND GENTLEMEN :—These are sounds I am so unaccustomed to hear directed towards me within these walls, that it would be folly to pretend ignorance of their cause. I am to attribute them to a misunderstanding between Mr. Wood and myself, relative to the word "Englishman," which I uttered when I last left the stage. Allow me to ask you whether the name of England is a disgrace. [No, Wemyss, no.] I am an Englishman, and now appeal to *you* as *Americans*—what would you think of an American, who, on the other side of the Atlantic, should have occasion to pay a compliment to his country, in these words, "Die as an American citizen ought," who should be told " It is my will and pleasure that you insert 'Englishman,' or I will snip your ears off;" what would you think of him who under such a threat, would be dastard enough to submit? [Bravo, Wemyss—well said—bravo !]"

Mr. Wood now made his appearance. In his address to the audience he stated that his predecessor, Mr. Wignell, had erased the words, which *he* with a pen, *scratched from the prompt-book, after our altercation had taken place,* and with his own hand wrote the word *brave* over the printed word *English.* Nor was this the only mis-statement which caused me to form the sudden resolution of placing the whole facts as they occurred, before the audience. When he had finished, the audience called loudly for the continuation of the play, when I requested their indulgence for one minute, com-mencing —

" LADIES AND GENTLEMEN,—Allow me *one* word. There is not a syllable of truth in what Mr. Wood has uttered. (Hisses.) He has boasted he can turn the Philadelphia audience around his finger at any moment. I acknowledge he possesses a fluency of language which I do not, but situated as I now am, it becomes necessary that the whole truth should be known. He said he had *cowed*.every Englishman he ever had to deal with, and he would *cow* me too. He threatened, if I dared to utter that speech, he would forfeit me. Under excitement I *did* say, if he did, I would thrash him, and so I will."

Here I was interrupted with a shower of hisses, cries of "go on with the play," &c., &c. My first appeal was received enthusiastically ; and had I stopped there, my triumph would have been complete and unalloyed ; but, in losing my temper as I listened to gross misrepresentation, I perilled my cause. My final triumph was more owing to the words of my author, than to my adroitness in managing my case.

In returning to my assumed character of Harry Herbert, my first speech ran thus :—" I have not had a bit of fighting for a long time, and damme, if this has *not* given me a relish for it."

Those only who were present can form an idea of the elec-trical effect produced upon the audience, the theatre fairly shook with applause and laughter. This turned the tide once again in my favour. When Mr. Wood appeared shortly after-wards as Columbus, the hisses were both sharper and louder than those directed against me, in the commencement of this disgraceful and humiliating scene, and so continued to the close of the performance.

On the following day, the *"row"* at the theatre formed the

general topic of conversation. Opinion being divided as to the justice of the decision of the audience, and a general belief that the contest between the manager and the actor would be resumed, became prevalent, my friends demanded from me a pledge that I would remain quiet and leave my cause as it stood, entirely in their hands. To this I could scarcely object, and I entered the theatre on the evening of the 18th, expecting, I hardly knew what, but determined to meet it boldly.

When I appeared as Captain Bolding, in the Rendezvous, there was a slight attempt to hiss, promptly silenced. As I raised my eyes, I saw two gentlemen, busily engaged with foot and hand, each ejecting from the pit an offender, the audience apparently enjoying the scene. The enemy being routed, my friends prudently desisted from showing any marks of disapprobation towards Mr. Wood; and so far as the public were concerned, the matter was set at rest forever.

This was the *Roland* dealt to me by Mr. Wood, for the *Oliver* administered to him by me in the affairs of Kean. However, he missed his calculation, as the event proved, but he made the attempt boldly.

In consequence of this fracas, for four years we acted together, in the same theatre, without exchanging words, off the stage; but like all other foolish quarrels, time has obliterated its recollection, and Mr. Wood and Mr. Wemyss are upon the same terms as when they first met.

CHAPTER XII.

Mr. Francis' Farewell of the Stage. Oh, Shame! where is thy Blush. First Appearance of Mr. E. Forrest as a Star. Portrait of the American Tragedian as Rolla. Account of his First Appearance in London.

On the 18th of May, Mr. Francis, the oldest actor in the United States, and one to whom the Philadelphians were indebted for many a hearty laugh, announced his farewell benefit, previous to his retirement from the duties of an arduous profession. I almost blush to write, that it was one of the worst houses, not only of the season, but which had ever been seen in the present theatre. I cannot better express my indignation than to quote from the correspondent of the United States Gazette. "Mr. Francis' unsuccessful appeal is a stigma on our city; but thus it ever is—the favour of the public is lavished on *stars*, while the deserving but less aspiring performer is neglected and disregarded. Although flattered and applauded, he is suffered to sink into want and

penury. This evening may afford the useful lesson to performers particularly, that public favour is no surety.

> ——He that depends upon 't
> Swims with fires of lead,
> And hews down oaks with rushes.

The current of popularity is as changeable as the winds which
blow from all points of the heavens, and he acts most wisely
who makes the best of it when it sets in his favour. The
public are neither just or generous in the distribution of its
patronage."

The performance selected for the occasion was the comedy
of "She stoops to Conquer," and a new farce which had been
written for me, entitled "Exit in a Hurry." Poor Francis
did not survive this mortification many months.

The 16th of May, 1826, is a night not easily to be forgotten
by those who take an interest in theatrical matters. It was
on the occasion of Mr. Porter's benefit, on this evening that
Mr. E. Forrest returned to his native city, which he had left
as a boy to seek for fame in the far West. His acting as
Jaffier, in Otway's tragedy of Venice Preserved, was warmly,
nay enthusiastically applauded, and as the curtain fell, an engagement called for, which was announced for Thursday,
Friday, and Saturday. The theatre, however, was closed on
Thursday, but Mr. Forrest acted Rolla, on Friday the 19th of
May, and repeated it again on Saturday, when the theatre
closed for the season.

When I first met

Mr. EDWIN FORREST,

behind the scenes of the Chesnut Street Theatre, in the month
of May, 1826. He was a modest, unassuming young man,
who scarcely mustered courage sufficient to enter the green-
room, where were assembled many of the best actors the
American stage could boast of. Mr. Charles Porter introduced
me to him, and expressed a wish that I should see him act
the part of Jaffier. I took my seat in the boxes, determined
to be pleased; and I was so. I expressed myself warmly in
his praise to Mr. Frederick Huber, who took much interest in
his welfare. He said, "Frank, if you really think what you
say, do me the favour to publish his likeness in the next
number of the 'Acting American Theatre;' it will serve a
very worthy young man, and do you no harm." "Very well,
you get his assent to sit for the picture; I will instruct Mr.
Neagle when he visits New York to paint it." I addressed a
letter to Mr. Forrest on the subject; the result was the

publication of the first engraved portrait of the American tra- gedian, as Rolla, in " Pizarro." Thus commenced an intimacy which has continued ever since.

Whenever chance and talent unite to place one member of a profession above all competitors, it is not surprising that weak mortals should have their brains turned by unlooked-for and unhoped success. When moving himself in a very humble position as an actor, he was loud in his denunciation of Mr. Cooper, for the "*brusque*" manner which he thought proper to adopt towards the members of the profession less fortunately placed than himself. Such conduct is any thing but becoming, and deserves not only the censure of the profession, but the public; yet Mr. Forrest has carried his rudeness to much greater extent than ever Cooper did in his haughtiest day of theatrical power. He possesses many excellent traits of character, and none more than his affectionate care and forethought for his mother and sister, to whom he devoted the first fruits of his rising popularity. He can also at times be generous to his late fortunate brethren of the sock and buskin. But there is one blot on his escutcheon which never can be erased; he suffered Mrs. Gilfert, the widow of a man to whom he owed both fame and fortune, to be buried by a subscription raised by the actors of the Philadelphia theatres, although he was aware of her distressed situation before her death.

Mr. Forrest owed his rapid rise in public favour as an actor, in the first place, to his birth as an American; secondly, to nature, for the endowment of great personal advantages; and thirdly, to that chance, without which the two former would have been useless. On opening the Bowery Theatre, in the city of New York, in 1826, Mr. Gilfert, the manager, (and as shrewd and capable a one as ever directed a theatre,) knew it was necessary to find some one whom he could place in a prominent situation, to arouse the curiosity of the public, and direct their attention to his new building. He found the material in young Forrest, and left the press and his own ingenuity to work out the result. His appearance at the Park Theatre, in Othello, for Woodhull's benefit, gave the *cue*, and Mr. Forrest was forthwith announced as a star of the first magnitude, and so upheld at all sacrifices, until he really became what in the first instance he had no pretensions to be considered. However, Shakspeare says, " some men are born to greatness, others achieve greatness, and some have greatness thrust upon them." Of this latter class was decidedly our young tragedian; but endowed with strong common sense, he watched his opportunities, and availing himself of every chance, he finally in his native city of Philadelphia obtained from Rufus R. Blake the enormous sum of two hundred dollars per night, to which he has since adhered, or only departed from for the still more ruinous terms to the managers of one-half of the gross receipts of each night's performance.

Keeping steadily in view the fortune he was determined to acquire, he offered a premium of five hundred dollars for the best play in five acts, written by an American author, of which he was to be the hero. The prize was borne off by Augustus Stone, who produced the play of "Metamora," in which Mr. E. Forrest has drawn more money than in all his subsequent efforts. His representation of the Indian Chief is a finished piece of acting, which may be equalled, but never will be excelled. His Spartacus, in Dr. Bird's tragedy of the "Gladiator," is also a part which, being his own by copyright, there will never be an opportunity of drawing comparisons ; and if there were, they certainly would not be to his disadvantage ; but as this was the character in which he staked his reputation before a London audience, I subjoin the account of his first appearance, taken from the London Times of the 18th of October, 1836.

"Drury Lane Theatre.—Mr. Edwin Forrest, who has established a high reputation in America, his native country, as a tragedian, appeared for the first time before an English audience at this theatre, last night. The character selected for his *debut* was that of Spartacus, in a tragedy of that title, written by Dr. Bird, also an American. Mr. Forrest was received with a hearty warmth, which, from the first moment of his appearance, left no doubt, if any could have been entertained, that the audience were well disposed to accept his exertions for their entertainment. He is a tall, rather robust man, of some thirty years of age, not remarkably handsome, but with expressive features, and that cast of countenance which is well suited for theatrical effect. His voice is remarkably powerful, his figure rather vigorous than elegant, and his general appearance prepossessing. The subject of the tragedy is one admirably adapted for scenic representation, and has already been essayed in the French and German theatres. Dr. Bird appears not to have borrowed from any of his predecessors, but to have preserved in the main features of the drama the historical facts relating to his hero. In concentrating the interest and the action of the play in the character of Spartacus, he has bestowed very slight pains in the delineations of the other characters. The consequence of this is, that all the scenes in which the hero is not in action, are languid, and all the other personages in the play are very faintly sketched. With such materials as history furnished him, he might easily have done more and better. The wife of Spartacus is said to have accompanied him in his exploits, and by her supposed skill in divination, to have prompted and encouraged some of his most daring enterprises. This hint might have sufficed to make Senona a more important personage than Dr. Bird's fancy has created. Our business, however, is with the play as we find it, not as it might have been. [Here follows a description of the plot of the play.]

"The latter part of the play is less vigorous than the former; but

F

there are some scenes of stirring interest in which Mr. Forrest made a powerful impression on the audience. The poetry of the drama is rather powerful than polished; and although it contains some passages of considerable beauty, it is more generally characterized by a rough passionate strain, in which gracefulness is sacrificed to force. One speech, in which Spartacus describes the beauty of his Thracian vallies before the invasion of the Romans, and contrasts it with the devastation which had followed their footsteps, struck us as being particularly happy. At the conclusion of the play Mr. Forrest was called for, and began to address the audience, a practice not usual nor safe, at least on this side of the Atlantic. He thanked them for the reception they had bestowed on him, and expressed his satisfaction at finding in that reception a proof of their good will towards America. Now, although their praises were warm and hearty, they were given to him personally, and simply because they thought he deserved them, and would have been just as freely bestowed if he had come from Kamtschatka as from New York. There are no national prejudices between an audience and an actor, nor any where else in this country, which could make it for a moment questionable that a deserving artist would be well received, from whatever quarter of the globe he arrived. When, however, Mr. Forrest, encouraged by the applause, began to thank them for the favours they had shown to the tragedy, he provoked some dissent, the audience not seeming to think as highly of the poet as of the player—so Mr. Forrest made his bow and retired.

" We shall be glad to see him in some other character, and if he acquits himself hereafter as well as he did on this occasion, he will have no reason to be dissatisfied with his voyage, and the theatre will have engaged an able performer, who, to very considerable skill in his profession, adds the attraction of a somewhat novel and a much more spirited style of playing than any other tragic actor now on our stage."

I will now give the cast of the play on its first representation on the London stage.

Marcus Lucinius Crassus, *Warde*; Gellius, *F. Cooke*; Lentulus, *Hooper*; Jovius, *Bartley*; Bracchius, *Matthews*; Florus, *Brindal*; Spartacus, *E. Forrest*; Phasarius, *Cooper*; Enomais, *Baker*; Crixus, *Duruset*; Mummius, *Mears*; Scropha, *Honner*; Boy, *Miss Marshall*; Centurion, *T. Matthews*; Julia, *Mrs. Hooper*, (her first appearance); Senona, *Miss Huddart*, (first appearance in five years).

Also the original cast in New York :—

Marcus Lucinius Crassus, *Richings*; Lucius Gellius, *Povey*; Scropha, *Wheatley*; Jovius, *Woodhull*; Mummius, *Hayden*; Baliatus Lentulus, *Blakeley*; Florus, son to Lentulus, *Field*; Bracchius, *Thorne*; Spartacus, *E. Forrest*; Phasarius, *Barry*; Enomais, *Nixsen*; Crixus, *Reed*; Centurion, *King*; Slave, *Bisset*; Boy of Spartacus, *Miss E. Turnbull*; Julia, *Mrs. Wallack*: Senona, *Mrs. Sharpe*. Gladiators, 20; Roman Guards, 16; Lictors, 6; Patricians, 6; Ladies, 8; 6 Female Slaves; 2 Children.

A fac-simile of the manager's announcement, in the underline of the London play-bills :—

Mr. Edwin Forrest,
The eminent American Tragedian,
Whose first appearance last evening on the British stage, (before one of the most crowded audiences ever assembled in this theatre,) elicited those enthusiastic testimonials
of success, which
have stamped him
one of the Greatest Actors
that ever graced an English Theatre, *will*, in consequence of the unbounded applause with which he was received in the
New Tragedy of
The Gladiator!
have the honour of repeating the character of *Spartacus* three times every week, until further notice.

Mr. Bunn was determined to make the most of his bargain, and doubtless reaped a rich harvest from the exertions of the American tragedian.

Mr. Forrest's Shakspearian characters, with the exception of Othello, where his terrific energy in the third and fourth acts holds his audience in breathless amazement, are not above mediocrity; his Richard the Third, and his Macbeth, do not even deserve that name; but in those characters which have been written for him, in which his physical requisites have been brought into play in the most favourable manner, he maintains a reputation which will be cherished so long as the American drama, of which he may be called the founder, shall exist.

There is no name I shall have occasion to refer to more frequently than Mr. Forrest's, as I progress, or of whom I shall have more to write.

The Philadelphia Theatre having closed for the season, the company proceeded to Baltimore, where we opened with the play of the "Stranger;" but our season was brought to an abrupt termination by the "Kean row." From the opening, there was a feverish anxiety to know when Kean's engagement would commence, or whether he intended to visit Baltimore. No sooner did the announcement of his name appear, than it became evident his reception would not be a friendly one, although he hoped, and his friends were sanguine the result would be the same as in New York and Philadelphia—an expression of public feeling which would subside. He had re-requested me to play "*Richmond*," knowing that so long as it was possible to hold our ground, I should never desert him, although the prospect of being hooted and pelted, was by no means a pleasant one. When he appeared as Richard the Third, the hubbub as usual commenced, but had apparently subsided during the third act, when every thing was so restored to quiet, that I left the theatre to obtain some portion of my

.dress from the Shakspeare, where I boarded. I was surprised
on my return to find the storm raging more furiously than
ever. This was owing to the injudicious conduct of Kean's
friends, who ruined his cause. During the early part of the
evening, they had displayed two placards in front of each
stage box, the one bearing the motto, "*Let the friends of Kean
be silent;*" the other, "*Kean for ever !*" Had they adhered to
their maxim of silence, their triumph would have been complete, but although their tongues were silent, their hands were
too active; on the slightest opposition, they seized the aggressor and ejected him from the theatre. Those treated in this
unceremonious manner, for exercising what they conceived to
be their right, formed a group before the doors of the theatre,
recapitulating their wrongs to the already excited populace,
waiting only for a leader to commence mischief; a brickbat
thrown at the windows of the saloon, was followed by a rush
towards the door. The theatre was saved from destruction
by the spirited conduct of Mr. Montgomery, the mayor of the
city, who interposed his person, assuring the mob, that none
could enter that building for the purpose of mischief, except
over his body; a pause took place, and that pause, in all probability saved the life of Kean—who was enabled to make
his escape from the theatre; every carriage was searched, and
it was not until assured that the object of their vengeance was
beyond their reach, that the crowd dispersed, some remaining
on the ground until daylight.

And where was the manager during all this riot and confusion? Mr. Wood, fearful of some serious mishap, left the city
in the steamboat at five o'clock, on a plea of business; thus
depriving Kean of the aid of that tongue, which for a long
series of years, had guided the taste and quelled the unruly
spirits of the theatre. Policy might have dictated his retreat,
but justice to those under his control, should have held him
fast at his post, in the hour of danger. He is a bad pilot who
deserts the helm when his vessel is in the neighbourhood of
breakers.

Thus ended Kean's performance at the Holiday-street Theatre, in June, 1826. On the following morning, Col. Benjamin
Edes, a respectable and respected citizen of Baltimore, called
upon me, and said, "Wemyss, if you are a friend of Kean's,
get him out of the city; if he attempts to play to night, we
shall *tar and feather him ;* and he may think himself lucky if
he escapes with no further injury." Assured it was useless to
endanger his safety, I proceeded directly to his hotel, told him
he had no time to lose, but must prepare to leave the city
without an instant's delay; that the excitement against him
was increasing every moment, and that violence would attend
any attempt to appear again upon the stage. He said, "My

God! what shall I do? I have not a cent with me; this is so totally unexpected, *where* is it to end?" I enquired what sum would be sufficient for his immediate necessity—he replied, about two hundred dollars; this I procured from my friend Conine, and succeeded in getting him safely out of the city. While many were enjoying, in anticipation, the scene they expected, Kean was safely on board the steamboat, on his way to Philadelphia. I accompanied him, leaving my wife and children in the charge of Mr. Jefferson. The Theatre in Baltimore was closed for the season, and the company returned to Philadelphia.

Kean was received in Philadelphia with open arms; a reaction had taken place in the public sentiment. Conceiving he had been sufficiently punished, pity resumed the place of resentment, and he was looked upon as an ill-treated man. The theatre was re-opened on the 12th of June, and he appeared as Richard the Third, with the tide of popular favour as strong in his behalf as ever it had been in his proudest days of success; and although he did shed tears at the idea of playing Shylock for a quarter of a dollar, all he received, (his terms being to share the receipts with the management, after deducting two hundred dollars, each night,) yet that night (the cause of which should be buried in oblivion,) erased from his engagement, his attraction continued undiminished. The last night he played in Philadelphia was on the 26th of June, 1826, when he appeared as Cardinal Wolsey, in "Henry the Eighth," and Sylvester Daggerwood, for his benefit, leaving the stage in what mountebanks call a *flip-flap*, really well executed. But what a ridiculous association in the minds of his audience; the great tragedian, and the clown of a circus, both seen in the same person, and for the last time. Before he left the city he sent me the following note, enclosing the money borrowed in Baltimore :—

" DEAR WEMYSS,

208 thanks !

" Take an opportunity of visiting our crib on the banks of the Hudson : you will find as honourable a gang as ever cried " stand " to a traveller, and fattened on pillage : though the captain may happen to be on duty, the troop delight in the swindling fraternity, and you will be truly welcome.

" Success, dear Wemyss,
(Signed,) " EDMUND KEAN."

Addressed thus :—
" —— Wemyss, Esq.,
" Tragedian, Comedian,
" Fencerenian, Lotterenian,
" Omnenian, *non*,
" Alterenian !!! Philadelphia."

I never had the pleasure of seeing him again. He was in Dublin when I was in England, in 1827; although hourly expected in Liverpool, I sailed, on my return, before his arrival. He never possessed a warmer friend, or more enthusiastic admirer. He sat for his portrait to Neagle, for the Acting American Theatre, which picture was afterwards purchased by George Munday.

Mr. and Mrs. George Barrett played a short engagement; after which Mr. E. Forrest returned and played his first regular star engagement, at the Chesnut-street Theatre, commencing on the 5th of July, with Othello; Rolla, on the 6th; William Tell, on the 7th; Earl Osmond, in the "Castle Spectre," on the 8th; Jaffier, on the 10th; and Othello, on the 11th; when the theatre was closed, and he accompanied us to Washington city, where he *first* acted Damon—since, one of his most favourite characters.

It was at the close of the summer season of 1826, that Mr. Wood retired from the management, having dissolved partnership with Warren. His situation as stage manager was filled by my old friend, Joe Cowell; and the season of 1826 and 1827, I may honestly say, was the most pleasant year of my American engagements. I heard with regret of his retirement, although I was fixed upon as his successor. In his "Thirty Years among the Players," he does injustice to Warren, and has made it appear that the actors engaged by Mr. Hallam, for Cowell and Simpson, surpassed in talent and attraction those engaged by me for the Chesnut-street Theatre; yet every play-goer knows he retired from the contest, and when he returned to renew it, after Warren's theatre had been opened thirty-five weeks, he was obliged to close; the "Gnome King" having so far surpassed his "Sleeping Beauty," that his theatre was deserted, while the Chesnut-street Theatre continued to be well attended to the close of the season.

CHAPTER XIII.

Baltimore Season not worth even a passing record. Cowell's management. Macready's first appearance in Philadelphia. His disagreeable manners producing quite an excitement among the Actors against him. Great Effect of his Colloquial Acting. Sensible Conduct under Undeserved Reproach. Note to the Author. First Appearance of Mrs. Knight, late Miss Povey. Her Great Success. Compliment to the Author. First Appearance of Miss Hester Warren. First Appearance of Miss E. Jefferson, afterwards Mrs. S. Chapman. First Attempt at Management in the United States. Preparations to cross the Atlantic. Instructions and Departure.

THE Baltimore season concluded, we opened in Philadelphia on the 4th of December, 1826, with the play of the "Stranger," and the farce of the "Turnpike Gate." The talent of the company was inferior to any season I had yet known, and complaints were loud in all quarters, yet Cowell's name was a tower of strength. He was deservedly popular, both with the actors and the public, and no one regretted more than I did his retirement, notwithstanding I was selected as his successor. Mr. Macready was the first star of the season. He opened on the 10th of January, 1827, as Macbeth, and at once received the approbation which his high character as an actor deserved. He played Hamlet, Virginius, William Tell, Pierre, Coriolanus, Damon, Petruchio.

It was during the performance of "William Tell," a circumstance occurred which might have proved fatal to his future prospects in the United States. The property man (worthy old Charley Ward) had, through negligence, forgotten to provide an arrow to break before Gesler, in the fourth act of the play, compelling Macready to devote from his own quiver, one so loaded and poised, as to prevent the possibility of a failure in the most critical situation of the play. Not being one of the mildest tempered men, and irritated at the moment by the loss of, to him, a valuable stage property, he said, in anger, to the property man, who was waiting to make his apology, "*I can't get such an arrow in your country, sir!*" which was thus translated for him, "*I can't get wood to make such an arrow in your country.*"

The anonymous letters sent to the then respectable conductors of the daily press, were enclosed to Mr. Macready, who, of course, disavowed their contents. He assembled the company upon the stage, by special request, read the accusation, and appealed to them, collectively and individually, to say, whether any one present had ever heard him make use of such an expression.

All remaining silent, he made a neat appeal to their feel ings, stating, that if he had personally offended any one of them, he regretted it, and held himself personally reponsible; but he hoped none who had heard him were base enough to make use of such means as the letter he held in his hand, in revenge for supposed slight.

It is really singular that, deriving all, or nearly all, the act ing plays from England, applauding and constantly in asso ciation with the best English actors, there should exist, behind the scenes of the American theatres, such an inveterate hatred to the foreign artist, that every little word uttered should be construed into an intentional national insult, which, magnified by the malign report of the lower order of actors and their tavern companions, is introduced before the curtain, to the annoyance of at least two-thirds of the audience assem bled for amusement; who, provided the actor entertains them for the moment, care nothing about him or his opinions, ex cept to furnish a subject of conversation for a few minutes at their next evening party. Had the penny press been in ex istence during Macready's engagement, a rash word, harmlessly spoken, to a negligent property man, would have been suffi cient to have terminated his career on the American stage. The poison once disseminated, no opportunity would have been offered for justification: he would have been driven home in disgrace for an offence—never committed.

In rehearsing the play of Virginius, an occurrence took place which caused a hearty laugh at the expense of Mr. William Forrest, (brother to the tragedian) who was the Icilius. Caught by the natural tone and manner of Macready, who, turning suddenly, said, "Will you lead Virginia in, or do you wait for me to do it." "Whichever you please, Mr. Macready," was the ready answer, followed by such a laugh as only actors can enjoy. He even deceived the acting man ager, Mr. Cowell, old and experienced as he was, in a similar manner in William Tell. When speaking to young Wheatley about his shoe being untied, Cowell said rather pettishly, "Don't keep us here all day, Mr. Macready, about the boy's shoe—go on with the rehearsal." These are compliments to the colloquial skill of Macready, as great as was ever paid to any actor by his professional brethren.

His Damon was by no means as good as Cooper's; it was too laboured, too cold and artificial, to reach the feelings of his audience. He confessed it was not a favourite character, and only assumed in compliance with the wishes of the manager.

He sat for his portrait to Neagle for the acting American Theatre, and the plates sent to him on that occasion produced the following note.

(COPY.)

Mr. Macready presents his best compliments to Mr. Wemyss, to thank him for his elegant collection of theatrical portraits. He can only regret that he has so little title to Mr. Wemyss's acknowledgments, and th at he has had no ampler occasion of testifying his respect for one among the few members of his profession whose deportment and manner he has observed as creditable to it.

Approbation from Sir Hubert Stanley is praise indeed!

The next star was Mrs. Knight, (late Miss Povey,) who made her first appearance in Philadelphia, on the 29th of January, 1827, as Floretta, in the "Cabinet." Who does not remember the bewitching simplicity of

Mrs. KNIGHT?

The archness and vivacity displayed in her acting, greatly enhancing the pleasure derived from the sweet tones she warbled forth in her ballads. She was the first female singer of cultivated taste, who had visited the United States since the days of Miss George, the Wowski of Coleman's "Inkle and Yarico." Her attraction and popularity remained undiminished for many successive seasons. It was not only in opera she was a universal favourite, but her acting in Kate O'Brien in "Perfection," and Betty Finikin in "Gretna Green," was truly excellent; it would have puzzled the most snarling critic to have found just cause for censure in the first named piece. So completely did she take her audience by surprise, that at the fall of the curtain, the Pit actually rose by acclamation, demanding a repetition, a compliment so very unusual in those days, when the habit of calling for every actor at the close of an engagement was not in vogue, that it was appreciated as no mean honour. She was pleased to thank me personally for my performance of Charles Paragon, insisting that I was entitled to my full share of the unexpected but highly valued compliment. Never was a more general shout of approbation heard within the walls of a theatre, than greeted my announcement of Mrs. Knight's compliance with the wishes of the audience. As I can call to mind no other instance on record, during my knowledge of the American stage, of such an occurrence, in justice to all concerned, I will record the cast. —Sir Laurence Paragon, Mr. C. Green; Charles Paragon, Mr. Wemyss: Sam, Mr. John Mills Brown; Kate O'Brien, Mrs. Knight; Susan, Mrs. C. Green. A more just estimate of the merit due to the actors, may be formed from the knowledge of the fact, that not one of them were in possession of their written parts, until the rehearsal on the day previous to the performance, which so gratified the brilliant audience assembled on the occasion of Mrs. Knight's benefit. It was a proud night for star, managers, and actors. It is needless to add, it was repeated to an excellent house, and has retained possession of the stage ever since. I have seen many Kate O'Brien's, including Miss Kelly, Clara Fisher and Miss Rock; but never one who approached Mrs. Knight in excellence. It was indeed " Perfection."

On the 28th of February, Booth acted the tragedy of " Scylla." Mr. E. Forrest appeared as Damon, on the 7th of March. And during his engagement, which was not a profitable one, he played Othello, Rolla, William Tell, Sir E. Mortimer, King Lear, Jaffier, and on the 14th of March, Richard the Third; the worst representative of that character I ever witnessed; nor do I think he has ever improved upon his first false conception of the character. I may be wrong— but such is my opinion.

Macready returned to us on the 26th of March, commencing with Othello—playing the Stranger, Hamlet, Cardinal Wolsey, Macbeth, Romont, in the revived play of the " Fatal Dowry;" Henry the 5th, Virginius, King John; and Felix, in the " Hunter of the Alps."

On the 16th of April, 1827, (Easter Monday,) Henry Wallack, who had become, since the death of Barrere, the lessee of Chatham Garden Theatre, was engaged to produce the spectacle of " Brian Boroihome," which had drawn crowds in the city of New York. It was well prepared, the scenery excellently painted, and would doubtless have been successful, with its play-bill surrounded with " Harps," and its " Erin Go Bragh," in flaming red letters;—but, Mr. Webb, an actor of some repute, who was to have been the representative of Voltimar, had been studying ancient history too closely, and came to the conclusion, taking Shakspeare for his authority, that the Danes were powerful drinkers, and therefore appeared upon the stage so perfectly undisguised in liquor, that the audience thought proper to hiss, which he resented, by walking out of the theatre. Mr. Heyl read the part; and the piece, in consequence of Webb's misconduct, was unequivocally damned. If ever a penal code should be enacted, for the sole punishment of actors, drunkenness should be a penitentiary offence, without the possibility of pardon. How many managers have had a prosperous season ruined, by the misconduct of *one* actor; and hundreds of dollars judiciously expended, lost for ever, by this worst of evil habits. The correction is in the hands of the public alone: while they permit an actor, who has thus insulted them, to appear again, as if no offence had been committed, reformation is hopeless. Had Booth been banished, the stage might have lost an admirable actor, but the example would have deterred others, who possessed not his talent, from venturing upon the experiment.—

George Frederick Cooke was tolerated in his brutality, which, if properly checked and rebuked, would have prevented Edmund Kean from offending in the same manner. It is said, genius will be erratic,—this may be true; but like the mad-ness of the confidant, in Sheridan's farce of the " Critic," let it, by request, be kept in the back ground.

For the benefit of Mr. Jefferson, whose name was sure to fill the house, his daughter, Miss E. Jefferson, made her first appearance upon any stage, as Rosina, in the "Spanish Barber." If Miss Warren was the best " debutante" I had ever seen, Miss Jefferson was decidedly the worst; she spoke so low, and so completely lost all self-possession, that, had it not been for her father, she would scarcely have escaped deri-sion. The only redeeming point was her song of " An old man would be wooing," in which she was feebly encored. From such an unfavourable beginning, little was to be expected.— But in the race commenced between Miss Warren and herself, although distanced in the first attempt, she far outstripped her in her future career; rising step by step, until she be-came, as Mrs. S. Chapman, the leading actress of the American stage, in the Park Theatre of New York, justly admired by every frequenter of the theatre; proving that the race is not always with the swift, or the battle with the strong. She married a second time, on the death of Mr. Chapman, Mr. Augustus Richardson, of Baltimore, retiring from the stage.

There was a similarity of fate in the career of these two ladies; both handsome, and both possessed of talent, both married to foreigners, both left widows at an early age, and both entering a second time into the state of wedlock; one dying in the zenith of her fame; the other having reached the highest goal of her ambition, voluntarily resigned the plaudits nightly bestowed upon her in the first theatre of her native country, to enjoy the blessings of domestic life, in retirement.

The play of " John Bull," established Mr. John Green in favour of the audience, as a good delineator of Irish character. His Dennis Bulgruddery was the greatest charm of the play, which was repeated four nights at the close of the season. Mr. Warren's benefit took place on the 12th of May, 1827 ; the theatre closing with the play of the " Cure for the Heartache," and the "Agreeable Surprise."

We proceeded as usual, to Baltimore, for the spring season, and while there, I was taken one morning by surprise, by an offer from Mr. Warren, to accept the acting and stage manage-ment of the theatres under his direction ; to cross the Atlantic and recruit his dramatic company, by engaging new faces from England. The offer he made was so liberal, that I desired a few days for consideration. My friends whom I consulted on the occasion, strongly urged my acceptance; among others Mr. Lewis T. Pratt, little dreaming that this arrangement would at no very distant period make him co-lessee of those very theatres.

My professional pride was also flattered by the idea, that Mr. Wood's assertion of my total failure in America, would be forever set at rest, by my appearance among my old associates after an absence of five years, as the manager of the Philadelphia Theatre. I therefore agreed to relinquish my lottery business, and on the 6th of May, 1827, made an engagement for three years with Mr. Warren, in which I promised to devote my time entirely to promote his interests.

On the 20th of June, I sailed from Philadelphia, in the Tuscarora, commanded by Captain Serrill, to return to my native country, full of hopes and fears for the success of my mission. My instructions, and my views of those instructions were as follows. How well I performed my duty, the public have placed on record, by their almost unanimous approval of those actors with whom I returned to open the season of 1827 and 1828.

(COPY.) MR. WARREN'S INSTRUCTIONS.

" MY DEAR SIR:

"In the mission you have so kindly undertaken for me, you will please to observe the following instructions—first, the performers:

" A gentleman capable of acting first tragedy, or young men such as Harry Dornton, Claudio, Laertes,—as to Hamlet, Richard, &c., you know since they have seen Kean, Macready, and such actors of the present day, to perform such plays without actors of that name and grade, would be useless.

" A man capable of sustaining heavy parts, which I am obliged to confer at present, on Wheatley.

" A young man who can sing,—on that subject you understand my views.

" A useful man to play low comedy, and if capable of playing Irishmen, the better; which will be four.

" A lady capable of leading in tragedy, Belvidera; also another lady, who would perform Lady Macbeth. If a woman of the time of life who could undertake both, it would be better.

" The salaries not to exceed thirty dollars. I would rather have it, not more than six guineas; but if an object is to be gained, two dollars will not make any difference.

" Passage, and any advance you may make to be repaid by a weekly deduction.

" Every engagement for two years, and the deduction shall be apportioned to the time. It may happen that some of the parties may be married. Any arrangement which you think necessary for their comfort, will be acceded to by me, as I am well convinced that you will do the best you can for the concern.

" With respect to Mr. Miller, you will please to enquire what he has sent ; and bring with you, what he has not, that you think will be useful ; but I don't want anything else. He can draw for the amount by way of Carey and Lea."

These instructions I was desired to show Mr. Richard Peters, Junr. of Philadelphia, and ask his advice upon the nature of them. On the 19th of June, 1827, he addressed me the following letter,

(COPY.)

" Philadelphia, June 19, 1827.

" DEAR SIR :—

" I have already delivered to you a bill of exchange for 75*l.* sterling, and have paid to you, by a check to your credit two hundred and thirty dollars. I now hand you a letter of credit from my friend, Mr. W. B. Evans, addressed to Mr. Grey Wilds, London, by which you will be enabled to draw 150*l.* sterling. These are on account of Mr. Warren, and will be accounted for to me, by him. I have also made arrangements with Messrs. Thomas P. Cope and Sons, by which all persons for whom you may request a passage on board of any of the Philadelphia packets by a line addressed to the captains, will be received, and the prices of the passage will be paid here by Mr. Warren. Captain West, of the Montezuma, has agreed to charge for the passages, the stipulated price payable at the par of exchange. This will be a saving of about fifteen dollars in each.

The other captains will do the same, if you insist upon it, and if they will not, there is another line, which sails from Liverpool the 20th of every month. I have thus completed all the arrangements assigned to me by Mr. Warren, and I trust they will be found satisfactory.

" A word or two about your project—as Mr. Warren has authorised me to speak of it. I think it fortunate that Hallam has been before you, and has made his selection ; you know the force of those he has engaged, and must go beyond him. You will be able to ascertain what the talents of all those he has brought with him are, and you must get persons who are superior to them in talent and in personal appearance, and in reputation. Do not let a guinea a week, or even more, separate you, if they can be obtained. I know Warren will confirm this, and I will get him to say so to you in writing. It will be all-important that you accomplish the object of your visit upon the principles I have stated, and succeeding in it, you will put Mr. Cowell and S. at defiance. Allow me to remind you, that with the audience, who are to be amused at the Chesnut Street Theatre, polished manners, good exterior, and a guarded sense of decorum are all-important. I claim no more than your knowledge of us will concede, when I say that an actor who does not appear as a gentleman will never succeed here; this deficiency has been the cause of the failure of many. It is not that he shall act the gentleman well, but that he shall be a gentleman who pleases us. Mr. Hallam has not competency to ascertain and judge of this matter, for his gentleman was vulgar, and his taste as low and as coarse as possible. I do you no more than justice to say, you have always exhibited the qualifications so necessary and important.

G

" Let your singer be a gentleman, and capable of playing the parts of opera, as such a person would exhibit their superior voice. High musical attainments are not so essential as expression, feeling, and vivacity; a good singer, not a superior one, who will maintain with respectability his parts in opera, will have much to do next season, with the Jefferson, who promises to be very attractive. I do not exactly understand what Mr. W. means by a female to play Belvidera, and another to play Lady Macbeth; the lady who can play the first ought to play the second. I think if you can get a lady to play high tragedy, of middle age, not old, of good appearance, and I should say a lady who can play Lady Teazle, and the females in very high comedy, you would do better. If you could find a person, who with low comedy, can play well in melo-drama and in pantomime, it would be well. Bring out the materials for two or more good pantomimes. Our friend Warren is too much disposed to confidence; I would advise you to establish an agency for him altogether independent of Price & Co., and the New Yorkers, and let it be private; they will bribe him off if they can, but this you can prevent, by a judicious selection.

" Arrangements should be made to have sent out all pieces which hit, if they are of a general nature. You may arrange with Mr. Curwin, to whom I give you a letter, to forward them from Liverpool, and let the agent send them to him; a little expense, &c., incurred, will be repaid. You remember you have active, enterprising, and skilful opponents; they are more—they are without principle, for so I must say of those, who, like Mr. Cowell, " have bribed off Mr. W.'s actors," and of Mr. Simpson, who said, " Let Warren get out who he will, I will have them in New York in a month." I say this to show you the necessity of exertion, of caution, and of making your contracts explicit and positive.

" I also say so to induce you to procure performers of more attraction than those which the circus habits of Mr. Hallam have enabled him to select. Remember the comparison will be between those selected by Hallam and Mr. Wemyss. It will be the test of your judgment and your taste, and I feel satisfied you will surpass in both. I recommend to you, and will get Warren to confirm it, if the payment of the passage out should be made an insurmountable objection, with a performer of high attainments, that you agree to pay it, stipulating that if Warren, to repay himself, desires to put up a benefit, in his or her name, he may do it. It will be very unfortunate, if, under such an arrangement, we would not be repaid the cost of the passage. The plan of making the weekly salary less, and paying the passage, is a good one.

" Wishing you a good voyage, and requesting you to say to Mrs. Wemyss, if I can be of any service to her while you are abroad, she may command me.   I am yours, very respectfully,
                    (Signed)   RICHARD PETERS, JUNR.

" P.S.—Let me recommend to you to call upon the stars in London, all you think may come here, and tell them not to sell themselves to Price and Co. Put an article in the Theatrical Messenger, stating what stars get here when they come on their own account. I will send you the materials for this by the packet from New York, which sails the 4th of July. This will break up the New York plans. This will let the *big fish* come here without Price and Simpson, and, in the end, will do more for Warren's scheme than they can counteract. You may leave the document, certified by Warren's treasurer, with the publisher of the article.

" Ascertain what agreement the stars would make with Warren, to come out here, and he may write them on your return, or before. This will have two effects : it will give you weight with them, give Warren a standing, and make them hesitate to sell themselves to Price." .

All the contents of this letter were afterwards approved by Mr. Warren, in a letter addressed to me in London. It will be seen that one of the great objects of my visit to England, was to place the Chesnut Street Theatre on the high ground from which it had lately receded, by treating directly with the stars, in London, instead of receiving them, second-hand, through the managers of the Park Theatre, New York, with whom it had become a fashion, to say, " you *must* receive Mr., or . Mrs., or Miss ———, on such a day, or they cannot visit Philadelphia at all." The general break-up in theatricals which took place in 1829 and 1830, alone prevented the suc- cess of this scheme. Mrs. Sloman's success induced Mrs. W. West and Mrs. Vining, to enter at once into terms, which, Warren retiring from the management, prevented from being carried into effect.

CHAPTER XIV.

Arrival in Liverpool. Meeting of Price and James Wallack. Stars in prospect. Miserable situation of the Provincial Theatres in regard to Talent. Journey to London. An English M. P. Offer of Alliance, Offensive and Defensive, with Dr. Hart, Agent of the Bowery Theatre. Engagement concluded with Mr. and Mrs. Sloman, Mrs. Austin, Miss George, and John Thompson Norton. Numerous Engagements with Clever Actors. Whole Ship-load of Actors for Philadelphia. Safe Arrival. Pleasant Voyage. Managerial Trouble commencing. The Opening of the Season of 1827 and 1828.

I ARRIVED at Liverpool on the 20th July, and as the vessel was made fast to the dock, the first person I saw standing on the wharf was Stephen Price, at that time manager of Drury Lane Theatre. He, and James Wallack, were anxiously ex- pecting Macready who, I informed them, I had left acting in Baltimore. They invited me to dine with them, anxious to hear all the news from America. I promised to see them in the evening, which we spent together, proceeding to the theatre, where I met my old friends, Meadows and Paul Bedford.

Price declared to me he had no connection with American theatricals, and knew no one, except Simpson, whom he would be more happy to serve than Warren, since he had cut adrift Mr. Lignum. I received much valuable information from him, as to the whereabouts of many actors I was anxious

to see; but I soon found, on my arrival in London, that Mr.
Price was still considered the manager of the Park Theatre,
New York; however, from him I learnt that Mrs. Sloman
might be induced to cross the Atlantic if I could make her an
offer worth accepting. Having been an intimate associate of
Sloman, when we were together in the Canterbury company,
I lost no time in addressing a letter to him, requesting to see
him as early as possible, after my arrival in London. On the
1st of August we met, and concluded an engagement for one
year, for the service of himself and Mrs. Sloman, for which I
agreed, on behalf of Mr. Warren, to pay him twenty-seven
pounds per week, and allow him all his travelling expenses.
This was one of the most important as well as most successful
engagements I made.

The mania for theatrical emigration to America was at its
height when I arrived in London. Dr. Hart of New York,
had engaged a strong reinforcement for the Bowery Theatre
of that city. The Boston managers were also exerting themselves to meet the opposition preparing for them by the erection of the Tremont Theatre, of which Pelby was to be the
manager. Hallam had engaged nearly an entire company for
the Walnut Street Theatre, Philadelphia, among whom were
Harry Smith and John Shefton. Applications from actors of
minor repute flocked in upon me by dozens, employing at
least an hour a day to answer. My first care was to see what
could be procured in the provincial theatres, but never was I
more disappointed; with the exception of Miss Huddart and
Miss Kenneth, both of Birmingham, and a Mr. Hammond, at
Liverpool, there was not an actor worth making an offer to,
and I was determined, if I could not meet with those whom
my judgment approved, to return to the United States without
forming any engagements at all.

Booth had strongly recommended to my notice Mr. S.
Chapman, as a young man of talent, worth enquiring after,
and I fortunately found him in the humour to answer my purpose. His brother William having been engaged for the
Bowery Theatre, I had no difficulty in forming an engagement
mutually satisfactory. I agreed to give him five pounds per
week, which he thought then a liberal offer, although some
time after his arrival in the United States, although regularly
paid, he grumbled at exceedingly, because he found others,
of less value to the theatre than himself, in receipt of higher
emolument.

My next enquiry was after Mr. Southwell, and I must confess my surprise was equal to my pleasure, in finding the
dashing Romeo, my old strolling acquaintance, Francis, whom
I parted with in Bolton, Lancashire. I had considerable
difficulty in prevailing upon him to listen to my proposal; he

laughed at the idea; nor do I think even our old friendship would have induced him to listen to my overtures, had he not have had a quarrel with Elliston upon the score of business, when, Irishman-like, acting upon the impulse of the moment, he came directly from the theatre to me, and to prevent the possibility of reconciliation, signed his articles before he left my lodgings, to my no small gratification, although much to the annoyance of Elliston, who threatened to arrest him for breach of contract, if he attempted to sail for America; and poor Southwell felt uneasy until he was safely at sea on board the Montezuma.

Mercer and family next engaged my attention, a most valuable acquisition to any theatre. I now tried Rowbotham, and was equally successful. Miss Emery, of the Surrey Theatre, I was also fortunate enough to engage, and on recounting my recruits, I began to feel proud of my success. A male singer was the only important person I now wanted, and here I was completely baffled, and at last imposed upon by Pearman, who recommended to me his pupil Hutchings, at that time engaged in the York Theatre. He was the only person to whose talent I was a stranger, until I had committed myself beyond the possibility of retracting, and bad as was the bargain, it was Hobson's choice, "*that or none.*" I now turned my attention to a machinist, and materiel for a good pantomime. Mr. Henry Lewis was recommended to me by Barrymore, a most able mechanic, whose failings rendered his talent a source of mortification more than profit, although he was of great service to the theatre. Master and Miss Kerr, and Miss Hawthorn, together with two young ladies named Minter, who failed to make their appearance at the appointed time, Mr. Willis as a melo-dramatic leader, completed my arrangements, and with a feeling of pride I wrote to Mr. Warren, informing him of my success in carrying out all his views.

I now received a note enclosed to Mr. Kenneth, from the Hon. F. H. F. Berkeley, requesting an interview, which I found was an application from Mrs. Austin, which I was most willing to entertain. She, was then singing at Vauxhall, where I went to hear her, and was so delighted with her voice, that on the following morning, after a few moments' conversation, I left two proposals for her consideration, to the last of which she replied,—

" Mrs. Austin is prepared to accede to an engagement at Philadelphia, as proposed by Mr. Wemyss, for twelve nights, at ten pounds sterling per night, and a half clear benefit, to take place on any day, Friday or Saturday excepted; the strength, or any part of the company being at Mrs. Austin's disposal on that night. Mrs. Austin to appear at Philadelphia (unless indisposed by the voyage) within a week after her arrival; not to play more than three times a week, and to be guaranteed an engagement at Baltimore sharing with the manager, after the expenses; the balance to be struck be" tween the parties each night; the payment either weekly or nightly, as may please the manager."

This was the substance of the engagement, which was finally arranged, with the option of a renewal for twelve nights longer, on the part of the manager, on the same terms.

(COPY OF MR. H. BERKELEY'S NOTE.)

" Mr. H. Berkeley's compliments to Mr. Kenneth, begs to acquaint him, that on Monday he will meet Mr. Wemyss and himself at Mrs. Austin's, at any time Mr. Kenneth may fix, finally to arrange everything. Mr. Berkeley sees no obstacle, but will make every remark on paper, to the most particular iota, for Mr. Wemyss' approval. Mr. Kenneth will be kind enough to acquaint Mr. W. that Mrs. Austin can get an engagement at either theatre in New York, and appear there *first*, but that she certainly shall consider herself bound to Mr. Warren, and respecting all other engagements in America, shall make a point to be guided by that which will be most agreeable or useful to the Philadelphia manager.

" Respecting the ten pounds, nightly, Mrs. Austin will be entirely guided by Colonel Berkeley, who arrives on Saturday at Berkeley House, and it was owing to his opinion, that she made the proposal; but it has removed much objection in her mind to find Mr. Wemyss ready to meet the terms, as it clearly proves his good opinion of the venture. In short, Mr. Berkeley merely proposes Monday, because of the arrival of his brother, the necessity of attending to whom, Mr. Kenneth can very well understand."

Here was a great point gained in a negociation for a *star;* the Chesnut Street Theatre receiving a preference to either the Park or Bowery Theatres of New York, and through a source which might hereafter be turned to great advantage. The patronage of Colonel Berkeley to theatres and theatricals in London, being too well known to require comment.

It was in consequence of this engagement, which was concluded on the Monday, that John Thompson Norton, the trumpeter, *par excellence*, was engaged to try his fortune in the western world—an acquisition to the orchestra of no mean value.

On the Tuesday, August 21st, I found the following note upon my table.

" Dr. Hart, of New York, has had the pleasure of waiting on Mr. Wemyss, on business relative to the Philadelphia Theatre. If it will suit the entire convenience of Mr. W., Dr. Hart will be glad to see him any time to-morrow, between 12 and 3 o'clock, at his residence, No. 14, Pall Mall.

" Tuesday, Aug. 21, 1827."

I waited upon Dr. Hart at the appointed time; the result was the engagement of Miss George, to appear in Philadelphia.

He made also an offer which I agreed to, subject to the final approval of Mr. Warren, in Philadelphia. *It was*, if the Bowery Theatre of New York, of which he was the agent in London, would receive such stars as we engaged, on fair and reciprocal terms that the Philadelphia Theatre would enter into an arrangement to exclude entirely every star known to be imported by Price and Simpson, and lend our aid to the engagement of Braham and Madame Vestris, for the Bowery and Philadelphia theatres. Dr. Hart further pledged himself, if Warren agreed to this arrangement, that the French Dancers, now on their way to America, or any auxiliary aid from their company, which could frustrate the views of the New York manager, in Philadelphia, should be at our disposal, by giving one week's notice. He honestly confessed these offers were not made that they loved us more, but that they hated the Park most.

This was a strong blow aimed at the prosperity of the Park Theatre, which, if the Boston managers, who were also tired of their thraldom, had entered into, would have placed Price and Simpson in the situation of suppliants, rather than the despots which they had hitherto proved.

Gilfert was the first to break this arrangement by an angry publication, stating that Miss George was engaged only for the Bowery Theatre, any other announcement to the contrary notwithstanding, while I had a written engagement in my possession, which, in justification, I published at full length in the newspapers of the day. E. Forrest also, whose movements were dictated by the Bowery manager, to whom he was then engaged, formed another obstacle to the fulfilment of the interests of both theatres, that no good was ultimately gained by either party from preliminaries which promised so fairly.

Had Gilfert acted in good faith towards Mr. Warren, the Park Theatre must have lost the omnipotent name of *the* Theatre; for, during the winter of 1827 and 1828, it presented the uncommon spectacle of being dependent, for foreign attraction, almost entirely upon the importation of other theatres; Clara Fisher and Mr. Horn being the only new stars over whom they exercised any control.

But the first proposition made to the Bowery Theatre, to exchange stars on fair and reciprocal terms, in the person of Mrs. Sloman for Mr. E. Forrest; (and every body who recollects any thing about theatrical representations knows that Mrs. Sloman's first engagement was a succession of well-filled houses, the worst of which was better than any house Mr. E. Forrest had ever attracted to the Chesnut Street Theatre, at *that* time, except on the occasion of his benefit,) was received almost as an insult, both to the lady and the management.

The disavowal of Dr. Hart's authority to enter into any such arrangement, and the coolness that followed, healed the breach which was threatened between the Park Theatre and the Chesnut Street Theatre; Mr. Warren being perfectly willing to form a treaty, offensive and defensive, with the Bowery Theatre, but by no means anxious merely to change masters, which appeared to be Mr. Gilferts's view of the alliance.

On the 8th of September, I embarked at Liverpool, on board the Montezuma, Captain West, on my return to Philadelphia, accompanied by Mr. and Mrs. Southwell, son and servant; Mr. S. Chapman and brother; Mr. Hutchings; Mr. and Mrs. Mercer, and son; Miss Emery; Mr. J. T. Norton; Mr. Willis; Mr., Mrs., and Miss Ker; Miss Hawthorn and Miss Worghman; Mr. and Mrs. Lewis, and family; leaving Mr. and Mrs. Sloman; Mrs. Austin; Miss George; Miss Minter; and Mr. and Mrs. Robotham, to follow as early as possible.

I must do Captain West the justice to say he made us all as comfortable, as it was possible under the circumstances, to be; a merrier set seldom crossed the Atlantic in company. We had one masquerade, two or three concerts, which, considering the musical talent, were excellent, indeed—better than an audience assembled on shore paid a dollar per ticket to hear— and several dances, which we must honour with the name of ball; all this tending to make a summer passage a pleasant voyage.

On the 17th of October, 1827, I left the ship, with the letter bag, proceeding up to town on the Norfolk steamboat, reported myself to Mr. Warren, found my wife and children in excellent health, and myself once more at my own fireside. If a man wishes to know the comforts of home, let him be absent three or four months, with a wide expanse of water dividing him from those he holds most dear. It was within one day of four months, since I parted from my wife, during which time I had not been stationary one day; having been either on board a ship, a steamboat, or a mail coach, at some period during each twenty-four hours of my absence from America.

Mr. Davis's company of French comedians were acting in the Chesnut Street Theatre. The policy of this movement has been much doubted; certain it is that the fashionables of Philadelphia mustered so strong in their support, that Mr. Davis was induced to repeat his visit each succeeding summer; but it had a most sinister effect upon the opening of the English season. Notwithstanding Mr. Warren had expended between five and six thousand dollars for auxiliary aid, the band having been augmented by recruits from Germany, under the direction of Mr. Braun, making the orchestra the the most complete ever assembled within the walls of an

American theatre, yet the receipts of the first week fell short of the nightly expenditure. It was not until the production of "Evadne," and the "Rencontre," that the season began to assume a favourable appearance, and was brought to a most successful close.

On the 24th of October, a concert was given, to introduce the new band with eclat; in which I had the satisfaction of hearing Mr. Willis *alone* encored. This I looked upon as a favourable omen, and received many congratulations from my friends.

The theatre was announced to open on the 29th, with "Romeo and Juliet," and "Is he Jealous," to give Mr. Southwell an opportunity of appearing in Romeo. I soon discovered that the stage manager's situation was not to be a bed of roses. I received no less than seven anonymous letters upon the subject of Miss Warren's playing Juliet.

Southwell, however, made quite a hit in Romeo, and Miss Warren, notwithstanding all the hints of secret foes, played Juliet very prettily. On the following evening Mr. Mercer and Mr. Hutchings made their bow; the former gentleman becoming at once a decided favourite. Mr. S. Chapman made his appearance as Pierre, in "Venice Preserved," under most unfavourable circumstances: Mr. Wood having been announced for the part, but unable from sickness to play. Miss Emery was the Belvidera. Mr. Norton also made his first appearance. The houses during these preliminary arrangements were very bad, but on the production of "Evadne," in which, for the first time, all the strangers were placed before the audience in one play, curiosity filled the house, and from that moment prosperity began to dawn. At the conclusion of the play Mr. Warren publicly returned me his thanks for the able manner in which I had accomplished his mission.

The next successful step was the production of a new comedy entitled the "Rencontre," which, with "Evadne," filled the house for several nights. The non-arrival of Mrs. Austin, as expected, by the Robert Edwards, had left me in uncertainty as to my movements with regard to stars; therefore, it was fortunate that the public appreciated the efforts of our really good stock company.

On the 14th of September Mr. Charles Horn made his first appearance in Philadelphia, as Young Meadows, in "Love in a Village," Mrs. Knight playing Rosetta; although the first stars of the season, they were not very successful.

On the 26th, I received the following letter from the Hon. F. H. F. Berkeley:—

" Algonquin," (at sea,) Sunday, Nov. 25th, 1827,

" My Dear Sir,
    " Mrs. Austin, Mrs. Sloman, and Mr. Sloman, are here, all in
health, as well as

                            " Yours, truly,
            (Signed)   " F. H. F. Berkeley."

This was a weight removed from my mind, although it was
unfortunate; the two stars, from whom I expected most,
arriving in the same vessel.   Had Mrs. Austin have come, as
arranged, by the Robert Edwards, the money paid to Mrs.
Horn and Mrs. Knight would have been saved to the treasury,
and her own reception would have been more to her satisfaction.   She made her first appearance in America, at the
Chesnut-street Theatre, December 10th, 1827.

Mrs. AUSTIN.

This lady, who became so popular in New York, as the first
representative of Cinderella in the United States, and who,
in conjunction with Mr. Jones, made English Opera fashionable, was engaged by me in London for the Chesnut-street
Theatre, Philadelphia.   She made her first appearance as
Rosetta, in " Love in a Village :" the brilliant style in which
she executed the music at once established her reputation as
a singer of more than ordinary talent, but the taste for music
and the opera was in its infancy; to Mr. Warren belongs the
credit of its cultivation.   The excellent orchestra of the year
1827 and 1828, provided for the Chesnut-street Theatre, deserved a better fate than to be scattered throughout the
Union.   Three years later, such music within the walls of a
theatre would have formed no inconsiderable portion of the
evening's attraction.

Mrs. Austin's engagement, although rich in reputation, was
a failure, in the most important matter to the manager,
"money."   Every body who heard her sing, praised her; but
circumstances, beyond the control of the theatre, and an unmanly attack in the columns of a newspaper, to gratify the
feelings of parties who must not be mentioned, induced the
ladies to absent themselves on the nights of her performance.
This prejudice, unjustly fostered against her at a later period,
she entirely surmounted, and became a great favourite.   She
played Rosetta, Lucy Bertram, Rosina, Margaretta, Florence
St. Leon, Diana Vernon, Mary Copp, and for her benefit revived Dr. Ames's opera of " Artaxerxes," in which she gave
the music of Mandane with splendid effect; Mercer playing
Artabanes; Hutchings, Arbaces; Miss. E. Jefferson, Artaxerxes;
and Mrs. Darley, Irene.   I question if the opera was ever better

performed in America than on this occasion. She proceeded to New York, where she became a reigning favourite, assisted by Horn and Mr. Pearman—repairing the wound Mrs. Sloman's success had inflicted upon her vanity, and turning the tables, as far as attraction was concerned, decidedly in her favour.

CHAPTER XV.

Mrs. Sloman's First Appearance in America. Great Receipts. Good Generalship. Ridiculous Habits. Mrs. Austin. E. Forrest. Play of the "Usurper." Grand Flare Up. After Thunder, Clear Weather Again.

THE 7th of December, 1827, was a day of anxiety. On that evening Mrs. Sloman made her first appearance as Isabella, in the "Fatal Marriage." To me her success or failure was a matter of great importance; for, as the first star imported for the Philadelphia Theatre, our future exertions would be *guided* by her reception. She was an old acquaintance; her husband had been an intimate companion, in the happiest days of my strolling career. Mr. Warren was pledged, through me, to pay her twenty pounds sterling per week, for one year; it cannot, therefore, be a matter of surprise that I exerted myself to the utmost in her favour, that I entered the theatre full of fears for the result, with the one hope, so spendidly realized, that she might please the audience.

The house was only indifferently filled, but the pit was overflowing, and her success triumphant.

MRS. SLOMAN

produced a greater sensation, and drew more money for thirteen successive nights, than any star who had hitherto graced the boards of the Chesnut Street Theatre. She was a compound of faults and beauties, in the art of acting—so blended that it was at times difficult to say whether her performance was really good, or very bad, but it seldom failed to please her audience.

When I first saw her, in Canterbury, in 1818, she was, as Miss Whitaker, a pretty and a clever girl, playing singing chambermaids, in which she was a great favourite; she then became the wife of Mr. Henry Dowton, (the manager's son,) and by her kindness and attention to his comfort, during a long and tedious illness, acquired the estimation of all who knew her. Some years after his death she became the wife of Mr. John Sloman, and made her appearance as a tragic actress, with success, at Covent Garden Theatre. Her reputation, aided by the recommendation of Mr. Price, induced me to make the offer, on behalf of the Philadelphia Theatre, which her husband accepted. On the first night of her appearance in America, very few ladies graced the boxes, but the impression made upon the audience, in the character of Isabella, was so favourable that at an early hour on the following morning the doors were besieged by an anxious crowd, waiting to secure places in the boxes, which, on her second appearance, were filled to overflowing, and so continued during her engagement. The receipts of her first performance were two hundred dollars less than any subsequent representation. The thirteen nights produced *ten thousand six hundred and thirty dollars and seventy-five cents*, or 817 dollars 75 cents per night—a result most gratifying to me and satisfactory to Mr. Warren, who again thanked me, by Judge Hopkinson, for the able manner in which he was pleased to say I had discharged my commission.

Mrs. Sloman played Isabella, Mrs. Haller, Belvidera; Jane Shore; Juliet, Mrs. Oakley, Lady Townley; repeating several of the characters by request. In "Jane Shore," where Miss Emery, (who had become an established favourite) played Alicia, there was quite an animated contest for superiority— Mr. Matthew Carey, whose opinion was of some value in such matters, openly declaring his preference for Miss Emery, who was a valuable actress. This difference of opinion was of service to the treasury.

Mrs. Sloman left us, for the Federal Street Theatre, in Boston, where the same success did not attend her efforts; while in the Park Theatre, New York, Simpson proved for once a good general, by crushing her with superior attraction, on the nights on which she did *not* appear: Mr. Horn, Mr. Pearman and Mrs. Austin, playing together in opera three nights a week, while Mrs. Sloman, unsupported, occupied the other three.

With her first success terminated her attraction. So fickle is the public mind, that on her return to Philadelphia, before the close of the season, she could not attract a single dollar. The same thing occurred to Clara Fisher, whose first engagement was only eclipsed by Mrs. Sloman's.

Mr. Sloman made his bow to an American audience, on the occasion of his wife's benefit, December 17th. His comic singing proved very attractive, giving a fresh impetus to the desire of the audience for a re-engagement of Mrs. Sloman. Mr. Sloman's acting, having the advantage of many original parts, was considered good by many critics; however, I cannot pronounce it so. His singing was excellent; and in that alone consisted the secret of his great benefits throughout the United States. It was only from this source in New York that the engagement of Mr. and Mrs. Sloman paid Mr. Warren.

While upon the subject of New York theatricals, the managers there have a foolish habit of announcing pieces for representation for the first time in America, which have frequently been played in Philadelphia, deceiving only themselves by this miserable trick, and provoking comparisons by no means favourable to their managerial enterprise. As thus : a Philadelphian visits New York, inquires for a play bill, sees a piece *thus* announced, and naturally enough says, " Why, have you not seen *that*, yet? your managers must have been asleep ; it has been acted in our city six months ago."

Mrs. Austin having proceeded to New York, the nights vacated were assigned to Mr. E. Forrest, on condition that he should return and finish the engagement, on the 26th of March. He appeared as Brutus, in Howard Payne's tragedy, on the 5th of January, but the houses were indifferently attended ; but it must be remembered at this time Mr. Forrest had not acquired the fame which afterwards enabled him to dictate terms to managers. He was climbing the hill with rapid strides, but had not reached its summit.

On the 26th of December, 1827, the long announced tragedy of the " Usurper," written by Dr. M'Henry, was produced. Ere I speak of its reception by the public, let me state that Dr. M'Henry *cast* the characters himself, selecting those actors he thought best qualified to give him support. I record this, to show the feeling which existed towards him as an author, and the disposition of the management to afford him every facility in their power, which could contribute to his success.

The Doctor received an assurance, that so long as the tragedy would draw the nightly expenses incidental to the performances, (300 dollars,) it should be repeated. The newspapers were zealous in their endeavours to aid his cause, and a writer in the Saturday Post went so far as to say, " In Europe, on a piece being more than commonly successful, it was the practice of the audience to call for its repetition by name." Here the cue of action was distinctly given. The night of performance arrived. The prologue, written by James S. Barker, Esq., fell to my lot. I will first give the dramatis personæ ; for since that eventful night, the infant, whose death is announced in the second scene, which incident had nearly upset the gravity of the spectators, has grown up and become a talker on his own behalf ; whether the play be improved by the alteration, I leave those who witnessed its performance, and (since the Doctor's resolution *" to print it, and shame the fools !"*) have had courage to read it, to decide.

THE USURPER.

Cobtha (*the Usurper*) Mr. Southwell; Labra, King of Munster, Mr. Brown; Mahon, (*rightful heir to the throne*) Mr. Mercer; Partholon, Mr. S. Chapman; Arch Druid, (*confidant to Cobtha*) Mr. Wood; Connal, Mr. Heyl; Athmore, Mr. Hathwell; Hermod, Mr. Drummond; Cathal, Mr. Darley; Clansagh, Mr. Wheatley; First Chief, Mr. Parker; Second Chief, Mr. Murray; Third Chief, Mr. Delarue; First Soldier, Mr. Klett : Second Soldier, Mr. Lyons; Third Soldier, Mr. Bengall; First Bard, Mr. Hutchings; Second Bard, Mr. Jefferson; Priestess, Miss Emery; Elifinor, Miss Warren; Moreat, Miss Darley; Servant, Miss Hathwell.

Music composed expressly for the piece by Mr. Willis.

The Prologue written by James S. Barker, Esq. to be spoken by Mr. Wemyss.

PROLOGUE.

From that romantic Isle, whose emarald plains
In smiling verdure, hide their sanguine stains ;
The land of heroes, and by patriots trod,
The land of lovers, and the bard's abode.
From-Erin borne on poesy's magic wing,
The chiefs of other days we hither bring ,
To claim within this hospitable dome,
A stranger's welcome, in a stranger's home,
The poet of the scene, who trembling woos,
To-night the favour of the tragic muse,
Though not unknown to you, his tuneful page,
For the first time presumes to tread the Stage ;
And conscious of the peril, suppliant bends
Before a jury of indulgent friends.
Not his the strain, where fabling numbers flows,
And turgid diction speaks fictitious woe ;
In nature's language he essays the art,
To reach the judgment, and to touch the heart.
From the historic page his theme he draws,
And days when Erin dared give Erin laws.
What time the sage's voice and soldier's call,
And bards' proud anthem rang through Tara's Hall ;
While Erin's priests yet held their Druid rite,
And Erin's warriors dared for Erin fight.
Our poet's pencil paints the moral scene,
Teaching what ought to be, by what has been.
Lo ! the red fratricide, whose regal vest,
Clasps scorpion conscience closer to his breast ;
Or the arch hypocrite, whose holy guise,
Cheats, for a season only, mortal eyes.
Hurl'd from a throne, or from the altar driv'n ;
Detested, scorn'd of man, condemned of Heav'n

While in the patriot prince, and faithful maid,
And generous friend, the living truths portrayed.
That virtue, friendship, and unspotted love,
On earth revered, draw blessings from above.
Such was thegenuine drama's moral School,
The drama scorned by bigot and by fool;
When with the energy of wisdom fraught,
The Addisons, and Steeles, and Johnsons taught.
And though to-night, we boast no golden name,
Like theirs, bright sparkling on the scroll of fame,
Let the endeavour to uphold the laws
Of the pure drama, and great virtue's cause,
Secure the patient hearing for our bard,
The candid judgment, and the just reward.

Well would it have been for Dr. M'Heny's cause, had his tragedy contained but half the merit of this prologue. Notwithstanding the exertions of his friends, I never witnessed a more complete failure. It is true, that as the curtain fell, many young men, fond of making a noise, and delighting in the prospect of a theatrical row, vociferously called for the author, and a repetition of the play, which I promised for the following Thursday, announcing it in the play bills as follows:

" The Usurper having been unanimously called for by the audience on its first representation, will be played again on Thursday next."

For this, I received the thanks of the author, and, until the termination of the next performance, I was every thing that gratitude could make me; I even received a present of one of the author's poems, accompanied with, "from his assured friend, Dr. M'Henry," written by his own hand, on the title-page. The second night, producing one hundred dollars less than the amount of the expenses, released me from all promises, and turned the gratitude of Dr. M'Henry to gall; and in an instant I was transformed from one of the best to one of the worst of human beings.

The play of the Usurper had been accepted for representation by Mr. Warren, previous to my return from England; the hope of success was deemed by Dr. M'Henry a sufficient remuneration. He now demanded a third representation, for the benefit of the author, founding his claim upon the usages of the large theatres, in London. To this arrangement, many objections presented themselves; one of the greatest magnitude was, the night wished was pre occupied. Mr. Matthew Carey, whose philanthropy frequently got the better of his judgment, prevailed upon Mr. Warren to let the author have the boon desired, he giving security for three hundred dollars. Having performed my duty to the author and the public, I

did not feel inclined to let the responsibility of this perform·
mance rest upon me : but without any intention of wounding
Dr. M'Henry's feelings, I announced his benefit in the fol·
lowing notice :—

"In consequence of the persevering and unceasing application of Dr.
M'Henry and his friends, the tragedy of the Usurper will be played for
the third and last time at this theatre, on Friday, the 1st of February, for
the benefit of the author.'"

My only object, in this announcement, was to prove to those
who were in the habit of frequenting the theatre—to whom
the play was really obnoxious—that it was the author's doing,
not the manager's. I was therefore surprised to read in the
United States Gazette of the 30th of January, 1828, the
following :—

"TO THE PUBLIC.

"It is well-known to the play-going portion of the inhabitants of Phila·
delphia, that a new tragedy of my composition, has recently been twice
performed at the Chesnut Street Theatre, and that it received on both
occasions the approbation of the audiences. A few days after the second
representation, I was induced by the numerous inquiries that were made
at my house by respectable individuals, relative to the time when a third
representation, which it was supposed would be for my benefit, would take
place, to apply to the managers for information. To this application, Mr.
Wemyss replied in a style of ambiguity, which occasioned me to require
from him a verbal explanation. This he gave in so abrupt a manner,
that I resolved to hold no more communication with him. *Some of my
friends,* however, conceiving that I was unjustly treated, took up the
matter, and *pressed upon the managers* the propriety of allowing me a
benefit. Friday evening was in consequence set apart for the purpose. In
appropriating to me that evening, I considered the managers to be acting
towards me not only with good faith, but with good will, and I looked
forward to the promised benefit for some remuneration for my labours.

"With these feelings, what was my surprise, when going on Monday
night into the theatre, I found the intended performance of 'The
Usurper' announced, in a manner and in terms, highly insulting to my
friends and to myself, and calculated to destroy all my prospects of profit
from a benefit. ' In consequence of the persevering and unceasing appli·
cation of Dr. M'Henry and his friends, the tragedy of ' The Usurper' will
be played for the third and last time at this Theatre, on Thursday next,
February 1st, for the benefit of the author.'

"Comment on the evident design and tendency of such an announce·
ment is unnecessary. It might be observed, however, that the foregoing
statement affords a positive contradiction to the assertion, that I had made
persevering and unceasing applications for a benefit; I had, in fact, never
applied but once.

"Under these circumstances, I hope an allowable degree of self-respect
will be admitted by those who are desirous to witness another representa]

tion of ‘The Usurper,’ as an apology for my prohibiting that representation, which I have done, in a note addressed to Mr. Warren.

“ From the sympathy and support of a generous and enlightened public—the public of Philadelphia—from whom I have never failed to receive justice and kindness, if I were to seek for redress in the present instance, I know I should find it. Many magnanimous minds would feel pleasure in taking part with an individual so clearly ill treated, and in teaching arbitrary managers of theatres, that they ought not altogether to disregard the approbation of a community, which can never approve of injustice and oppression. But I ask no redress. My fellow-citizens, I am persuaded, will continue to manifest towards me that good will, which I have experienced from them, and which forms, at this moment, my pride as well as my consolation.

“ Jan. 30th, 1828.”   (Signed)   “ JAMES M‘HENRY.”

Here is as pretty a piece of incendiarism as ever emanated from the pen of mortal man ; the object decidedly “ a row.”

Dr. M‘Henry asserts to the public that he made but one application for a benefit. Mark his own words : “ not content with my answer to his application, he sought a personal interview, and after that resolved to hold no further communication with me: but (mark this) his *friends* conceived he was unjustly treated, and from his statement it appears, *they* took up the subject, which he had resolved to abandon, and pressed upon the managers the propriety of allowing me a benefit.”

Bah—nonsense ! If he had not urged the matter, few of his friends would have cared a straw about either the Usurper, or the theatre ; and if this be not perseverance for the attainment of an object, I am at a loss to know what is.

But to dismiss the Doctor and his tragedy, on whom I have already wasted too much space.

On the evening following the 1st of February, the night originally appropriated for the author’s benefit, previous to the play of “ The Wonder,” a placard reading thus :—

“ Usurper.
Benefit
For the Author,”

was placed in my hands, which was freely distributed in the front of the theatre. Now, what will an enlightened and liberal public say of the man who, after publicly relinquishing his right to a benefit, should take such means to obtain it. The late Samuel Chapman very facetiously interlined this placard, thus :—

“ The Public is respectfully informed that the
“ Usurper
declines taking any
Benefit
Dr. M‘Henry being ashamed of passing
For the Author.”

In which state it remained in the green room for several days, and was enjoyed, even by the Docter's friends, as an excellent joke.

This was the first time I had incurred the displeasure of the audience, as a manager; and never, in any case, was it less deserved. I had performed more than my duty to the author; I had devoted my time, and Mr. Warren had expended his money, on a thankless speculation.

Dr. M'Henry has since thought proper to alter his first hantling, as he terms the Usurper, and produced it at the Arch Street Theatre, where its reception was less equivocal; and nothing can rescue it from the oblivion to which it is now consigned, with the pleasing recollection to the author, of being twice damned; although in his preface he asserts it was received by two audiences, at the Chesnut Street Theatre with every mark of approbation, and only withdrawn because he considered the conduct of the acting manager, (meaning me,) to be grossly insulting towards himself and his friends; although in doing so, he was aware of making a considerable sacrifice of his pecuniary interests.

"Nil fuit tam impar sibi."

I have proved that every exertion was used by him to reap, if possible, the pecuniary advantage, alluded to, and the most unfair means resorted to, to make the public aid his design. His attempt to create a disturbance in the theatre failed; but the first fruits of his bitter enmity were severely felt by me in my position as manager.

The old story of slighting native talent, (native talent, in this instance, at least, born in Ireland,) and treating America with disrespect, was revived; some persons carrying their malignity so far as to accuse me of having forbidden the orchestra to play the national airs, nightly called for by the audience.

To shield myself from this unmanly and insidious attack, I was compelled to address the public, at the end of the play-bills, which I did on the 3rd of February, thus:—

TO THE PUBLIC.

"A report being in circulation, that I had forbidden the orchestra to play the National Airs, I beg leave respectfully to inform the public, that so far from forbidding them, I have frequently given orders that one or more should be played every evening; and from this date, the following arrangement will take place previous to the commencement of the play:— The band will perform the overture of the piece, or such overture as the leader of the orchestra may see fit to substitute. Between the play and the farce, each night, the time will be exclusively appropriated to

NATIONAL AIRS.

I trust this arrangement will prove satisfactory to all parties, and at once disprove the *monstrous calumny.* It is my sincere wish, and Mr. Warren's interest, that every individual who contributes in the slightest degree to the support of the theatre, should leave, if possible, perfectly satisfied with the evening's amusement.

" F. C. WEMYSS,

" THEATRE, Feb. 2nd, 1828." " Stage Manager."

This order, publicly given, annoyed poor Braun, the leader, who could not endure the frequent repetition of " Yankee Doodle," to the exclusion of Mozart, Weber, &c.; not entering into the national feeling, which made it the most agreeable to an American ear.

I do not accuse Dr. M'Henry or his friends, of circulating these reports; but it is an unfortunate coincidence, that the accusation in the newspapers appeared simultaneously with Dr. M'Henry's appeal; and since the fracas about Harry Herbert, a predilection for England and her institutions has been received as *my* creed. Love of our native country is implanted by nature in our bosoms, and I most warmly applaud it, wherever met. Much as I have suffered from wilful misrepresentation, I admire that feeling of patriotism, which will not brook even a breath of insult from the lips of a foreigner. I have always regarded the institutions of America with pride, while I never shrink from defending my native England, when unjustly assailed. My feelings towards America and England cannot be better expressed, than in slightly altering the toast of a worthy Irish baronet, in the farce of the "Sleep-Walker." Speaking of England,

"May the gentlemen of your country, and mine, never meet in altercation, but in good humour, over a bottle."

Such should be the feeling of every Englishman towards an American, and every American towards an Englishman.

CHAPTER XVI.

On the 10th of January, Miss George, of whom so much had been said, made her appearance in Philadelphia, as Susanna, in the opera of the " Marriage of Figaro." She was much inferior to Mrs. Austin, as a singer; attracting but little notice, except in the petite comedy of "'Twas I, or the Truth a Lie," in which she sung "The Bonny Breastknots," much to the satisfaction of the audience. Miss Kelly played a very successful engagement, commencing on the 2nd of February, with Donna Violante in the "Wonder." On the 17th of February, quite a novelty was placed before the audience, in the shape of a new opera, by Kotesbue, in German, in which Mr. Braun and Mr. Mercer, were particularly happy. The overture was performed entirely by French horns, and enthusiastically encored.

On Wednesday, the 20th of February, 1828, Reynolds' comedy of "The Will," was performed, for the purpose of introducing

MISS CLARA FISHER.

Although in France, "*the children's theatre*" frequently produces an extraordinary juvenile actor, precocious dramatic talent has rarely met with success in England or the United States, where people generally have something of more importance to occupy their time, than listening to children assuming the garb and manners of men and women.

Master Betty, the young Roscius, so termed; the young lady whose name I am recording; and Master Burke, whose musical talent enlisted public curiosity in his favour, are exceptions to this general rule.

Miss Clara Fisher, when only six years of age, was indeed a *rara avis*; and the judicious manner in which she was placed before the public, aided her success. In Lord Flinnip, her assumption of the character of Richard the Third, surrounded by her pigmy warriors, was perfect; as the performance of a Lilliputian, it was faultless; as a child apeing a man, it would have been ridiculous. No child was better schooled, or reflected more credit on her preceptor; her powers of imitation were carefully developed, exciting the wonder of the critics of London, who pronounced her a Kean in minature.

But like all other cases of precocity, premature decay follows; either the public are too exacting, or the mind of the juvenile player breaks down from over action, ere it reaches maturity—there being no case on record of a child acquiring popularity at so early an age who retained it in after life. When Miss Clara Fisher first visited the United States, her youth and reputation induced crowds to visit the theatre whenever her name was announced. Now, how changed her destiny—surpassed by many who, in her early career, never dared to think of approaching her in the favour of the public.

I can scarcely conceive a more painful situation to an actor possessing a sensitive mind, than the consciousness of having made a retrograde movement in public opinion at the very time his utmost exertions have been used to maintain a position which all conceded him entitled to. Yet how few escape this mortification, who commence at the top round of the ladder of fame. Neglected as Clara Fisher now is, her name will descend among the few who have arrived at eminence, when those who enjoy a short-lived triumph, from her supposed humiliation, will be forgotten. By her exertions, a large family have been respectably educated, and established in life, while in private society, no one in the whole profession is more universally esteemed. This must be her consolation in retirement, for that fortune which she ought to have possessed.

Her first engagement in Philadelphia averaged upwards of seven hundred dollars per night, out of which she received nearly four thousand dollars; but as, in the case of Mrs. Sloman, when she returned, all curiosity to see her had subsided; nor do I remember that she ever afterwards played a profitable engagement in Philadelphia—that is, profitable to the treasury of the theatre. Her Four Mowbrays will long be remembered as a finished specimen of comic acting.

Mr. Burroughs played a night or two; but his houses, after the great business we had been acting to, appeared really worse than they were.

On the 21st of February, the "Red Rover" was produced. Messrs. Carey and Lea, the spirited booksellers and publishers, having announced Cooper's new novel of the "Red Rover" as nearly ready for delivery, a thought struck me, that if a copy of the novel could be procured, in advance of the publication, and a nautical drama founded upon it, it would be productive both of reputation and money.

I waited upon these gentlemen, who, in the kindest manner, granted my request, stipulating only that it should not be seen by any person except those concerned in our preparations. With my prize in my possession, I returned triumphantly to the theatre. I offered Mr. S. Chapman twenty dollars a night, for every night it should be acted, if he would compile a drama, (for which he possessed an apt talent,) such as should meet my approbation, from the "Red Rover," retaining such scenes as I pointed out—the moving panorama being intended for the great scene, as a novelty. Here was a field for manager, author, painter, and machinist; and well did each acquit themselves, not forgetting the excellent music of Mr. Braun. Never in any theatre was a more successful piece produced; enabling us to act on the Tuesday and Thursday nights to five hundred dollars per night, against the brilliant success of Miss Clara Fisher. The Prologue, written by Richard Penn

Smith, was spoken with much eclat, by S. Chapman and myself, in our characters of Author and Manager.—Let it speak
for itself.

PROLOGUE TO THE " RED ROVER."

*Spoken by Mr. Wemyss and Mr. S. Chapman ; written by
R. P. Smith, Esq.*

ENTER THE MANAGER, FOLLOWED BY THE CALL-BOY.

MANAGER.—Another author ! what is this you say,
    Another author, with another play,
    Who vows with all the vehemence of rage,
    That I *must forthwith* bring it on the stage ;
    The fellow's mad—stark mad—to brave the town,
    And *vi et armis*, force his rubbish down ;
    But show him in—(exit boy ;) they shall not make me fear
    Tho' authors now like Banquo's race, appear
    A moment, and then vanish.
                (Enter author.)—Sir, your most—
    A virgin author, to give up the ghost.
AUTHOR.—You're wrong, my friend, my drama ;—(offers MS.)
MANAGER.—   Let me see !
AUTHOR.—We'll charm the town, and fill your treasury.
MANAGER.—A modest youth—the town—I understand ;
    But genius-like, you write a d——d cramp'd hand,
    Which I cannot decypher ;—Sir, no doubt
    You can explain what this is all about.
AUTHOR.—The title will explain ; there—there, turn over ;
    One leaf speaks volumes.
MANAGER.—(Reading.)—" The Red Rover."
    A cunning rogue, the critics to confound,
    Here builds his fabric on another's ground ;
    But let us hear what arguments you bring,
    By way of recommending this strange thing.
AUTHOR.—Our scenes are drawn from Cooper's graphic page,
    Sufficient passport, surely, to the stage.
    Sublime his taste—in beauty e'en profuse ;
    Yet yielding little to the Drama's muse.
    For these descriptions, which with nature vie,
    The painter's brush but feebly can supply ;
    Yet much depends upon the painter's art ;
    And how—the plane—and saw—perform their part.
    So critics who uphold the stagyrite,
    May close their ears, and shut their eyes to-night.
MANAGER.—Zounds ! how is this ?
AUTHOR.—Be patient, you shall see,
    A scene to tickle the catastrophe ;
    " One," as Bays says, " shall set the audience mad,
    And pit, and box, and gallery it, egad,
    With anything extant."

MANAGER.—(Surprised.)—You mean to say,
    With hammer, paint, and boards, you wrote *this* play.
  AUTHOR.—Precisely so.
MANAGER.—And should it chance to hit,
    Of course you'll lay a claim to toast and wit.
  AUTHOR.—You're right again.
MANAGER.—Modest,—but if it fails—
  AUTHOR.—Well! damn the carpenter, the boards and nails.
    But that's impossible—impossible.
MANAGER.—Indeed!
  AUTHOR.—My dukedom to a dernier, 'twill succeed.
    A showy drama from a native tale,
    In this fair city, ne'er was known to fail.
MANAGER.—We'll try that point.
  AUTHOR.—Perhaps 'twill be the rage;
    The " Rover"—what! already on the stage—
    This looks like expedition, cries that *beau*,
    While sauntering in the lobby, to and fro,
    A wish to please the town; egad! that's right—
    A native play—I'll take a box to-night.
MANAGER.—To please the town, has been, I here declare,
    My proudest study, and my hourly care;
    And when I prove imperfect in the part,
    The fault lies here; (touching his head,) but comes not
        near the heart.
    The wish to please, at least all must allow:
    The " Rover," shall be done—so make your bow.

                          Exeunt together.

Lewis, for his manner of sinking the Caroline, and his arrangement of the deck of the Dart, with the whole plan of his panorama, deserved and received unqualified approbation, both before and behind the curtain. The effect produced on the audience by the first representation, was capital. Being taken by surprise, many declared the ship was positively in motion, the optical delusion practised being so perfectly arranged.

One incident only occurred, which might have ruined our success. At the night rehearsal for the scenery, everything had succeeded beyond my most sanguine expectations; when Mr. S. Chapman, elated by the approbation bestowed on his exertions, suddenly said, " Mr. Wemyss, expend fifty dollars more, and I will astonish you; I will make a shower of rain which shall induce the audience to look for umbrellas; but I must have three gauze curtains. As I never saw but one good effect by gauze, (the dream scene of " Cherry and Fair Star,") I hesitated; when, with his characteristic humour, he said, " Don't spoil our ship at last, for a half penny worth of tar; let me have my way; if it don't succeed, I will pay for it myself. Mr. Warren, who was within hearing, and pleased with the appearance of success, which every thing promised, called out; "Let him have it, Wemyss." The order was given, and on the following evening, the rain descended amid thunders of applause from the audience,—enveloping the boat, in which Wilder and his lady-companions were rescued, in a dense fog, in which they were likely to remain. The effect not having been tried, no means was provided for removing the unfortunate gauze, and the rain, after having performed its part to admiration, had to ascend again to the skies, amid the laughter of the audience, and the mortification of the author. The stirring incident of the piece restored the good humour of the audience; but the shower of rain was dispensed with in the future representations. Southwell, by his refusal to act the part of Wilder, fixed upon me a most unpleasant duty, which prevented that attention to many minor details, which would not have occurred had I been out of the dramatis personæ. As we contrived to sink a ship, covering it with foaming billows, surely we could have removed my friend Chapman's shower of rain, without the necessity of restoring it to the clouds.

It was in the month of February or March, 1828, that Mr. M'Geary, a bookseller, from the city of New York, issued proposals to erect a new theatre in Philadelphia. The location chosen was in Arch street, near the corner of the 6th street. After all the preliminary arrangements were agreed upon, Mr. M'G. either *could* not or *would* not, give the security demanded by the subscribers of the stock, for the fulfilment of his promises: and the project would have been abandoned had not Mr. W. B. Wood stept forward with an offer to proceed, which was accepted, in the sequel, ruining him, and every other manager who was unfortunate enough to occupy it. It was built by Mr. Strickland, the architect of the Chesnut Theatre, but he did not improve upon the model of the latter house. Mr. Wood took his farewell benefit at the Chesnut street Theatre, on the 14th of April. "Adelgitha" and "Mr. H." were the pieces selected. At the close of the performance, the audience called loudly for Mr. Wood, who addressed them in his usual happy manner. To do him justice, I never saw a man who made an extemporary address with a better grace, or possessed so happy a facility of moulding an audience to his own peculiar views.

Miss Rock, the first failing star of the season, appeared as Letitia Hardy and Jenny Transit. She was a clever actress, but her appearance was by no means prepossessing, and the manner in which she dressed, so ancient, compared with the dashing Miss Kelly, that she excited little or no interest in the audience.

Celeste—the divine La Bayadere, whose career has been one

of the most fortunate in the annals of the American Drama, made her first appearance, on the 18th of March, at the Chesnut Street, in a Grand Pas Seul. Her poetry of motion was not at this time appreciated; and when she appeared as Myrtillo, in the "Broken Sword," her acting was the cause of more mirth than sympathy. Who can forget her exclamation of "*My fader's murtherer,*" and repress a smile at the announcement of the playbills—"*Celeste in a speaking character.*" Her husband, Mr. Henry Elliott, very soon discovered the secret of success was not so much in appearing before an audience, as in preparing that audience for her reception by the puff preliminary; and by his judicious newspaper arrangements, succeeded in placing Celeste foremost in the ranks of those whom managers were anxious to engage, because their engagements were always profitable to the theatre. Her popularity remained undiminished to the last hour of her appearance on the American stage; and the announcement of her name, at any moment, will secure a well filled house.

On the 26th of March, Mr. E. Forrest was announced to act in Boston, in New York, and in Philadelphia. Not being blest with the power of ubiquity, he remained in Boston, while we were placed in a two-fold dilemma. Having engaged Mr. Forrest to finish the number of nights due at this time, we could make no other arrangement without violation of contract, while Mr. Gilfert (for I will do Forrest the justice to think it was not his arrangement) did not condescend to inform the management of the change which had taken place in his views. To the Philadelphia Theatre it was a loss of time which could have been profitably employed; and disappointment was prevented by an announcement in the playbills, that should Mr. E. Forrest arrive, as expected, he would appear, but that the "Red Rover" would be the substitute. Thus I adroitly avoided the possibility of incurring the displeasure of the audience on the sensitive point of native talent, leaving the matter to be settled by Mr. Forrest and his audience when they next met.

The benefits of the actors were very well attended this season. W. Chapman, a very good comedian, acted Crack for his brother Samuel's benefit. Miss Southwell aided her brother in the opera of Malvina, while Mr. M'Cahen made a second attempt for Mr. Brown's benefit; but the Colonel makes a much better politician than an actor; his first appearance was in Young Norval, on the 29th of January; after which he played Murtoch Delany, in the "Irishman in London." On the 25th of April, Mr. Cooper made his first appearance in Macbeth, on his return from England, after his unsuccessful attempt on the London stage. The house was

H

crowded to give him a welcome. One of those laughable
occurrences which sometimes take place in a theatre, produced much amusement, but robbed Mr. Cooper of half of the
enthusiam of his reception. Mr. Brown, who played a minor
part, appearing on the bridge from whence Cooper was expected, was mistaken for him, and received with cheers by
the audience, who, when they discovered their mistake, enjoyed a hearty laugh at the expense of poor Brown's feelings,
which was only interrupted by the appearance of their favourite, who received their acclamations with much satisfaction. I was in hopes that this feeling in Cooper's favour,
would have caused the theatre to be filled nightly, during
his engagement; but, although aided by Mr. E. Forrest, it
was a most unprofitable one to the treasury; yet the attraction of Cooper and Forrest, in the same plays, should have
been powerful enough, in the worst of times, to insure success
to any manager bold enough to present it to the public, at
the cost to himself of fifty per cent on the amount which he
received for admission. Ruinous terms—as all managers have
since learnt, to their sorrow, but which some stars still demand, and what is more extraordinary, receive.

Plantou, the dentist, attempted Richard the Third, on the
6th of May, to the amusement of those only who can derive
gratification from very bad acting, and who discovered that,
Oh, go a head, was not Shakspeare, a discovery Mr. Plantou
made before them, as he searched the book diligently to assure
himself the prompter had given him the wrong word, concluding with, "*I no see him—he is not there—go-a-head—your
Shakspeare is too hard for me,*" and the curtain fell amid
roars of laughter, groans and hisses. Nor would the audience
suffer the farce of "Where Shall I Dine," to proceed, until I
made an apology for what they deemed a piece of impertinence, in permitting Mr. Plantou to perform. What a pity
they do not retain the same notions of propriety now,—the
theatres would be better worth attending.

Mr. and Mrs. Sloman appeared for my benefit, to a full and
fashionable house; the more gratifying to my feelings, from
the numerous mortifications I had experienced during the
season in the discharge of my duties as stage manager. Like
the man and his ass, in the fable, I found that to endeavour
to please every body, was the sure method to please nobody.

Notwithstanding the extraordinary exertions made by the
management, and the continued novelty presented to the
audience, much dissatisfaction was expressed, that English
opera, which had been produced at the Park Theatre, New
York, with Messrs. Pearman and Horn, and Miss Austin, supporting the principal characters, had not been tried at the
Chesnut Street, where they were convinced it would be sup-

ported. Mr. Warren, anxious to please all parties, entered
into an engagement with the lady and those gentlemen,
agreeing to provide and pay for a suitable chorus, and such
additional instrumental music in the Orchestra as they might
require; indeed, the arrangements called forth the praise of
Mr. Berkeley, to whom the details were intrusted. All parties
were sanguine in their expectations; but by this engagement
Mr. Warren lost upwards of a thousand dollars, (only two
nights producing the expenses, and one of these a benefit,) and
I lost—*my reputation, Iago.* During these unfortunate operas,
the sons of harmony were out of tune. Mr. Horn brought ac-
cusations against the integrity of the theatre, which brought
blows in return for impertinence. During the melee, *he* received a black eye, and *I* had the mortification of being
paraded before the Mayor of the city, on a charge of assault
and battery, with threats of further violence, and bound over
to keep the peace, under a penalty of one thousand dollars.
This did not add to the attraction of the opera or the reputation of the theatre; but such things will happen occasionally
in the best regulated families, and such occasions are better
met with the old proverb of "least said, soonest mended."

On the 13th of May, Mr. Rowbotham, one of the most useful actors attached to the theatre, made his first appearance
as Dumont, in "Jane Shore." It will be scarcely credited by
those who afterwards were his warm admirers, that it was
with difficulty I could prevail on the newspaper critics to
give him a fair chance. There was but one feeling among the
corps editorial toward him, and that one of the most un-
friendly nature. He afterwards became a great favourite, and
died Manager of the Chesnut Street Theatre, universally regretted. Mrs. Rowbotham appeared as Lucretia in the farce
of the "Rendezvous," on the 19th of May, rising by rapid degrees, in favour with her audience, until her loss was felt
more severely by the play-goers, than any one of her predecessors. She was engaged by me in London, for a comparatively insignificant situation, but became one of the greatest
favourites of the really talented company of the Chesnut
Street Theatre. Death made sad havoc in a few years among
those who crossed the Atlantic during that season. Mr. and
Mrs. Rowbotham, Mr. Southwell, Mrs. S. Chapman, Mr. Kerr,
Miss Emery, and Mr. Willis, all paid the debt of nature
within a few years after their arrival.

On the 3rd of June, Miss Warren eloped with Mr. Willis,
during the performance of "Clari," leaving the theatre for
the time being, minus a leader of the orchestra and a Leoda
in the Episode. This foolish marriage broke the spirit of Mr.
Warren, who never recovered from the shock his feelings sustained upon the occasion; although reconciled to his daugh-

ter, it preyed upon his mind and impaired his health ; he was never the good-humoured Sir John Falstaff more.

Mrs. Sloman and Miss Clara Fisher, were the last stars of the season, their attraction completely gone, both engagements commenced and concluded to a beggarly account of empty boxes, with the exception of Mrs. Sloman's benefit— never known to fail.

Mr. Cowell having returned from Baltimore, (where his season had been a most brilliant one) opened the Walnut Street Theatre, announcing that, with the aid of the brush of Mr. Walker, the talented scene painter of the Park Theatre, New York, he would produce a spectacle which should eclipse everything heretofore seen in Philadelphia, for beauty of scenery and machinery.

Possessing, as I did, the aid of Lewis in the mechanical department, and of Chapman in the arrangement of melo-drama, I was determined that the well merited reputation acquired by the "Red Rover," should not be wrested from us without an effort. I accepted the challenge, and held a consultation with S. Chapman, Lewis, H. Warren, and Griffith, the stage-carpenter, to find some piece which should enable us to retire from the contest of the longest season ever known in Philadelphia, not only with honour but with victory. The "Gnome King," presented itself, as furnishing the greatest scope for not only inventive faculty, but scenic effect. With Mr. Warren's approbation, I gave orders to prepare it for representation, in the most perfect manner. It was produced on the 10th of June, completely annihilating the "Sleeping Beauty," which was well got up at the Walnut Street Theatre, thus closing the first season of my management, on the 21st of June, with flying colours. The "Gnome King" was acted eleven nights, and when the theatre closed, I entertained sanguine hopes it would be a card to open with for the following season.

The theatre was open two hundred acting nights, during which not one week had elapsed without the appearance of a "star." Notwithstanding the rapid succession with which all the talent that could be obtained was placed before the public, I produced the dramatic spectacle of "Peter Wilkins," "The Red Rover," "Thirty years of the Life of a Gambler," and the "Gnome King," *four* heavy scenery pieces in one season, despatch hitherto unknown in an American theatre ; *four* new tragedies ; *two* full operas of three acts each, and *one* entirely original, of one act ; *eighteen* new farces ; *one* musical comedy ; *one play*, (the "Usurper,") in five acts ; and *three* domestic melo-dramas ; in all thirty-four new pieces, eleven revivals of pieces previously acted in Philadelphia, but almost forgotten. The receipts were great, beyond previous seasons ;

averrging very nearly five hundred dollars per night. The amount paid to "stars," the expenditure necessary to renovate the wardrobe, which was almost entirely new, and the expenditure incurred in England and the Continent, left only a small balance in the treasury, (but a good stock of reputation,) to commence the following season.

The stars of the season recorded, many of whom played two and three engagements, were Mr. Horn, Mrs. Knight, Mrs. Sloman, Mrs. Austin, Mr. Sloman, Mr. Hackett, Mr. E. Forrest, Miss George, Miss Kelly, Mr. Burroughs, Miss Clara Fisher, Miss Rock, Mr. Cooper, Mademoiselle Celeste, and Mr. Pearman—an array of talent not often offered in the same period, and rarely, if ever, supported by a stock company of excellent actors.

At the conclusion of this season, Mr. R. Peters, jun., expressed to me Mr. Warren's unqualified approbation of the manner in which I had conducted the business of the theatre; and, as a proof of his sincerity, proposed, if agreeable to me, as Warren was getting too old for active business, that he should take me into partnership. This was the first idea I had of becoming manager, on my own account. Flattering as the proposal was, with the prospect of two new theatres in the field for the following season, I decided to reject it; but circumstances occurred in rapid succession, which induced me to alter that resolution.

During the visit paid annually in the summer to Washington city, by the members of the Philadelphia Theatre, Mr. Cowell suddenly declined proceeding with the alterations commenced at the Walnut Street Theatre. Had I taken what he rejected, how different would have been the result, both to Mr. Warren and myself; by acting in concert and not in opposition, we should have secured an undivided field. One expression of Mr. Warren's altered my intentions; he said, " Wemyss, don't leave me." " Warren, I will *not :* we sink or swim together." I wrote to Mr. Peters on the subject of his proposition, at Mr. Warren's desire; and from that letter may be dated the unfortunate partnership of Pratt and Wemyss, attended with one slight gleam of *sunshine*—the sequel, *desolation* and *ruin.*

CHAPTER XVII.

Battle! Battle! Battle!   Three Theatres, when one was deemed suffi-
cient.   A Firmament of Stars.   " Lay on, Macduff."   Blow for Blow.
Madame Fearon's First Appearance in Philadelphia. E. Forrest. French
Dramas and German Musicians.   Unfortunate Accident.   Preparations
to Close the Season.   " He that Fights and Runs Away," &c., &c.
Hardly Used, but not Beaten.

At the close of the Washington season, Mr. S. Chapman left us
to join Mr. Wood, whose new theatre, in Arch Street, was to
open on the 1st of October, 1828 ; the only actor, and I record
it with pride, whose sense of honour was not strong enough to
resist the offer of increased emolument for decreased reputation, in the violation of contract, to assist a rival establishment, built with the avowed purpose of ruining (if possible)
Mr. Warren, from whose enterprise they were at present in
the United States.

That Mr. Chapman had no cause of complaint, the following
letter from him, after Mr. Wood relinquished the management
of the new theatre, and he wished to return to the service he
had deserted, will prove :

(COPY.)

" Philadelphia, December 12, 1828.

" Sir—I write by the desire, and at the suggestion of Mr. Jefferson. It
is his wish that I should again enlist under your banners; and from the
gentlemanly treatment I met with from yourself and Mr. Wemyss, I must
acknowledge that nothing would give me greater pleasure, provided I
received a fair remuneration for my services.   I understand you are about
to take a part of your company to Baltimore; should that be the case, I
should like much to become a member of it; and should any hostility exist
between Mr. Wemyss, or yourself, and me, most happy to consider it (as I
always have) a matter of business, and forget it.   You know, I believe,
my willingness to serve, and my ability, and how anxious I am to forward
the interest of that leader, whose officer I consider myself.   Mr. Jefferson
has kindly offered to deliver you this, who will perhaps state more fully
my wishes on the occasion.

" I am, sir,
" Yours, truly,
(Signed) " SAMUEL CHAPMAN.

" To WILLIAM WARREN, Esq.,
Chesnut Street Theatre."

Mr. Chapman was of much importance to the theatre.   To
him I had confied the arrangement of melo-dramatic spectacle,
which he executed with credit to himself and the theatre.
He had, since his arrival in the United States exhibited much

discontent at what he was pleased to term his paltry salary, (one of his own proposing in London, and higher than he ever before received.) So well satisfied with his exertions was I, that I recommended Mr. Warren, before we had the slightest idea of his intended treason, to place his salary on the list for the following year at twenty-eight dollars per week, instead of twenty-two, the terms of his unexpired contract. This intention was communicated to him, and met by the information that he did not intend to remain in the theatre unless his salary was advanced to the same amount offered him by Mr. Wood.

It is not, therefore, to be wondered at, that even the respect of Mr. Warren for Mr. Jefferson, whose daughter Elizabeth, Chapman had married, could not prevail upon him to accede to any proposition for one who had so unceremoniously violated existing contracts. Chapman possessed literary acquirements of no mean order. The cessation of friendly intercourse between us was matter of regret, but being in some measure bondsman for his fidelity, it was the only course could pursue; and from the hour of his desertion until his death, we never exchanged a passing salution, although I do not believe any ill-feeling existed on either side. My position as manager of the Chesnut Street Theatre rendered it impossible to receive his visits, without apparently countenancing his dereliction from the strict path of rectitude, which should have guided his business transactions; while, as he says, he looked upon it as a matter of business and laughed at it.

We commenced the winter campaign of 1828, in Baltimore, early in the month of September; and notwithstanding the attraction of a new and also a good stock company, the aid of Mr. and Mrs. Sloman, Miss Rock, Mr. Cooper, Mademoiselle Celeste, and the successful melo-dramas of the "Red Rover," "Gambler's Fate," and the "Gnome King," *the season was a failure.* Indeed, experience proves that Holliday Street Theatre commences its season with bad houses, which gradually grow worse, until it closes, leaving the actors unpaid, and the manager always in difficulty. The one hundred and twenty-six free admissions, transferrable once in each season, explain the cause. No sooner is an attractive bill laid before them, for a theatrical campaign, with the price of admission fixed at one dollar to the boxes, than the newspapers teem with advertisements offering stockholders' tickets at 25 cents per night, for the season. The only great house was Sloman's benefit, which, as usual, was filled to overflowing.

Battle—battle—battle.—We now approach the season 1828 and 1829, in Philadelphia, where we shall find three theatres and a circus struggling for existence, where, heretofore, *one* was deemed sufficient. Mr. Wood opened the Arch Street Theatre on the 1st of October, 1828, with the comedy of the "Honey Moon,' and the afterpiece of "Three and the Deuce." The French Opera was placed in the Chesnut Street Theatre to check this move, until Mr. Warren was ready to commence his season, which we did on Thursday, the 13th of November; opening with the play of the "Gamester," in which Mr. Cooper and Mrs. Sloman appeared, and "Fish Out of Water," for Mr. Sloman, as the farce. *Three* stars to commence with ! ! !

The stars announced by Mr. Wood as engaged to appear, were *Celeste*, and her sister Constance, Mr. Holland, Miss Kelly, Mr. Horn, Mrs. Austin, Miss Rock, and James Wallack. From the last-named gentleman much was expected. His popularity was great, and he might be considered as the only antagonists we had to fear. He had previously written to Mr. Warren, offering his services for twelve nights for five hundred pounds sterling, which terms were not accepted. Mr. Wood agreed to give him two hundred dollars per night, which he would have been foolish to reject. I now turned my attention to Mr. E. Forrest, as the only star most likely to occupy the nights of Wallack's engagement in Philadelphia, with profit to the Chesnut Street Theatre. To my surprise I received a proposition asking two hundred dollars per night. I laughed at this proposal, and in reply stated he must be either mad, or think me so, to *make* such a proposition; which, to have yielded an equal sum to the management, must have avaraged nightly *seven hundred dollars ! !* He succeeded in obtaining these terms from the manager of the Walnut Street Theatre. All these engagements will account for the speedy bankruptcy of the managers throughout the United States, and the fortunes acquired by " stars" through their downfall.

On the 6th of November, Maywood appeared at the Arch Street Theatre, as "King Lear !" and from that time became identified with the Philadelphia stage, but not as a tragedian. No—to New York we resign all the laurels he boasts in *that* way. As the representative of Scotchmen, he is a valuable actor ; but it is as a manager and an active business man, that his reputation is based in this city : for the opportunity he is indebted to me, as I appointed him acting manager of the Washington and Baltimore theatres, in 1829.

On the 17th of November, Mrs. Knight opened in Adela, in the "Haunted Tower." It will scarcely be credited, that the second night of her engagement yielded only eighty dollars; while Cooper and Mrs. Sloman were not doing much better. On the 2nd of November, a novelty was presented in the person of Herr Cline, whose graceful movements on the elastic cord, (what a fashionable title for the tight rope !) astonished the good people of Philadelphia.

The commencement of our season was a bad one. Notwithstanding Mr. Warren paid Cooper fifty dollars per night, Mrs. Knight fifty dollars per night, and Mr. and Mrs. Sloman one hundred and twenty dollars per week, in addition to the current expenses of the theatre, the receipts did not average more than one hundred and fifty dollars per night, to meet an expenditure of 350 dollars. The only consolation was to be found in the fact, that the Arch Street Theatre was not doing better, although Mr. Wood had the advantage of a prosperous opening.

My whole energy was directed to divide the town, if possible, during the engagement of Mr. Wallack, whose first appearance was announced for the 26th of November, as Hamlet. I was certain if this engagement could be broken down, the fortunes of the Arch Street Theatre would be broken with it; I therefore announced Herr Cline's benefit, with a grand ascension from the back of the Stage to the gallery, surrounded by fireworks, for the 29th of November. Aided by Mrs. Knight, and the new farce of " The Invincibles," which had made so decided a hit, the admirable manner in which the ladies went through the manual exercise, being marked by the long-continued applause of the audience, the whole available talent of the theatre being brought to bear, had the desired effect: we triumphed, and it was a triumph well worth the sacrifice made to obtain it.

But as one good turn deserves another, Mr. Wood prepared a similar reception for Clara Fisher, from whom we anticipated a few nights of good business. On the 3rd of December, the night announced for her first appearance, Mr. Wood announced *his own name* for a benefit, with the powerful aid of Mr. Wallack, as a volunteer; but neglected to act on the occasion himself, an omission so singular, as at once to open our eyes to the real intention. I therefore, after much persuasion, induced Warren to announce *his* benefit on the same night, with Clara Fisher as a volunteer.

The gauntlet of opposition was thus boldly thrown; although many were foolish enough to blame Mr. Warren for allowing his name to appear in opposition to his late partner, but now rival. *The only business answer is,* Mr. Wood announced his name to strengthen Wallack's engagement, which began to be known as a failure; and Mr. Warren met this *ruse de guerre* by a similar announcement, to strengthen the engagement of Miss Clara Fisher. In the whole course of my management, I never exercised a better piece of generalship, as the event proved.

The contest was so close, that the houses were as near *a tie* as possible; but it was a death blow to the Arch Street Theatre, under Mr. Wood's management. After trying the reduction

of the prices of admission, (of which Mr. Wood enjoys the
honour, for to him and not to me, it belongs,) in the middle
of Mr. Wallack's engagement, the theatre closed, never to be
opened again under Mr. Wood's management, whose reign, in
his new theatre, had been a short and *not* very merry one.

Mr. Wallack made an application to me, to play at the
Chestnut Street Theatre, in consequence of Mr Wood's failure
to comply with the terms of his contract,—*he could not pay
him*;—and on the 20th of December, 1828, he appeared as
Brutus, in Howard Payne's play, at the Chestnut Street
Theatre ; and on the following night, as Charles Surface,
and Michael, in the "Adopted Child." Thus terminated his
visit to Philadelphia, most unprofitably to him.

MADAME FEARON

made her first appearance in Philadelphia, at the Arch Street
Theatre, on the 9th of December, as Floretta, in "The Cabinet." This lady was decidedly the best English singer who
ever visited the United States; although one who never
played a successful engagement. Her appearance was not in
her favour; her figure was too much *enbonpoint* for an American eye; she was really fat, fair, and past forty; but in the
science of music, I doubt whether Malibran herself excelled
her. The young ladies, who are taught to beat a tune upon
the piano for the amusement of papa and mamma, could not
appreciate the difficulty of her "cadenza," or the study required to form a perfect singer : nay, they had the bad taste
to laugh at some of the most beautiful and difficult passages,
which she executed with such precision and brilliancy.

The taste for opera (and even now, it is more a fashion than
a taste,) had no existence then; La Somnambula and Norma
had not become familiar to the ear; Mrs. Wood, Miss Sheriff,
and Mrs. Seguin had not charmed all our fashionable ladies
into ecstacies. The prima donna of the Neapolitan theatre
was doomed to return home, mortified with her reception,
with no very exalted opinion of the American taste for music.

She declared this to be the country where mediocrity of
talent was paid beyond its worth, but where excellence in
music, painting, or poetry, would pine and decay for want of
patronage; and there is too much truth in the assertion.
The fact is—neither the English or the Americans can boast,
phrenologically, of the bump of music ; the sound of pounds,
shillings and pence, with the one, and dollars with the other,
is the sweetest music their ears can listen to.

The last night of the present season at the Arch Street
Theatre, was announced for Roberts' benefit, on the 22nd of
December. On the 25th it closed ; re-opened, with Roberts

announced as manager, and finally closed on the 29th of December, for Mrs. Blake's benefit, with "Alexander the Great," and the "Turnpike Gate."

So far, so good. Mr. Warren had made great exertions' and those exertions had succeeded. He now engaged Mr. Hunt, Miss Philips, and Miss Clara Fisher, to produce the opera of "Native Land," which had failed at the Arch Street. When produced for Mrs. Austin's benefit, it made a decided hit; and the prospects of "Old Drury," as the Chesnut Street was now termed, began to assume a profitable aspect. Blake was unremitting in his exertions to procure a good company for the opening of the Walnut Street Theatre, on the first of January, which the closing of the Arch Street, rendered an easier task than he had any right to expect.

Warren became frightened at the prospect of further opposition; the price demanded and obtained by the stars, he refused to comply with; this threw Monsieur and Madame Charles Rouzi Vestris, and the corps de ballet, from the Lafayette into the arms of Blake, who eagerly secured their services at any price. With the failure of Wood before his eyes, Warren wished to retire from the contest; he said, "You are young and enterprising; fight the battle, and leave me as an older general, to give you advice: two thousand dollars will relieve me from all present difficulty; now if you can advance that sum, I will let the whole concern upon reasonable terms.

In an evil hour for all parties, I induced Mr. Lewis T. Pratt to join me in the offered speculation; and on the 25th of December, 1828, the lease of the Chesnut Street Theatre was by consent of the stockholders, assigned to Pratt and Wemyss; we paid two thousand dollars, cash down, and agreed to pay the rent of the Chesnut Street Theatre, and allow Mr. Warren three thousand a year for the use of his theatrical property, including the rent of Baltimore and Washington theatres; in addition to which, he was to receive forty dollars a week, as an actor, during the continuation of the lease; possession of the property to be given on the first of January, 1829.

Warren took his farewell benefit, as manager, December 30th, 1828; the play of "Merry Wives of Windsor," and the spectacle of "Illusion," most beautifully got up, and intended for the New Year's pageant, had no alteration in the management, taken place. The last night of Mr. Warren's management, was the play of "Adelgitha," and "Illusion."

On the first of January, 1829, Pratt and Wemyss commenced their career, with an address, written by James S. Barker, the grand spectacle of "Illusion," and a new pantomime, entitled "Philip Quarle." The Walnut Street Theatre opened for the first time, since its alteration from a circus to a theatre, under the management of Inslee and Blake, with the "Honeymoon," and the "Lottery Ticket:" their house was filled to overflowing, while ours yielded only four hundred dollars.

In the commencement of our undertaking, difficulty surrounded us at every step—Mr. Warren having declined the aid of stars, at the exorbitant prices demanded. Had we even been willing to comply, the most attractive were engaged to the managers of the Walnut Street Theatre. We were therefore compelled to find the attraction in melo-dramatic spectacle. Mr. Warren had despatched Mr. Wepfer to Germany, at the close of last season, for the purpose of bringing over a full and efficient corps de ballet, for whom we had kept the season open from any entangling engagements, and who were hourly expected.

He arrived without a single dancer, and an addition of five musicians to our already excellent orchestra, who were only wanted in the event of his success with the dancers. However, I shall here record the names of this orchestra, because I do not believe such an efficient one was ever assembled, before or since, within the walls of an American theatre. Leader, Mr. Braun; Mr. Willis, Mr. Wepfer, Mr. Dielman, Mr. Meigner, Mr. Skenlocker.

We were compelled to keep the Baltimore and Washington Theatres open during a winter season. At Baltimore, the management was entrusted to Mr. John Sloman, who resigned it into the hands of Mr. Maywood. In Washington, as members of this company, were Mr. and Mrs. Thomas Flynn, Mr. Stone, (author of "Metamora,") and his wife, Mrs. M'Clean, and many other actors of talent. Our hopes of success, in Washington, were built upon the crowds which would assemble at the metropolis to witness the inauguration of General Jackson, on the 4th of March, 1829, as President of the United States. Unfortunately for our hopes, Mrs. Jackson died, and mourning, not festivity, was the order of the day.

On the 6th of January, Madame Vestris and her husband made their first appearance at the Walnut Street Theatre, Philadelphia, attracting within those walls the fashionable society, on which the Chesnut Street Theatre alone can depend for success. The Rubicon once passed, the difficulty vanished; attraction alone was required to induce them to repeat their visit—and yet the leaders of fashion, through Mr. Walsh, at that time their organ, cautioned the managers of the Chesnut Street Theatre against engaging French dancers, as no ladies could visit the theatre to witness such an exhibition.

On the 8th of January, Richard Penn Smith's drama, in

honour of General Jackson, was produced to a house of one thousand dollars, *the first and last of the same race.* On the 12th, the "Battle of Waterloo," with the aid of seven volunteer companies, was brought out with great success, and on the same night Mr. E. Forrest made his appearance at the Walnut Street Theatre, as Damon, for which he received two hundred dollars ! ! ! The town, for a time, was Forrest mad, and the managers reaped a rich harvest from their mad speculation. Without wishing to detract from Mr. Forrest's merit, it was a lucky circumstance that Madam Vestris preceded him. He deserves his good fortune, and long may he live to enjoy it; I know no one who has encountered more difficulty from managers, to establish his position ; and that *knowledge* makes *me acknowledge* he is right, now the tables are turned, to squeeze as much out of them as possible, although I have suffered in the process. The idea that Mr. Forrest could be worth 200 dollars per night, while Mr. Cooper, in his brightest day, never *asked* more than 50, is a riddle, for those only who paid the money, to solve.

Our piece of the "Battle of Waterloo," was as successful as we could wish, and would have continued to crowd the theatre, but for a melancholy accident. On the 15th of January, Mr. Tryal Deves, a member of one of the volunteer companies, was shot upon the stage, during the performance ; he lingered until the 16th, at 2 o'clock, but never spoke after the fatal accident. Such an occurrence within the walls of a theatre, was well calculated to strike the audience with dismay. They retired immediately, but to me the horror of the scene was increased by the fact that the unhappy man, who had thus met his death in the performance of an act of kindness to the managers, had left a wife and nine children, (the youngest not six months old,) who were entirely dependent on his exertions for their daily bread.

The only reparation in my power I offered to the widow—a benefit, free of any expense whatever ; and wishing to have the house crowded, I addressed a note to the managers of the Walnut Street Theatre, requesting, if compatible with their arrangements, they would close their Theatre, and add to the attractions of the evening, by allowing the members of their company to unite with ours. Mr. Blake declined closing their doors, but kindly offered to appropriate a night at the Walnut Street Theatre, at no distant period, for the same benevolent purpose, for which Mr. E. Forrest volunteered his gratuitous aid.

The benefit took place at the Chesnut Street Theatre when Mrs. Sandford, the daughter of Mr. Holman, volunteered her services. The play was "Every One has his Fault," and

I

the afterpiece the "Adopted Child." Each actor resigned his night's salary; the carpenters and doorkeepers also tendered their mite, which I added to the gross receipts.

The Washington Circus also gave a benefit for the same purpose, from which Mrs. Deves realized about one hundred dollars, thus proving that actors, with all their faults, are not devoid of charity to their fellow men in distress.

I now approach a blot upon this subject I would willingly obliterate. Messrs. Inslee and Blake announced their benefit; I permitted Mr. E. Forrest to return one night earlier from his engagement at Washington, for the purpose of lending his aid to the charitable purpose, when, to the astonishment of the whole city, the boxes being taken for the aid of the widow and orphans, and an overflowing house expected, the managers, (*shame upon them!*) not content with deducting their nightly expenses, announced in the bills of the day that one-half only of the gross proceeds would be given to Mrs. Deves and her children, thus turning the misfortunes of the widow and orphans into a vile source of profit to themselves. No one was more indignant than Mr. E. Forrest at such conduct, and it is only to be regretted he did not demand from Inslee and Blake 200 dollars for his performance, and have given it as a donation from himself to those he intended to serve.

Whether Mr. Inslee or Mr. Blake have the credit of this arrangement, as Rob Roy says, "is between their conscience and the long day," but money so obtained could not prosper.

I am perfectly aware a justification of this measure has been attempted, on the miserable plea that the widow had no claim upon them, her husband was not shot in *their* theatre. *All this is true:* but the benefit advertised at the Chesnut Street Theatre was rendered less productive by their announcement that a benefit would *also* be given for the same object at the Walnut Street Theatre—thus preventing those who would only have deserted their theatre on such an occasion from visiting the Chesnut Street Theatre at all. Certain it is their house was crowded, and that they pocketed between three and four hundred dollars designed for the children of Deves.

Mr. E. Forrest had not the most distant idea he was presenting his services to Messrs. Inslee and Blake, but travelled upwards of an hundred miles, in a severe winter, with the laudable purpose of aiding those unhappy children who were suddenly deprived of their natural protector in an awful and unexpected manner. He expressed his indignation loudly to his friends upon the subject.

From this truly lamentable occurrence may be dated the long train of misfortune which assailed the management of Pratt and Wemyss. By no exertion could we possibly raise a house sufficient to pay the expenses; our capital was dwindling away, while the play of the "Rivals," cast thus: Sir, Anthony Absolute, *Warren:* Captain Absolute, *Wemyss:* Fag, *Hathwell:* Faulkland, *Southwell:* Sir Lucius O'Trigger, *Mercer:* Acres, *Jefferson:* David, *J. Jefferson:* Mrs. Malaprop, *Mrs. Francis:* Lydia Languish, *Mrs. Rowbotham:* Julia, *Mrs. Darley:* Lucy, *Miss Hathwell:* for the benefit of a star, (*Madame Heloise,*) produced only *twenty-two dollars and fifty cents!!* Alas! for the legitimate drama. One of the finest comedies in the British language, acted as well as it could be at any theatre in the United States of America, to such a sum!

Misfortunes never come single. Mr. E. Forrest who attracted admiring crowds in Philadelphia, could not play to an average of one hundred and thirty dollars a night in Washington city! during the session of Congress. Mr. Wallack played to still less, and on one occasion not a single individual presented himself to inquire whether the theatre was open, when his name graced the head of the bill. The inauguration week was supported by the aid of Herr Cline, and Washington did, certainly, with the aid of Mr. and Mrs. Sloman, Miss Clara Fisher, Ronzi Vestris, Mr. E. Forrest, and Mr. Wallack, yield a profit of five hundred dollars in a season of three months. Well done! Washington. It is more than either Philadelphia or Baltimore did to—Pratt and Wemyss.

On the 28th of January, 1829, the Chesnut Street Theatre closed for the season, for my benefit, with the comedy of "Wild Oats," and the drama of the "Bottle Imp." All bills paid, and no outstanding demands against the treasury.

CHAPTER XVIII

Full Cry for Baltimore. More difficulties. Waggons fast in a Snow-Storm. Theatre Opened. Magnificent Plan for re-decorating Old Drury. Return to Philadelphia. In at the Death. Walnut Street Theatre closed for ever, under the Management of Blake and Inslee. Fresh Start in a very Rainy Night. Play of the "Poor Gentleman," and Farce of the "Invincibles." The First full Opera ever acted in Philadelphia in the Italian Language. The two Theatres springing up in existence again, under fresh Management. The Beginning of the End. Close of the Management of Pratt and Wemyss.

WITH an unwilling heart, but yielding to necessity, we resolved to leave a clear field to our successful rivals, and try what Baltimore would accomplish for a winter season, aided by Wallack. Herr Cline, Vestris, Monsieur and Madame

Achille, Mr. and Mrs. Pearman, and Mrs. Hamblin, as stars.
We therefore closed "*Old Drury.*"

In Baltimore, a new difficulty met us; the stockholders of
the theatre contended that although Mr. Warren had a right
to occupy it free of rent, excepting only the season tickets, he
had no right to tranfer that privilege to a third party, that
we could not open unless we agreed to pay fifteen dollars per
night, which, added to a license demanded by the corporation
of the city of Baltimore, amounting to ten more, made twenty-
five dollars per night for the privilege of opening a theatre in
the worst theatrical town in America.

Our engagements being made, we could not stop to argue
points of *right*, but agreed to the demand as a matter of expedience, and on the 30th of January, 1829, I started for Baltimore on as fine a winter morning as ever dawned. At Lancaster I met Mr. and Mrs. Rowbotham; we slept at York, and
when we arose in the morning the ground was covered with
snow, which continued to fall during the day—a fair specimen
of the weather we were doomed to encounter during the winter.

The first news I heard on my arrival at Baltimore was, that
the trustees refused to give possession of the theatre, under
Warren's lease, and a report prevailing that we should not be
allowed to open on Monday night. With Mr. Wallack engaged
at a nightly salary of one hundred dollars, and the company
assembling, it may be imagined I was in no very enviable situation. I waited upon Mr. Lucas, jun., and Mr. Cohen, who
called a meeting of the trustees, and all difficulty was satisfac-
torily arranged.

I commenced the season on Monday, the 2nd February,
under every disadvantage. The snow-storm had so retarded
the waggons that they did not reach Baltimore until four
o'clock in the afternoon. Mr. Mercer had not arrived, and we
were compelled to bustle through the play of "Pizarro" in the
best manner we could, I playing at least four parts. An apology was due to the audience, which they received with much
good nature, knowing how we had contended to open at all.
It was an awful night, the snow drifting in every direction,
yet the receipts amounted to 203 dollars, which, for Baltimore,
augured well. Herr Cline played the following night to 65
dollars—his second night only yielded 48 dollars; while
Wallock only played to 165 dollars. An effort was necessary
to rouse the Baltimoreans; therefore I tried Wallack, Mrs.
Hamblin, and Herr Cline, on the same night, to which I added
Monsieur and Madame Achille—the receipts, 836 dollars.
This was ruinous—Wallack 100 dollars, Herr Cline 50 dollars,
Achille 60 dollars, Mrs. Hamblin 20 dollars, two hundred dollars for extra aid. Vestris and Rosalie, still worse—and now
hold up your hands in wonder, and then blush for the spirit

of your monumental city: Monsieur Vestris, Madame Vestris, Mademoiselle Rosalie, Mr. and Mrs. Peerman, *all in one night* —gross receipts, 84 dollars ! ! !

"*It is impossible!*" And so would *I* have said, had I not seen it. Here, then, we were on the high road to ruin; but let me do the trustees of the Holiday Street Theatre justice. Seeing and approving the efforts made, they desired the weekly rent to remain until we heard from them on the subject. This was a seasonable relief, although a small one; but heretofore we had met all payments.

Misery loves company; and it was with a feeling of satisfaction, on the verge of ruin ourselves, we heard that Inslee and Blake, whom we had left in Philadelphia in the full tide of success, were unable to pay their actors; and, to add to their pecuniary difficulties, were at personal enmity with each other.

We resolved to be in at the death, and came to the bold resolution of re-decorating the Chesnut Street Theatre, and making one desperate effort for masterdom.

Mr. Pratt hinted to me, that a new name might possibly be serviceable as stage manager, and proposed Mr. John Jefferson; the popularity of his father's name pointing out the propriety of the choice. I named Rowbotham, as having more experience in the direction of the stage; and he was accordingly announced as stage manager, on the 9th of April, 1829.. How he treated me for my kindness on every occasion to him, will appear hearafter;—"Seek fire in ice; but seek not gratitude in a white man's bosom." So says Lewis, in the "Castle Spectre;" and he had a tolerably fair estimate of mankind.

The plan furnished by Lewis, our machinist, for the decoration of the Chesnut Street Theatre, was magnificent. Had the agents not interfered and prevented the removal of the canopy over the dress boxes, it would have been the most beautiful theatre in the United States. We were compelled to alter our plans, and neatness was substituted for display; the dome alone retaining its originality of the burnished rays of a golden sun. It cost us two thousand dollars, and we had the use of it exactly ten weeks.

But leaving Mr. Pratt to superintend his carpenters at the Chesnut Street Theatre, in Philadelphia, let us return to Baltimore, where the season continued as disastrous as ever: but to the citizens of Baltimore, for their kindness to me as an individual, I must ever be grateful. The directors of the Fancy Rag Ball, requested me to announce my benefit, and they would visit the theatre in character, filling the pit at box prices. This plan was afterwards abandoned, each member being at liberty to visit any part of the house. The receipts were five hundred and fifty dollars; the pieces were,

"He lies Like Truth," and "The Bottle Imp." To my friend Boole, the auctioneer, I was indebted for this house; not the only favour I have received at his hands, for which I have nothing to offer but the assurance his kindness is gratefully remembered.

Richard Penn Smith's play of "the Prodigals," was by me re-christened "The Disowned," to avail myself of the popularity of Bulwer's novel of that name. I produced it for the first time, at the Holiday Street Theatre in Baltimore. The exertions of Mr. Southwell and Mr. Jefferson saved the piece, before the excellent acting of Mr. Rowbotham had an opportunity of rendering it triumphantly successful. It was afterwards performed in London.

During this whole season, the weather was our greatest enemy. A good box book was the sure forerunner of a snow-storm, or a deluge of rain, which continued during the evening.

Now for a marvellous story, but a true one. Mr. and Mrs. Pearman having been engaged to perform the opera of "Der Freyschutz," some difficulty occurred with Mr. Braun the leader of the orchestra and Mr. Pearman, which ended with Mr. Braun leaving the orchestra and taking with him nearly all the German musicians. Mr. Dielman took the leader's chair, and with five instruments, we actually played the opera of "Der Freyschutz," in the city of Baltimore, three successive nights, to houses averaging two hundred dollars—Mr. Meignen carrying us thus through a difficulty which appeared insurmountable.

The season was thus brought to a close. On the 9th of April we re-opened the Chesnut Street Theatre, with the "Poor Gentleman" and the "Invincibles;" the rain descending in torrents during the whole of the day. The Walnut Street Theatre closed on the 14th of April, with an announcement, that Mr. Blake's benefit would be postponed until the re-opening of the theatre; which never took place under the management of Inslee and Blake.

As our former failure had been attributed to want of attraction in the shape of stars, we resolved to make a vigorous effort to restore the fortunes of Old Drury. The attraction offered, even satisfied the stockholders, and their representative season tickets, (the bane of all theatres;) but this likewise failing, the cry was, "Why did you not do this before you went to Baltimore?"

Wallack and Hamblin in the same plays; the French Corps de Ballet; Italian opera; and even fancy dress Balls, were all offered in vain.

The theatre was re-decorated in handsome style; but another opposition awaited us, and like Banquo's issue, followed by a third. Mr. Aaron Philips opened the Arch Street

Theatre on the 15th, and closed it on the 25th. The Walnut Street Theatre opened immediately as a dramatic commonwealth, under S. Chapman, Green and Edmonds, on the 27th of May, the day we closed, to open no more.

On the 28th of April, we announced a Grand Fancy Dress Ball, where everything was abundantly supplied but dancers. We could not muster two quadrilles upon the floor. This was repeated, by desire of those who witnessed the arrangements, on the 2nd of May; but here we had dancers enough, but so few spectators, that it proved a losing concern.

Mr. James Craig having received a letter from Mr. Horn, touching the performance of an Italian opera at the Chesnut Street Theatre, an arrangement was entered into for the services of himself, Madame Fearon, Madame Brichta, Signor Rosich, Signor Augrisani, and "La Triumphe del Musica" was produced on the 5th of May, with the following cast :— Aristea, Madame Fearon ; Celestina, Madame Brichta ; Count, Caroline C. Horn ; Don Febeo, Signor Rosich ; Briscoma, Signor Augrisani.

As this was the first Italian opera acted in Philadelphia, it gave great satisfaction, and in this worse than wretched season, produced four hundred dollars nightly. Could the parties themselves have varied the piece, they would have attracted fashionable audiences to the end of the season, the receipts increasing each night. As it was, Mr. Horn received eight hundred dollars for four nights, while the management, in receiving an equal sum, did not receive sufficient to defray the expenses of extra music, and incidental charges. Thus it is, when stars appear, and draw crowded houses, they not only pocket the profits, but leave the manager *minus ;* as it seldom happens, the nights on which they do play, yield money sufficient to meet the necessary expenditure ; which deficiency must be supplied from the manager's share of his stars' houses.

Until this system be reformed, adieu to any well-conducted theatre. If the public will be content to see one part preeminently acted, in preference to the whole play supported by medicore talent, they will continue to patronise the stars ; but if they wish for the rational amusement of a well-acted play, they will desert the stars, no matter how brilliant, to support the manager, who will secure to them such a stock company, as used to grace the boards of the Chesnut Street Theatre, when Warren, Wood, Duff, H. Wallack, Wemyss, Jefferson, Blisset, Burke, Francis, Mrs. Entwistle, Mrs. Wood, Mrs. Darley, and Mrs. Francis, with a host of minor names, equal in merit to many that figure as stars at the present day, all of whom appeared in one play, without exciting the least astonishment.

At that time, a play was cast properly in every depart-

ment; at present, the minor parts are filled in such a manner,
that all gratification derived from the talents of a superior
actor, is marred by the miserable bungling, and worse
grammar, of those who are deemed of too little importance,
to attract the notice of even a paid critic.

The public must correct this evil for themselves. While
managers can procure actors—(no, not actors—*individuals*,)
for three or four dollars per week; and the public allow such
gentlemen to strut their brief hour upon the stage, murder-
ing English grammar at every sentence, there is no hope of
amendment.

But, if those persons who condescend to write about the
drama would ｛unveil this system, they would do more good
in one month towards the cause they profess to support, than
will be accomplished in one year, by puffing a manager, or
lauding a "star," who needs not such praise, or dreads their
censure.

On the 27th of May, Pratt and Wemyss closed the Chesnut
Street Theatre, and terminated their management with the
"Rencontre," "Wandering Boys," and "Fortune's Frolic."
From the 1st of October, 1828, until the 27th of May, 1829,
the struggle for ascendancy had been maintained throughout
a cross fire. Wood opened the new theatre, and was the first
to retire from the contest; Warren followed; and Pratt and
Wemyss succeeded him. Inslee and Blake, Aaron Philips,
and the Commonwealth, formed from the broken and scattered forces of all the theatres, alone remained—the success of
their summer's season causing their dissolution.

The stockholders of the Chesnut Street Theatre, re-entered,
and took possession of the theatre. The terms of the original
lease not having been complied with, the sub-lease, of necessity, became void. The only regret I experienced, was, Mr.
Warren had not continued the management; old recollections
might have operated in his favour, and prevented the sacrifice
of his theatrical property,

He felt keenly the neglect of his rich, and apparently once
kind friends—his misfortunes hastening his death.

During the summer, the Washington Circus was altered
into a Theatre which, for a few weeks, was very successful;
aided by the talents of Isherwood, Walstein, Mr. and Miss
Wells; Mrs. Maywood, Mrs. Stickney, Somerville, and Heyl.
I played Marplot there, on the 23rd of July, for the benefit of
Mr. Huddy, the artist, who had been unfortunately burnt out
of his home. For Heyl's benefit, Warren and myself, and Mr.
Rowbotham, played in "The way to get Married." It was a
very pretty little theatre, and well conducted. I shall have
to say a few words about it, at the close of the next season.

CHAPTER XIX.

Mr. Pratt in the field Alone. Mr. Philips at the Arch. Davis's French Opera Company at the Chesnut Street. The Walnut Street. Chapman, Green and Edmonds. A French Corps de Ballet at the Tivoli in Market Street. Thus began the Flourishing Winter Seasons of 1829 and 1830. Metamora. Faustus. Theatrical Fund. Apparent necessity for such an Establishment. Coldness and Apathy of Actors in its behalf.

MR. PRATT made an application for a new lease to the board of agents, with the understanding, that if I made no application and he obtained the theatre, the outstanding debts of the firm should be assumed by him. In making this arrangement and retiring from the management, I intended to leave the city of Philadelphia; but fate would not permit me. I applied to every manager in New York and Boston, without success. Theatricals were in that state, that theatres were closing, and managers becoming bankrupts every day.

The winter season of 1829 and 1830, was commenced by Mr. A. J. Philips, at the Arch Street Theatre, on the 31st of August, with the play of the "West Indian," and the melodrama of "Luke the Labourer." He introduced to the Philadelphia audience, Mr. Archer, Mr. Walton, Mr. Andrews, Mr. Charles Young, Mr. Hazard, Mr. John Fisher, Mr. Jervis; Mrs. Young, Miss Hamilton, Mrs. Vernon, Miss Coleman, and many other actors of merit. He really had an excellent company; and what appeared to promise success, many new faces.

The French opera company, so termed, under Mr. Davis, opened the Chesnut Theatre, on the 7th of September, and Mr. Pratt commenced his season, on the 20th of October, with the "Honey Moon," and "A Roland for an Oliver."

The Walnut Street Theatre also opened under the management of S. Chapman, Green and Edmonds, on the 7th of September, with the play of "She would and She would not;" and the farce of the "Turnpike Gate," Miss Clara Fisher being the star of the evening.

Messrs. Fogg and Stickney, opened an Amphitheatre; and a very inferior French corps de ballet, tried their fortune under Monsieur Babiere, at the old Tivoli, in Market street. It may be said, with truth, that Philadelphia was this season the emporium of all the regular dramatic talent of the United States; yet it was the most disastrous one ever known; the actors being literally in a state of desperation. For myself; for seven weeks I never received one cent from the treasury; and I have reason to know, others were not paid in better proportion.

English opera was the attempted attraction of the Chesnut Street Theatre, with Mr. and Mrs. Pearman. It was produced with every proper attention to rehearsals; but met with little success.

This season was marked by the production of Stone's prize tragedy of " Metamora," by Mr. Philips, at the Arch Street Theatre, on the 22nd of January, 1830. The anxiety to see Mr. E. Forrest in the original character thus prepared for him, crowded the theatre on each night of the performance, adding to his reputation as an actor, as well as to his private fortune, as a man. It is a very indifferent play, devoid of interest; but the character of Metamora is beautifully conceived, and will continue to attract, so long as Mr. E. Forrest is his representative; it was written for him, and will, in all probability die with him. Few actors would have the hardihood to risk their reputation in a character, so decidedly known as the best performance of the first tragedian of the American stage, provoking comparison to their disadvantage.

" Faustus," too, formed quite a topic of conversation. Philips had spared no expense or exertion to produce this drama in a style worthy of a metropolitan theatre. Coyle's scenery was delightful; but the tact of Mr. S. Chapman, turned the puffing of his antagonist to his own advantage. Possessing the aid of Lewis, he forestalled public opinion, by producing this piece at the Walnut Street Theatre, on Saturday, December 12th, 1829, in such a manner as to satisfy the public, and ruin the prospects of the Arch Street Theatre, where every thing that scenery, music, costume, or machinery could do, was *perfect*. But it was not played until the 16th of December, when, for the cause here stated, it did not repay the manager for his labour. This was a fair business rivalry for which S. Chapman deserved great credit. He reaped by promptitude, the reward which belonged to Philips. While these two theatres were thus employed in the endeavour to neutralize their attraction, the Chesnut continued to drag on from week to week, without a chance of success.

Mr. James Murdock made his first appearance at the Arch Street Theatre on the 13th of Oct., 1829, as Frederick, in " Lover's Vows," a performance of much promise, and his judicious choice of De Camp for his first manager, enabled him to reach, in a few years, a respectable position in his profession. He is decidedly the best juvenile actor on the American stage.

THEATRICAL FUND.

Actors are proverbial for their improvidence in all money arrangements: honest in principle, where they receive their income, but living up to the full amount of it. Should a season overtake them, when the manager is unable to pay their weekly salary, a few months will involve them in debt, from which they experience more than ordinary difficulty to extricate themselves; their vocation renders them also liable to accidents, and when ill health assails them, they are indeed helpless mortals. With the knowledge of these facts, it is not strange that every effort to establish a fund for the relief of distressed and decayed actors in the United States, should prove abortive. It was attempted in Boston, where Matthews left all the proceeds of premium sales for tickets, on the nights of his performance, to be devoted to such an institution.

In New York, large sums have been contributed, of the disposal of which no person can or will give an account. In Philadelphia, we thought we had hit upon the right plan, by appointing a majority of the trustees from the walks of private life, but our funds were suffered to remain idle for seven years in the Philadelphia Bank, and when finally invested in the loan of the Lehigh Coal and Navigation Company, no interest was added to the principal, while the depreciation of the stock renders it doubtful whether the original investment will ever be paid.

The prospects of the fund, commenced in Philadelphia on the 6th of December, 1829, were most flattering. The depression of the interests of the drama made a collective movement of vital importance; a committee of five met from each theatre for the purpose of forming a "General Theatrical Fund." From the Chestnut Street: Jefferson, Wemyss, Kilner, Maywood, and Rowbotham. From the Arch Street: Archer, Walton, Andrews, Roberts and Foot. From the Walnut Street: S. Chapman, John Jefferson, Clarke, Green, W. Chapman. After preliminary arrangements, on the 20th of December, 1829, a set of rules and regulations for the government of the association, were formed, and signed by the following gentlemen:— W. B. Wood, E. Forrest, F. C. Wemyss, Joseph Jefferson, J. Green, S. Chapman, John Jefferson, Thomas Kilner, R. C. Maywood, G. Andrews, Thos. Archer, W. B. Chapman, J. H. Clarke, H. H. Rowbotham, J. F. Foot, T. J. Walton.

An election was held for officers, which resulted in the choice of James N. Barker, Edwin Forrest, Quintin Campbell, as Trustees; John Henry Clarke, as President; William B. Wood, as Secretary; R. C. Maywood, J. F. Foot, F. C. Wemyss, Thomas Archer, Samuel H. Chapman, Standing Committee.

The Fund association being thus organized, the following circular was addressed to every theatre in the United States, with a printed copy of the Rules and Regulations:

Sir, or Madam,

Your attention is earnestly requested to the enclosed Rules and Regulations of the General Theatrical Fund.

The list of members will convince you of the readiness and sincerity with which its objects have been entered into; the expedience and necessity of such a society, I trust, will induce your hearty concurrence and co-operation; and I an authorized to add, that many liberal donations already have been bestowed.

By order,
(Signed)   JOHN FORRESTER FOOT.
Secretary, T. F.

Mr. E. Forrest, with a promptitude which did honour both to his head and heart, tendered his gratuitous services for one night, at every city or town in which he might be engaged, in aid of the receipts, added to which, he gave a donation of fifty dollars; Miss Clara Fisher and Mrs. Sloman gave each a similar sum.

Messrs. E. L. Carey, Pierce Butler, W. E. Bridges, W. E. Israel, C. Alexander, J. Savage, F. A. Huber, P. Wetherall, C. Wetherall, G. D. Shaeff, of the city of Philadelphia, each gave a donation, several of them expressing their intention to repeat the same annually, until the Fund should be firmly established. The first benefit took place on Tuesday, March 26th, at the Arch Street Theatre, on which occasion the Chesnut and Walnut were closed, and the actors of the three theatres employed in the performance. E. Forrest played Macbeth; the farce was the " Lancers;" and the first address on behalf of our infant association, was delivered by Mr. Archer, the stage manager of the Arch Street Theatre. The receipts were six hundred and five dollars; thus in less than three months, paying all expenses incurred, we had a balance in bank of seven hundred and sixty-five dollars, the most kindly feelings for our success in the community, during the worst theatrical season ever known in Philadelphia, when actors were suffering distress from the non-payment of salaries, and managers relieving themselves from the anticipated horrors of a prison, by the benefit of the insolvent laws.

All our labour was thrown away by the apathy of those most interested. The money obtained was permitted to remain idle in bank, the opportunity lost of receiving donations from the stars who visited us from Europe; the actors, one by one, declining to pay their dues, and the chance of realizing fifty thousand dollars, which would hourly have increased, forming a Fund to which every deserving actor could have looked with confidence for support in old age, placing him beyond the reach of misfortune, was lost!

Many years will elapse before so favourable an opportunity will again present itself: should it occur, I hope the actors will profit by experience, and establish a General Fund, which shall be as lasting as the profession, and to which each may point with pride and say, " *This is my work.*

CHAPTER XX.

No Song no Supper. Jefferson leaves the Theatre, and never afterwards Acts in Philadelphia. Plenty of Hard Work. No money. I give up at last in Despair, and come out with an Advertisement, "Starved Out." Man of Business behind a Counter. Calvin Edson, the Living Skeleton, turned Actor. Horrible Destitution of the Philadelphia Actors during this Season.

DESOLATION and misery was now the order of the day. Lucky was the actor who could realize a few dollars from his benefit : as to salary, it was insanity to look for such a thing. To change your situation was by no means to better your position. But when it is known that the actors of the Chesnut Street Theatre, performed the opera of " No Song no Supper," without a note of instrumental music, the orchestra having struck, because they were not paid, some idea may be formed of the state of the theatres. The audience permitted the vocal music to proceed, and even honoured one or two pieces with an " encore."

Booth, who was engaged, was attacked with one of those fits of periodical insanity, to which he is subject, and was chained down to his bed, thus injuring instead of aiding our cause.

Jefferson, whose benefit was announced with the new play of "A School for Grown Children," could scarcely muster enough to pay the expenses, and resolved to leave the theatre. The manager having demanded and received the full amount of his nightly charge on such occasions, offered him but half his income at the treasury, on Saturday. This was a blow the favourite comedian could not brook. The success of Sloman, an actor so greatly his inferior, had irritated him both with his manager and the audience ; but what must have been the apathy of the public towards dramatic representation, when such a man, whose reputation shed lustre on the theatre to which he was attached, was permitted to leave the city of Philadelphia with scarcely an inquiry as to his whereabout, two-thirds of the audience ignorant of his departure. The last time he acted in Philadelphia was for my benefit, kindly studying the part of Sir Bashful Constant, in " The Way to Keep Him," which he played admirably.

Mr. JOSEPH JEFFERSON

Was an actor formed in nature's merriest mood, a genuine son
of Momus; there was a vein of rich humour running throughout all he did, which forced you to laugh despite of yourself.
He discarded grimace as unworthy of him, although no actor
possessed a greater command over the muscles of his own face,
or the faces of his audience, compelling you to laugh or cry
at his pleasure. His excellent personation of old men acquired
for him, before he had reached the meridian of life, the title
of *Old Jefferson*.

The astonishment of strangers at seeing a good looking
young man pointed out in the street as Jefferson, whom they
had seen the night previous, at the theatre, tottering apparently on the verge of existence, was the greatest compliment
which could be paid to the talent of the actor.

His versatility was astonishing; light comedy, old men,
pantomime, low comedy, and occasionally juvenile tragedy.
Educated in the very best school for acquiring knowledge in
his profession, his father being an actor of no mean repute in
Drury Lane Theatre, during the reign of Garrick, Jefferson
was an adept in all the "trickery" of the stage, which, when
it suited his purpose, he could turn to excellent account. He
was the reigning favourite of the Philadelphia Theatre for a
longer period than any other actor ever attached to the city,
and left it with a reputation all might envy.

In his social relations he was the model of what a gentleman
should be, a kind husband, an affectionate father, a warm
friend, and a truly honest man. He died at Harrisburg,
where he had been playing, at his son's theatre, but no stone
marks the spot where moulder the remains of one of the
brightest ornaments of his profession.

"Alas! poor Yorick!"

During no period of my theatrical life did I work harder or
receive less money than during the season under Mr. Pratt's
management of 1829 and 1830; it was no uncommon occurrence to appear in two new characters on the same evening,
and on more than one occasion, "three." So long as there
appeared the slightest chance of resuscitation to the fallen
fortunes of the Chesnut-street Theatre, the actors laboured
diligently, but when after all their toil, *no money* could be
obtained for weeks in succession, one by one dropt from their
allegiance; for myself, I abandoned the theatre in despair, my
benefit alone preserving me and my family from actual starva-
tion. In this situation of affairs, I turned my thoughts to my
old vocation of selling lottery tickets, and on the 22d of March,

1830, much to the annoyance of many of my professional brethren, I issued the following advertisement:—

"STARVED OUT!

" The unprecedented depression of Theatricals in the city of Philadelphia having deprived the managers of the different theatres of the means of paying their actors, or fulfilling their contracts, the profession no longer affords the means of pro- curing the humble fare of bread and cheese for the support of a family. Under these circumstances, am I compelled to seek for other means of subsistence, and to exclaim reluc- tantly—

" Othello's occupation's gone!"

" F. C. Wemyss, grateful for past favours, again solicits the patronage of his friends and the public, having opened a lot- tery office in the Arcade, No. 34, East Avenue, and 35, West Avenue, where, by strict attention, he hopes to merit support. Having been three years out of business, he can only at present refer to prizes sold in days of '*Auld lang Syne;*' and many whose fortunes have been amply increased by their purchases from him, can bear testimony that Wemyss' office was *fortune's own abode.* He has sent a most pressing invitation to her, and doubts not she will return to her old quarters."

[Here followed a scheme of the Union Canal Lottery.]

The heading of this advertisement gave particular offence to the managers. To their remonstrances I could only answer, *Is it not true?* and then laughingly using the language of Shakspeare, say, " I am not bound to please thee with my (answers) advertisments."

I now made known my terms for acting, to be five dollars per night, payable in advance, for any parts I had previously acted, and ten dollars if required to study a new character. Although I could receive money from the treasury, as a regularly engaged actor, yet this arrangement yielded me an average of from fifteen to twenty dollars per week, and was a most seasonable supply to aid my new business. It was thus I became a member (for occasional aid only,) of the seceders, who opened the Washington Theatre, in York Road; and those who witnessed the performance of the comedies of " John Bull," and " The Rivals," left the theatre delighted with the representation. Mr. Duff, Mr. Wemyss, Mr. Foote, Mr. Clarke, Mr. Webb, Mr. Logan, Mrs. Wheatley, Mrs. Stick- ney, Mr. and Mrs. C. Durang, were members of the company. It was here that Mr. David Ingersoll, a young man of much promise, and well known in New York as an excellent actor, made his first public effort. Dissipation finished his career at an early age, which common prudence would have made a brilliant one. What a pity it is, that while so many actors have imitated Mr. E. Forrest *on* the stage, so few have imitated his admirable example of sobriety and economy, in private life. Mr. A. Adams, his only successful rival, would have possessed a fortune equal to the great tragedian, had his conduct off the stage been marked by the same correct demeanour.

> "Alas! that a man should put an enemy
> Within his mouth, to steal away his brains."—SHAKSPEARE.

One of those outrages upon public decency, too common in the minor theatres of London, but which had hitherto never been attempted in America, was perpetrated at the Walnut-Street Theatre, in the production of a piece under the title of the "Mail Robbers," while Porter and Wilson were upon trial for their lives, for the commission of the crime of robbing the United States mail; both being found guilty and sentenced to be executed. Can anything be more revolting than making such a subject the theme of dramatic representation, while the victims were awaiting the penalty due to their crimes, among the community whose laws they had outraged. Surely this is a case in which the authorities of the city should have interfered, to prohibit such an exhibition; that they did *not* do so, is a lasting disgrace. The crime, however, did not go unpunished.

Mr. S. Chapman, the manager, having, with his artist, visited Turner's Lane, where the robbery was committed, to give an exact scenic view of the spot, contracted a violent cold, which terminated his existence on the 16th of May, 1830. By a singular fatality, his last appearance upon the stage was in the character intended to represent Porter, who was afterwards hanged. Poor Chapman! he was a man of varied talent, of much literary knowledge, and an universal favourite: with all his faults, the stage "could have better spared a better man." Had he lived, he would have produced an entire revolution in the minor drama of America; with his death, ceased the prosperity of the theatre; he is buried in Ronaldson's cemetery, where a neat monument records his memory, erected by friends he had gained during a sojourn of two years and eight months in the city of Philadelphia.

The death of Mr. Chapman proved the service that a well regulated theatrical fund must be to actors in distress. No sooner was it known, than a special meeting was summoned, and the following letter was addressed to his widow:—

(COPY.)

"Philadelphia, May 18, 1830.

" MY DEAR MADAME,—

" In deep condolence for your late bereavement, the members of the General Theatrical Fund respectfully tender their assistance, professionally, in aid of a benefit, should you feel disposed to avail yourself of their exertions. With best wishes for your prosperity, we remain

Your obedient servants,

(Signed,)   J. H. CLARKE,
FRAS. C. WEMYSS.

" J. T. FOOT, Secretary."

On the 26th of May, this benefit took place at the Walnut Street Theatre. The pieces selected, the "School for Scandal," and "High Life Below Stairs;" every member of the Fund affording their gratuitous services, thus placing five hundred dollars at the disposal of the widow.

Before the close of this calamitous season actors were to be seen walking the streets of Philadelphia, with their toes protruding from their shoes, their elbows from their coats; and their hats, which had once been black,—oh! name them not—

" ———— I had a hat,
Yet it was not all a hat:
The rim was gone.'
(Vide) Parody on Lord Byron's "Darkness."

Eagerly seizing the occasional chance of obtaining a dollar, for acting, as the substitute for one whose indisposition (to act without being paid—ha! ha! ha!) prevented their appearance; forcing the manager into an apology, which the audience knew to be untrue, and sneered at accordingly.

The last attempt in this scale of degradation, was the reduction of the price of admission to the boxes, to fifty cents, and the production of Calvin Edson, the living skeleton, as an actor. In the burletta of "Rochester," on 24th of June, 1830, he appeared as Jeremiah Thin; but even this failed to relieve the manager from any portion of the difficulty he laboured under: bad became worse, until the doors of the Chesnut Street Theatre closed for the season, under Mr. Pratt's management, with a bill of performance announced, which could not take place, because actors, musicians and carpenters, were worn out by hope delayed and broken promises, of—money tomorrow never came.

If matters fared thus badly with the performers of Old Drury, they were not much better at the other houses. Mr. Philips, after a disastrous season, attempted to open again; but closed for want of an audience, on the fourth night. The Walnut Street Theatre, whose chance of success ended with

the death of Samuel Chapman, lingered open to the last, closing with a load of debt which forced the managers to shelter
themselves under the benefit of the insolvent laws.

If the season of 1828 and 1829, saw the retirement of Wood,
Warren, Blake, (Ainslee,) Inslee, and Wemyss, 1829 and 1830
terminated the career of S. T. Pratt, A. J. Philips, Green,
Edmonds, and poor Sam Chapman; for their successors, I refer
you to the next chapter.

CHAPTER XXI.

Campaign of 1830 and 1831. Non-payment of Salaries. Charles Kean.
Master Burke. The Star System.—Rush-lights. Mademoiselle D'Jick,
the *great* actor. Tyke, in the "School of Reform."

THE campaign of 1830-'31, was opened on Saturday, the 28th
of August, by the Chapman family at the Walnut Street Theatre with the "Heir at Law," and "Love Laughs at Lock-
smiths." The company was really one of talent, and merited
a better fate than non-payment of salaries.

But *novelty, new faces, strange faces,* has ever been the cry
in Philadelphia when amusement is proposed, which desire is
no sooner complied with, than a wish succeeds for the faces
of their old favourites, whose absence is lamented when too
late, and comparisons instituted by no means favourable to
the new comers. It appears almost incredible, after the
misery of the spring and summer season of 1830, that any
capable actor should have been found hardy enough to venture upon management; yet all three of the theatres were
occupied, and ready for a fair start in this road to ruin.

The present season was marked by the appearance of the
smallest and the largest star that ever graced the same
theatre—Master Burke, the Lilliputian musician and actor,
and Mademoiselle D'Jick, the elephant of Siam, who both
appeared at the Arch Street Theatre, which opened on the
30th of August, under the management of Archer, Maywood
and Walton, with the "Bride of Lammermoor," and "Turn
Out;" Hyatt and Kilner being added to the names familiar to
the citizens of Philadelphia.

Davis, of the French opera, opened the Chesnut Street
Theatre for a short season.

Messrs. Lamb and Coyle made me an overture to enter into
partnership with them in the Chesnut Street Theatre, or to
take the stage management. I recommended Mr. W. B.
Wood for that situation, as I believed his name associated
with the theatre was most likely to command the support of

the fashionable circles in aid of the drama; but the revival of that taste, which appeared extinct, for theatrical representations, was reserved for the appearance of Miss Fanny Kemble, at a later period, of whom hereafter. I declined their offer, but accepted an engagement in the theatre, which opened on Monday, the 18th of October, with the "Heir at Law," the "Lottery Ticket," and the "Young Widow;" an address, written by W. C. Bridges, was spoken by me, of which I regret I did not preserve a copy. John Mills Brown and Mrs. C. Young were the only strangers of any reputation who possessed the charm of novelty, although the season commenced very prosperously.

The first announcement which excited attention, was the name of *Mr. Charles Kean*, (son of the great tragedian,) at the Arch Street Theatre, on the 23rd of September, to perform the part of Richard the Third. The house was well filled, and I took my seat in the boxes, with a feeling of regret that Mr. C. Kean had not selected the Chesnut Street Theatre to make his first appearance. Old recollections, and the warm friendship I entertained for his father, rendered me anxious for his success. I left the theatre with a feeling of disappointment, and a conviction that the mantle of the father had not descended upon the shoulders of the son. The performance was weak throughout, painfully reminding the auditor of his father's excellence, only to recal his own want of physical power to act such a part as Richard the Third; it was a failure which no subsequent effort could eradicate. And had Mr. C. Kean's pretensions to be ranked among the first actors of the British stage rested upon his *first* visit to the United States, his claim could not have been recognized; to his *name* alone was toleration conceded, added to which, he possessed a rival in the person of Mr. E. Forrest, a young man of his own age, rapidly rising in popularity with his countrymen, and between whom and himself comparisons were instituted on all occasions. It was, therefore, a fortunate circumstance for his reputation, that he paid the United States a second visit when his position as an actor was more definitively fixed, but he will never prove an attractive star. In the Atlantic cities he played Richard, Sir Giles Overreach, Shylock, Othello, Hamlet, and Reuben Glenroy. On the 14th of December,

MASTER BURKE,

the Irish Roscius, appeared for the first time in Philadelphia, at the Arch Street Theatre, in the character of Young Norval, in "Douglas," leading the overture of Guy Mannering, and playing Dr. O'Toole, in the "Irish Tutor." The house

presented any thing but a flattering appearance, the Phila-
delphinsa having no peculiar relish for precocity; but his
success was great, and the remainder of his engagement must
have amply compensated for any little mortification he may
have experienced on his first reception. The sweet tones of
his violin, and the graceful manner in which he handled his
bow, created a sensation in the musical world. He left the
city with his pocket well filled with dollars, and a reputation
which rendered it difficult to procure a seat in the boxes,
when he returned. [Against his acting I must be allowed
to enter a protest—it was so inferior to that of Clara Fisher
at a [much earlier age, it excited no astonishment, and
was tiresome to the audience, but to his musical abilities I
render a willing homage. He was a *prodigy*, deserving the
success which crowned his efforts.

A new tragedy, from the pen of David Paul Brown, Esq.,
a distinguished member of the Philadelphia bar, was produced at the Chesnut Street Theatre, on the 14th of December, 1830, entitled " Sertorius." Booth played the hero in a
manner which would have commanded success for any piece;
the beautiful poetry of this play, flowing from his lips must
have gratified the fastidious taste of any author—how, then,
must it have delighted the audience. The play wanted *action*
—there was too much declamation. It was received by a
fashionable audience with every mark of success, and repeated
several times, being withdrawn only by the termination of
Mr. Booth's engagement—another of the blessings of the star
system entailed upon managers, who are thus prevented from
reaping the harvest of their exertions, even from a successful
play, the engagement of the *star* elsewhere precluding the
possibility of prolonging an engagement.

Richard Penn Smith also produced a new piece, for Christmas Night, founded on Cooper's novel of the Water Witch, in
which I had to play Tom Tiller. Mr. Young, for whom the
part was originally compiled, returning it to the managers at
the eleventh hour, as too long, he being utterly unable to
commit the words to memory. My faculty, in that respect,
being notorious throughout the profession, it was useless to
say I *could* not do it, and I was unwilling to say I *would* not ;
but after labouring successfully at my task, I could not conceal my mortification to find I was the only person in the
piece conversant with the language of the author. Instead of
receiving help from those who had less to learn, I was obliged
to prompt others, and bear the whole burthen of a three act
melo-drama on my own shoulders. It was a fortunate circumstance that the holiday folks who composed our audience
were too noisy to observe our delinquency, or the piece would

have met a different fate. It passed off with *eclat*, and then passed on to the managers' shelves.

On the 8th of January, Charles Kean commenced an engagement at the Chesnut Street Theatre, but the error he had committed in not choosing it as his first ground, was not to be repaired. His houses were worse than he attracted at the Arch Street Theatre. Throughout this season, the stars were continually running from one house to the other; so that, as Jack Falstaff has it, "*you knew not where to have them.*"

Mr. E. Forrest, after playing at the Arch Street Theatre, also came for a few nights to the Chesnut Street Theatre; so also Madam Fearon, Hackett, Finn, Mrs. Austin, and others.

On the 10th of January, 1831, I revived, for my benefit, the good old comedy of the "Suspicious Husband," and a new piece entitled "Free and Easy," heading my play-bill thus:

No Stars,
But a host of approved Rush-lights.

Wood,	Wemyss,
Roberts,	J. M. Brown,
Young,	Green,
Mrs. Darley,	Mrs. Wood,
Mrs. Young,	Mrs. Willis,
Miss Kerr,	Mrs. F. Durang.

Rushlights! Most of them better stars than those who grace the play-bills nightly, with their names in large letters, in *these* degenerate times. The play was judiciously chosen, well acted, and presented to a fashionable audience, but the manager pocketed the proceeds, kindly allowing me to call upon my friends to make up the deficiency, by taking a second benefit. This was the first time I ever knew the proceeds of an actor's benefit to remain unpaid; it had always been considered a trust, sacred in the hands of the manager. Misfortune may render a man unable to meet his payments of weekly salary, but to refuse to pay over the proceeds of an actor's benefit, is a crime, a breach of trust of the blackest kind, seldom practised by the most unprincipled manager.

On the 5th of April, I appeared at the Walnut Street Theatre, in the character of Tyke, in the "School of Reform," which I had promised to act, to oblige a very worthy friend of mine, (whose name I do not feel authorised to mention,) to whom I once stated I thought I could play the part.

Before the curtain rose, I would willingly have paid fifty dollars to have escaped the effect of my folly, in making a rash promise. Fancy a light comedian, held in high estimation by the audience of the Chesnut Street Theatre, attempting to perform the most difficult part in the range of domestic tragedy, requiring a broad Yorkshire dialect to afford even a chance of success. By one of those freaks, which frequently make or mar an actor, I was successful, beyond my most sanguine expectations.

The difficulty of the task ensured my triumph : the audience expected, and came prepared, to witness a failure ; but when the curtain fell on the second act, the applause was so hearty that I felt I was sure of success. When I appeared again, I was greeted by three distinct rounds of applause, and was offered, at the close of the performance, one hundred dollars to repeat the character on the following Saturday night.

So much was said out of the theatre about this performance, that when I was in treaty with Maywood and company, Rowbotham made a positive stipulation, that I should open in Tyke, which I agreed to do, on condition that he gave me a Saturday night at the Walnut Street Theatre for my benefit, and should not ask me to repeat the part.

My second attempt was by no means so successful as my first ; six weeks had elapsed, during which time all my theatrical friends had been urging me to turn my attention to what are termed the "Heavy Countrymen," of which Tyke is the best specimen. The audience expected too much, and were disappointed. In the first instance they were agreeably surprised, and in the second, proportionately disappointed, although they warmly applauded the effort. Three times in the course of my theatrical career, I have received the marked approbation of the audience, for acting parts totally dissimilar to my usual cast of characters, and from which I expected to reap anything else than reputation. *Dr. Cantwell,* in the "Hypocrite," *Tyke,* in the "School of Reform," and *Old Nelson,* in "Jonathan Bradford," will ever be remembered by me, as characters which proved to the audience I was capable of affording them amusement in a more varied line of the drama, if I chose to turn my attention to them.

The seventh of May, 1831, is deserving of record, as being the day which gave birth to the firm of Maywood & Co., the only management assuming anything like stability since the days of Warren and Wood ; they opened the Walnut Street Theatre with the "Foundling of the Forest," and the "Sleep Walker," remaining open until the 31st day of July, at which time they obtained possession of the Chesnut Street Theatre also.

CHAPTER XXII.

New Management: Stars announced. Forrest and the Gladiator.
Warren's last appearance as an Actor.

THE season of 1831—32, was opened by Maywood and Co., on
Saturday, the 27th day of August, at the Walnut Street
Theatre, with the melo-drama of the "Heart of Mid-Lothian,"
and the farce of "Raising the Wind," in which I personated
Jeremy Diddler.

On the Monday following, Messrs. Jones, Duffy, and Forrest,
opened the Arch Street Theatre, with Sheridan's comedy of
"The Rivals," and "Black-Eyed Susan."

On the 17th of October, the Chesnut Street Theatre once
more opened its doors for the season, announcing as stars engaged, Mr. Sinclair, Miss Hughes, Master Burke, Mr. C. Kean,
Mr. Anderson, Madame Bartalozzi, Mr. Finn, Mr. Hackett,
Mrs. Barrymore, Miss Clara Fisher, and Mr. Booth.

They say the first blow is half the battle: but should that
blow fail, what becomes of the aggressor? The first star presented to the public was

Mr. SINCLAIR

who was announced to play Francis Osbaldistone, in "Rob
Roy," on the 17th of October. As a singer, he was once the
pride of the London stage; the successful rival of Braham,
whose triumph in English music, in conjunction with Miss
Stephens (the Countess of Essex,) in "Guy Mannering" and
"Rob Roy," form the subject of many a pleasing reminiscence
in the musical world. Thirty nights was announced as the
utmost limit to which his present visit to the United States
could possibly extend, (at least so said the play-bills, which,
like the newspapers, *never lie*). The prices of admission were
raised to the old standard, and public expectation wrought
up to the highest pitch. This unnatural excitement proved
the grave of his reputation: he fell a victim to his own fame.
The wreck of his former self, he was called upon to realize
the most extravagant expectations, and failed most lament-
ably, sealing the fate of the Chesnut Street season, whose
prospects appeared so brilliant. His voice had fled; in vain
the managers endeavoured through the columns of the newspapers, to persuade the public he sung as well as ever he did
—the man was there, 'tis true, but the voice, which could
keep a crowded theatre in breathless silence to hear, "*Pray,
Goody, please to moderate,*" was gone; his climacteric was

passed, and he was rapidly descending to that position, where
managers become fertile in framing excuses to avoid entering
into engagements which they knew must fail.   It is a
source of regret to the admirers of Mr. Sinclair—"and their
name is *legion*,"—that he did not retire when he could have
done so with eclât.   His visit to the United States was injudicious; he must have been aware that his powers were impaired, if not entirely lost, and that no recollection of what
he had been could be brought forward to shield him before
the audience of the New World, where he presented himself
as a candidate for public approbation, relying upon the force
of his reputation for a favourable reception, furnishing another proof of the tenacity with which public performers
cling to that applause they have been accustomed to receive,
until sounds of an opposite nature awake them to the unpleasant truth, that their attraction is gone, fled like a dream,
never to return.

I have heard Mr. Sinclair sing, when admiring crowds
could scarce obtain admission within the spacious walls of
Covent Garden Theatre; when his name was sufficient to fill
a concert room to overflowing, and his ballads the theme of
praise on every tongue; but I should never have recognized
the gentleman who appeared this evening as Francis Osbal-
diston, as the John Sinclair, claimed as the Scottish Minstrel,
and the King of Song.

The failure of this, their first star, and the greatest name
they could offer, had a most sinister effect on the future prospects of the managers during the season.

Messrs. Jones, Duffey, and Forrest were active and enterprising opponents, watching to take advantage of every false
move their adversaries might make.   Mr. E. Forrest played
"Metamora" on the same evening at the Arch Street Theatre,
which terminated so fatally for the treasury of the Chesnut
Street, and on the following Monday they produced Dr. Bird's
tragedy of the "Gladiator," (24th of October).   The reception
it met with was enthusiastic, and notwithstanding the opinion
of the London critics to the contrary, its success was well
deserved.   As a first attempt at dramatic composition, it reflected honour on its author.   Accustomed as an actor is to
striking scenes, I was taken by surprise, at the effect produced
at the closing of the second act, the rising of the Gladiators
in the arena, and the disposition of the characters as the act
drop fell, I do not believe was ever surpassed in any theatre
in the world.

But the author committed a blunder in composition : unless
he was prepared with something more vigorous, he should
have ended his plot here, instead of commencing it.   The
very excellence of the situation and action just depicted;

prepared you for something more startling yet to follow, while the third act, which immediately follows, is the worst act of the whole play, as if the author had exhausted himself in the commencement of his task; and instead of rising gradually to the point oi excellence he here acquired, he sinks below mediocrity, and, with the exception of the description of Phasarius and the death of Spartacus, he never again rises above it.

It would be superfluous to say one word on the subject of Mr. E. Forrest's performance of Spartacus: it was the perfection of melo-dramatic tragedy, to the excellence of which every frequenter of the theatres bears willing testimony. J. R. Scott merited the thanks of the author for his performance of Pharsarius, and the managers for the scenery and dresses. The play was produced in a style worthy of the reputation of the actor, by whose liberality it was presented to the public. It was repeated almost every night during Mr. E. Forrest's engagement, and retains its popularity undiminished to the present day (1843).

On the 14th of September, I had a misunderstanding with Maywood & Co., which led to my retirement from the Chesnut Street Theatre; the cause, an attempt to forfeit me one dollar, by the management, for having prevented (by the loss of a night's sleep,) the necessity of their changing the pieces announced for performance. Without the usual notice in the Green-room, but on the mere supposition that I had played the part, Mr. Rowbotham, the stage-manager, sent my name to the press for Mandeville, in the "Young Widow," not only a long but a difficult part; the first intimation I had of it was the printed bill, at half past ten o'clock, on the evening preceding. I told Rowbotham, at once, I would not do it. My unfortunate (*many might think it fortunate*) faculty of committing a given of number of words to memory in the shortest space of time, was too well known to the managers, who, after many kind phrases, and the "blarney" which usually proves successful with an actor, when a manager is anxious to coax him into a disagreeable thing, I agreed to attempt it, on condition that a rehearsal was called at one o'clock. The performance of the evening, in which I sustained a principal part, was not concluded until half-past twelve o'clock, when, with the prompt-book in my possession, I left the theatre, not to seek repose, but to read incessantly for three hours. By four o'clock, I had completed my task, and retired to bed, when in the morning I was summoned to attend a ten o'clock rehearsal. Notwithstanding this was a violation of terms on which I consented to study the character, it was my intention to have been there—accident alone prevented it. "*I fell asleep,* and did not awake until after eleven o'clock. Finding it impossible to be at the theatre in time to rehearse a piece, which does not occupy an hour in acting, I devoted the forenoon to reading the part attentively, and to my great satisfaction, found I was perfect. I told Rowbotham the reason of my absence, who laughed, and thanked me at the end of the performance, with the remark, that he did not know how the devil I got the words into my head. Having fulfilled my promise, I could scarcely expect punishment, where I was fairly entitled to remuneration for extra services; therefore, on Saturday, I was not only surprised, but indignant, to find a dollar retained from my salary, with the notice on a small piece of paper, explaining the cause, which read thus :—"Mr. Wemyss, one dollar, keeping the prompt book of the 'Young Widow,' from rehearsal." I refused to submit to this act of injustice; the managers seemed to treat it as a good joke; but I had not inclination to be joked out of my money. I made a formal demand for the restitution of the dollar, which being refused, I told them that I would commence a suit for its recovery, if it cost me twenty times the amount. I received a reply from Mr. Maywood, stating that the rules and regulations of the theatre were imperative, and binding upon all; that they would be enforced in every case, without reference to persons; that the money could not be returned; that I was at liberty to adopt any course I might think proper. I therefore, forthwith, issued a summons against Maywood, Rowbotham and Pratt, for the *enormous sum of one dollar,* unlawfully by them detained. Before the day fixed for the hearing before the magistrate, they cooled a little. Fearing to risk an exposure which must have proved most discreditable to them, they sent me the money, with the costs, to the magistrate's office, and contented themselves with addressing me a letter, stating my services would not be required in the theatre at the expiration of the present week. Nothing would have pleased me better than such an arrangement at the commencement of the quarrel, for I never could forgive the meanness of the act; but now, my character as an actor, and a man, required I should submit to no measure which could appear to place the managers in the right, and myself in the wrong, in a cause so oppressive and tyrannical. I refused to accept this discharge, as it was termed; but the breach of contract, it actually was; my engagement being for ten months, and not for one week—we tried this question also, which was decided in my favour, by arbitration. I returned to the theatre, on the 27th of October, after an absence of four weeks, during which, they had to pay me my stipulated income, for doing nothing; until their inability to pay their salaries, left me at liberty to turn the tables, and discharge them from being my masters, instead of their discharging me as their servant. The hostility thus engendered, continued in active operation for years. Considering Mr. Pratt had been my partner ; Mr. Maywood, the acting manager of the Baltimore and Washington Theatres, on my account; and Mr. Rowbotham was the stage manager of my creating, in the Chesnut Street Theatre, I was, even if in the wrong, from old associations, entitled to some little courtesy. But when, by express stipulation of engagement, I was exempted from attending more than one rehearsal of a new piece, and not bound to attend an old one at all, except at my own pleasure and convenience, I am at a loss to account for this transaction. It is true, Mr. Rowbotham said he had selected me as an example, that he might say to others—"Why, we forfeited Wemyss. How then can you expect to escape?" Good logic, this ; but applied to a bad subject, when he proposed to make me a victim to frighten others into the performance of their duty.

Early in November, I received from Warren the following letter, dated Baltimore :—

" DEAR WEMYSS :—

" What are you about—are you a Walnut Street play-actor, or a Chesnut Street play-actor, or no play-actor at all ? Do write, and let me hear the news. Do you think there is a possibility of my acting at either of the theatres in your city, during the present season ?

" Yours, very truly,

(Signed,) " WILLIAM WARREN."

I showed this letter to Mr. Maywood, and the result was an offer of an engagement at the Chesnut Street Theatre, the last he ever fulfilled, commencing with Falstaff, on the 19th of November, 1831, and terminating on the 25th of the same month, when, for his benefit, he appeared as Sir Robert Bramble, in the " Poor Gentleman." I played Frederick, and in the last scenes of the play it was evident that the old gentleman's memory was failing. In the beginning of the fifth act, he suddenly laid his hand upon my shoulder, and said, " Frank, lead me off the stage, for I do not know what I am talking about." He finished the part, committing blunder upon blunder, until it became evident to the audience, who kindly cheered the last moments of his public career with their long and continued approbation. He never acted again—and thus closed the theatrical life of William Warren, one of the greatest favourites, both as a man and an actor, the Philadelphia stage ever possessed. As a manager, he long and ably directed the theatre in its brightest days; universally respected, his misfortunes in the latter part of his life, met with universal commiseration, but little assistance. He died in Baltimore, on Friday, October 19, 1832, aged 66 years, regretted by those friends who best knew his worth, and remembered by all, as the only representative of Shakspeare's inimitable Sir John Falstaff. The last time his name was announced, was at the Arch Street Theatre, on the 8th of December, when he intended to take leave of the audience in an address, in the character of Falstaff. He was too ill to appear, and I regret to state the amount of the house for his last benefit, was a disgrace to the frequenters of the theatre— leaving him, in sickness, to regret he had suffered his name to be announced, and that his friends, in the hour of his utmost need, had entirely deserted him.

Miss CLIFTON

appeared as Lady Macbeth, on the 10th of December. She failed to excite the slightest attention, possessing no requisite for an actress but personal appearance, and deserving only of notice, as the first lady belonging to the American stage, who was born in the United States, and put forth pretensions to be considered a star. Her first benefit in Philadelphia, took place at the Chesnut Street Theatre, and (with the exception of Madame Heloise) was the worst house ever seen upon such an occasion, within the walls. The performance was " Bertram," and the " Lottery Ticket;" Hamblin playing Bertram to her Imogene. It is an ungracious task, to speak of any lady in other terms than those of praise, therefore I must be excused from entering into any further discussion, upon Miss Clifton's merits as an actress. She played Astarté, in London, in Lord Byron's "Manfred;" and lattely supports Mr. Forrest during his star engagements; but owes her position entirely to the system of newspaper puffing, so fatal to the real interests of the drama.

On the 17th of January, 1832, R. T. Conrad produced a five act tragedy of some merit, for Mr. Murdoch's benefit, under the title of " Conrad of Naples," at the Arch Street Theatre. Murdoch as the hero, acquired a goodly share of reputation, and certainly acted this part better than J. R. Scott, who afterwards attempted it.

I must not forget to mention a row which took place on the 17th of December, at the Walnut Street Theatre, in conse- quence of Mr. Hamblin breaking down in the character of Richard the Third, his old enemy, the asthma, preventing him from proceeding beyond the third act. An apology was made to the audience, who quietly sat out the new piece of " The Evil Eye;" but when the curtain rose upon the farce of " Raising the Wind," in which I had to perform Jeremy Diddler, the audience gave strong proof of their determination to see the last two acts of " Richard the Third." From the violent disapprobation, I ventured to expostulate with Mr. Rowbotham upon the folly of attempting to proceed; but he asked me if I was afraid—I said " No; but the ladies are." "Go on !" said he. " Up with the curtain," said I. But no sooner had we commenced the second act, and the determination of the management to proceed in spite of opposition became manifest to the audience, than some gentleman blackguard, (aside) threw a large piece of plaster, extracted from the roof of the pit passage, with some force upon the stage. It fell at the feet of Mrs. Charles Green, who was acting Peggy, and whose face miraculously escaped the contact. Her husband, who was on the stage, representing the character of Old Plainway, in an instant seized the offending missile, and hurled it back upon the audience with the emphatic phrase, that the man that threw it, was a blackguard and a coward. A general row ensued, in which stoves were overturned, hot coals distributed, and the melee ended by leaving actors and audience in the dark, the lights being rapidly extinguished. How many black eyes, and how many useless threats were uttered I stop not to detail. That Mr. Green was wrong in throwing a handful of rubbish among the audience, is not the question. He was undoubtedly right, in protecting his wife from insult; and his noble expression, that he cared for no danger; he only wished to be placed before the scoundrel who threw the plaster, or any one who would justify him ; and as far as strength remained, he would protect a woman against the whole assembled crowd, one after the other, gained him a host of friends, and saved the manager much future annoyance form his ill-judged perseverance.

Miss Hughes appeared at the Chesnut Street Theatre, as a vocalist : her success was not equal to her merit. Blanchard, one of the glories of the British stage, in its best days, also appeared on the 23rd of January, at the Chesnut Street Theatre, which was now opened ; one company doing double duty, playing at both theatres on the same night ; very amusing to the actors, not unprofitable to the managers, but decidedly deprecated by the audience, who could not discover why an actor, passing from the corner of Ninth and Walnut Street, to Sixth and Chesnut Street, should be worth double the price of admission, in a farce, which they had paid to see him in a full play, in the early part of the evening.

Blanchard opened as Don Lewis, in " Love makes a Man." To say that it was an excellent piece of acting, would only be to reiterate what every body, conversant with the stage, has already said; but it wanted actors of the same school, now, I am sorry to say, fast fading from existence in the counterparts.

The play is obsolete to the present generation; and Mr. Blanchard's failure to attract was owing to no want of merit on his part, but a want of judgment to appreciate such acting by the audience, who prefer "Napoleon," "Zanthe," or any dramatic representation, where the eye can be gratified, to smart dialogue and repartee, which form the essence of comedy. By the old authors, therefore, Monsieur Gouffe, with his imitation of the Monkey tribe, would fill the theatre, while an effort "to raise the genius, and to mend the heart," would fail.

The 18th of February, 1832, should be marked in the dramatic calendar with "a white stone," having introduced a young lady of superior talent, in the person of

Miss VINCENT,

who made her first appearance on any stage, at the Arch Street Theatre, in the character of Clari, taking not only the audience, but the actors, by surprise, who, while congratulating her upon her merited success, felt that the profession had acquired a gem of talent of the highest order. To Mr. Hamblin the public were indebted for the introduction of this young lady, whose short but brilliant career forms an epoch in the history of the American stage. From the night of her debut, she rose in favour with the audience, who felt justly proud of their countrywoman; until the citizens of New York and Boston, confirming the opinion of the critics of Philadelphia, placed her, by unanimous consent, at the head of the arduous profession she had chosen. Had her life been spared, she would have created in London as great a sensation in the dramatic world, as did Miss Fanny Kemble in the United States, or Madame Rachel in France. Her person was small; her features not remarkable for beauty, yet bore the stamp of intellect, which, when lighted up by the enthusiasm of her assumed character, captivated the hearts of the audience. She died before her reputation had reached its zenith, lamented by all who knew her, occupying without a rival the proud station of the first actress in America.

It is singular, that while female talent, (previous to the appearance of Miss Fanny Kemble,) was at the lowest ebb upon the London stage, the native actresses of the United States should have presented a galaxy of talent, in the persons of Miss Vincent, Miss Ann Waring, Mrs. Richardson, (Miss E. Jefferson,) Mrs. Willis, (late Miss Warren,) all the Placide family, Miss Pelby, (Mrs. Anderson,) Mrs. Kent, Miss Mary Duff, Miss Riddle, Mrs. Flynn, and others. Had the managers of the London Theatres been aware of its existence, many would have been translated to the great metropolis, as attrac-

tions of rare value. I have been surprised that Mr. Price'
while furnishing the American stage with European talent'
did not attempt the task for which he was so well qualified, of
introducing some of these young ladies to a London audience.
The speculation would have been a profitable one, for talent of
the highest order in England is always sure to command
success.

The season of 1831 and 1832, was also marked by another
addition of value, in

MR. G. H. HILL,

better known as Yankee Hill, who, from a very humble position in the Arch Street Theatre, in which he was frequently
insulted by the derision and disapprobation of the audience,
suddenly became a *star*, and what is more extraordinary, a
good one too. Discharged in disgrace from his situation, for
refusing to assist as a courtier, in the coronation scene of the
" Exile," glad to escape from an audience who ridiculed him,
desperate in his circumstances, and reckless of consequences,
he applied to Mr. Simpson, of the Park Theatre, New
York, for permission to attempt a Yankee character. His
success at once enabled him to enter the lists, as a star,
to share the praise already bestowed upon Hackett in this
new species of dramatic character. Making the best of his
time during Hackett's absence in England, he proved a formidable rival to that gentleman, on his return, beating him on
his own ground, in the very characters of his own creating.

There is a quiet, natural manner in his acting the " Down
East Yankee," which takes possession of the risible faculties
of his audience, giving them full employment during the time
he continues on the stage. He is the best representative of
what may be styled American comedy. His success in London
was a just compliment to his talent. The stage is indebted to
him for the possession of several good acting pieces, written to
display his peculiarities. He proved for many seasons one of
the most attractive stars, until forgetting what he had been,
in what he was, he aimed at an unenviable notoriety out of his
profession, which has materially injured his prospects of
future success. Had Mr. Hill been a man of education, he
would have supported himself with credit in the position he
had suddenly reached. Having boldly breasted a storm, which
threatened to annihilate his claims as an actor, and triumphed
over it, an overweening vanity has proved more detrimental
to his fame, than all the artifices of his enemies could ever
have accomplished.

What an agreeable thing it is for a manager to be compelled,
against his will, to retain an actor, and what a pleasant life the

actor leads during the period ! Every day I experienced some
annoyance, of which I could make no formal complaint, but
which I knew was done with an intention to promote misunderstanding. Mrs. Knight being engaged at the Chesnut
Street Theatre, wished to open in Kate O'Brien; knowing I
was a member of the company, and remembering the manner
in which this piece was received on its first representation,
naturally wished me to act Charles Paragon. I had caught
a severe cold, which, affecting my throat, compelled me to
remain in the house, when I received a letter from Mr.
Maywood, requesting I would make an effort to come out
upon the present occasion. I replied that I would do so, on
condition I was not requested to act any other part on that
evening, as I did not feel sufficiently recovered to resume my
duty in the theatre. With this understanding, I suffered my
name to be announced. Mr. Booth having arrived unexpectedly, "Hamlet" was announced for the play, in which I had
usually acted Ostric. Much to my mortification, I found my
name in the play-bill, but was assured by Mr. Rowbotham, the
stage-manager, it was a mistake, and that Mr. Mercer would
act the part. I was not even called upon to rehearse it, and
certainly should not have consented to stand upon the stage,
an inactive spectator, for half an hour, with a bare neck and
an ulcerated sore throat. But so good an opportunity to mor-
tify me was not to be lost. At the end of the third act of the
tragedy, Mr. Maywood came to me to know whether I intended
to play Ostric; I replied decidedly not; when Mr. Rowbotham
appealed to the audience to be suffered to omit the second
scene of the fifth act, in consequence of my indisposition. I
was not even aware that such a request had been made,
until when discovered as Charles Paragon, I was astonished
to hear a few sharp hisses, perfectly unconscious that they
were directed towards me, until after the scene was finished,
when I was informed of what had taken place. I wasted no
words, but sent a card to the newspapers the following morning, in explanation, stating the fault was with the management, not the actor; that the whole part was not forty lines,
and that any actor could have easily committed them to
memory during the fourth act of the play; that Maywood &
Co. were in possession of the knowledge that I would not do
it, early in the morning; that I regretted the interruption
which had taken place, but that I was certainly not the offending party, having left the sick chamber to aid the management, which had endeavoured to represent me in a most
offensive position before the audience; that the Chesnut
Street Theatre must indeed be reduced in respectability, when
such a request, as to omit a scene with such an actor as Mr.
Booth, was resorted to, to gratify a petty spirit of revenge

upon an actor. This, however, was the last scene of the contest. I agreed to cancel my engagement, receiving my benefit on the 10th of February, on which occasion I revived Goldsmith's comedy of the "Good-natured Man," and left the Chesnut Street Theatre, after ten years' service.

On the 14th of March, I entered into an engagement with Duffy, Jones, and Forrest, for a few nights at the Arch Street Theatre, opening in Roderigo, in "Othello," and Delaval, in "Matrimony," in which Miss Mary Duff was the Clara. It was during this short engagement as a *star in the city of Phila-delphia—g-o-o-d gra-ci-o-u-s!*—that I had the pleasure of acting Count Valentia, in the "Child of Nature," for the benefit of Miss Vincent, who represented Aramanthis with all that simplicity which had already won the hearts of the audience.

Early in the month 'of April, I paid a flying visit to Albany for twelve nights, where I made my bow as Charles Paragon, in "Perfection," Mrs. Knight being the Kate O'Brien. Mr. E. Forrest, Mrs. Pelby and Miss Pelby, were also there, playing on the same nights, so that if the citizens of Albany did not visit the theatre, it was not for want of attraction.

As the English tragedian Kean, was driven from the American stage, for refusing to act Richard the Third in Boston to a *handful* of spectators, I was surprised that the American tragedian, E. Forrest, ventured to dismiss an audience, whose paucity in numbers he did not choose should interfere with his desire to witness a little *fun* at the circus, where the "Greek," a well-known billiard-marker in the city, was advertised to play Richard the Third. The theatre being closed, the manager, Mr. Forrest, and myself repaired to the circus, without a comment from the disappointed few, who laughed at it as a 'good practical joke on a rainy night.

" That such a difference there should be,
Between tweedle dum and tweedle dee."

The fortnight I spent in Albany was delightful recreation, parties of pleasure being formed to Troy, the Shaker Settlement, and other places of interest in the immediate neighbourhood, every day after rehearsal ; and although I did not return to Philadelphia much richer, I was gratified with the hospitality displayed towards me by the Albanians, and look back with pleasure on my short visit to their city.

On my return, I became regularly attached to the Arch Street company. The season closed on the 18th of June, when, for the first time for several years, the actors were regularly paid, all demands honourably settled, and Messrs. Duffy, Jones and Forrest in high credit both within and without the walls of the theatre. It was at the Arch Street

Theatre that Sheridan Knowles' play of the "Hunchback" was first acted in the United States, J. R. Scott being the Master Walter, and Miss Riddle the Julia; the play was as well, if not better acted, as a whole, than I remember to have seen it since, although "the *Julia*" had not yet given to it the stamp of fashion, which crowded every Theatre in the United States when Miss Fanny Kemble was announced to act the part.

It was in 1832 that the Anderson Row took place at the Park Theatre, New York, where the worthy citizens made the unwonted call for Mr. Price, that they might hiss him. What the exact nature of Mr. Anderson's offence was, has never been ascertained by the profession; so many rumours have been afloat, that I should be afraid to assign a cause. It is sufficient to record the fact, that he was not permitted to act in the United States—rather a heavy sentence for a private quarrel. But his behaviour was not calculated to conciliate, but rather to irritate his opponents. He paid the penalty of his folly and rashness. The audience lost the opportunity of hearing a clever singer, and he returned to London, to rail against America and its democratic institutions, on all occasions, for the remainder of his life, and then to be forgotten.

It was in the summer of 1832, that

MR. THOMAS RICE,

better known as Jim Crow, made his appearance at the Walnut-Street Theatre.

" Did you ne'er hear of a jolly black diamond?"—*Tom and Jerry.*

This gentleman, whose representation of the character of a negro raised him to affluence, made his first appearance in Philadelphia in the summer of 1832, at the Walnut Street Theatre. The roars of laughter with which his extravaganza of Jim Crow (the original of which was a negro of Pittsburgh, known as Jim Cuff,) was received, his excellent acting as well as singing, soon induced offers from managers, which filled *his* pockets and *their* treasury. He was for a time the " *lion*" of the minor theatres. With an innate tact for business, he improved the opportunity his popularity afforded, by collecting all the really beautiful airs which the negro sings while performing his daily labour, and writing himself the " libretto," to introduce a novel species of entertainment, with the imposing title of Ethiopian opera. His " Bone Squash" was an amusing affair, the music truly delightful, and ably executed. The " Virginny Cupids," although vulgar even to grossness, met a good reception. With this capital, Mr. Rice crossed the

Atlantic, and turned the heads of the chimney sweeps and apprentice boys of London, who wheeled about and turned about and jumped Jim Crow, from morning until night, to the annoyance of their masters, but the great delight of the cockneys. That his financial affairs have been improved by the trip there is little doubt, but his popularity in his native country has been lost, by his endeavour to ingraft the English dandy with the American negro.

In London, where a black man is scarcely seen, it might be remarkably "*funny*," but the broad caricature of the American negro was the attraction of Jim Crow at home, who, when converted into an English gentleman, was a most insipid creature. As an actor, Mr. Rice's reputation depends upon his black face; and how he contrives to keep it white, might be matter of grave debate, begrimmed as it has been for the last ten years, at least three hours in each of the twenty-four.

In private society, Jim Crow is a "*first-rate*" companion: full of anecdote, possessed of vocal abilities, and agreeable in conversation, he makes a valuable member of any social club.

I have paid him many hundred dollars, during my management, and am proud to say, in business he is both just and liberal, never attempting to squeeze the last dollar from a manager with whom he may have contracted an engagement which proved a losing speculation. His practice on such occasions having generally been voluntarily to resign a portion of his right, by good humouredly observing, in his negro slang :—Lookye here, my master, this has been a bad job—I don't think you ought to suffer to this tune; live and let live is a good motto—hand over——, and I will give you a receipt in full, and wish you better luck another time." The few dollars remitted, unasked, in this manner, have been repaid, with interest, by engagements when he was not actually wanted, but always cheerfully received by those managers who knew how to appreciate an act of kindness cleverly proffered, and when accepted never forgotten.

He played in " Whirligig Hall," for the managers' benefit, on the 28th of July, closing the season of the Walnut Street Theatre with eclat, the last of distinction, to managers and actors, for many years. The fall of 1832 witnessed the general revival of the drama throughout the United States, by the arrival of Mr. Charles Kemble and his daughter, and a succession of stars, of more than common brilliance, from England.

As a specimen of the distress which actors endured during these three years, I give a copy of a letter written by one of the oldest, as well as respectable members of the profession. The name I withhold, in respect to his feelings.

(Directed,) To MR. WEMYSS, present.

" SIR :—I am in a state of mental agony, debating whether I shall
" play the Roman," or " nobly live and see my family starve." Do, for
Heaven's sake, render me a *small* pecuniary assistance, *any* you think
proper—we are destitute. By so doing you will greatly oblige your old
friend."

I need scarcely add the letter produced the desired effect,
and the gentleman, when I last saw him, was as hearty and
good humoured as if he had never known an hour's distress.

CHAPTER XXIV.

Commencement of the Season of 1832—33. Rivalry between the Arch and
Walnut Street Theatres. Mr. and Miss Kemble. Dr. Bird's Tragedy
of " Oraloosa." Disagreeable Accident. Mr. Kemble's Acting in different Characters. Death of Mr. Warren. Treatment of his Family
by the Managers of the Chesnut Street Theatre. Statement of Facts.
Building of a Theatre in Pittsburgh. Offer of its Management. Tragedies by Dr. Ware and Jonas B. Philips. Fanny Kemble and her
Journal.

I now approach the period of a revival, when actors were no
longer to be seen lounging about without employment, but
when really clever actors were eagerly sought for. Jones,
Duffy and Forrest had contrived to pay their performers, with
regularity; Maywood & Co., by placing their actors on two-
thirds of their actual engagements, also received receipts in
full, and both parties commenced the season of 1832—33 with
every prospect of success. At the Chesnut Street they announced Mr. Charles Kemble, and Miss Kemble, Mr. Sinclair,
the Ravel family, James Wallack, Miss Vincent, Madam
Fearon, Mrs. Austin, as the stars; while at the Arch Street,
it was known Mr. E. Forrest was the chief attraction, Mr. and
Mrs. Hilson, J. R. Scott, Mr. Hill, Mr. C. Kean, Mr. Cooper,
presented a formidable array in opposition.

The campaign was commenced by the Arch Street managers,
on Wednesday, the 5th of September, 1832, with the comedy
of the " Poor Gentleman," and the farce of " How to Die for
Love." The company consisted of Mr. W. Forrest, Duffy,
Jones, Murdoch, Wemyss, J. R. Scott, D. Reed, H. Knight,
T. Placide, Horton, John Green, Thayer, James, Thompson,
and Howard; Mrs. Stickney, Miss Riddle, Mrs. Jones, Mrs.
H. Knight, Amelia Fisher, Mrs. J. Greene. On Saturday, the
8th, the Chesnut Street opened with Barrymore's military

spectacle of "Napoleon," and the farce of the "Lottery Ticket," in which Roberts—the true successor of Jefferson, and the only one.deserving of that title, until the arrival of W. E. Burton—played Wormwood. Thus the race was fairly commenced, each striving for ascendancy; the location of the Chesnut Street Theatre giving it the preference with strangers, because the Arch Street was difficult to be found, unless you left your home for the purpose of going there.

The first grand struggle took place on the 10th of October, when Mr. Charles Kemble made his first appearance in Philadelphia, in the character of Hamlet, at the Chesnut Street Theatre, and Mr. E. Forrest produced Dr. Bird's tragedy of "Oraloosa," at the Arch Street. With attraction so equally balanced, the town was fairly divided. Every body was anxious to see Mr. Kemble, whose reputation as an actor stood higher than that of any performer of the present day, while Dr. Bird's great success in the "Gladiator," ex. cited an no less degree of curiosity to witness his second at. tempt as a dramatic poet. The result of this exertion on the part of the management of both theatres, was full houses for a succession of nights, during the respective engagements of the Kembles and Mr. E. Forrest.

Dr. Bird's tragedy of "Oraloosa" did not increase his reputation. From the author of the "Gladiator" something better was anticipated; while the present play fell below the previous production of the doctor's muse. Neither plot, incident, or dialogue would bear comparison with his former self, while the same glaring error, of producing a climax at the end of the third act, by the death of Pizarro, in the banquet hall, beyond which he could not rise, was again committed. The audience were evidently disappointed, and Mr. E. Forrest judiciously struck it from the roll of his acting characters, after the first season, conscious it was unworthy the fame of the author, and would never produce anything but mortification to the actor.

To me the 10th of October, and the tragedy of "Oraloosa," form no pleasing remembrance, although they can never be forgotten—having caused me, in mimic fight, (too real for fancy,) the loss of two front teeth, which Mr. E. Forrest, in the furor of acting, displaced from their original stronghold in my mouth, by a thrust from his sword at the head of Don Christoval, occasioning some of the wags of the green-room an opportunity of making a bad pun, by declaring that Forrest wished to teach me the proper pronunciation of the name of the play, by forcing me to say to him, " *Oh-they-are-loose-sir !*" I confess, I could see little merit in this, but it served to

L

make a laugh at the time, and perhaps diverted an angry feeling from an awkward accident.

On the 12th of October, Miss Fanny Kemble appeared as Bianca, in "Fazio." Strange as it may appear, connected as I have been with the American stage for twenty years, I never met Mr. Charles Kemble, or his daughter, in the United States, either as actor or manager.

I never had the pleasure of seeing Miss Fanny Kemble on the stage but once, for a few minutes, in the second act of the "Hunchback," when, in anticipation of a treat of no ordinary nature, I was summoned by the call-boy of the Arch Street Theatre, to which I belonged, by the pleasing intelligence that an unexpected change of performance required my presence there immediately. I left the theatre in a very ill-humour, consequently am unable to offer an opinion upon the acting of the young lady. I therefore take it for granted she was a prodigy. That she revived the prostrate fortunes of the drama in the United States, admits not of a doubt; her popularity, and the name of Kemble, made the theatres once more a fashionable place of amusement.

I had long known Mr. Charles Kemble as the best representative of high comedy belonging to the British stage. He was acting at the Glasgow Theatre, in 1814, when I made my first appearance as an actor. I received from him, at that period, much good advice, which, like all advice offered upon the same subject, was disregarded. But no one who was ever devoted to his profession, can hear the name of Kemble, without pointing to it with a feeling of pride, to prove that the profession of an actor is not incompatible with the bearing and manners of a gentleman. The society of "the Kembles" has been courted by all classes, and their fame is interwoven with the history of the stage for upwards of half a century.

As an actor, Mr. Kemble enjoys a popularity that may well be envied. If I were asked to designate the most finished piece of comedy acting I ever witnessed, I should say the Lovemore of Mr. C. Kemble, in "The Way to Keep Him." There was such an exquisite ease about it, which divested the mind of the idea of acting, and presented the reality—you forgot Mr. C. Kemble, and saw only before you the heartless man of fashion he represented. Here he was without a rival, but like all—(managers, shall I say, or)—actors, vanity induced him to attempt Macbeth, Hamlet, and Richard the Third, recalling the excellence of his brother, (John Kemble,) in those parts; producing a feeling of disappointment, that one so perfect in his own walk of the drama should render himself almost ridiculous, by attempting the hero of tragedy, beyond his grasp. In Romeo, Heeneya, or Lord Hastings, he is equally at home as in comedy; but beyond that, in tragedy, he should never attempt to soar, and whenever he does, failure is sure to follow.

When he arrived in the United States, he perhaps did wisely to act as a foil to his daughter's excellence, but, with his Benedict, Mercutio, and Young Mirabel fresh in my re-collection, I experienced a feeling of regret that he should have placed himself before the audience in such a situation as to detract from the high position he justly holds as a finished comedian. The delight with which his performance of Mer-cutio, on the 3d of November, was hailed, and the change of opinion it immediately produced in the minds of his audience, as to his ability as an actor, must have proved to him that the Philadelphians knew how to appreciate what was really excel-lent. It was the theme of conversation throughout the city: "Did you see Kemble last night?—you lost a treat! I never saw Mercutio acted before!—hope he will repeat it." This was enthusiasm, compared with the faint praise reluctantly yielded to his Sir Thomas Clifford, and the downright abuse bestowed upon his Hamlet.

On the 19th of October, we received the intelligence of the death of poor Warren. Duffy, Jones, and Forrest, always fore-most in deeds of charity, at once offered the theatre for a bene-fit to the widow and family, which took place on the 27th, Booth playing Old Norval, to the Young Norval of William Warren, who made his first appearance upon the stage on the occasion. The conduct of the managers of the Chesnut Street Theatre was of a widely different character towards the widow of the one who had directed the theatre in their possession, in its brightest days. Having in my possession a pamphlet, published at the time, I shall transcribe the whole as an act of duty, to the memory of one whom I called friend during life, and the recollection of one whose kindness can never be ef-faced. That the insolence of those in power, received no re-buke from the audience, is another proof of the ephemeral existence of an actor's popularity. Scarcely cold—and already forgotten,—farewell to thee, Warren.

TO THE PUBLIC—STATEMENT OF FACTS.

Having been advised by many of my late father's friends to withdraw my mother's name from before the public, on the occasion of a benefit an-nounced by the managers of the Chesnut Street Theatre, it becomes an imperious duty to show that public, before whom my lamented father was for upwards of thirty years an approved actor, the reasons which forced me to adopt my present course.

As soon as my father's death became known in Philadelphia, the mana-gers of the Arch Street Theatre, in compliance with a wish expressed through Mr. Booth, in the kindest manner appropriated an evening for the benefit of my mother; and in order to secure the aid of Mr. Booth, Saturday the 27th of October, was fixed upon. The result is well known. I arrived from Baltimore on the Thursday previous, and on the following evening, Mr. Rowbotham of the Chesnut Street Theatre, informed me that the managers intended to give a benefit at their house. This was thankfully accepted on my part, as it was voluntarily offered upon theirs. The success of Mr. Kemble and his daughter, suggested the idea of an application to the former gentleman, for his aid upon the occasion. Mr. Maywood the acting manager, approved of it, and advised me to do so. My surprise was, therefore great, on the receipt of Mr. Kemble's answer, which follows, to find that the managers had thrown an insurmountable obstacle in the way of my wishes; notwithstanding, it has since appeared that Mr. Kemble played two nights after the expiration of his engagement on Thursday, the first of November.

COPY OF A LETTER ADDRESSED TO MR. KEMBLE.

"October 29th, 1832.

"SIR :—It is with reluctance that I trespass upon your attention, personally unknown to you as I am; but my motive will, I trust, prove a better excuse than any other I could offer.

"My father, the late William Warren, with whom I believe you were once acquainted, after a series of misfortunes resulting in a total ruin, became through the failure of his health, incapable of assisting his family by his professional exertions. His distresses accelerated the work of time, and after a long and painful illness, he expired a few days since at Baltimore, leaving his family dependant upon the resources of those members of it, who in consequence of their youth and peculiar situation during the sickness of their father, are now in some degree unfitted for the task of suitably providing for them.

"The managers of the Arch Street Theatre, with the greatest kindness, devoted an evening—Saturday last—to their benefit; and the managers of the Chesnut Street Theatre have made a similiar offer; but unless backed by some strong attraction, I fear that it will not be essentially serviceable, and therefore, I have ventured to ask, if it be not incompatible with your engagements, that you, sir, will lend your powerful aid on the occasion.

"You will materially oblige me by leaving a line containing your decision, at the box office of the Chesnut Street Theatre.

"I am, Sir,
"Your's most respectfully,
(Signed) "WILLIAM WARREN."

COPY OF MR. KEMBLE'S ANSWER.

Mansion House, Oct. 30th, 1832.

"SIR :—I am favoured with your letter, and regret that circumstances should have made such an application necessary. On speaking with the manager of the Chesnut Street Theatre upon the subject, he informs me that it is his intention to appropriate a night for the benefit of your family; but that it cannot take place this week on account of previous arrangements. My engagement in New-York, will take me from Philadelphia in a few days, so that it will not be in my power to comply with your request. Hoping that the public will be more mindful of the pleasure which they have derived from the talents of your late father, than your letter seems to anticipate, and fill the house to overflowing, on the night devoted to his family,

" I am Sir, your obedient servant,

(Signed) "C. KEMBLE."

COPY OF MR. WARREN'S LETTER TO MAYWOOD & CO.

" Thursday Nov. 1st, 1832.

" GENTLEMEN :—As previous arrangements have prevented your devoting a night for my mother's benefit this week, I wish to know definitively, what night next week will be convenient to you, and the terms on which it is your intention I should take the house. The earliest night that your arrangements will permit you to dispose of, will be the most agreeable to me. Your answer early enough to afford an opportunity of advertising the result in the papers of to-morrow afternoon, will oblige,

" Your's respectfully,

(Signed) " WILLIAM WARREN."

This letter remains unanswered.

On Saturday, about noon, I waited upon Mr. Rowbotham, who verbally informed me the benefit would take place on Tuesday or Thursday, but which, he could not say. I then enquired the terms, to which, he gave me no satisfactory answer; but merely replied, " This is for *your* benefit, not *ours*, and you shan't lose anything by it." I saw Mr. R. again at the theatre in the evening, and he there told me that Tuesday was the night determined on. I asked what pieces, and he enquired whether I intended to play myself. I told him no; and he then said something about " The Good Natured Man." I told him I could not advise about the pieces, but to play any five act comedy which embraced the strength of the company. This was the last interview I had upon the subject. Although I wished my card to have appeared in the newspapers, of the city on Friday afternoon, their delay rendered it impossible to insert one before Monday, which would have been useless altogether. Thus I was completely ignorant of the entertainment selected, until the playbill appeared :—" Simpson & Co !"—", A Hornpipe ! !"—" The Peasant Boy! ! !" As the terms of the night were still unknown, it became obvious to all my friends, that the benefit was intended merely to produce the nightly charges to the managers, through the use of my mother's name.

A gentleman was deputed to wait upon Mr. Maywood, under these circumstances, and urge a a postponement, to which Mr. Maywood replied, such arrangement was impracticable ; and Mr. Pratt added as an objection that there would not be twenty dollars in the house.

Following the advice of my friends, I declined the benefit altogether. Mr. Maywood's opinion being—" That the pieces were as good as any thing that could be done." Mr. Rowbotham's—" That I was badly advised." Mr. Pratt's—" That I had no claim; but it was a matter of charity altogether."

(Signed) " WILLIAM WARREN."

November 7th.

N.B.—I made no application to the managers of the Chesnut Street Theatre; it was their own offer, and *accepted—not claimed—*by me.

Comment is unnecessary; but it is surprising that a feeling of public indignation at such wanton insult did not overwhelm the managers. They wisely attempted no explanation.

I copy the following compliment from the National Gazette :—

" TO MR. WARREN.

" Full many an actor have I seen,
Who ranted till his face was black.
But none, methinks, e'er trod the scene,
I liked so well as thee—Old Jack.

Let Thomas Cooper walk the stage,
Or Edmund Kean again come back,
To fret, and strut, and fume and rage ;
Thou'rt worth a thousand such—Old Jack.

Thy jokes are new, tho' often told,
Thy merry wit is never slack,
Thy sterling worth, like wine that's old,
Is better every year—Old Jack.

Then let me see thee once again
At Gadshill—swiftly fly the track,
And tell how many thou hast slain,
To keep thy credit up—Old Jack,

I wish to view thy waggish air,
To see thee drink thy fav'rite sack:
And, mug in hand, devoutly swear
Thou had'st not drunk to-day, Jack.

I wish to see thee slay the dead,
And gravely take him on thy back,
And swear that human valour's fled,
Or only lives in thee—Old Jack."   P. E. T.

A young musician, named Allen, produced quite a sensation at the Arch Street Theatre; playing on the violin a là Paganini, on one string. As a boy, he was quite clever, much applauded, but did not draw money; youthful prodigies rarely succeed. He was, however, deserving of success.

The Kembles having made quite a sensation in the fashionable circles of society, were not long absent from the city. They returned again on the 5th of December, after an absence of little more than four weeks. Charles Kean was engaged at the Arch Street Theatre as a counter attraction, and answered the purpose of the managers, if not his own.

It was during the month of January I received a letter from my friend, George A. Cooke, of Pittsburgh, requesting me to furnish him a plan for the building of a theatre, proposed to be erected in that city of smoke and industry : the management of which he wished me, when finished, to undertake, if I had nothing better in view. I was too glad to accept the proposition, and applied to Mr. Haviland, the architect, for assistance. From the plans furnished by him was erected what may justly be termed the model theatre of the United States—elegance and comfort being combined, both for the auditor and actor. Of this I shall have to speak more at large.

The course of true love never did run smooth ; and no actor ever attained the highest honours granted to his profession, that envy and malice did not attempt to wither "the bays" that encircle his brow.

After a career of success, which might truly be termed the Kemble mania, the divine Fanny was accused of having spoken disrespectfully of the Americans in their own capital, the city of Washington. Among other charges, the serious one of having said, the Americans did not know how to sit a horse correctly, and to maintain that the left, and not the right, should be the path the law ought to direct as the rule of the road. For this terrible crime of entertaining an opinion of her own, and daring to express it, she was to be doomed and called upon to give an account at the bar of public opinion assembled within the walls of the Walnut Street Theatre, where placards were distributed with the intention of proving, in this land of freedom, that a lady's tongue, from time immemorial her weapon of offence as well as defence, must be bridled, and not be permitted to wag in ridicule of any thing American.

CHAPTER XXV.

J. P. Wilkinson. Journey to the West. Beautiful Scenery. Fine Situation of Pittsburgh. Dramatic Festival. Opening of the Pittsburgh Theatre. Tyrone Power.

JONES, Duffy, and Forrest, at the close of the season, were presented by the actors, and others, with a silver cup, valued at one hundred dollars, for the honourable manner in which they had discharged all their obligations, since they undertook the management of the Arch Street Theatre. The cup was

presented by Morton M'Michael, Esq., in one of his happiest
speeches, and received by Mr. Jones, the senior partner, with
a suitable reply—nearly one hundred gentlemen being assembled on the stage, where an elegant cold collation was prepared; and the song and anecdote enlivened the company,
who dispersed about two o'clock, A. M., highly pleased with
the events of the evening.

On the 26th of March, my old friend,

J. P. WILKINSON,

made his first appearance in Philadelphia at the Walnut
Street Theatre, as Ephraim, in the "School for Prejudice,"
and Geoffrey Muffincap, in "Amateurs and Actors." Occupying, as he did, in London, with Arnold of the English opera
house, a high station among his contemporaries, for many
seasons, and being known as the original representative of
Dr. Logic, of universal renown, it would have been reasonable
to suppose a full house would have assembled on the occasion.
On the contrary, the meagre appearance of the audience was
sufficient to damp the energy of any actor. That Wilkinson
should have been so coldly received, and wholly neglected,
was a slur on the dramatic taste of the city. The character
of the Parish Charity Boy, so well understood in the British
metropolis, and so totally unknown in the United States, the
representation of which made Wilkinson the magnet of attraction for a whole season, in a London theatre, produced not
the slightest approbation. The feeling of the audience was
one of disappointment, which must have been mutual. If
they thought the actor dull and prosing, he must have thought
them cold and ungenerous. The dogged stupidity of the
Charity Boy, kicked and cuffed by every body in a London
lodging-house, was not appreciated by an audience ever ready
to laugh at the air and smartness of a Lissardo.

Wilkinson bore his disappointment like a philosopher,
giving proof of his judgment and good sense, by fulfilling all
his engagements, giving utterance to no complaints, and returning to his native country—to forget the folly which induced him to travel, as Murtoch Delany says, "to see foreign
parts"—to enjoy his reputation at home, in the bosom of a
happy family circle, of which he is not only the head, but the
pride—an honourable and an honest man.

On the 5th of July, 1833, I started for Pittsburgh, accompanied by my wife, my two youngest children, and their
nurse, wisely resolving not to abandon housekeeping in the
city of Philadelphia, or to remove my family, until I saw whether the prospects of success, so brightly painted, would be
realized.

A journey to the West, in 1833 was not what it is now—railroads were not so numerous. The whole 300 miles was performed in stages, without a single stoppage throughout the route, which was advertised to be performed in four days and a half.

We started rather in melancholy mood—shaking hands with one, nodding adieu to another, and kissing the tears from the cheeks of the children about to be separated for the first time from their parents—these thoughts occupied our minds for the first few miles. We had but two passengers, besides our own party, who left us at Lancaster, so that we were undisputed masters of the vehicle until we arrived at Carlisle, rendering the first night's journey very comfortable. At Chambersburgh, where the two routes from Philadelphia and Baltimore joined, we received an addition to our numbers, by no means pleasant, six grown persons and three children, increasing the party. Thus, with every seat occupied, containing nine passengers, and the addenda of five children, the remainder of the journey was to be performed. Thus crowded, we commenced the ascent of the mountains. Fortunately the weather was fair, and never shall I forget the grandeur and beauty of the scene which met my eye, as I reached the summit of the Cove Mountain. The amphitheatre of forest, with all its rich and varied foliage, the farms in the valley beneath, the village at the foot of the mountain, made us all forget every annoyance in exclamations of wonder and surprise—our fellow-travellers, like ourselves, crossing the mountains for the first time. The rapid descent, continuing for three miles, without interruption, alarmed the ladies, but delighted the children, and as darkness began to shadow the earth, at the close of the second day, the rain fell in torrents, continuing with slight intermission to the close of our journey, banishing the prospect of further comfort, and affording no opportunity of enjoying the mountain scenery as we progressed.

When we arrived at Bedford, we were detained two hours, a most seasonable relief to the ladies. We should have supped here, but being heavily laden, and four hours behind our time, every body had retired to rest, but those whose duty it was to attend to the stage, on its arrival. A glass of milk-punch, and a cracker was all that could be obtained in the way of refreshment; thankful for that, I was too old a traveller to render a disagreeable situation more irksome by the exhibition of bad temper, where I knew there was no remedy but endurance. Mrs. Wemyss, too, although much fatigued, laughed at every thing with that happy disposition which enabled her to convert present annoyance into food for amusement to the whole party, and suffocated as we all were, she declared that never in her life did she behold so beautiful a scene as the setting sun, in passing through Mount Pleasant.

On the morning of the fifth day, we entered the city of Pittsburgh, about seven o'clock, the rain descending rapidly, and giving to the Birmingham of America a desolate and dreary appearance, speaking any thing but welcome.

We drove to the Exchange Hotel, where the hospitality which we received at the hands of Mr. M'Guire, soon restored us to good humour. My friend, Mr. George Cook, was at the hotel before we had finished breakfast, and by 10 o'clock on the morning of the 10th of July, I found myself within the walls of the theatre destined to be the field of my future operations.

Here carpenters, painters and gilders were busily employed upon what appeared to be a shell, which would scarcely be ready by the first of September. The activity and business habits of the contractors, Messrs. Roseburgh, Scott, Reynolds and M'Cullough accomplished the task in the given time, to the surprise as well as gratification of the citizens of Pittsburgh.

Pittsburgh, at this period, was at the height of prosperity, resembling a beehive, where no drone is suffered to exist. The roaring of the furnaces, the clank of the hammer, were unceasingly heard, day and night, while the activity on the banks of the river, and of the canal, the constant train of drays laden with merchandise for the West, moving slowly along the streets, furnished a novel and pleasing sight—while the ringing of steamboat bells, and the roaring of the high pressure steam engines in the boats, as they arrived and departed, gave the best assurance of the prosperity of the city, and the business enterprise of its inhabitants.

No city in the United State is more romantically situated, or can boast of finer scenery in its immediate neighbourhood. Situated on the banks of the two rivers, the Monnogahela and Alleghany, whose junction at this point form the Ohio River, the City of the Three Rivers, clouded as it is in endless smoke from its factories, possesses advantages not often met with in a manufacturing town. A walk of a quarter of an hour in any direction places you above the smoke, so much complained of by strangers, and presents to the view landscapes in which the eye of an artist revels with delight, and shady retreats upon its hills, where, free from observation, they can wander, and ponder upon the endless source of wealth which the coal mines beneath their feet pour daily into this city of industry. And here it was I expected to take up my future residence.

Whoever is acquainted with the duties of a manager of a theatre, will know that during the last few weeks of building there is no time for the director to be idle. Six weeks had

flown over my head, when by the arrival of a few members of my company, I was made aware that the time approached for the opening of the theatre rapidly approached.
On Wednesday, the 21st of August, I received an invitation
from the directors of the theatre company, to meet them at
the Shakspeare House, to commemorate the completion of
their labours. I cannot give a better description of the
evening, than I find in The Statesman of the 28th of August,
headed :—

NEW THEATRE—DRAMATIC FESTIVAL.—On Wednesday evening, the directors of the Pittsburgh Theatre gave an excellent supper to Mr. Wemyss,
and the contractors, to celebrate the completion of one of the handsomest
buildings which the city of Pittsburgh ever boasted. At nine o'clock,
about sixty gentlemen sat down to supper, at the Shakspeare House,
provided in Mr. Wilson's best style. Harmony and good humour per-
vaded throughout; no one left the table but with a feeling of regret that
the hours had passed so rapidly, on an occasion devoted ' to the feast of
reason, and the flow of soul.' The company retired at a late (early) hour,
mutually pleased with each other's company. The following regular
toasts were given from the chair, on the occasion :—

THE DRAMA—Its agency in exerting a salutary influence is to be esti-
mated not by the standard of possibilities, but by that which is incorpor-
ated with its design.

WILLIAM SHAKSPEARE—The child of nature—he represents her as she is,
without often marring the chasteness of her colouring, or the simplicity of
her imagery.

THE CONTRACTORS OF THE NEW THEATRE—The skill and promptitude
which completed it, are in good keeping with the taste which furnished the
model.

THE WESTERN DRAMA—May it reflect the warmth of genuine feeling,
united with radiations of classic taste, upon the emporium of arts and the
workshops of industry.

MR. WEMYSS, THE PRESENT MANAGER OF THE PITTSBURGH THEATRE—
With pleasure we greet his presence, and trust that his urbanity and anxiety
to please, will meet the reward due to his individual and professional
merit.

After the applause with which this toast was received had subsided,
Mr. Wemyss rose, and in a neat speech, of which we can only give the
substance, returned thanks as follows :—

GENTLEMEN.—In rising to acknowledge the favour you have just conferred upon me, perhaps the best method of returning my thanks, would
be to assure those gentlemen, many of whom I see around me, (to whose
undaunted perseverance in the good cause we owe the erection of a theatre,
which I may boldly affirm, in point of elegance of structure, decoration,
convenience, and comfort, both to auditor and actor, is not surpassed by
any in the United States;) that so long as it remains under my direction,
no exhibition shall ever take place within its walls, calculated to cause a
feeling of regret to any individual who may have contributed a single dollar towards its erection.

Gentlemen, as far as one man's efforts can be directed to render your
amusement a source of gratification, mine will be devoted to that end.

Overtures will be made to every actor of superior talent, who may be at present, or shall hereafter arrive, in the United States; and I doubt not that many, if not all, will be induced to visit your busy and prosperous city.

For the kind manner in which you have been pleased to receive the toast of our worthy President, relating to my humble self, I can hardly thank you as I ought. I will not longer trespass on your time, but will, with your permission, propose the health of the ' President and Directors of the Pittsburgh Theatre.' With all the honours, drank with three times three, and one cheer more.

The following volunter toasts were given on the occasion.

EDUCATION—The only moral steam that will work without friction; the engine of the world.

THE LADIES OF PITTSBURGH—Where they take the lead, who will fear to follow.

Mr. J. R. Smith, the Scenic Artist of the Pittsburgh Theatre—In this instance he has demonstrated by the touches of his skill, that the warmth and aspirations of the youthful imagination can be transferred to canvas. In the language of Shylock to Portia, "How much older art thou than thy looks?"

THE NEW THEATRE—The elegance of the structure and the rapidity of its completion, proves that Pittsburgh, in point of taste, skill, and enterprise, is not surpassed by any city in the Union.

THE MARCH OF REFINEMENT AND LIBERALITY—We hail those lovely harbingers of a " New Era," even amid clouds of smoke and the fulminations of intolerance.

THE PRESS—As connected with the drama, the devil is said to be in both, but is harmless so long as he is bound by *boards*.

THE OCCASION OF OUR MEETING—May we all continue to be stockholders in fellowship and good feeling, and ever ready to pay our instalments on each share of the good things around us.

THE ENCOURAGEMENT OF THE DRAMA—The strongest evidence of a refined civilization in every age coincident with the progress of literature and the arts.

THE AUTHORITY OF CRITICISM—When prompted by spleen, though it may slightly wound, the missile generally rebounds upon the hyper-critic; but when guided by science, taste and impartiality, it exerts a salutary force in meliorating literary society.

PITTSBURGH—Her moral force, without classic taste united with practical exhibitions of it, would be deficient in an important fellow-lever.

The theatre being finished, was opened on Monday, the 2nd of September, with an address, written by N. R. Smith, Esqr., of Pittsburgh and spoken by myself.

ADDRESS.

When Genius, hovering in his native sky,
O'er climes untutored cast a watchful eye,
As yet, while thought was cradled by the Nine
And fanned by zephyrs from Olympus' shrine,

He sank at length from his empyreal height,
And shed o'er Greece the rays of classic light.
The Muses triumphed and the Graces smiled,
As brightened forth the dawnings of their child;
The plastic power of Genius entertwined
Strength, fervour, beauty, in the infant mind;
And reason, memory, judgment, formed the skill
To curb the passions, and control the will.
Still as the urchin Thought grew up, he knew
No art to bring men's foibles into view,
Nor yet their virtues, that this moral plan
Might meliorate, exalt immortal man.
To give perfection to the skill *their* muse,
Thalia and Malpomene infuse.
Greece rose in splendour as the lambent flame
Which Genius kindled, blazoned forth her fame;
Arts, science, arms, possessed the aspiring soul,
And the bright Drama crowned the boundless whole.
The Nine survived the ravages of time,
And waved their trophies in another clime.
Rome caught the Grecian spirit, and her pride
Conceived new honours, spread her laurels wide,
And triumphed long the mistress of the sphere,
Till ruthless ruin checked her high career.
The torch of Genius, though its flame had waned,
Was not extinguished, for the spark remained;
And fanned by breezes from the Muses' bower,
Relumed at length with renovated power.
To Gothic night succeeded all the fame,
And more, that gave to Greece and Rome a classic name;
The crest of Europe rose as Science spread,
And o'er the world its light and lustre shed;
Shakspeare appeared the Drama's claim to try,
Gave it new worth, and fixed its destiny,
At length, when Freedom planted here the Tree,
And called our soil the Home of Liberty,
Beneath its shade she fixed the Drama's seat,
Where all the kindred ties of Nature meet.
Hail to Columbia, free and unoppressed,
And hail the rising glory of the West!
Queen of the West, we trace thy rapid rise
From forest gloom beneath inclement skies.
Prophetic vision did not ken this age—
He—an enthusiast—madman—to presage,
That thirty years would throng a bleak, wide waste
With wealth and pride, with fashion, beauty, taste.
Taste and refinement here have joined to rear—
Adorn a Dome, that pleads *your* guardian care,
Taste shall unfold what taste alone imparts,
Enlightened intellects and generous hearts;
And here the Drama shall display confessed,
The Nine still vigorous, the Muses blest.

The play was the "Busy Body," and the afterpiece, "Of Age To-morrow." The company consisted of Mr. Addams, Mr. John Sefton; Mr. Charles Green, Mr. Henry Eberle, Mr. George Smith, Mr. William Smith, Mr. D. Rice, Mr. Hubbard, Mr. Bannister, Mr. Spencer, Mr. Wallace, Mr. M'Dougal, Mr. W. Sefton, Mr. Gifford, Mr. Parsloe, Mr. Hathwell, Mr. Warren, and Mr. Wemyss; Mrs. J. Sefton, Mrs. Green, Mrs. Smith, Mrs. Turner, Miss Julia Turner, Miss Turner, Mrs. H. Eberle, Mrs. M'Dougal, Mrs. Hubbard, and Miss Hathwell. There were also engaged; who never made their appearance in fulfilment of their contract, Miss M'Bride, Mr. and Mrs. Stickney, Mr. Milliken, Mr. Mllor, and Mr. Cuddy.

I had made my arrangements upon a scale much too large for the population. Half the number of actors would have been sufficient. It is therefore, not surprising, that the first season was by no means productive; and my Pittsburgh friends, (who are numerous,) will excuse me for the declaration, that their judgment in theatrical matters was most singular. The company would bear comparison with the best in either of the Atlantic cities; yet they selected the worst actors, (with the exception of Mr. A. Addams,) as their especial favourites, and even hissed poor Spencer, (who afterwards perished with Fanning, like a hero, in Texas,) from the stage, because he dressed like a gentleman, and would persist in wearing white kid gloves in the street. Another amiable trait in their character, was a practice they had of hissing the manager on the last night of the season, merely in wanton sport, always salving his feelings with a good house. Booth they pronounced a bad actor; E. Forrest they did not support during his first visit; and yet several years afterwards they crowded the theatre nightly to witness the performance of both these gentlemen; although the former disgraced himself as usual, by appearing in "Hamlet" in a state of intoxication. Yet this theatre, when I became acquainted with the taste of the citizens, and experience taught me how to manage it, proved the best and most profitable, ever under my control.

The receipts of the first night amounted to 392 dollars 62 cents, which fell to 101 dollars, on the second. Forrest's first night was 394 dollars 25 cents; yet he was the first actor of repute, who played under one hundred dollars, ("King Lear," the character,) while Mr. Booth's first night was 348 dollars; yet he played Reuben Glenroy to 112 dollars, and Pescara to 106 dollars. Mr. Power's first night was 353 dollars, his second, 119 dollars 25 cents. In fact, the worthy citizens of Pittsburgh seemed to think their duty performed towards the manager, if they received a star of the brightest nature with one good house, and made him a great benefit, on the system—one for you, the other for him.

The following letter of Booth's deserves a place from its singularity. It bears the Baltimore post mark of the 3rd of December.

(COPY.)

" TUESDAY NIGHT,
" Stage Office, once more:
"I am, as the French say, *en route*, and hope to reach Pittsburgh in time to begin on Monday night—bar sickness, my lord judge, and other delays. Messrs. Managers of the West, you are partly the cause of _____. Had you not announced Mr. Booth as being engaged in Pittsburgh and Cincinnati, Hamblin never would have *cotched* me here as he did. It is best, in my humble opinion, not to announce until the beast arrives.
" Your's as in duty bound,
(Signed) " J. B."
" Good!—commence with I am—conclude with J. B.—he conjugates the villain!
" To F. WEMYSS, ESQ.
"Theatre, Pittsburg, Pa."

During the time the theatre was building, the stockholders were anxious that nothing should be left undone to render it as perfect as possible. And entering into this feeling, I resolved the arrangements of the interior should be made worthy of imitation by larger establishments. Every dressing room was carpeted and furnished. The green room furnished in the style of a modern drawing room, with piano, ottomans, chairs, looking-glasses, &c. The whole costing upwards of a thousand dollars.

During the first season, from the 2nd of September, until the 8th of January, upwards of four months, the receipts amounted to seventeen thousand six hundred and twenty-seven dollars and thirty-seven cents; to which is to be added, one thousand dollars for season tickets; making in all, 19,327 dollars. Out of which the stars received 3291 dollars, and the actors from their benefits, 846 dollars.

Notwithstanding one or two unpleasant occurrences, I was enabled at the close of the season, to state, that during one hundred and eleven nights, not a single change had taken place in the pieces announced to be performed, which for variety, could challenge competition.

On the 10th of January, 1834, I took the company down the river for six weeks, to Wheeling, where we acted to an average of seventy-five dollars a night, in a large room, miscalled a theatre. Russel Smith painted some very pretty scenery, and I escaped with a loss of three hundred dollars, which enabled me to keep the company together, until my return to Pittsburgh on the 23rd of February, for the purpose of presenting to the citizens the inimitable

TYRONE POWER.

Who that ever saw his laughing face, but must regret his lamentable end, as one of the "ill starred" passengers of the lost steamship President—the ocean for a grave. When I first saw Power act, he was considered a light comedian of mediocre talent, possessing so much quicksilver, that it was impossible to keep him quiet in any one spot of the stage for two consecutive seconds. This failing he never entirely divested himself of; it was conspicuous in the "Irish Ambassador," in Ratler, in "How to Pay the Rent;" or in Pat Rooney,—annoying to every actor who had to support a character in the piece; but not unpleasing to the audience.

Chance installed him as the Irish comedian when poor Connor died so suddenly. His success at first, was by no means extraordinary; it was tolerated as a good natured effort of an actor, to aid the management in a dilemma. He rose in public favour slowly, and it was not until his return from the first visit to the United States in 1833, that he became an actor of consideration in London, where, prior to his death, fame and fortune were struggling who should crown him fastest. He was a noble, generous-hearted fellow, always willing to do a charitable action without making a parade of it, to form theatrical capital upon.

His career in America was brilliant beyond comparison, seldom playing to a bad house; frequently crowding the theatre to excess. An universal favourite with actors, managers, and the public; good humoured Paddy Power, his cognomen behind the scenes as well as before the curtain. His last appearance but one, in Pittsburgh, was marked by one of those disgraceful scenes which render theatres, and all connected with them, a bye-word for the finger of scorn. In the play of the "Irish Ambassador," Mr. Green and Mr. Hubbard were both so intoxicated, as to render it necessary to remove the first named from the theatre; and the latter actually fell upon the stage during his performance. Mr. John Sefton read the part of one delinquent, while I had to officiate in a similar manner for the other.

Power bore the mortification with remarkable good nature; having been in a great measure to blame, for dismissing the rehearsal at 12 o'clock with one of those complimentary speeches yclept "blarney," which he knew so well how to use on all proper occasions. Whether he felt what he so neatly expressed, or wished himself to take the ride for amusement he recommended to the actors, is a matter of no importance. In following his advice, Mr. W. Sefton, Mr. A. Addams, C. Green, and Hubbard returned to the city, as Bob Logic would say, in prime order—the consequence of which has been narrated.

The theatre was filled with ladies, which I need scarcely add, did not occur again during the season. It was a death-blow to our reputation, and resented as every similar exhibition should be, by every respectable citizen absenting himself from the theatre; although, as the manager, I was the innocent sufferer. I bowed with respect to the decision which I felt to be just, and recommended the course adopted by the Pittsburgh audience, as worthy of imitation; it is the only one to prevent a repetition of insult. It should have been carried one step further, by a marked determination never to permit the offenders again to appear upon the stage of the Pittsburgh Theatre.

I had used every endeavour to induce Power to visit Pittsburgh, had teased him into compliance, and was sorry to part with him on such terms, just as the audience were beginning to appreciate his merit. He agreed to play one night more, to prove to the public that he acquitted me of all blame, and rather accused himself as the author of the evil which thus brought his engagement to a premature close. He alludes to it jocosely in his Recollections of America. Poor fellow, his fame is cherished in the old as well as the new world, and many a heartfelt sigh has been breathed to the memory of—Poor Power.

He commenced his engagement on the 31st of March, with Sir Patrick O'Plenipo, in the "Irish Ambassador," and finished with Paddy O'Rafferty, in "Born to Good Luck." He was delighted with the theatre, and makes honourable mention of it in his account of Pittsburgh.

I subjoin his letter, upon the subject of his engagement:—

(COPY.)

"MY DEAR MR. WEMYSS:—

"I perceive that you purpose re-opening the Pittsburgh Theatre, in February. Now, I shall be here in April, and if, about the end of that month, or in May, you think a visit from me to my countrymen there will answer our mutual end, I shall be most happy to meet you on the banks of the Ohio. I congratulate you on the terms you appear to part with your constituents—and in the way of news from England, have only to tell you Bunn & Co. are gone to the devil. Never was failure in quackery more absolute than this attempt to "gag" the profession, by joining the two theatres in one. Allow me to beg an early reply. I act here until the 7th of February, and on the 17th open in Boston. With best wishes, believe me, "Truly Yours,

(Signed,) "TYRONE POWER."

"MANSION HOUSE, Philadelphia,
January 23, 1834."

CHAPTER XXVI.

Removal to Pittsburgh. Visit from the Author's Brother. Lake Erie.
The Falls of Niagara. Bad Roads. The Ohio River. Cincinnati.
Commencement of the Fall Season at Pittsburgh. Strange Changes.
Lease of the Walnut Street Theatre. Burton, as an Actor and Author.
Mr. and Mrs. Wood. Miss Philips. James Sheridan Knowles.

FINDING the theatre with careful management could afford a
comfortable livelihood, I lost no time in sending for my family
from Philadelphia. I hired a house in Liberty Street, and
made up my mind to a long residence in the city of Pittsburgh. How little do we know of our future destiny, which,
in despite of our daily labour, urges us on to the fulfilment
allotted by fate to every member of the human family.

We soon had the pleasure of beholding our children seated
once more at the table, from which they had been daily
missed, and again under the eye of their ever anxious and
affectionate mother.

During the summer, I had the addition of a fine little Pittsburgh boy to my family, and a visit from my brother, Captain
Wemyss, of the British army, whom I had not seen for
twenty years. We parted as boys, and met—he, a veteran
officer, and I——but no matter. If my position in society
was altered, my pocket had been replenished by my long
course of buffoonery.

In his company, I travelled through the State of Ohio,
finally taking a steamboat on Lake Erie, in which we descended
to Buffalo, and so crossing into Canada at Black Rock, proceeded to the wonder of the world, the Falls of Niagara,
which every Englishman, travelling for pleasure, takes the
earliest opportunity of visiting. If I attempt no description
of them, it is because they cannot be described. I was fool
enough to venture under the mighty cataract, which feat of
daring is daily practised; and only those who have stood upon
the rocks, and seen the mighty flood, which in an instant
might overwhelm them, can form any idea of the various feelings which in so short a space of time crowd into the human
mind. How insignificant does man appear when thus braving
his Creator—placing his life in jeopardy—for what? to say,
"*I have been under the Falls of Niagara.*" What romantic
folly!

From Fort George, we crossed Lake Ontario to Toronto,
where Captain Wemyss met some of his old military companions, in whose society we spent a delightful evening. The
following morning we retraced our steps, returning towards

Pittsburgh through the country of the Seneca Indians, paying for our ride, but dragging the coach two miles for one it dragged us. Never did I see such roads; every five minutes was heard the driver's summons to dismount, for we were *stalled* again; so with the assistance of a rail, we contrived to extricate the lumbering vehicle, in which we had engaged a passage to the town of Erie. We returned by this route, preferring it to the Lake conveyance; during a high gale of wind, and as we progressed along the margin of that sheet of water we beheld so placid a few days previously, we beheld it lashed into fury by the wind, exhibiting one vast crest of turbulent foam on this inland sea.

After a delightful trip, we arrived in Pittsburgh, from whence we proceeded in a few weeks to Wheeling. On my return, Captain Wemyss took his departure for the West Indies, and left, for a time, a void in our family circle, which he had enlivened during the summer.

My wife and the little Pittsburgh stranger accompanied me on a visit of business to Louisville, Kentucky. In our passage down the Ohio, we enjoyed the beautiful scenery of that splendid river. At Cincinnati, where we remained one night, I of course paid a visit to the theatre, then under the direction of Russel and Rowe, of New Orleans. The proud Queen of the giant West is a Philadelphia in miniature; the same regularity of building, the same cleanliness of appearance, and the same industrious population. The citizens who founded such a place may well feel proud of their handi-work. Louisville, although a more active place of business, is far behind Cincinnati in what may be termed the picturesque and beautiful. We remained there one week, and ascending the Ohio, returned to Pittsburgh to make preparations for the fall season at the theatre, which commenced on the 8th of September. The company, Mr. John Sefton, William Sefton, Oxley, C. Porter, J. G. Porter, Schinotti, Kent, Lewellen, De Cordova, J. Reed, C. Green, Harris, and Wells, Mrs. C. Green, Mrs. Kent, Mrs. Roper, Mrs. Lewellen, Mrs. La Combe, Mrs. J. Sefton; new faces, and many of them actors of talent. At the commencement of the season an effort was made by a committee of those who took an interest in the welfare of the theatre, to secure the performance of one legitimate five-act comedy in each week, the play to be chosen by the committee, who affirmed that this species of dramatic representation was most congenial to the taste of the citizens of Pittsburgh. The night selected was the Wednesday in each week. The first play, the "School for Scandal," a judicious selection, which filled the lower boxes, but the pit, gallery, and upper boxes were e-m-p-t-y. The second comedy, "She stoops to Conquer," was followed by the like result, whereas the repetition of the

"School for Scandal," as the third attempt, failed to procure even the attendance of the committee themselves, who gave up any further attempt in despair, leaving me for the future to manage the theatre in my own way, with the promise of their future support in any effort which should not be considered as degrading to a temple dedicated to the muses.

The failure of this attempt to make one decent house each week, induced me to turn my thoughts to other cities for permanent support, convinced, thereby, that Pittsburgh could not be relied upon for a longer season than six weeks or two months at any one time.

Since my departure from Philadelphia, strange changes had taken place. Duffy and Forrest had abandoned the Arch Street Theatre, which Maywood and Co. had taken, leaving the Walnut Street without a tenant, which being advertised to let, I was deliberating whether to return to the East, or to bend my course still further to the West, towards Cincinnati and Louisville, where the theatres leased by Russell and Rowe, were offered to me for the winter season, when my friend George Cook, unexpectedly made his appearance at my house, and during dinner, on the Sabbath day, issued his orders for my immediate departure for Philadelphia, thus:—
"Frank," said he, "I have been thinking over your affairs, and I am afraid the Western theatres won't answer your purpose, you must go over the mountains this evening, and at once secure the Walnut Street Theatre; this city, it is evident, will not by itself support a company of actors, and as I brought you here, I feel in duty bound to see you placed in as good a position as I found you, when you adopted my advice to try your fortune in this city of iron and smoke."

In eight hours I found myself comfortably seated in the Pittsburgh mail coach, "en route" for Philadelphia, to propose for the lease of the Walnut Street Theatre in that city. So suddenly are resolutions taken, which alter the course of events in man's life.

When I arrived in the city of brotherly love, the first person I surprised by my unexpected appearance, was my worthy friend Louis A. Godey, who had become a "Benedict" since we parted. I at once communicated to him the object of my visit. He did not seem to think very highly of the speculation, and even dissuaded me from making an offer; but a letter from Pittsburgh, with orders all but peremptory, decided the matter.

In forty-eight hours after my arrival, all the preliminaries were agreed to. Rent four thousand one hundred and fifty dollars per year, exclusive of the rooms occupied as bars, which, on account of a recent law, prohibiting the granting of tavern licence to theatres, I refused to have anything to do with, and the stockholders received three thousand dollars per year, for breaking a law which the manager thought proper to obey. More of this hereafter.

I agreed to pay one thousand dollars in advance upon signing the lease, and the stockholders agreed to re-decorate and paint the theatre according to a plan furnished by myself. I left them to prepare the lease for signature, while I proceeded to New York to complete my arrangements. I remained there two days, where Thomas Flynn, on behalf of Mr. Hamblin, promised many things which his proprietor afterwards failed to ratify.

I returned to Pittsburgh on the twelfth day after my departure, with my lease in my pocket, to prepare for opening what was now first christened the American Theatre in Philadelphia.

While I was in Philadelphia, I visited the Arch Street Theatre, where Power was performing as usual, to good houses, and I learnt that Mr. Maywood was hourly expected with recruits from England, for the stock company. These were Mr. Hamilton, Mr. Lindsay, Mr. Brunton, Miss Pelham, Miss Elphinston, and Mr. W. E. Burton. The last, the only one destined to add to the resident talent of the American stage; although, on his first appearance in Philadelphia, he did not meet with a very favourable reception. No sooner had he played Guy Goodluck in "John Jones," than the Philadelphians discovered they had acquired an actor worthy to succeed Jefferson; and he rapidly rose in estimation, assuming at no distant period, the proud title of a successful star; rather an unusual honour to a stock actor on the American stage. With him originated the Gentleman's Magazine, which he sold to Graham, the present proprietor, to turn manager; an unfortunate exchange in a pecuniary point of view. However, his pride might have been flattered in converting Cooke's Circus in Chesnut Street, into the most splendid theatre the United States could boast, where for a short period he was pre-eminently successful; but finally sank under an effort to sustain a fourth theatre, where those already established were rapidly changing hands for want of support. Mr. Burton as an author, possesses talent of no mean order, and whether as manager, actor, or author, is alike indefatigable. His industry deserves that success which the writer sincerely wishes may ultimately crown all his efforts. As an actor, he is entitled to the first rank in his profession; however public opinion may vary upon some points, all will admit his title to be just, when pronounced the best low comedian of the American stage.

My first business after my arrival at Pittsburgh, was to despatch my artist, W. Russell Smith, (a name since well known in the annals of fame,) to Philadelphia, to decorate the interior of the theatre. And well did he execute that work. The design was formed thus: each tier of boxes was decorated with paintings representing some celebrated battle in the history of the United States; around the dress circle were placed medallions of the heads of the Presidents; around the second tier, the heads of celebrated generals, and around the third tier, the heads of the naval heroes; between each medallion and its corresponding painting, was a large burnished gold star, the whole forming on a pink ground, the most pleasing interior I ever saw. I have seen them more gaudy, but never one so chaste.

The time for opening was fixed for the 22d of December, 1834, the Monday previous to Christmas Day, giving me ample time to bring my season to a successful termination in Pittsburgh, and to make the necessary arrangements for returning to the city of Philadelphia after an absence of eighteen months, during which Duffy and Forrest commenced the campaign of 1833 and 1834, at the Arch Street Theatre. On the 28th of August 1833, with the "Iron Chest" and the "Young Widow;" J. R. Scott playing Sir Edward Mortimer. The stars announced, being E. Forrest, Master Burke, and Mrs. Conduit, who afterwards became notorious as the cause of Mr. and Mrs. Wood's fracas in New York, and this may be the most appropriate place for the following remarks.

MR. AND MRS. WOOD.

These distinguished vocalists made their first appearance in the United States, at the Park Theatre, New York, on the 19th of September, 1833, as the Prince and Cinderella; and at the Chesnut Street Theatre, as above related; here their first engagement was not a profitable one. It was not until the following season, when they produced "La Somnambula,' that the theatre was nightly crowded with delighted auditors. The lady, as Miss Paton, had long enjoyed the reputation of being the best English singer of the day. How well she deserved that title, let those decide who have heard her in "Norma." As to her merit, there is no divided opinion; but as to the merit of Mr. Wood, there are as many opinions as critics; no two agreeing upon the exact rank he ought to hold as a vocalist.

To the Woods belongs the credit of establishing what Mrs. Austin and Mr. Berkeley commenced—a taste for English Opera, on so firm a basis, as to render it essential to the success of a theatrical season. They made the citizens of these United States in love with music, paving the way for the success of Mr. and Mrs. Seguin, Miss Sherriff, Mr. Wilson,

Giubelei, Miss Poole, &c. The only thing now wanting to place the American theatres in the same rank as the best in Europe is "The Ballet," for which Fanny Elssler has left a hankering wish, as Malibran did for the Italian Opera.

No person has been treated so harshly by the American public as Mr. Wood; twice driven in disgrace from the stage, and on both occasions without cause, or even reasonable complaint, on the part of his persecutors.

Mr. E. Forrest refused to act for the benefit of the poor, in his native city of Philadelphia, during a winter of more than common severity; but nobody dreamt of hissing him from the stage, or forcing him to retire from his profession, because he denied the right of any committee to dispose of his services as they thought proper, or to exact from him two hundred dollars, (the compensation he received for acting nightly,) for the same purpose to which they generously proposed to contribute the price of a box-ticket. As a matter of *business* he refused his professional services, which nobody presumes to say he had *not* a right to do; but he offered publicly, through the newspapers, to *double* any sum that either of the gentlemen who were so clamorous on the subject of his refusal *would give for the relief of the poor, from one hundred to five hundred dollars;* but they declined this just mode of testing the sincerity of their charity, designating the proposal as an insult from a purse-proud actor. Much undeserved obloquy has been cast upon Mr. Forrest's name for the want of feeling he exhibited in refusing his professional aid for this benefit; but I can see no evidence of want of feeling in the proposition which accompanied the refusal. It was a determination to maintain the right of control over his business capital (*i. e.,* his talent,) at the same time that he was willing to contribute generously to the wants of the poor.

The demand made upon Mr. Wood was of a similar nature, but the exercise of the same control was refused. It was intended as charity to an individual, a member of the profession, who had not the slightest claim upon his consideration that she should expect, and her friends demand, the gratuitous services of Mr. and Mrs. Wood on her benefit night. Was Mrs. Conduit the friend or associate of Mrs. Wood? *Assuredly not.* They possessed nothing in common but the unenviable title of *actress.* The attack made upon Mr. Wood was followed up with the ferocity of savages, and disgraceful to a civilised community. He was, perhaps, unwise, for he might easily have turned the tide of popular *indignation* into *admiration,* by at once acceding, in bland terms, to the wishes of those assembled for the avowed purpose of insulting him, and offering the services of himself and Mrs. Wood for the *lady's* benefit; but he preferred his independence to his interest, refusing to yield to threats what he had already declined to entreaty. His subsequent conduct, in spitting in the face of the reporter of the *Courier and Enquirer*—the newspaper which produced the mischief—admits of no excuse ; but it was a manly feeling which prompted the act. He was too young and powerful to attack an old man, for the purpose of castigation, without a charge of cowardice ; to have challenged him would only have been to have subjected himself to a column of abuse in the newspapers, on the audacity of an actor, whose profession, it would have been said, excludes him from the title of gentleman, daring to seek the redress of one. He did it, therefore, to provoke from the reporter a demand of that satisfaction for an insult no gentleman could brook, which he was anxious and willing to afford him. But these wholesale assassins of reputation always shrink from the responsibility of personal encounter ; in a court of law, and not the court of honour, he sought his redress, receiving several thousand dollars for preventing Mr. Wood from peacefully pursuing his profession. Hard sentence this, for an assault unattended by violence. Had the reporter spat upon the actor, the judge, I am inclined to think, would have pronounced no such heavy penalty. The courts of New York fined Bennett of the *Herald* five hundred dollars for libelling a judge, and Wood, the actor, thousands, for spitting in the face of "one of the *gentlemen* of the press," who had not only libelled him, but through the influence of the newspaper for which he wrote, fomented a conspiracy which drove him from the stage.

The sober second thoughts of the people convincing them that Wood had been most hardly dealt with, and wishing once more to hear the syren notes of Mrs. Wood, he was invited to cross the Atlantic, with an assurance that the past was buried for ever in oblivion. In an evil hour he consented again to visit the United States, to be again insulted, without having given any cause of offence ; but Philadelphia, not New York, was the scene of his last degradation.

The Opera of "Norma" had been produced at the Chesnut Street Theatre, as opera alone can be rendered effective, with a full band of instrumental music, and a full chorus of well-drilled singers ; but the result proved that the managers did not reap a full harvest. The receipts were unequal to the expenditure ; they could not pay their singers and musicians ; and because Mr. Wood would not consent to do it for them, by sacrificing his share of the proceeds to the necessity of the theatre, he was, a second time, compelled to resign his professional engagements ; the only offence laid to his charge being a refusal to proceed with the opera without being paid for his services, according to contract. When the managers and himself agreed to bring what they represented to be a losing engagement to the theatre, to a termination, no allusion was made by either party to the fact of the following night being the one appropriated for the benefit of Mrs. Bailey. Mrs. Wood at once volunteered her services for a concert, to be given by Mrs. Bailey, at which Mr. Wood was not permitted to sing; he prudently declining to appear when rumour pointed out "a row," without an object. Thus the Woods were, a second time, driven from the shores of America, victims of unjust persecution. Kean, who had offended, was severely, but perhaps justly, punished; Anderson merited his fate, and courted it; but Wood was the victim of newspaper violence and misrepresentation, and, to crown all, he had invested the greater part of his professional earnings in the stock of the United States Bank—lost—all lost; so that his recollections of the United States must be very agreeable; and if the notes of himself and his wife were now considered as of little or no value, those he received in return proved more worthless.

The death of Mr. William Forrest caused the Arch Street Theatre to close for the season as early as the 4th of February. On the 11th of June, Mr. Duffy produced Dr. Bird's new play of the "Broker of Bogota," written for Mr. E. Forrest. Why it has been so seldom acted, might well be asked; for as an effective acting play it is superior to either the "Gladiator" or "Oraloossa," from the pen of the same author.

On the 23rd of August, 1834, Maywood and Co. commenced their season, in the Arch Street Theatre, with the play of "Man and Wife," and "Simpson and Co." Maywood having visited England during the vacation, sent over, as recruits, Mr. Burton, Mr. Hamilton, Miss Pelham, and Miss Elphinstone, who made their first appearance in the United States thus: on the 25th of August, Mr. Hamilton as Sir. B. Backbite, and Miss Pelham as Lady Teazle, in the "School for Scandal;" on the 26th, Miss Elphinstone as Juliet; and on the 3rd of September, Burton, as Dr. Ollapod, in the "Poor Gentleman," and Wormwood in the "Lottery Ticket." Power and James Wallack played each for a few nights; and on the 13th of October, the Chesnut Street Theatre opened with "Romeo and Juliet,"

Miss PHILIPS

acting the part of Juliet. This young lady's fame in the theatrical world was of very recent date, and, although supported by Wallack, always a favourite with the Philadelphia public, her engagement was not an attractive one. The

M

managers had raised the prices—to one dollar, boxes, and
fifty cents to the pit, which, might have caused the failure,
more than any want of talent in Miss Philips, who is universally respected for her private worth; and having retired
from the stage, is scarcely a fair (yet she is a very *fair*) subject for criticism. .

The stars announced were Matthews, J. Wallack, James
Sheridan Knowles, Mr. Ternan, Signor Lauza and pupils,
Miss Philips, Miss Fanny Jarman, and Herr Cline.

On the 27th of October, 1834,

JAMES SHERIDAN KNOWLES

played Virginius, in his own play of that name. We had always supposed Virginius to be a Roman; but to use a little
Irish slang on this occasion, he was "a Greek"—what a delightful Irish brogue he had. This was not tragedy upon
stilts, but upon "hand-crutches." Mr. Knowles has been
justly termed the Shakspeare of the present era of the drama,
and to carry the similitude a little closer, he determined to
prove, like the immortal bard who preceded him, that a divine author may be a very bad actor. The London critics,
when they permitted, or tolerated the performance on the
stage, of this truly good author, permitted him to exhibit
himself in a position which his vanity made him fancy he
was fitted for. I will not do him the injustice to follow him
through the career of antics he was permitted to play; but
turn with pleasure to the record of the reception given to his
literary talent, leaving his acting where it is, and from whence
no labour can remove it—the theme of laughter to those
whom he has made his brethren of the sock and buskin—the
actors.

On the 8th of November, a public dinner was given to the
dramatist, at the Masonic Hall, by many of our first citizens,
at which Matthews was present; and where justice was
awarded to one whose plays had for years delighted his hosts.
Upon this occasion, and in such a scene as this, Knowles was
at home—his good humoured blarney making every one
present pleased with himself, and consequently pleasing
everybody. Whoever had the good fortune to be present at
this dinner, will remember it with feelings of pleasure—
where the feast of reason and the flow of soul imparted
warmth and hilarity to the dullest present.

On the 10th of November, Matthews, after an absence of
eleven years, again appeared before many of his old friends.
In 1827, he told me in London, that if his life should be
spared long enough, he was determined to contradict in person, the calumny circulated, by playing his "Trip to Ame-

rica," word for word, before an American audience, and leaving them to judge on their own soil whether he had designedly misrepresented them. His expected acquittal was but a disagreement of his jury; and the result aided the speedy dissolution which followed his return to England. It is a subject of regret to me, that I arrived from Pittsburgh twenty-four hours too late to shake hands with him. He started for New York the very day I returned to Philadelphia.

CHAPTER XXVII.

Return from Pittsburgh. Eclipse of the Sun. Opening of the American Theatre, Walnut Street. Gratifying Reception. Mr. Oxley. Mr. A. Addams. Firemen's Fund Benefit. "Zanthe." "Tom and Jerry." Awkward Accident. Misconduct of Actors. "Last Days of Pompeii." E. T. Conner's Performance of Glaucus. Sheridan Knowles. Miss Emma Wheatley. Coney and Blanchard, with their Dogs. Close of the first Season. Introduction of Mr. Hadaway to the Walnut Street Theatre.

On the 29th of November, 1834, the Pittsburgh Theatre closed its third Season, having been open seventy-five nights, during which Gouffeé, (the Monkey man,) Miss Mary Duff, Mr. Charles Mason, Mrs. Sharpe, Mr. Cooper, and Miss Priscilla Cooper, (Mrs. Robert Tyler,) Mr. A. Addams, and Mr. Hill appeared.

On the 1st of December, I started with my family in the Good Intent Mail line, for Philadelphia; and in our progress, witnessed an eclipse of the sun at the top of the Alleghany mountains, the most beautiful and sublime sight ever seen from such a position—the shadow of darkness on the trees, looking indeed like the shadow of death, as described in the Pilgrim's Progress.

On Monday, the 22nd of December, 1834, according to previous announcement, I opened the American Theatre, Walnut Street with the following company:— John Sefton, William Sefton, E. Connor, John Mills Brown, Charles Porter, J. G. Porter, Charles Thorne, A. Jackson, W. Kent, Schinotti, De Cordova, Lewellen, Rodney, Caldwell, Mestayer, Sprague, Fenner, Forrest, Wemyss, and Barrymore; Prompter, Mr. Huntley; Miss Mary Duff, Mrs. Duff, Mrs. Kent, Mrs. Thorne, Mrs. Conduit, Mrs. Cooke, (Mrs. Roper,) Mrs. La Combe, Mrs. Brown, Mrs. Jackson, Miss Charnock, Miss Ruth, Miss Pearce, Miss Gillespie. Barrymore was the stage manager; Clemens, the leader of the orchestra; the play, "Wild Oats," and the farce, the "Dumb Belle." When I appeared as Rover, my reception was most gratifying to my professional pride. Not content with the usual demonstration on the appearance of an old favourite, as the curtain fell upon the last act of the play, I was loudly called for, and received by such applause as rarely falls to the lot of an actor. The farce of the "Dumb Belle" introduced John Sefton, after an absence of some years; it was admirably acted, and at the close of the performance, I was again called before the curtain, and while bowing my acknowledgments, an auditor proposed three cheers for the success of Mr. Wemyss and the American Theatre; which were given with a hearty good will.

The first drama I produced, was "The Golded Farmer," in which Mr John Sefton laid the foundation of his theatrical fame. To him this part, which he at first refused to play, and to the last moment grumbled about, has put more money into his pocket, than all the catalogue of parts he ever acted, put together. At the Franklin Theatre in New-York, under the management of Dinneford, he played this part one hundred times, during the first season, a thing without precedent in the annals of the American stage, either before or since. Mr. Sefton had a clause in his articles of agreement with me, by which he had the right to choose his part in the dramatis personæ, where there was more than one low comedy part in a piece, and he insisted on playing Harry Hammer; but Barrymore insisted that he was the only man in the theatre fit for his "thief" in the "Golden Farmer." It was finally left to my decision, and although John Mills Brown played Hammer, much to the mortification of Sefton; yet I do not think my friend John has any cause to complain of the result, offended although he was by the choice, and first played Jemmy Twitcher as an act of favour towards me in the management of the theatre. "*Vell, vot of it,*" we know what we are; but the best among us know not what we may be.

I laid out a plan from which I never departed, to produce a new piece every Saturday night, and the steady perseverance in this plan, first gave the Walnut Street Theatre one night in the week, on which the manager could depend upon a good house by very moderate exertion. And Saturday still preserves it prerogative in that theatre.

On the 29th of December, I introduced to the Philadelphia public, their townsman, Mr. John Oxley, as a star, (one of minor importance; but who still continues to sparkle, while brighter constellations have been totally eclipsed.) As an actor, he was unknown; but he made an impression which has since enabled him to wander about, with the admitted right of having his name placed in large letters on the playbills, whenever he performs.

The "Amazon Sisters," followed the "Golden Farmer," in

which Miss Mary Duff and Mrs. Kent sustained the heroines
in a masterly style. On the first of January, 1835, the
" Deep, Deep Sea" was produced; but notwithstanding Barrymore's acknowledged tact, it failed to please, and was withdrawn after the second night. On the 5th of January,

MR. A. ADDAMS,

after so long an absence from Philadelphia as to have been almost forgotten, made his bow to a crowded house, in the
character of Hamlet. Had he permitted me to choose, it
would have been either Damon or Virginius. He pleased his
audience, but in either of the latter characters he would have
carried them away with him triumphantly. Why Hamlet
should be selected by so many clever young men to try their
powers, is a subject upon which pages might be written. Of
all the characters of Shakspeare, the melancholy Prince of
Denmark is the most difficult to attain excellence in. John
Kemble, Charles Young, Edmund Kean, and Junius Booth,
are the only actors who have, in my mind, approached the just
conception of this part. I do not like Macready, with all his
study—he is too cold and constrained; and although A.
Addams' representation is on a par with E. Forrest's, yet they
both want that finish so requisite to complete the picture, neither of them having any pretensions above mediocrity in this
character. Addams played twelve nights, on each successive
performance rising in favour, until he was fixed so firmly in
the good opinion of the audience, that nothing has been able
to destroy his popularity, and no man has laboured harder to
effect it—disappointing his audience frequently, yet always
forgiven, and always received with kindness on his return to
reason, to offend in a similar manner on some occasion when
his services were most needed.

Gifted by nature with a commanding person, not only a
handsome, but an expressive countenance, a voice capable of
being modulated to the tones of the softest flute, yet powerful enough to out-rant the loudest lungs of any actor who ever
tore a passion to rags, Mr. Addams should have distanced all
competitors. He is the only one who ever had a chance of
shaking Forrest in his position, and made him tremble for
his title of *the* (" par excellence") American tragedian. The
genius of Addams is superior to that of any American actor,
but the study and application requisite to make that genius
available, was wanting. While Forrest, by tact in the management of his affairs, was accumulating wealth, Addams was
destroying both his pocket and his health by a course of dissipation which placed public opinion at defiance. His engage-

M 5

ment with me, which should have been profitable to us both'
was of no service *to him*, and a positive loss *to me*. No one laboured harder than myself to reclaim him. That he has
chosen to throw away such advantages is a source of regret to
all his friends.

On Tuesday, the 27th of January, took place the first
benefit in aid of the Fund for the Support of Disabled Firemen. The house was filled; Addams acting Damon, and
Oxley, Pythias. The following Address was written by Robert
T. Conrad, on the occasion, and delivered by F. C. Wemyss :

ADDRESS.

The city slumbers : o'er its silent walls
Night's dusky mantle, soft and silent, falls ;
Sleep o'er the world slow waves its wand of lead
And ready torpors wrap each sinking head ;
Still'd is the stir of labour and of life,
 Hush'd is the hum, and tranquilliz'd the strife ;
Man is at rest, with all his hopes and fears,
The young forget their sports, the old their cares,
The grave or careless, those who joy or weep,
All rest contented on the arm of sleep.
Sweet is the pillow'd rests of beauty now,
And slumber smiles upon her tranquil brow ;
Bright are her dreams—yes, bright as heaven's own blue,
Pure as its joys, and gentle as is dew ;
They lead her forth along the moonlit tide,
Her heart's own partner wandering by her side ;
'Tis summer's eve : the soft gales scarcely rouse
The low-voic'd ripple, and the rustling boughs,
And, faint and far, some melting minstrel's tone
Breathes to her heart a music like her own.
When, hark ! oh, horror ! what a crash is there !—
What shriek is that which fills the midnight air ?
'Tis fire—'tis fire ! She wakes to dream no more ;
The hot blast rushes through the blazing door,
The room is dimm'd with smoke, and, hark, that cry !
 " Help ! help !—will no one aid ?—I die ! I die !"
She seeks the casement, shuddering at its height—
She turns again—the fierce flames mock her flight !
Along the crackling stairs they wildly play,
And roar, exulting, as they seize their prey ;
" Help ! help !—will no one come ?" she can no more,
But, pale and breathless, sinks upon the floor.

Will no one save thee ? Yes, there yet is one
Remains to save, when hope itself is gone ;
When all have fled, when all but he would fly,
The fireman comes to rescue, or to die !
He mounts the stair—it wavers 'neath his tread,
He seeks the room, flames flashing round his head,

He bursts the door, he lifts her prostrate frame,
And turns again to brave the raging flame.
The fire-blast smites him with its stifling breath,
The falling timbers menace him with death,
And sinking floors his hurried steps betray,
And ruin crashes round his desperate way;
Hot smoke obscures, ten thousand cinders rise,
Yet still he staggers forward with his prize;
He leaps from burning stair to stair—On! on!
Courage!—one effort more, and all is won;
The stair is passed, the blazing hall is braved,
Still on—yet on—once more! thank heaven, she's saved!

The hardy seaman pants the storm to brave,
For beck'ning fortune woos him from the wave;
The soldier battles 'neath the smoky cloud,
For glory's bows is painted on the shroud;
The fireman also dare each shape of death,
But not for fortune's gold, or glory's wreath;
No selfish throbs within their breasts are known,
No hope of praise or profit cheers them on,
They ask no meed, no fame, and only seek
To shield the suffering, and protect the weak;
For this, the howling midnight storm they woo,
For this the raging flames rush fearless through,
Mount the frail rafter, head the smoky hall,
Or toil, unshrinking, 'neath the tottering wall;
Nobler than those who, with fraternal blood,
Dye the dread field, or tinge the shudd'ring flood;
O'er their firm ranks no crimson banners wave,
They dare, they suffer—not to slay, but save:
At such a sight, Hope smiles more heavenly bright,
Pale, pensive Pity trembles with delight,
And soft-eyed Mercy, stooping from above,
Drops a bright tear—a tear of joy and love.

And should the fireman, generous, true, and brave,
Fall, as he toils the weak to shield and save?
Shall no kind friend, no minist'ring hand be found
To pour the balm of comfort in his wound?
Or should he perish, shall his orphan say,
" He died for them—but what for us do they?"
Say is it thus we should his toils requite?—
Forbid it justice, gratitude, and right;
Forbid it, ye who dread what he endures,
Forbid it, ye whose slumbers he secures,
Forbid it, ye whose hoards he toils to save,
Forbid it, all ye generous, just, and brave;
And, above all, be you his friends, ye fair,
For you were ever his especial care;
Give to his cause your smiles, your gentle aid—
The fireman's wounds are heal'd, the orphan's tears are stayed.

At the close of the performance I was called before the curtain, to return thanks on behalf of the committee, which I did.

On the following evening, I produced "Zanthe," founded upon Kenney's tragedy of "Hernani," which had failed at the Chesnut Street Theatre, with Mr. Charles Kean for the Hero. The secret of this splendid drama, which is now vivid in the recollection of the audience, was simply this:—I was preparing "Gustavus," with a Ball Masqué, to surprise the citizens, when by some means Maywood & Co. were apprised of my movements, and endeavoured to forestal them. Much to my annoyance they announced "Gustavus," and produced it on the night of my benefit. Barrymore, whose fertile genius in a theatre was never at a loss, came in, and perceived by my face that something more than common was the matter. I handed him the play-bill containing the announcement of what we intended to be *our great card*, and for which Russel Smith, Landers, and the wardrobe keepers, had been working incessantly from the night the theatre opened. He burst out into a hearty laugh, and slapping me upon the shoulder, said, "Never mind, governor, we will give them a Roland for an Oliver; let them have 'Gustavus,' we will give them a coronation as well as a ball masque, and not lose an hour either. Io triumphe !"—and away he went. In something less than an hour, he returned in high glee. "All right, my master, and Wednesday shall see us in a new style before this audience, or I will forfeit my head." Wednesday did see us triumphantly successful. For eighteen nights "Zanthe" crowded the theatre; but all is not gold that glitters. Notwithstanding we received in four nights, two thousand two hundred and sixty-five dollars, yet the average was unequal to the expenditure. The extra expense nightly, was—brass band, 20 dollars, four drummers, 3 dollars, one hundred and twenty-five supernumeraries, 26 dollars 25 cents, wax candles, 140—35lbs every three nights, say 7 dollars, two pound red fire, at 3 dollars, 50 cents—7 dollars; in all, 63 dollars, in addition to the dresses and properties, which were in Barrymore's usual style of extravagance. And if "Zanthe" was found at the end of the season in debt to the treasury, it had given us a reputation for spectacle which has served the Walnut Street for capital, ever since the memorable 28th of January, 1836. Its success was perfect, and taught the managers of the aristocratical theatre, "prudence." They never attempted the same thing again; but quietly suffered me to enjoy my reputation as a *minor* theatre.

The favour with which "Zanthe" was received, induced me to revive "Tom and Jerry" with new scenes, and every property on the same scale as when first produced at the Chesnut

Street, in 1828, under Warren and Wood. The 9th of February saw the curtain ready to rise upon a house of 482 dollars. Every thing promised a rich harvest; all was marred by the misconduct of Mr. William Sefton, who was the Jerry of the evening. His brother John first called my attention to him during the opening chorus. It was evident he was in such a state of intoxication, that if he got through the part, it would be a miracle. My piece was evidently sacrificed, and I made up my mind to endure the mortification as best I might, resolved that in his person, such an occurrence should never take place again. At the conclusion of the second act, while I was giving some directions to the master carpenter, being dressed at the time for Falstaff, in the "Masquerade," one of the carpenters in running across the stage, slipped and fell between my legs. In endeavouring to rise, he brought me to the floor with him, falling on me and twisting my leg under him. This accident lamed me for life. For twelve months I was unable to walk without the aid of a stick, and never perfectly recovered the use of my knee. Therefore, I have cause to remember, "Tom and Jerry."

On the 23rd of March, "The Last Days of Pompeii" was produced with twenty-two new scenes, painted by Russel Smith. The design of the last scene was truly magnificent; but whether by accident or design, failed on the first night. I was present at this representation, for Barrymore had promised to outdo himself: and he certainly kept his word. The three first acts had proceeded much to the satisfaction of the audience, when Barrymore came forward and prepared them for a failure, by stating that his last act had never been rehearsed. Blunder succeeded blunder, until, to crown the whole, the quick match which should have fired Vesuvius, was cut, and passing backwards and forwards on the traveller like a squib, was the only eruption which was to bury Pompeii. Down came the curtain amid the jeers and laughter of the audience. Barrymore, half crazy, seized one of the side lights, and, at the risk of having his eyes blown out, held the lamp until the powder ignited. A most brilliant display of fire-works succeeded. Elated, and determined that the audience should see what effect his last scene had been intended to produce, he insisted upon raising the curtain; but the carpenter, whose duty it was to attend to this matter, had left his post. Up went Barrymore himself, the fireworks blazing away all this time; and very well worth seeing they were—but powder won't burn for ever. Just as he succeeded in raising the curtain, the last spark exploded in a puff of powder, and all was darkness. Such a roar of laughter, and such a shower of hisses followed, that Barrymore ran out of the theatre to avoid the shame and mortification of meeting any of the actors. Of course the fate of the "Last Days of Pompeii" was sealed. It cost twenty-three hundred dollars, and was played six nights only. This induced me to hurry on the benefits as fast as possible; and the season closed on the 11th of April, with Connor's benefit—a young man who, from this very failing piece, in which he acted Glaucus, became one of the most popular stock actors ever known in Philadelphia: thus proving that it is indeed an ill wind that blows nobody good. The receipts of the season amounted to twenty-seven thousand nine hundred and twenty-five dollars, which, for ninety-six nights, gives an average of 291 dollars per night.

The theatre opened again on the 2nd of May, with Yankee Hill, who played to a succession of bad houses; followed by Mr. and Miss Cooper. Sheridan Knowles played Icilius, for Cooper's benefit—rather an ancient looking lover for Virginia; however, it proved the kindness of the author's heart. Miss Emma Wheatley and Master Bowers, Mr. Charles Eaton; and finally, Ooney and Blanchard, with their dogs Hector and Bruin, and Jim Crow Rice. This season was injudicious. Having succeeded in establishing the Walnut Street as a winter theatre, I should have been content; but the summer season having been looked upon heretofore as exclusively belonging to this theatre, I was induced to make the trial, which cost me eleven or twelve hundred dollars during the fifty-six nights it was open, and is only remarkable for having introduced Hadaway to this theatre, who became a reigning favourite during the whole of my career as manager.

CHAPTER XXVIII.

Madame Celeste. "The Blind Beggar of Bethnal Green." Sheridan Knowles. Emma Wheatley. Mrs. Austin's Farewell Benefit. A sad disappointment. Miss Booth. Abbott as "Hamlet." Balls. John Reeve. Actors, and their Imitators. Complimentary Benefit to Mr. W. B. Wood. Brough. Mr. and Mrs. Wood. Great Success of "La Somnambula."

I MUST now proceed to trace the progress of the Chesnut Street Theatre, from the time of my opening. On the same night, Dec. 22d, Celeste, whose career in Europe had added to her previously acquired fame, played in the "Wizard Skiff," and the "Wept of the Wish-ton-wish." Elliot offered to come to the American at the conclusion of his present engagement. I unfortunately declined the proposition, because I considered the terms exorbitant, thus losing a good auxiliary, and, what would have been of far greater consequence, depriving May-wood and Co., as the sequel proved, of their most attractive, and always to be relied upon, star of the season. On the 29th, Miss Philips was announced to play Mrs. Beverly, but did not arrive, in consequence of some accident on the rail-road; she, however, appeared the following evening. On the 7th of January, "Gustavus" was produced. On the 12th, Emma Wheatley, and on the 14th, James Sheridan Knowles, with the wonderful Diavolo Antonio, and his equally wonderful sons. On the 20th, Knowles produced his own play of "The Blind Beggar of Bethnal Green," playing Lord Winford himself, Emma Wheatley supporting the character of Bess. The play made no great impression, and was acted only a few nights. After this, Knowles gave a series of lectures on dramatic literature. Here "Richard was himself again;" in such a sphere he moved without a rival, and those who heard these lectures were warm in their expressions of admiration; but I doubt if the author realised much money, however he increased by them his literary fame. Mrs. Austin's farewell benefit, and last appearance, was announced for the 16th of February, the lady playing Ariel in the "Tempest," and Zulima in "Abon Hassan." The house was a very indifferent one, the weather very bad: and the managers announced another night for that purpose, Feb. 19th, when she made her last curtsey to the Philadelphia public, as the Princess in "Massaniello," and "Cinderella," after a residence of eight years in the United States, during which time she laboured hard, and successfully too, to establish a taste for English opera; and her reception induced others, of higher talent, to cross the Atlantic in search of fortune. The Chesnut Street Theatre closed for the season on the 21st of February, with Mrs. Ternan's benefit; the pieces, "Fazio," and "The Young Widow." The purpose of closing, the avowed *necessity* of reducing the price of admission to the standard of last year.

I must now travel across the Alleghanies, and bring my fall season in Pittsburgh to a close, which commenced on the 17th of October, 1835, with A. A. Addams as Damon. He was always a sure card with the citizens of Pittsburgh; and started the season with a house to the tune of 259 dollars; his benefit 313 dollars; after which I despatched him across the mountains to play "Jack Cade" at the Walnut Street Theatre. Murdock made his first attempt as a "star," aided by Miss Vos, Hill, and afterwards by Conner and Miss Mary Duff: he was not considered of sufficient importance. He had two benefits, neither of them worthy of a stock actor in common favour with his audience. Aided on the occasions by other stars, the first house amounted to 185 dollars 50 cents, and the second to 158 dollars 75 cents.

Music being the order of the day, I made an arrangement with John Thompson Norton, Hunt, Trust and Cioffi, on their way to New Orleans, to stop four nights at Pittsburgh. A subscription paper was well filled to insure me from loss in this attempt, and on the second of November my box-sheet presented the unusual spectacle of five hundred places secured : even what are termed the " flies" were taken. Night approached, but with it came not the stars of the evening ; the canal boat bringing me the very consolatory information, that my party, in despite of warning, had insisted on taking Leech's line of boats instead of the Express line, and that in all probability the gentlemen would arrive about four o'clock on the following morning. The deception practised by this line often proved a source of annoyance from which there was no redress ; but I had cautioned Mr. Norton in Philadelphia, and he therefore sinned with his eyes open. I had to call upon Murdoch to aid me by playing Dick Dashall in " My Aunt," and returned between two and three hundred dollars at the doors. Nor was this the worst of the loss : at least half of those who had subscribed for the four nights at once withdrew their names, and several were so much offended as to abstain from visiting the theatre again during the season ; it was not, therefore, in the best of humours that I met the " absentees" at the breakfast table. They performed on the second of November to 280 dollars, on the fourth to 191 dollars, and on the fifth to 132 dollars. The three houses scarcely yielded as much as the first would have done, and one night out of the four lost altogether. For this disappointment I received only an allowance of fifty dollars from our original engagement.

On the 7th of November Mr. and Mrs. Ternan appeared in " Fazio" and " Personation." On the 20th of November, Miss Booth (now Mrs. Charles Burke) took her first benefit. This young lady improved rapidly in her profession, and at this early period of her career gave promise of her future popularity. She was a great favourite with a portion of the audience, although her style of acting was by some considered as coarse and vulgar—wanting the refinement necessary to personate a lady upon the stage, and approaching in assumption of character nearer to the manners of a chambermaid. Logan beat us all this season in the receipts of his benefit ; and on the 28th of November the theatre closed, as usual, with my benefit, Miss Ann Waring playing "Therese." In six weeks Addams, Murdock, Miss Vos, Hill, Norton, Hunt, Trust, Cioffi, Mr. and Mrs. Ternan, Mr. Conner, and Miss Mary Duff appeared, so that the worthy citizens of Pittsburgh could not with justice complain of the want of attraction.

On the 19th of October—"Tell it not in Gath, publish it not in the streets of Ascalon!" Mr. Abbot made his first appearance at the Chesnut Street Theatre as Hamlet. "*Oh Crickee!*"

Do the actors in England suppose that Americans are totally ignorant of the position they occupy in their profession in their own country? Abbot, in his best day, never aspired to even second rate parts in tragedy in London, where he was admitted to be the best walking gentleman belonging to the British stage, and capable of better things, having pretensions as a genteel comedian of repute. We could have tolerated him as a light comedian, superior in every respect to Mr. Balls, who followed him to this country, and allowed his claims to the foremost rank in that walk of the drama; but as a tragedian, capable of playing Hamlet, it was impossible he could succeed, and any mortification he may have met in this career is to be attributed to his own foolish vanity. Whoever had the pleasure to meet him in private society must remember him with feelings of regret, that he is not longer spared to occupy a place at the festive board, he so much graced, where few men possessed so happy a talent of making himself generally agreeable. Whatever may be the opinion of his merit as an actor, placed beyond the sphere of his ability, as a companion all must yield to him their full approbation.

"He was a fellow of infinite worth."—SHAKSPEARE.

Miss Emma Wheatley was the next star, followed by the ever successful Celeste, producing with great effect the "Devil's Daughter," and commencing the announcement of her one hundred and one (more or less) farewell benefits, with "Victorie," and the "Spirit Bride."

Balls made his first appearance in Philadelphia on the 16th of November, as Vapid, in the "Dramatist," and the Three Singles, in the "Three and the Deuce." He was a sprightly, dashing, good-looking fellow, possessed of more impudence than talent, seldom knowing the words of his part, and keeping the audience in good humour by never allowing them an opportunity of discovering his weak point. His first engagement was, I am told, a profitable one to the theatre; but, the novelty worn off, such a result could never be expected again. How I hate bastard starring! Why don't the public finish the matter by turning a few of them adrift? Where talent is really overwhelming in its effect, the starring system may be endured; but if ever a well regulated drama is to take root and flourish, the profession must be stripped of all exotics.

On the 17th of December, 1836, one of the drollest of all droll comedians appeared in the person of

MR. JOHN REEVE,

another, and a bright victim to conviviality. From an actor whose gibes and merriment did keep his audience in a roar, descending to the besotted buffoon, uttering his own coarse and vulgar jokes to make the million laugh, and the judicious grieve; rarely treating his audience to the words of the author, but by his rare comic powers, retaining possession of their kindly feelings to the last moment of his career. Nature had endowed him with such rich powers of mimicking, that he dared to enter the field against the *Matthews*, on his own ground, and with success, in a piece called "1, 2, 3, 4, 5, by Advertisement," in which he acted on his first appearance in Philadelphia.

As an actor, he was a spoilt child. From the night of his first appearance in the English Opera House, he gained a place in the good graces of his audience; and as a "droll," was little inferior to Liston, the great buffoon of the English stage. Reeve never knew the excitement or privation of the strolling actor's career. His first attempt was made in the metropolis; and notwithstanding his erratic course, to the last of his professional existence, he possessed the undiminished favour of the audience at the Adelphi Theatre. When he played Bob Acres, in Sheridan's play of "The Rivals," in Philadelphia, he found himself charged with the high crime and misdemeanour of being an imitator of *Burton*, whose popularity had been acquired by a close imitation of the best points in Reeve's acting. This is not an uncommon occurrence in theatricals; first impressions, if favourable, bearing great weight in the minds of auditors. Miss O'Neil is said to have formed her style of acting from Miss Walstein, who was rejected in London, as an imitator of Miss O'Neil—Elliston, in the same manner, of Tom Cunningham of Bath—Mrs. Jordan, of Mrs. Brown, of the York Theatre, who, in comedy, shared the same fate as Miss Walstein before the London public. While the imitators reaped golden opinions, the real Simon Pures were rejected as base counterfeits; but Reeve's failure in America was owing more to his intemperate habits, than any other cause; increased, perhaps, by the mortification of finding himself considered second to an artist whose greatest merit was, that he *could* imitate such an actor as John Reeve successfully.

On the 18th of January, Mr. and Mrs. Wood appeared in the opera of "The Maid of Judah," aided by

Mr. BROUGH,

who made his first appearance on the Philadelphia stage, in this opera.

> "There was a jolly miller once lived on the River Dee,
> He drank and sang from morn to night, no one more blythe than he;
> And this the burden of his song, forever used to be—
> I care for nobody, no not I, since nobody cares for me."

Here is at once a character of my good-natured friend Brough, a better companion over a boon or a bottle, than an actor upon the stage. As a singer, a valuable adjunct to Mr. and Mrs. Wood, and like a satellite, deriving lustre from their superior fame. He has travelled throughout the United States, respected wherever he went, and his absence regretted as the loss of a capital good fellow, ever ready to perform a generous action, seeking his reward in the consciousness of having performed a pleasing duty to one of his fellow beings. Long may his jovial laugh ring over the board of festivity, and success crown him wherever he goes. His name in theatricals must be associated with "La Somnambula," and will descend to posterity, so long as the charming music of that opera retains a place in every lady's musical port-folio.

"La Somnambula" was acted for the first time in Philadelphia, on the 11th of February, 1836, and for fifteen consecutive nights held possession of the town—the Chesnut Street Theatre closing on the 25th of February, for the season, the engagements of Mrs. Wood elsewhere, preventing a longer stay; having acted in Philadelphia, from the 18th of January until the 25th of February.

CHAPTER XXX.

Discoveries in the Moon. Sol. Smith *vs.* the Man-monkey. "The Spirit of '76." Coney and Blanchard. The "Infernal Machine." Opening of the Theatre in Washington. A Drunken Ghost in "Hamlet." "The Jewess." Mr. Murdoch. A Curious and Interesting Scene. News of the Capture of Santa Anna. Close of the Walnut Street. The Wilmington Theatre. Indifference of the people of Wilmington to Theatricals.

The American Theatre in Walnut Street opened for the season on the 22nd of August, 1836, with "Richard the Third," Booth playing Richard to 556 dollars; quite a cheering prospect. On the 30th, Addams played Othello to Booth's Iago, to 591 dollars. Mr. Forbes, Miss Vos, and Rice, (Jim Crow,) succeeded Addams and Booth.

On Saturday, the 5th of September, the first new piece was produced under the title of "Discoveries in the Moon," (Rice was the author,) founded on the well-remembered *hoax*. It was very successful, and withdrawn only because Rice's engagements would not permit a longer stay. "Bone Squash Diabola," for which Clemens had written the music, and Landers prepared the machinery, was transferred to the Bowery Theatre, New York. Thus we lost the credit of its original production.

Forbes and Miss Vos did not add to the receipts of my treasury; but on the 15th of September, Sol Smith, the cherished favourite of the south-western theatres, made his bow in Philadelphia, as Mawworm, in the "Hypocrite." Gouffe played on the same occasion; and here we see the difference of value between intellectual and physical acting,. (I am indebted to my friend Oxley for the observation). The gentleman and actor received from the citizens of Philadelphia, on his benefit night, 140 dollars, while the man-monkey, on the previous night, received 444 dollars. *O tempora! O mores!*

On the 23rd of September I produced a National Drama entitled "The Spirit of '76," in which the costumes, scenery, &c., of the times were carefully preserved. It was played seven nights, to an average of 257 dollars, and was then withdrawn, to make room for Coney and Blanchard, and their dogs, who held possession of the theatre for fourteen nights. On the 16th of October, Mr. Ward took his benefit, previous to his departure to join Maywood and Co., at Baltimore and Washington. Mrs. E. Knight and Mr. Hill both played a short engagement. On the 24th of October, Mr. Benjamin Brewster, a young lawyer of much promise, dramatised the "Infidel," from Dr. Bird's novel of that name. I regret that I was in Pittsburgh on this occasion, for I think that his play deserved a better fate than it met at the hands of my stage manager.

The next piece was a horrible perpetration, under the title of "Fieschi; or the Infernal Machine." All I can say about it is, that it was played to infernal bad houses, and consigned to the infernal regions, with the *blessings* of the actors. Hacket played one night, on the 18th of November; and on the 21st, Addams attempted Richard the Third. Booth and Rice, (Jim Crow,) played: the former, Sir Giles Overreach, and the latter in "Oh, Hush!" on the 28th, to 857 dollars.

On the 25th of December, 1835, I opened the Old Theatre, in Washington city, with "Therese," and "Kill or Cure;" following it by Booth, who played an engagement, profitable to me as well as himself. Everything seemed to promise a good season; but, notwithstanding the aid of A. Addams, Mrs. E. Knight, Mary Duff, Signor Vivalla, and many others, the first fortnight was the only one attended with profit, and I closed it on the 8th of February following; one incident only occurring worth record—a drunken ghost, in "Hamlet !"—A spirit steeped in spirits ! Poor Paddy Field, could you have found no other part to disgrace yourself in? Although no subject for laughter, yet it was too comical to see this ghost staggering across the stage, and then, in despair, missing the entrance by which he should have left it. A fellow-feeling for a fellow-failing, I presume, alone induced Booth to proceed, who laughed as heartily as any of the audience.

On the 15th of February, James Wallack commenced a short and very unprofitable engagement. I thought I had achieved a great triumph in obtaining his services. Had I known what I discovered afterwards—that in concluding this engagement I was enabling Maywood & Co. to continue, for twelve nights longer, their successful career with the Woods, which Mr. Wallack's time would have interrupted, I should not have been so well pleased with the idea. People are sometimes too cunning for themselves.

The Annual Benefit promised to the Firemen's Fund took place on the 18th of February, and even with the aid of Mr. Wallack, I am sorry to add, was a failure, 39 dollars, 25 cents, being all the money I had to pay over to their treasurer on the occasion. Wallack's last night, on which occasion he played Rienzi, was only 68 dollars. He never on any engagement proved a fortunate star to me.

On Monday, February 29th, "The Jewess" was produced. This was an alteration by myself from a drama called "Esther the Jewess." The only merit it contained was its pageantry, which was the most superb of any thing yet offered to the public of Philadelphia. The allegory, headed by Time, representing every nation on the face of the globe, was of such an imposing nature, that I boldly assert, the last scene has never been equalled in America, or surpassed anywhere. The beauty and variety of costume, formed a tableaux on which the eye rested with feelings of delight. The far-famed "Naiad Queen" had no single scene that could compare with the last scene of the "Jewess," although as a whole it far surpassed it, having something like interest attached to its plot, and a succession of brilliant scenes, while the "Jewess" boasted of but one, but that one was a *chef d'œuvre.* It was played fourteen nights, and withdrawn to make room for "Norman Leslie."

This piece was dramatised by F. C. Wemyss, in consequence of Hamblin demanding half the receipts of each night's performance for the use of Miss Medina's drama from the same novel.

Murdoch, with whom I had entered into an engagement to pay him 275 dollars per month, for three months, and take the proceeds of his benefits, made his first appearance at the Walnut Street Theatre, under my management, as Rover in "Wild Oats," on the 12th of March. He told *some one*, in particular confidence, and *that somebody* repeated it to *every body*, that *he* had *no* interest in the receipts on his benefit nights, so that all the advantage I expected to reap from the engagement was lost, and at the expiration of the time I declined renewing it, or making him any further offer, but such a one as I made to Hadaway, Conner, and others regularly engaged in the theatre. Thus terminated, on the 2nd of July, the attempt to make a "star" of Mr. James E. Murdoch in his native city—not much to the satisfaction of either party. That pear was not ripe.

On the 25th of May a scene occurred of such a character, not often witnessed within the walls of a theatre. The performance announced was "Othello," and "Perfection;" the proceeds to be appropriated in aid of the people of Texas, the public sympathy being deeply excited by the fall of the Alamo, and the inhuman butchery of Fanning and his associates. News of the capture of Santa Anna arrived in the city, and Mr. Coffee, of the Exchange Reading Room, knowing that Colonel Childers of Texas was at the Walnut Street Theatre, with the Texan Committee, came directly to the theatre with a slip received from New York. Colonel Thomas Florence, a member of the Committe, read it from the boxes, eliciting the most enthusiastic cheers. Colonel Childers addressed the audience in a complimental strain, and alluded to the threat made by Santa Anna, "to place his blood-red banner of Mexico on the dome of the Capitol of Washington;" and reversing the picture, adverted to the period, when it was not improbable that the Star Spangled Banner, aiding the Lone Star of Texas, would float from the gilded domes of Mexico, as a sign that the tyrant had fallen—that the people were free.

The theatre closed on the 4th of July, with the "Boston Boys in '76," and "Black Eyed Susan."

The Pittsburgh Theatre opened on the 2nd of April, for the spring season, and closed on the 14th of May. The stars who appeared, with the exception of Herr Cline, presented not a very brilliant array.

On the 29th of May I opened the Theatre in Wilmington, Delaware, a very little, snug affair, but out of place in such a city. Notwithstanding Conner, Miss Mary Duff, Murdoch, Oxley, and even Miss Fanny Jarman appeared, in six weeks the whole receipts amounted only to 886 dollars, an average of

24 dollars a night. Booth could only play to 33 dollars. It was impossible to excite sufficient interest about the drama. With the exception of a few, the citizens neither cared about the actors or the theatre.

CHAPTER XXXI.

On closing the season, on the 4th of July, 1836, I applied to the stockholders to replace the stage, which had become positively unsafe. They refused; but Mr. Henry G. Freeman *kindly* gave me permission, if I thought proper, to do it at my own expense. As I intended to open my season with the "Bronze Horse," I was compelled to forgo the exhibition of scenic pieces, for which the Walnut Street had acquired a reputation, superior even to the Bowery, in New York; or have the stage relaid. Of two evils I chose the least; and, at a cost of one thousand dollars, Mr. Sanders, and his assistants, completed the alterations.

A new difficulty now arose. Miss Waring, upon permission, had been acting for six weeks in New York, with Mr. Hamblin, in the music composed by Mr. Henry Allen, expressly for her voice. I now wanted her assistance; she refused to return, and fulfil her engagements. Mr. and Mrs. Muzzy, also, having had overtures from Mr. Barry, also violated their contract. Mr. and Mrs. Houpt, who were engaged, also refused to come to Philadelphia, having made their arrangements with me the means of obtaining their own terms with Pelby. Mr. Collingbourne, and Mr. and Mrs. Watson, I had voluntarily released. Mrs. Willis was engaged at the Park Theatre, New York: and to her kindness in foregoing, under these circumstances, a more eligible situation, was I indebted for the means of opening at the appointed time, but not with the appointed piece. The "Bronze Horse" was not produced until the 31st of August; and is the first piece upon record that ever ran fifty nights, in one season, in the city of Philadelphia.

I opened on Saturday, the 27th of August, with the "Fate of Calais," and the "May Queen." The money saved by the misconduct of these actors proved a source of profit on the season, which, for the first time, netted nearly five thousand dollars; the success of the "Bronze Horse" rendering it unnecessary for me to supply the place of any of the delinquents until after Christmas. "Verily, out of evil sometimes cometh good." Russel Smith increased his reputation tenfold by the scenery; and repaired to Boston, to the New Theatre, (The Lion,) to paint the scenery, and also superintend the machinery. Mr. John Wiser supplied his place during his absence; and in the Walnut Street Theatre acquired the first practical lessons in the art of scene-painting, in which he, also, has become an adept.

Booth was the first star, commencing with the "Stranger," on the 6th of September. I did not wish to break off the connection of Booth's name and the Walnut Street Theatre, or I should have declined this engagement; it was paying a premium to keep him from performing at any other theatre in the city. Mr. and Miss Cooper followed—the "Bronze Horse" still continuing his career. On the 3rd of October, Mr. Finn appeared in the "Clandestine Marriage;" an actor, whose dreadful fate in the Lexington steam-boat makes his a name which never will be forgotten. To me he addressed the last letter he ever wrote upon the subject of theatricals, and, in all probability, the last he ever penned; and I cannot do better than subjoin it, although it was two years from the present time. He was ice-bound on the western side of the Alleghany mountains, and from Pittsburgh had addressed me a letter of complaint; the subject of which I was anxious to remove. He remained to act (as he passed through Philadelphia, returning from that unfortunate engagement), for Celeste's benefit, at the Chesnut Street Theatre; and, so delayed, became a passenger on board the Lexington; whether perishing by fire or water has never been ascertained.

"United States Hotel, Saturday Evening.

"DEAR WEMYSS,

"I did not receive your letter till after I had finished acting, or should have replied before.

"I think my explanation of circumstances will exonerate Mr. Jackson from having unnecessarily communicated the contents of your 'confidential letter.' From the tenure of your first letter, he naturally concluded it was left optional with him to renew; which he had no hesitation in doing, previous to the receipt of your counteracting letter; and on my claiming the fulfilment of that promise, he was obliged, in self defence, to state your sentiments. Nor did he consent to make another engagement till the Wednesday following, and then only after consulting with Mr. Simpson.

"You admit that the failure of the mails was the cause of his not receiving the one assenting to the renewal. This did not reach him till last Sunday; but what was he to do, in the absence of all information, but decide for the best? I pass by the circumstance of taking a long, expensive, and hazardous journey; the one from Pittsburgh being the most dreadful I ever encountered—two nights out, in an open board box, half froze to death, and nearly buried in snow—because they were the first, though severe penances, for committing a most glaring act of folly. I took exception to what seemed a capricious movement without sufficient motive, because the time subsequent to the expiration of the first week was unfilled by any one else, and had, (apparently, at least,) a wish to exclude me from participating in the next, for the mere purpose of exclusion. I have no reason to complain of Pittsburgh; bad as it was, it was better than I anticipated; the people suffering, and those who could afford to pay for amusement preferred sleighing. In better times, and at another season, I have no doubt the arrangement—even after sharing 150 dollars—would have been a paying one; but I am convinced it is the wrong season for Pittsburgh. The navigation is stopped, there are no boatmen or travellers, the labouring classes are out of employ, and I defy the power of any professional locomotive to draw them.

"Mr. Jackson told me the whole of your communication about myself, ' also the words, until you hear from me again;' but this did not alter the position in which I was placed, because we had no reason to suppose that it would be in *two* days, as you did not state when. It is evident there was a conspiracy of the elements to thwart our prospects, in which I was a material sufferer in mind, body, and estate; and we can only fall back upon the melancholy consolation afforded by the proverb, ' bad now, better another time;' but that other time must be the better by being milder.

"Yours ever (December excepted),
"HENRY J. FINN."

Old associations had rendered me anxious to continue in the good opinion of Finn. Strange as it may appear, he had been the *tragedy hero* of Butler's Company; had been at the Haymarket Theatre, in London, where he was the original Thomas in the "Sleep Walker," and by his excellent acting of an insignificant part, aided materially in the success of the piece. He then returned to his native country, (for Finn was an American actor, although he never laid claim to any indulgence upon that score, but stood before his audience on his own merit,) and became one of the managers of the old Federal Street Theatre in Boston, and finally a "Star," and one of the brightest in the galaxy. No *one* need shrink to have their merits weighed by the standard that gave pre-eminence to Finn : his Lord Ogilby, his Philip Garbois, his Paul Schack, his Beau Chatterley, have never been equalled on the American stage ; and although it has latterly been the fashion to laugh at his Hamlet and his Romeo, I have seen them worse acted by gentlemen who claim the dignified appellation of tragedians. During this engagement, he acted Lord Ogilby, Paul Pry, Philip Garbois, Paul Schack, Dr. Pangloss, Billy Black, Beau Chatterley, Mawworm, Jack Humphries, and Richard the Third!!

On the 12th of October, Mr. and Mrs. Ternan played a short and profitable engagement, proving that it may be advantage-

N 5

one sometimes to descend from the stilts, and change your ground in the same city. No one understands this better than Mr. E. Forrest, who tries the market all round, and sometimes, although rarely, refuses a *better* for a *worse* offer, by this means keeping up the excitement that adds to his popularity.

Mr., Mrs., and Charlotte Barnes, played three or four nights, and now the " Bronze Horse" was suffered to rest, to make way for " Lafitte," the piece which caused the destruction of the Bowery Theatre, New York, in 1836, and the announcement of which here created more than usual excitement. It was first acted on Friday, October 28th, the audience leaving the theatre with a determination to hiss it on the following night. But a few judicious alterations, the chief one the arrangement of the Pirate's Island, altered the sentence. What failed so signally on the previous night was received with cheers on its second representation, and keeps possession of the stage to the present hour, as a favourite drama. It was played for twenty-one nights: Conner, Mrs. Willis, and Mrs. Preston, not forgetting Woodhull, gained much credit, while Percival, by whom it was patched together, as Cudjoe, made quite a favourable impression on his audience. The music was well selected, and what is of more importance, well sung; and no piece could be more satisfactory to the management, after having so narrowly escaped total damnation.

On the eventful 7th of November, the night the Pennsylvania Theatre opened, " Lafitte" was played at the Walnut Street to 628 dollars, a proof that the audience who support it, do not come in such numbers as supposed from the northern Liberties; a little tact and better judgment in the building, would have rendered a Theatre of their own profitable. I was very sanguine in my hopes, and felt the disappointment : it crippled my resources. But the general crash,—suspension of bank payments, desolation and ruin in the community,—not the building of this place, from the loss of which I had perfectly recovered,—caused my future difficulties.

On the 18th of December, Mr. Denville, a gentleman whom I had known with Macready under the name of Stuart, appeared in a well-written drama, entitled " Minerali." In what position to place him as an actor, would puzzle a Philadelphia lawyer : at one moment he would strike out some point so excellent, that the audience testified their approbation in a burst of genuine applause, the sound of which had scarcely subsided, when he would do something so totally ridiculous, as to raise doubts as to his sanity ; and *so* laughed at, and *so* applauded, he continued to act for six nights, when Richard the Third and Shylock convinced the audience he was *non compos mentis*, in which opinion, however reluctantly, I am compelled to acquiesce. Bunn got up " Manfred" for him and Miss

Clifton at Drury Lane, which had a most successful run, and there ended his reputation as "*a star.*"

After a short interval, during which hammer, paint, and nails were busily employed, "Thalaba" was placed before the audience on Monday, the 20th of February, producing in six nights, 3285 dollars, the greatest average of any piece I ever played at the Walnut Street Theatre. It did not cost one-third of the money expended upon "Zanthe," bringing a return, as compared to that much-talked of drama, into the treasury, during the run, of more than double the amount of money. On the 20th of March, David Paul Brown's play of "St Paul the Prophet," was acted for Conner's benefit to 728 dollars. How the accomplished author, who was present, bore the butchery,—for it was worse than murder,—of this his second-born, lives in his own recollection. Whatever he thought, he uttered no complaints; but I will entrust him with a secret, which, if he continues to write for the stage, may atone for the mortification he must have endured, and prevent the possibility of a similar occurrence: Never permit a play to be brought forward for *an actor's benefit night,*—it never *does* receive the necessary attention, either of scenery or dresses, added to which the performers seldom know the words of their parts, and more than two rehearsals can *never* be obtained. The manager feeling no interest in the result, beyond receiving his nightly charges for the incidental expenses of the theatre, will not lay aside his *own* business to promote the advantage exclusively of one member of his Company.

———

CHAPTER XXXII.

A Liberal offer ! Suspension of Specie Payments. Mrs. H. Lewis. "The Vision of the Sun." Conner, as Richard the Third. Mr. Walbourne. His Failure. The Ravel Family. An Amusing Declaration. E. Forrest. Mr. and Mrs. Keeley. Miss Ellen Tree. Mrs. Gibbs. Cooke's New Circus in Philadelphia. Mr. Vandenoff. Public Dinner to E. Forrest. Non-attendance of the Profession.

On the 31st day of July, 1837, my first lease of three years expired. The gas was to be introduced at the Chesnut Theatre in the fall, and I also wished the stockholders to introduce it into the Walnut St. Theatre at the same time. Whether it was finesse on the part of Mr. H. G. Freeman, who, although only the treasurer, was in fact the sole director of the place ; or whether it emanated from the board of directors, consisting of Messrs. Montelius, Wickersham, Peddle, Lajus, Donaldson and Freeman, the proposition made to me was, to renew my lease at an advance rent of one thousand dollars, for one year only, and they would introduce the gas.   Liberal! thrice liberal offer. A noble return for all my exertions—for all the improvements I had made to their property—but not an unusual one with landlords, and associated companies are the worst of landlords. You can fix the evil upon the shoulders of no one individual; but every act of grace is the work of each particular agent. It would not at that time have answered my purpose to throw up the theatre; but if I had done so, as the result proved, it would have saved me from ruin.   Mr. Cooke, whose equestrian company had been so successful in New York, came over to see me, in company with Mr. Amherst, on the subject of occupying the Walnut Street Theatre as a circus. My lease forbidding me to under-let the theatre, without the written permission of the board of agents, rendered it necessary to consult those gentlemen.   Mr. Cook's offer was a most liberal one—three thousand dollars, for three months, with full security, to be deposited in any bank of Philadelphia, nominated by the stockholders, to leave the property in the same condition he should receive it.—The conditions of my lease, requiring an advance payment of 1000 dollars, and 200 dollars per week after that, until all paid, the first payment commencing at the expiration of one week after the opening for the winter season, left the stockholders in advance payment six months, from the 31st of January. Unfortunately, all the rent was paid before this ofter was made; and, not satisfied with a rent which they have never received before or since, and the profit which would accrue to them from the rent of the bars, which would have been 1000 dollars, they refused their assent, unless I agreed to pay them 1000 dollars for it.   As they had already 2000 dollars of mine in their hands, I declined, stating at the same time, that if they refused their consent, arrangements would be made by Mr. Cooke, before he left the city, to build a circus in Chesnut Street.   Mr. Freeman laughed at the idea; but I had pledged myself to Messrs. M'Intyre and Rogers, who held control of the lot, in the event of our negociation being broken off, that I would bring Mr. Cooke to them.   I apprised Mr. Henry G. Freeman of the fact; he was still obstinate, reminding me of the lawyer introducing his client: "I send you a fat goose, pluck him, he will bear it." But I was tired of being plucked in so barefaced a manner. The stockholders of the Walnut Street Theatre, or their agents, were the sole cause of the erection of Cooke's circus, since altered by Burton, and now possessed by Welsh and Co., Mr. Cooke was anxious to occupy the Walnut Street Theatre: the fame of his New York exploits had made the citizens of Philadelphia anxious to see him.   The avarice of Mr. H. G. Freeman and his associates forced him to erect another building.

I introduced him to the gentlemen named above, and all the preliminary arrangements were made before Mr. Cooke left the city. When past recal, the agents told me they would give their assent, if I could prevail on Mr. Cooke to stop operations. This 1000 dollars I had denied, they were determined to have, and so proposed and so obtained in increase of rent for the year 1837, with the fact of a new circus staring me in the face by way of a pleasant opposition. This was my punishment, fool that I was, with a building in the city, of my own, which might have answered my purpose, until I could obtain a better one. I should have said "no;" as it was, for 12 or 1400 dollars outlay in gas fixtures the stockholders received an interest of 1000 dollars per year!!! Is it wonderful the manager should have been ruined? He ought to have been a wiser man, and said, "no: the gas I must have, but I will pay no more rent; or, at most, the interest on the cost of introducing it"—and *I would have got it*. But, throughout my whole dealings with the board of agents, the more I yielded, the more they demanded, until, provoked by insolence, I hastily severed a connexion, in which they seemed to think I had too large a stake, to be driven away from the possession, so long as it was in my power to retain it.

While Cooke was erecting his building, I made up my mind to a long summer season and a late opening in the fall. Here again I decided wrong. My season could not have been worse; and, by not being open at the usual time, the pit audience had found another place of amusement; and thus the main support of the Walnut Street Theatre was for the present destroyed.

In proceeding to Pittsburgh, I adopted the resolution of having no Stars; but taking my whole Walnut Street Company to produce, in rapid succession, those pieces which had been most successful in Philadelphia; and Russel Smith and his brother were started off, one month in advance, to prepare the scenery.

On the 10th of April, I opened to 300 dollars. Mr. Conner not arriving, the Wrecker's Daughter was changed to the Stranger; and so well was the play acted, that, for once, the Pittsburghers burst out into a hosannah for their manager. This was, numerically, the strongest company ever seen in the Iron City, accompanied by the adjunct, for the first time, of a corps de ballet. The company with which I opened the theatre possessed more talent; but the orchestra never was so complete, and now the efforts of actors were appreciated, not as four years ago, laughed at. The first week's business produced sixteen hundred and twenty-three dollars and seventy-five cents, or an average of two hundred and seventy dollars per night.

Well done, Pittsburgh—this, too, without the aid of a Star.
The first drama was "Zanthe," not liked; a little grumbling;
but the first night's receipts 423 dollars 37 cents. The
next was "Lafitte"—house, 461 dollars 87 cents; a great
hit. Then came the "Bronze Horse;" but, as if from *perver-
sity,* it was pronounced "a humbug," and the manager's character, in consequence, at fifty per cent. discount. It was excellently done. But the secret, it must be told : Madame Celeste, on her way to the West, had arrived, wanted to play,
and her services were declined ! ! ! She, or rather her husband,
Elliot, went grumbling on his way, leaving me to meet all
sorts of "*blessings*" for my refusal. But I had determined no
Star should act during this season; for I well knew, if I took
one, I must, perforce, take all the rest, or give offence. Besides, I had, at a very early period of my management, made
known to all these "*wanderers,*" that, as my time in Pittsburgh
was always limited to a certain number of weeks, announced
at the beginning of the season, they must make their engagements with me before I left Philadelphia, or make up their
"*books*" without Pittsburgh. To this rule I rigidly adhered;
and to that, more than any other cause, were the citizens of
Pittsburgh indebted for the visits of the brightest Stars, while
their fame was at its height. Serjeant Talfourd's play of "Ion,"
brought one good house ; and "Norman Leslie," four ;—quite
complimentary to my pride as an author.

"The Jewess," on the 13th of May, brought 358 dollars
62 cents, with an excellent box sheet for Monday ; but here,
a "malignant star" crossed my path. On Sunday, the 14th, I
first heard of—THE SUSPENSION OF SPECIE PAYMENTS ; and, on
the 15th of May, actually turned from the doors over 200
dollars, for want of change. Such a row—such swearing—
some at the banks, others at the theatre,—all declaring I had
specie enough and would not pay it out. I might have had
specie for 300 dollars I had deposited with Mr. Cooke that
morning, which I could have had, and as much more, for asking ; but I was so amused by the quaint speeches—half funny,
half threatening, that I heard at his counter during the day
—as every new refusal for change was answered with—banks
stopped payment, that I forgot my own business, until the
doors of the theatre opened, and I found myself in a very
awkward predicament. One hundred dollars of specie, which
I promised to return in the morning, was all I could raise ;
and I only made bad worse by paying that out. If the thought
had only struck me in the afternoon, I might have sold tickets
by the handful, by promising silver in change to parties of
four or more, that is, a front bench. Under this arrangement
—during the panic—I might have filled the house every night
at the slight cost of " thirty dollars discount." Two hundred

and fifty dollars of specie, nightly, would have secured me five hundred dollars per night. How readily a mistake may be pointed out, after the fact becomes apparent to every one. It was a decided miss; for the citizens had the theatrical mania so strong upon them at this time, that, specie or no specie, they were determined to come, buying two tickets, one for present, one for future use, when they could not obtain change for their notes.

Mr. James Wallack was permitted to pass through without being allowed to play, declaring it was the first time in his life a manager had ever refused his proffered services, in a city in which he had never acted. My worthy friend, Finn, also used his rhetoric, to convince me I ought to relax in his favour; and, when I would not, "then," said he, "I'll relax in yours—dine with me, and I will make you drunk, if I can, out of spite." I don't know whether he kept his word: but I saw him comfortably seated in the stage, at four o'clock in the morning, on his way East.

"The Jewess," was below par. "Thalaba" mustered only 250 dollars: and the "Last Days of Pompeii," 218 dollars; "The Star Spangled Banner," 257 dollars; and "Abon Hassan," for my benefit, on the 3d of June, 1837, only 175 dollars. NOTE: *They did not hiss me this season—this accounts for the badness of the house! !*

Thus was the most brilliant season ever anticipated cut short, by a circumstance which could neither be foreseen or prevented, in which I had not the slightest agency; but, like many more, was finally engulphed in ruin, without even sympathy, while the course of the banks was legalized, or galvanized. They were suffered to proceed with their business, without interruption—no charter was declared forfeited.

This season, with the disasters of the last eighteen nights, produced ten thousand seven hundred and forty-six dollars, making an average 223 dollars 75 cents per night; but at one time the average was over 300 dollars, and a prospect of continuance: but I had only seen the beginning of the end in Philadelphia. I had the prospect of a season which would require sacrifices, which, having so lately escaped from the difficulties of building the Pennsylvania Theatre, I was not prepared to meet.

To prepare for the continuance of my season, so as to avoid, if possible, the success which every body anticipated to attend the opening of the New Circus, Russell Smith and Landers had been preparing the "Vision of the Sun," with which we were to have opened: but delay—excitement out of doors—always apathy within—the piece was not ready till the 30th of June. So I opened the Walnut Street Theatre on the 17th, persuading Conner to attempt Richard the Third ! !

Shade of Shakspeare, forgive me ! He did it—and "*did it brown.*" The pit boys were vociferous in their applause ; and he has played it on one or two occasions since, when, I thank my lucky stars, I was not present. For "Thalaba," or "Lafitte," I want no better or more efficient man ; but the idea of Conner, as a tragedian—don't let me pursue it. On the 19th, Mrs. Henry Lewis, an actress of the Cobourg school, but a good one, and one whose value I appreciate, opened in Bianca, in "Fazio." On the following evening, she played Matilda, in the "French Spy ;" she also played Richard the Third, Virginius, and Othello ; and to say how the audience liked her, is only to say, she had 472 dollars on her benefit night, notwithstanding the thermometer was ranging at 82°, a pretty good proof of success.

"The Vision of the Sun" had been looked for and expected, as the opening piece : the scenery, machinery, &c., could not be excelled. But the disappointment—always throwing cold water upon any piece—showed me the receipts of *one hundred and fifty-four dollars,* as the first return of a piece, the last scene of which cost nearly three times the money. The second night—*Saturday night, too,* was twenty dollars worse. On the 4th of July, it was to 456 dollars, and the following night 97 dollars. It was played altogether ten nights, two of which, the 4th of July and the 18th—the night the Pennsylvania was launched—produced 1009 dollars 75 cents. Any other piece would have possibly produced more on these two holiday gala nights; and the other eight nights, collectively, yielded 961 dollars 25 cents. A heavy blow to the treasury. "*Damn the Banks*"—ALL caused by the banks. This was the general cry, and why not join it : for, seriously, they deserved a little harder treatment than harsh words.

Monday, the 10th of June, introduced to the Philadelphia audience one of the most astonishing men that ever trod the stage, whose fame was made by and expired with Tom and Jerry.

Mr. Walbourne was the original Dusty Bob ; and Pierce Egan, in his "Life of an Actor," classes his performance of this part, as giving him a title in the niche of fame beside John Kemble, Mrs. Siddons, and all the great actors contained in his "Catalogue of Parts Acted"—which can never be forgotten by those who witnessed them. Here is the note, page 14 :—"Mr. Walbourne's personation of Dusty Bob has been unanimously decided by the public, as one of, if not the greatest triumph of the histrionic art ever exhibited upon the stage." Kean, the first tragedian of the day, with the utmost liberality, gave it as his opinion that, during the whole course of his theatrical career, he had never seen any performance equal to it. Murden, a comic actor of great celebrity, exclaimed—" Good heavens ! is it possible—do not my eyes deceive me? Most certainly, it is a real *dustman* they have got upon the stage. I am very sorry the profession has descended so low as to be compelled to resort to the streets to procure a person of that description, to maintain the character." He left the house in disgust—nor was it until introduced to Mr. Walbourne, behind the scenes, that he would believe it was an actor. *Further praise than this is superfluous.*

Booth played a few nights, and then with J. R. Scott. Henry G. Pearson, formerly of Philadelphia, now of the New Orleans Theatre, also played with Scott; but his acting appeared to the audience an attempt at burlesque. If such was his motive, he was most successful; but his reason for such a course seems mysterious—very.

On the 13th, I opened in Pittsburgh, with the Walnut Street company, with " Damon and Phythias," and the " Agreeable Surprise." On the 16th of September, Mr. Connor resigned his situation, because I would not take Mr. Proctor out of the part of Gaulantus, which he had played in Philadelphia— quoted precedents never heard of, and, if allowed, only proving him to be wrong in the construction placed upon them by the usages of all well regulated theatres. I endeavoured to combat this folly in vain; he was obstinately bent upon carrying a point which, in the relative position of the two actors, would have been unjust to Mr. Proctor in every sense. I had taken no part in the foolish quarrel, which had driven people from the theatre in disgust; hissing and applauding both of them every night; and I resolved I would not now interfere. To Mr. Connor I had resigned my position in the theatre as an actor, permitting him to play all the light comedy, as well as the leading melo-drama. He had become a great favourite; and at the very time his services were most needed, he thought proper to withdraw, which he did, at the close of the season. Mrs. Lewis, the Ravel family, (with Gabriel,) the Ninth Wonder of the World, Master Meer, Mr. Marble, and Master Burke, were the stars of the season, which closed on the 4th of November, 1837; when they paid me their usual compliment of hissing, which they neglected last season, and gave me 378 dollars for my benefit. There was nothing heard but—how bad the company is—nothing to compare to last season; until, one Sunday afternoon, when the subject was being discussed, I asked for a sheet of paper, recapitulated all the names, and, to the utter confusion of the grumblers, proved that they had only lost Mr. and Mrs. Green, and had acquired Mr. and Mrs. Herbert, Mr. and Mrs. Meer, and Mr. and Mrs. Kent. To their being caught in this trap, I owed the exertion they made for my benefit night; for Pittsburgh was labouring under frightful pecuniary difficulty, from the ruinous rate of exchange, and almost total absence of specie funds in their business transactions.   Notwithstanding this general depression, in seven weeks and a half I took 10,604 dollars—an average of 230 dollars per night.   It is true I paid to the Ravel Family their own terms, and the other stars received a considerable portion of the money; but I here wish to draw a comparison, being forty-six nights in Pittsburgh, and the same number of nights in Philadelphia, the Walnut Street Theatre having been closed during the time the company were in Pittsburgh; 7,940 dollars—an average of 172 dollars 60 cents; a difference in favour of the small city over the large one of 57 dollars 40 cents per night, notwithstanding Booth, Rice, (Jim Crow), Marble, Connor, Murdoch, and Scott, and a new scenic piece; and, strange as it may appear, Booth's benefit yielded 475 dollars 75 cents, and my own, the following night, 483 dollars 25 cents—equal to 969 dollars, in two nights, or one-eighth part of the whole amount of the forty six nights' receipts!!   This was generally the case; the money made in Pittsburgh was lost in the Walnut Street Theatre; whose doors must have closed but for the timely aid received, in cash, from my western friends; yet it is but justice to state, that the expenditure for producing pieces, in the regular course of business, was charged to the account of the Walnut Street Theatre—the Pittsburgh Theatre receiving the advantage derived from scenery and properties, also dresses; and, most of all, the travelling reputation of such pieces as " Zantha," " Thalaba," " Norman Leslie," &c., &c.   For many seasons, Pittsburgh was a source of profit and pleasure; but when the tide did turn, I must show a different statement for forty-six nights.   Locked in by ice on the Ohio, Alleghany, and Monongahala rivers, shut out by snow upon the mountains, 2,308 dollars was all that was received during forty-six nights of a winter season, at the doors of the Pittsburgh Theatre! Unfortunately, the Walnut Street Theatre could not return the compliment of a cash remittance, to make good the deficiency; the season in Philadelphia being almost equally disastrous during the severity of this more than usually severe winter of 1839–1840.

The Chesnut Street Theatre opened, for the fall season of 1836, on the 20th of August; Mr. Robert Hamilton, Mr. Brunton, Mr. Lindsay, Mrs. Broad, and Miss Morgan, were announced as additions to the regular stock company; with Power, Mr. and Mrs. Keeley, Ellen Tree, Madame Celeste, Miss Philips, James Wallack, Dowton, and Gabriel Ravel, with a French troupe.

General Harrison visited the Chesnut Street Theatre, to witness Power's first appearance for the season, in the " Irish

Ambassador.' On the 14th of October, Power's engagement closed; the actor more popular and as attractive as ever: and on the following evening

MR. AND MRS. KEELEY

appeared, the former as Peter Spyke in a "Loan of a Lover,' and the latter as Lucille in a drama of that name, and Gertrude in the farce. Little Bob Keeley, and his still less wife, (Miss Goward,) were a pair of turtle doves worth caging. He is not the only actor who owes his first approach to fame to "Tom and Jerry." His admirable performance of Jemmy Green was one of the gems of the piece; quickly bringing the representative before the audience, as an actor possessed of more genius than heretofore conceded by the public. He was transplanted to the English Opera House, where he became a universal favourite. Mrs. Keeley was there received nightly with smiling faces, and applauding hands, as the soubrette, worthy of a place by the side of Miss Fanny Kelly, imparting such a vigour of colouring to every part she undertook, as to win the hearts of all, both male and female. The popularity of the Keeleys in London induced the offers, which for a time placed them before an American audience; where, if in a pecuniary point of view they were not benefitted as largely as they should have been, they have left a reputation which, should they again visit the United States, will make them the most profitable stars a manager can engage. Unfortunately, it was not until they were on the point of leaving us, the audience began to appreciate their value, and utter useless regrets that they had not availed themselves of the opportunity offered, to witness the performance of these talented artists, who must have returned to England with no very high idea of the judgment of our citizens in theatrical affairs. They continued to act during their first engagement in Philadelphia, until the 29th of October, when they were followed by Mr. James Wallack and Miss Clifton.

The Bowery Theatre in New York having been burnt to the ground after the second performance of "Lafitte," on the 23rd of September, a dramatic festival took place within the National Theatre, (Thomas Flinn, the manager,) as a farewell benefit to Mr. Thomas Hamilton: and no one ever better deserved such a compliment, for his integrity in all business transactions; the 15th of November the night selected—the volunteers on the occasion, Power, Dowton, Hackett, George Barrett, Miss Clifton, Miss Watson, Madame Celeste, Hamblin, and Miss Charlotte Cushman, who sung "The Open Sea;" the pieces—"Henry the Fourth," "Wept of the Wept-on-Wish," and "Three Weeks after Marriage."

On the 28th of November, Celeste produced "La Bayadere," under the title of "The Maid of Cashmere," which has retained its hold in the affections of the people from that date. On the 6th of December, Talfourd's play of "Ion" was first acted in America at the *Walnut Street Theatre !* Mrs. Ternan being the original representative in the United States. For the copy of the play I was indebted to Pierce Butler, Esq.

On the 17th of December, Celeste took another farewell benefit, (*Query,*—what number was this? I have lost count,) and on the 20th, the Ravel family, with the *immortal Gabriel,* commenced a career in Philadelphia, closing the year 1836 in a perfect blaze of theatrical success. The 1st of January, 1837, fell upon a Sunday, and the new year introduced as Julia, in the "Hunchback,"

Miss ELLEN TREE:

an actress who does not impress her audience violently in her favour at first, but gradually increases in their estimation, until finally having obtained a place in their hearts, there she remains in defiance of their better judgment. She must pardon me if I do not entertain so great an opinion of her talent as many of my contemporaries : my admiration of her sister, Miss M. Tree, (Mrs. Bradshaw,) whose performance of Clari and Zaide, in the "Law of Java," placed her so high in my estimation as a tragic actress, that I forgot her fame as a singer in my eulogium upon her acting—may render me an unfair judge of her merit ; her best points painfully bring to my recollection "the light of other days." I have never seen Miss Ellen Tree perform any part in the numerous range of characters she sustains, that left such an impression upon my mind, as to make me desirous of witnessing it a second time. She came to the United States heralded as the best actress of the English stage, (yet strangely enough her great fame in England was acquired after, and not previous, to her first visit to America,) which, being tacitly admitted, no critic was ungallant enough to analyse her claim ; besides her charming affability in private life turned the heads of half the editors, who bit the other half, and thus she triumphantly acquired golden opinions everywhere. May she long continue to convert them into eagles ! She acted during her first engagement, Julia, Rosalind, Lady Townley, Letitia Hardy, Mrs. Haller, Marianna, Beatrice, Juliet, Lady Teazle, Portia, Mrs. Oakley, Donna Violante, Juliana, Viola, Donna Olivia, Kate O'Brien, and Mary in the drama of "The Daughter." If variety be charming, surely here is enough to charm any one ; few stars favour their visitors with such a list.

Mrs. Gibbs, formerly Miss Graddon, played for Walton's

benefit, in "Cinderella," on the 25th of January, and Miss Grove, on the 30th, played Juliet. On the 14th of February, 1837, poor Rowbotham, one of the firm of Maywood and Co., died. He was one of my oldest theatrical friends: I induced him to cross the Atlantic, in 1827. Few actors have left behind them a name more universally respected. His loss will be severely felt in the Chesnut Street Theatre, as an able and strict drill serjeant.

The Arch Street opened on the 1st of May, 1837, with "Paul Pry" and the "May Queen." Power, James Wallack, Mr. and Mrs. Keely, Miss Ellen Tree, the Ravel Family, Miss Turpin, and Celeste, all played short engagements; the last named lady closing the theatre on the 8th of July, with another final leave of her American friends, written by a deaf and dumb poet, and presented to Celeste by General Morris, of the *New York Mirror*, as the play-bills politely informed us.

The Chesnut Street Theatre opened for the fall season, full of mystery. Not a star announced as engaged, but brilliantly lighted with gas on the 18th of August, 1837; the play, "Every one has his Fault" in which Mr. Harrington, one of the most sensible actors to be found among us, made his first appearance as Lord Norland, assuming a position which he held while he remained in the United States. On the 29th, the Budget promised made its appearance: E. Forrest, Hackett, Rice, (Jim Crow,) Ellen Tree, Charles Horn, Bedouin Arabs, Miss Horton, Mr. Brough, and Mr. and Mrs. Wood.

To oppose this galaxy, was offered the horses, ponies, clowns, and equestrians of

COOKE'S NEW CIRCUS.

which opened on the 28th of August, 1837—the most perfect affair of the kind yet offered for support in Philadelphia; but as the Yankees never saw anything upon which their inventive genius could not improve, so the style so new to them was, before Cooke's departure, thrown entirely in the shade. He had opened the eyes of Welsh, Raymond, Bancker, and other equestrian managers, and discovered to them a mine of wealth, which they have been working successfully ever since. No foreign circus can ever again compete with them—so it should be; and their enterprise and energy deserve the success they have met. For a short period the circus was the rage, the fashion, the everything. It continued open until the 21st of December, when, followed by the good wishes of the community, Cooke, and the different members attached to his establishment, proceed to Baltimore to reap fresh honours.

Miss Horton was the first star of the season at the Chesnut Street Theatre; she appeared as Cinderella on the 30th of

August. Hill, the best of all Yankee comedians was the next; then James Browne, a genteel comedian of the first rank; he played Bob Acres and Baron Frederick Willinghurst, on the 18th of September, inducing Mr. W. B. Wood to remark, that he belonged to the breed of actors that he feared was extinct—great praise, Mr. Browne, from such a source. I never heard a fault found with Mr. Browne's acting by any person in the city; but I do not recollect ever to have seen him play, except upon the occasion of some actor's benefit, to a tolerably filled house: indeed it was one beggarly account of empty boxes succeeding another, each night of his engagement—a striking proof that Philadelphia has receded from the high and honourable post she once occupied, which induced actors to look up to her decision of their talent as the pass-word to success. Alas! the same educated class of society rarely darken the doors of the theatre; and I fear the breed of the audience, as well as the actors, is fast becoming extinct. On the 25th of September, Miss Ellen Tree played a round of her favourite characters, and on the 9th of October one of the most extraordinary men belonging to the stage appeared among us—

Mr. VANDENHOFF.

This gentleman for many years enjoyed a high reputation as an actor, in Liverpool and Manchester. In an evil hour, anxious to increase his fame, he accepted an engagement at Covent Garden Theatre, where he made his appearance as King Lear. The press treated him with much severity, but with more civility than the audience. The manager, disappointed in his expectations, tried every annoyance to induce him to abandon his contract. I remember seeing him in a very indifferent melo-drama, founded upon Scott's novel of "Kenilworth," in which he acted the part of Leicester, the audience hissing him regularly as he left the stage. If this also was a managerial device, it failed; he had evidently made up his mind to receive, at least, the wages of his fall. His look of indignation plainly said, "Insult me if you please, I am defenceless; but I can't afford to relinquish my bond: the sovereigns I must have;" and he got them. A compromise took place; for a stated sum of money he agreed to leave the theatre. He returned to the country, hoping to receive from his former patrons sympathy and support. Here he was doomed to meet another disappointment. The fate of all unsuccessful aspirants for theatrical honours awaited him. During his absence Mr. Salter had so well supplied his place, that the audience would not permit the managers to discharge him, or to place him again in a second-rate position, to make an opening for their former favourite. The Montagues and the Capulets of old never carried their feuds to greater length : blood flowed, drawn by the fist instead of the sword, of the opponents. In 1822, every dead piece of wall in Manchester bore an inscription : *Salter for ever—Vandenhoff for ever—No rejected Actors*—giving the town an appearance of an election, during the discussion of some popular question. In Manchester, Salter was the favourite, but in Liverpool the odds were as decidedly in favour of Vandenhoff. The managers were compelled to retain both the actors—at Liverpool Vandenhoff taking the lead, and in Manchester Salter was to be the hero. After a short lapse of time, Vandenhoff returned to London, making now the Haymarket the scene of trial, with no better success : but with the iron nerve of a man of genius, conscious of having been unfairly treated, he made the third attempt, and succeeded, being considered one of the best tragedians of the English stage—indeed we may class him next to Mr. Macready. Not having been announced at the commencement of the season, he appeared without the usual preparation of *puff, puff, puff*. As an actor of cold declamation, he stands unrivalled—his Cato, and his Adrastus in "Ion," may be quoted as specimens of excellence. He made his first bow to a Philadelphia audience in Coriolanus, producing neither wonder nor displeasure. Mrs. Flynn supported him throughout his engagement. Jim Crow (T. Rice) was the next star. The traitor! the deserter! the black varmint!—what induced him to go to the Chesnut Street Theatre? Poor Gumbo Cuff! thy fame has gone—perished, thy broad humour : converted into a Bond Street dandy—Jim Crow turned aristocrat!! At the Walnut Street Theatre, a star of the first magnitude—on the boards of Chesnut Street, a thing to frighten the audience from the boxes. Mr. Rice found this secret out too late : after one good engagement—the reward of his English fame,—he was consigned with diminished attraction, and almost annihilated popularity, to the minor theatres, which he should never have left. All the new farces he brought with him, were formed for the meridian of London : too genteel for American negroes, and, consequently, troublesome only to the actors, and unproductive to the treasury. Rice's excellent performance of Othello in the "Black Opera," has redeemed his reputation. Why don't he associate himself with Palmo's "Ethiopean Opera Company?" His splendid voice and business tact will create for him, under such an arrangement, another fortune.

On the 15th of December, a public dinner was tendered to Mr. E. Forrest, by his fellow citizens of Philadelphia, for the able manner in which he had acquitted himself upon the London stage, claiming as an American, in the metropolis of the British empire, the right to be enrolled as an actor with their own Garrick, Kean, and Kemble. Nicholas Biddle, at this time a great man, (alas! for human greatness; had he died before the suspension of specie payments by the banks, what a reputation had been his in the history of after ages,—now the finger of scorn is pointed at his memory, as a financial Charlatan, who, by his wild theory and speculation, ruined thousands of his countrymen ! ! !)—was announced to take the chair; but being prevented by sickness, his place was supplied by Chief Justice Gibson, supported by Judge Roger, Mayor Swift, Joseph R. Ingersoll, Morton M'Michael, Louis A. Godey, E. Holden, &c., &c., &c. Mr. E. Forrest, and his friend, Mr. Leggett, of New York, being duly introduced by the Committee, the good things provided for the occasion by mine host of the Merchants' Hotel, (Mr. Sanderson,) were dispatched with the usual celerity on such occasions, and the speeches, which were excellent, commenced. Mayor Swift's allusion to the first attempt of Forrest to act in public, under the influence of the laughing gas, at the Tivoli Garden, in Market Street, caused a roar of laughter, in which no one joined more heartily than the tragedian himself. Forrest's speech had in the delivery too much of the Metamora style about it, but the matter was decidedly good; and although protesting that he was no actor here, (at the festive board,) yet he never acted so well in his life, as during this reply to the compliments profusely showered upon him.

When a public dinner is given in honour of a naval or a military hero, their professional brethren are sure to muster in their strength,—nothing but *duty* can induce them to absent themselves: the same "esprit de corps" governs statesmen, lawyers, and politicians; but a dinner to an actor, as the reward of literary service rendered to his country, was such an unusual event, that the novelty should have induced the attendance of every actor who respected his profession—their numbers should have spoken their feelings in this just cause of triumph to their art. In the days of Jefferson, Francis, Warren, and Burke, what a display would have graced this table; but while the bar, the press, and even the pulpit, were represented fully, the stage alone was numerically absent— W. B. Wood, Maywood, myself, E. S. Conner, Charles Porter, and Howard the vocalist, were the only members of the profession present. A deputation should have been there from the theatres of Boston, New York, Baltimore, and Washington, anxious to avail themselves of such an opportunity of proving that the stage was, and is, a profession that any man of learning might feel proud to embrace.

As a compliment to Mr. E. Forrest, this dinner was a flattering mark of the estimation in which his talent was held in his native city; but I should have preferred recording

that he was to be found as the esteemed guest of those gentlemen who met here to do him honour at their private dwell-
ings, giving to the actor a claim to the position of a gentleman, in the society of gentlemen, upon terms of admitted·
equality—respected and respecting. Is this for ever to be
forbidden ground? It has been asserted, that the conduct of
the foreign actors has been such as to close the doors of society
against their admission; but gentlemen, in mercy, visit not
these sins on the heads of your own countrymen. The time
is fast approaching when all your actors will be Americans;
give them, then, an inducement to elevate their profession—
show them that the doors of society are thrown open to them,
courting their admission. You will find them then rational
companions, eager to wipe out the stain of vagabondism
unjustly stamped upon their brow for ages.

CHAPTER XXXIII.

Opening of the American Theatre. "The Destruction of Jerusalem."
Introduction to Captain Marryatt. Destruction of Cook's Circus.
Movement of Managers in his behalf. Pittsburgh again. Mr. Parsons,
the actor and preacher. A Curious Letter. A Rebublican Lady.
Madam Augusta. Bad management of her husband. A Letter of E.
Forrest's.

On the 15th of November, 1837, I opened the American
Theatre in Philadelphia, with Booth as Hamlet, followed by
the farce of the "Welsh Girl;" receipts, 344 dollars. I had
hoped, by remaining in Pittsburgh, to have escaped the run
of success which Cooke commanded with his New Circus; my
company, too, had undergone a change not much for the
better; Conner had left me for the Chesnut Street Theatre.
My force stood thus: James Anderson, stage manager, Messrs.
Hadaway, Proctor, William Warren, C. Porter, Addams, Rice,
Joseph Smith, Kent, Herbert, Vaché, Grierson, Percival, F.
Myers, Wemyss, Wilks, Jackson, Mc Conachy, J. Van Stavo-
reen, Crouta, and Bannister; Mesdames Kent, Proctor (Willis,)
Bannister. Herbert, Wilks; Misses Warren, Price, C. Price,
Packard, White, and Ruth.

On Monday, the 20th of November, Bannister's play of the
"Destruction of Jerusalem," nicknamed the "Destruction of
the Walnut Street Theatre," was produced; the scenery, by
Russel Smith, was grand and imposing; the temple of Solomon, and the market-place of Jerusalem, with the last
scene, an exact copy of Martin's picture of Satan in Council,

o

surpassed anything I had seen for effect. Unfortunately, I
made Satan an angel of light; had I represented a devil,
with horns, hoof, and tail, the piece would have succeeded;
but a hue and cry was raised that it was the spirit of truth
and not the spirit of evil I raised. This proved fatal; pro-
fanity, sacrilege, contempt of religion, and a catalogue of un-
heard-of crimes were laid to my charge. The Press thought-
lessly joined the foolish cry; and after the sixth night, the
piece was withdrawn—yielding, in six nights, 1161 dollars to
pay 2700 dollars, a loss, in the second week of the season, of
1539 dollars. On the following Monday, by hard labour, a
new drama, the "Demon of the Desert," was produced—*failed.*
Mr. Booth was sent for, arrived on the 11th of December,
and played Richard—*he also failed.* By the six nights
engagement I lost 356 dollars, a very pretty beginning of
a season. Marble played three nights—*worse and worse;* the
receipts of the engagement, including his benefit of which he
received half, amounted to only 321 dollars. Christmas night,
another new piece, 196 dollars; but "Thæuba" was not more
fortunate than its predecessors. A host of benefits followed,
most of them *loss-ions*—Proctor's and Mrs. Kent's the only profitable ones. I now tried Porter the giant, and Major Stephens
the dwarf—*no use.* On the sixtieth night of the season I announced "Scotch Clans and Irish Chieftains," in which Mr.
Anderson's stage arrangements were admirable; but the 23d
of January *fixed their doom.* Nothing could succeed; the
"Destruction of Jerusalem" had, indeed, spread a blight upon
the theatre; 30 dollars, 40 dollars, and 50 dollar houses were
more frequent than agreeable spectacles. The first glimpse of
success was my complimental benefit, the arrangements for
which having been completed on the 8th of February, I had
the pleasure of seeing 1,084 dollars in the house—the pieces
being the "School for Scandal," and "State Secrets." The
volunteers on the occasion were, W. B. Wood, R. C. Maywood,
E. S. Conner, Mary Anne Lee, James Howard, W. C. Brough,
W. E. Burton, Thomas Faulkner, H. G. Allen, George Taylor,
Mrs. Hamilton, Mr. Walton, and Mr. Pearson. On this occasion I had the pleasure of an introduction to Captain Marryatt,
who, be his faults what they may, is an excellent companion.
Who brought him behind the scenes I do not know, but he
did not leave the back of the house as straight as he entered,
sundry glasses of champagne having elevated him to a state
of happy forgetfulness for the time being. This seasonable
relief to the funds of the treasury, although not as large as I
and my friends had calculated upon, was most serviceable.

On the 3d of February, a most appalling calamity took place
in Baltimore, the destruction, by fire, of Cooke's Amphitheatre, and all his splendid stud of forty horses—not one

saved! In twelve hours reduced, from comparative wealth, to want and misery in a foreign country. A meeting of the citizens was held in his favour, and resolutions passed to open books of subscription in his behalf; to apply for the use of the Holiday Theatre for a benefit—prices of tickets to be 2 dollars each; and a circular to be addressed to managers of the different theatres, to co-operate in measures for his relief.

Managers needed no prompting to such a deed. Before the resolutions were passed, Mr. Cooke was in possession of a letter from me, placing the Walnut Street Theatre at his disposal for any night he chose to name, without reference to my engagements, which I undertook to regulate, so that they should not interfere with any action for his immediate relief.

Hamblin, of New York, presented him forthwith with his original theatrical horse, Mazeppa; which induced others to offer him splendid horses; so that the great burnt-out was shortly on his feet again, and able to open his Circus, in Philadelphia, on the 6th of March. He met little or no encouragement; even the benefit at his own theatre was a failure. Oh, Philadelphia, this was not thy usual mode of treating misfortunes!—where the sufferer, too, was admitted on all hands to be worthy of thy sympathy.

In answer to my letter, I received the following:

"February 8th, 1833.

"MY DEAR FRIEND,

"I am requested by Mr. Cook to say that the anguish of his mind, and bodily illness, have jointly been the cause of his delay in answering your kind and welcome letter.

"Mr. Cooke accepts your offer, and will be happy to hear when the night is appointed. If "Monsieur Tonson" will give you no additional trouble, I will come over and act Monsieur Morbleu, as I have never appeared in Philadelphia. Mr. Cooke acknowledges your kindness most gratefully, as the first manager who has stept forward, and will always acknowledge the real obligation. Be kind enough to reply as early as possible, and probably I shall set off on the receipt of your answer, to make whatever interest I can among Mr. Cooke's friends.

"I am, for poor Cooke,

"Your very obedient servant,

(Signed) "J. W. AMHERST."

"P. S. Address Mr. Thomas Cooke, Gay Street, Baltimore.

"To Francis C. Wemyss, Esq.,

"Walnut Street Theatre, Philadelphia."

The benefit took place at the Walnut Street Theatre, on the 21st of February, (Wednesday). "The Battle of Poictiers," Herr Cline, and "the Weathercock;" receipts 600 dollars, 25 cents. Mr. and Mrs. George Jones acted three nights, and Booth once more—three nights, 184 dollars, 56 dollars, 174

dollars. Oh dear! oh dear! "Battle of Poictiers," produced
in lavish style, by Barrymore, with the ceremony of the In-
stallation of the Knights of the Garter, on the 19th of
February. *A more horrible failure than any thing yet!* Mrs.
Barrymore, four nights, only 220 dollars; and on the 21st of
March I brought this ruinous season to a close, with the
"Poor Gentleman," and "Sam Slick," for my benefit—279
dollars. Oh what a house.

Never did I turn my face towards my Pittsburgh friends
with so joyful a heart, as I stepped into the stage, on the 26th day
of March, to commence my spring season, which opened on the
31st of March, 1838, with "Faith and Falsehood," and "The
Secret;" house, 253 dollars. Monday, 2nd of April, 239 dollars—manager and actors elated by the view of full houses.
Nothing raises the spirits of an army so much as a sudden
victory. In the midst of gloom and defeat, the same result
followed in the theatre. The actors seemed to have acquired
new energy; and for eleven weeks, good humour, good houses,
and good living made every one happy and contented. The
benefits this season were all good. In this the citizens of
Pittsburgh evinced good judgment. Nothing makes a clever
actor more desirous of returning to a city than this attention
to his interest on the night of his benefit. I wish the example was followed elsewhere. My good friends of Philadelphia,
adopt this, even if it does proceed from the West of the
mountains; the talent of your stock actors will be materially
improved by it. On the 12th of April, Mrs. Watson played
Diana Vernon, in "Rob Roy," and treated the citizens of
Pittsburgh, for the first time, to an opera: playing "The
Barber of Seville," on the 16th, to a house of 348 dollars. Dr.
Valentine was the next star: but his eccentricities did not
seem to meet the expectations of his auditors. On the 7th
of May, Mr. Parsons commenced an engagement: this gentleman was a favourite—but, on the following season, provoked
the wrath of the Pittsburghers, by a very foolish speech,
which they resented, by throwing a portion of one of the
benches at his head. If I, as the manager of the theatre,
could laugh at their fun, and turn the practice of hissing me
at the end of each season, into a good-humoured joke, perfectly
understood between the audience and myself, surely he, as
my representative, should have possessed more sense than to
notice as an insult what was intended as "a lark"—a foolish
one if you please, but not a justification for the impertinent
speech he thought proper to address to them, and which they
so promptly resented. Mr. Parsons is now engaged in preach-
ing the Holy Gospel, and has learnt, I hope, that soft words
frequently turn away evil designs. May his ministry to his
Heavenly Master prove more successful than his stewardship

did to me, as his earthly one—and, above all, let him remember he cannot serve God and Mammon ! ! !

Here is a letter from a gentleman studying theology, with a view to being ordained a minister :—

(COPY.)

"MY DEAR WEMYSS:—Mrs. Shaw's engagement, no go. First night, 105 dollars; second night, "Lady of Lyons," 126 dollars; third night, "Ion," 80 dollars. What do you think of that? This place of Pittsburgh is not worth the attentions of any manager. I am disgusted with it, and never again in my professional character, will I visit it. A monkey show, at a fip a head, is equal to their deserts, and fully adapted to their intellectuality—more is beyond their conception; blast them. I am almost sick of the ways of management, if such is to be my success, and I think you will agree with me too. Therefore, if I was not already engaged to you, for Baltimore, I should, I think, decline the whole matter; but, as it is, I will do all I can to make things go right.

"Please write me by return, and give such instructions as you may think proper.

"Yours truly,
"PITTSBURGH, Nov. 16, 1838." (Signed,) "C. B. PARSONS."

On the 18th of May, 1838, Bulwer's play of the "Lady of Lyons" was acted, for the first time in the United States, at Pittsburgh—for my benefit ! Mrs. Proctor (Mrs. Willis, Miss H. Warren) was the Pauline, and Bannister the Claude Melnotte. Jim Crow Rice was the last star of the season, which closed on the 16th of June, 1838, with Mrs. Kent's benefit, "The Rent Day," and "The Pet of the Petticoats,"—amount of house, 306 dollars. I returned to Philadelphia and opened the American Theatre in Walnut Street, on the 23d of June, 1838, commencing a season which lasted for three hundred and eighty-five consecutive nights, or sixty-four weeks and one night, unprecedented in the annals of theatricals—once more rising to the height of popular favour as a manager. Oh, fleeting fame ! how evanescent ! The "Comedy of Errors" and "Jim Crow in London"—the houses very bad indeed.

On the 10th of August, in face of remonstrance from all quarters, I produced a pageant, entitled "the Coronation of Queen Victoria—IT WAS SUCCESSFUL. I followed, as nearly as I could recollect, the arrangement of Elliston's grand spectacle of the "Coronation of George the Fourth," refreshing my memory from the London newspapers, which were filled with the accounts of the coronation of Britain's youthful queen. It taught the audience once more the road to the Walnut Street Theatre, which they appeared to have forgotten; yet,

Mrs. Bannister's (Mrs. Stone's) republican feelings were so much annoyed, that she so far forgot her position to the manager and the audience, as to hiss the last verse of God save the Queen for several nights, inducing a few in front of the theatre to follow her example—rather an hazardous experiment, and perfectly uncalled-for. Her livelihood depended upon the success of the theatre which she thus tried to embarrass.

On the 24th of September,

MADAME AUGUSTA

appeared to a house of 877 dollars, filled with ladies, wherever a seat could be obtained. She was young, handsome, and possessed talent of the first order in her profession. The announcement of La Bayadere, under such circumstances, created an excitement which the folly and stupidity of Mr. St. James overturned. He engaged to furnish the services of his wife, (Mrs. Bailey,) as Ninka; Mr. Bishop, as the Unknown; and Mr. Archer, as Olifour, with twelve ladies as a corps de ballet. He arrived in Philadelphia with Mrs. Philips, in the place of Mrs. Bailey; *no Olifour;* and Mr. Horncastle, lent by Mr. Wallack, for one night, from the National Theatre in New York. Mr. Pickering, at the last moment, stepped forward and read the part of Olifour, from the score : but for this act of kindness, the audience must have been dismissed; yet Mr. St. James never offered him the slightest compensation. Horncastle being compelled to return to New York, Madame Augusta was announced in *Three Dances;* the engagement destroyed; for La Somnambula, as a ballet, did not prove acceptable in face of such a disappointment.

On the 19th of September, I received from Mr. Forrest the following letter, in answer to a question, why he was not announced as engaged at the Chesnut Street Theatre? where they had been so anxious to secure his services a few months before, when he so misled me as to his intentions.

"MY DEAR WEYMESS :—A press of business prevented my answering your letter yesterday.

"As to J. R. Scott, I have a rule which forbids my playing for any benefit but the benefit of the Theatrical Fund." I shall be most happy to pay him, out of my own purse, fifty dollars a week during the engagement, and I have no doubt that a like sum paid by you, would secure his services.

"In answer to your question, why I have not performed at the Park Theatre, listen—Mr. Price, to suit his own purposes, chose to infer that I would quit the profession this year, and so engaged the best of the season to foreigners, and to the exclusion of all native histrions. I always take pleasure in welcoming to our shores any exotic talent; but certainly not to the entire exclusion of that which is "native and to the manor born."

"I went to the National Theatre, where I was offered my own time.

"As for Maywood, he did not offer me an engagement, *of course*, as you must be aware that arrangements of the Chesnut Street Theatre are made in subservience to the wishes expressed or implied of the Park manager. Perhaps, however, his anti-republican principles were so shocked at my consenting to deliver a fourth of July Oration before the democracy of New York, that he determined to punish me for my offence, by excluding me from the Chesnut Street Theatre. But whatever motives operated with him or others, thanks to the "real people," I have, so far, been going on swimmingly.

"Last night, my benefit was between 1400 and 1500 dollars.

"Yours sincerely,

"New York, Sep. 18, 1838.   (Signed,)   " EDWIN FORREST."

CHAPTER XXXIV.

Return of Forrest to the Walnut Street.   "Amilie."   The Front Street Theatre and Circus in Baltimore.   A losing Concern.   Parsons study-ing Theology.

ON the 25th of October, E. Forrest returned to the theatre, where he first received those exhorbitant terms which swelled his fortunes; and the patrons of which he had displeased, by breaking a pledge made by himself—unsolicited by the audi-ence—that so long as the doors of this theatre (the Walnut Street,) were open to him, he wanted no other home, &c., &c. (See his address in 1829, at the close of his engagement with Ainslee and Blake.)   We have him here again, and so let *by-gones* be *by-gones*.   He played Othello in a masterly style, to 573 dollars; Damon, to 515 dollars; Claude Melnotte, to 553 dollars; Macbeth to 379 dollars; Metamora to 654 dollars; Metomora to 703 dollars! and Claude Melnotte and William Tell, for his benefit, to 862 dollars.   As the price of admission was only fifty cents to the boxes, and twenty-five cents to the pit, I may assert that more persons visited the theatre during this engagement, than on any previous occasion for the same length of time.   He repeated Metamora on Tuesday, the 23rd, to 413 dollars; Gladiator, 589 dollars; Claude. Melnotte, 375 dollars; Gladiator, 477 dollars; Richard III., 428 dollars; Gladiator and Carwin, for benefit, 851 dallars.

So determined was he at this time, in his opposition to May-wood, that when I laughingly proposed to cut him out of " Amilie," if I could get the music, he turned jest into earnest, by stating he knew Simpson had it; and if I would really do it, he would undertake to get it from the Park Theatre.   *Done*, and it was *done*—well *done*, on the 19th of November, in eighteen days from the time of this conversation. Forrest left Philadelphia for New York, on the 30th of October; on the 31st, I received this letter—

MY DEAR WEMYSS :—Simpson has promised me the words, music, &c., complete, of the opera of "Amilie," with this provision, that I pledge myself that what he lends shall not be copied, or used in such a way, that any other theatre may appropriate it to its use. I have pledged myself to this, and I expect the same pledge from you. Mr. Brough will be the bearer of "Amilie" to you.   "Yours respectfully,
" New York, October 31, 1838.   (Signed,)   EDWIN FORREST."

This was, indeed, quick work. Brough returned to New York to engage Bishop and Mrs. Charles Horn ; but some misunderstanding about terms with this lady, whose husband first demanded one thing, and then another, nearly overturned the whole arrangement. I proceeded to New York, and succeeded in obtaining Bishop and Madam Otto, engaged several chorus singers, and returning, commenced active preparations. The Walnut Street Theatre presented the appearance of a large academy of music—every room had a piano going; Mr. Taylor, Mr. B. Cross, Mr. Allen, and Mr. Bishop, each plied the chorus, from nine in the morning, until four in the afternoon of each day, while Brough and Madame Otto, with Bishop, devoted every hour to acquire their parts : the painting room was all activity, and the wardrobe presented a lively scene ; and at half-past eleven o'clock, on Monday night, the 19th of November, I had the satisfaction to hear the curtain descend upon the finale, followed by cheers, and such applause as rewards a manager for past labour, by the knowledge that the receipts of his treasury will be increased. Congratulations poured in from all quarters; for twelve nights. "Amilie" retained triumphant possession of the stage, and was reluctantly laid aside, to make way for the second engagement of Mr. Forrest, which, by contract, commenced on the 3rd of December. Bishop, as the Chamois Hunter, established himself as a tenor singer of taste and judgment ; the broken English of Madame Otto threw a pleasing charm around the part of Amilie, while Brough did his best to aid the efforts of the other two : the object was the result ; and the great object effected, the charm of novelty was gone, and the love-spell which held the city of New York captive so long, was broken before it was half done by the playing of Wilson, Seguin, and Mrs. Sheriff, in their unrivalled English opera ; as will presently appear.

in the United States, erected by Minifee, was opened to the public, with a large dramatic, as well as equestrian corps; the latter under the direction of S. Nichols,—the pieces of "Loan of a lover," equestrian exercies, and the farce of Raising the Wind"—amount of house, 525 dollars; the company, Mr. Parsons, Mr. J. Smith, Mr. and Mrs. H. Eberle, Mr. and Mrs. Rowe, Mr. Russell, Mr. Winans, Mr. Peceval, Mr. and Mrs. Anderson, Mrs. Proctor, Mrs. A. Knight, Mrs. Cramer, Plumer, Mr. Collins, Mr. and Mrs. Jackson, Mr. Vanstavoren, Mr. Woodbury, Mrs. Groves, Mr. Barry, Mr. and Mrs. Foster, Joe Murphy, and a strong corps de ballet; the equestrians, J. Aymar, Whittaker, Nichols, Knap, Hows, Andreas and Son, Miss Nicholas, Mr. and Mrs. Cole, R. Myers, Lipman, Mr. Woolford, ring-master, and a corps of Lilliputian dancers, under the direction of Amherst; Gossin, and Mr. and Mrs. Gardner, were engaged, but did not come. My nightly expenses were three hundred and twenty-eight dollars; the consequence was, in nine weeks I lost 2,768 dollars: the whole equestrian department, horses and riders, were a dead weight upon the stage performance; the "Bronze Horse," for ten nights averaged 400 dollars, I despatched the horses to Philadelphia, and endeavoured to retrieve losses by a succession of show pieces. Parsons who was the acting and stage manager, at a salary of fifty dollars per week, was studying theology in the theatre; neglecting the business, and caring about nothing but receiving his money from the treasury in which he was, punctually personified; I gladly cancelled his engagement, and have never met him since. In the pulpit his labours may be more successful; but from his career—his sudden return to the stage—I fear the love of notoriety, not religion, is the guiding principle.

I ought to have known Baltimore better; but I thought a *dash*, with everything of the best around me, would have made at least one brilliant season. It was a fatal error: had I confined my efforts to the stage alone, and followed that season by a circus, without dramatic performance, I should have hit the right nail upon the head. At the end of a season of one hundred and twenty-one nights, they made me a benefit of 751 dollars, for which they have my thanks; although they would not come to see Burton, Balls, J. Sefton, Marble, Wood and his dogs, Emma Ince, and Mary Ann Lee.

On the 3rd of December, at the American, in Philadelphia, Forrest, Oxley, and Mrs. Shaw, played seven nights, yielding to Mr. Forrest 1,467 dollars but to the treasury of the theatre —*nothing!* deducting the amount paid for the services of Oxley and Mrs. Shaw. Mr. Forrest's second engagement entailed a loss upon the theatre.

On the 9th of February, Nichols and his horses, from Balti-

mere, commenced an engagement with the " Forty Thieves ;"
and if in the Front Street Theatre they had proved a most
unprofitable speculation, at the Walnut Street Theatre, for
seven weeks, they continued to draw good houses, not only
retrieving all losses, but leaving a surplus in the treasury.
This season was one of singular changes : commencing on the
23rd of June, 1838, the middle of October found a deficiency
of over five thousand dollars ; the 20th of March found the
whole loss retrieved, and a continued gain to the termination
of the season, on the three hundred and eighty-fifth night, the
14th of September, 1839 ; the best, and, in fact, the only great
season I ever had in the Walnut Street Theatre, which was the
sink that swallowed up all the gains of Pittsburgh, and continually cried *more, more !* The equestrian drama produced,
was " Forty Thieves," " El Hyder," " Timour the Tartar,"
" Cataract of the Ganges," " Lodoiska," " Blue Beard," and
the " Tiger Horde." During this engagement, my master-
carpenter, James Landers, left me to build the stage of the
new Bowery Theatre ; he was a loss, indeed ; he is the best
theatrical carpenter and machinist in the United States.

The Pittsburgh Theatre, this spring, opened on the 13th of
May, 1839, with " Laugh when You Can," and " Raphael,"
Balls playing Gossamer. The citizens of Pittsburgh almost
killed him with kindness out of the theatre, if they did not
answer his expectations behind the curtain ; his head was not
hard enough to attempt the game he nearly fell a martyr to ;
to see a Pittsburgh *bon vivant* under the table, is a task few
attempt who knew them, and fewer succeed in accomplishing.
My friend Balls was a child at this game, and they laughed at
him for his folly, until an attack of *mania-a-potu* turned a joke
into earnest, and both parties withdrew from the contest,
equally ashamed of having participated in it.

On the 22nd of May, the Bedouin Arabs astonished the
natives, while Miss Mason, Mr. and Mrs. Sloman, John Sefton,
and Mr. E. Forrest, kept up the ball most successfully ; the
season closing on the 29th of June, with " A Lesson for Ladies,"
and " Cramond Brig," for my benefit ; a little hissing, as usual,
and a splendid bottle of Champagne to wash it down afterwards : this was my last visit professionally to Pittsburgh.
Mr. Parsons superintended the following season, and Mr.
Jackson finished the game, in 1840, with a loss of four thousand
dollars in seventy-two nights, the greater portion of which,
unfortunately, remained unpaid.

CHAPTER XXXV.

The Walnut Street Leased to Cooke. Opening of the Chesnut Street.
A Galaxy of Stars. Madame Vestris. Mr. Seguin. Miss Sheriff.

On the 2d of April, 1838, by permission of the board of agents, I let the Walnut Street Theatre to Cooke, for the production of horse pieces. This consent, gentlemen, twelve months sooner, would have been worth several thousand dollars a-year to you, prevented the building of the Circus, and saved your tenant from ruin. Now it was a matter of indifference, and yielded by you for the sake of the income derived from the bars, the theatre being closed at the time. He produced "Mazeppa," in splendid style, followed it with "Napolean," so well done by Barrymore, which failed; and on the 25th of April, the "Cataract of the Ganges" sharing a similar fate, he closed his doors on the 25th of May, never to open them again in America; returned to his native country with blighted prospects and ruined fortune, to commence a new career, at a time when age should have been rendered comfortable in retirement. He left behind him a name respected by all with whom he had the slightest business transactions. May success attend his future movements.

On the 28th of April, Mr. Vandenoff appeared as Cato. A new piece entitled "Sam Weller," from the Pickwick Papers, seems to have been very successful at the Chesnut Street Theatre, rather an unusual occurrence there with that style of dramatic literature. On the 1st of June, Conner played Richard the Third, to how many spectators is not recorded; and on the 26th, Mr. W. B. Wood claimed the honour of being the first representative in Philadelphia of Claude Melnotte, in "The Lady of Lyons,"—sixty won't do for twenty-six years of age! Why did he not try Col. Damas?

On the 25th of August, 1838, the Chesnut Street Theatre was announced to open with a host upon host of various attraction; but one damper to the whole—*the prices were again to be raised,* of course to be again lowered. The list of stars ran: Mrs. Matthews, late Madame Vestris; Miss Sheriff, Madame Celeste, Mademoiselle Stephon, and a corps de ballet Tyrone Power, Charles Matthews, Wilson, Seguin, Mons. Hazard, Bedouin Arabs, James Wallack, and Hackett. The pieces on the first night, "Wives as they Were, and Maids as they are," and "The Ladies' Man;" a very good house.

The 8th October brought before us

, MADAME VESTRIS, (MRS. CHARLES MATTHEWS,)

who appeared as Gertrude, in "The Loan of a Lover," and
Julia, in "One Hour, or the Carnival Ball." Without
entering into any defence of the faults of Mrs. Charles
Matthews, to her the American theatres are indebted for the
improvement so apparent in the arrangement of the stage,
carpets, ottoman's, grates, fenders, centre-tables, &c., in
drawing-rooms; gravel-walks, beds of flowers, hot-house
plants, in gardens, are all her work. Among the number
of ladies who have attempted the difficult task of managing
a theatre, she alone has succeeded. Look at the perfect manner in which the light pieces were produced at the Olympic
Theatre, in London. Every thing requisite to complete the
illusion of the scene *was there*—and she insisted, as a "sine
qua non" with the American managers, that they should *be
here also*. For this alone she deserves the gratitude as well as
admiration of every visitor of the play-house. As an actress
in the varied extent of the drama, she has *no* superior: and
any auditor who could listen unmoved to her "Clara," in
"The Barrack Room," may for ever renounce all claim to taste
or judgment in theatrical matters. The prejudice excited
against her by an unfortunate expression, said to have been
uttered by her at Saratoga, prevented her from receiving an
impartial hearing at the hands of an American audience; her
engagement was a failure both in money and reputation. But
this is not to be attributed to want of talent in her profession.
The absurd cry that she was no actress, and unworthy of the
reputation she enjoyed, was raised by prejudice, and was anything but creditable to the judgment (which was never used)
of the American public. The manner in which she resented
the mortification she experienced was ill-judged; and her attack upon Jim Crow Rice, although not intended as ill nature,
was so construed, and gave him an opportunity to lampoon
her with effect, in what he termed his own lyric style, turning
all her efforts into ridicule. Every body joined in the hue-
and-cry against her, and seemed determined to prevent her
success: every opportunity was eagerly seized to wound her
pride. How well this succeeded, her speedy return to England
proclaims; but this result was the effect of accident, not design. A brilliant campaign was anticipated for her; and her
failure is to be attributed to occurrences which took place out
of the theatre. To her husband, Mr. Charles Matthews, the
audience was better disposed: every thing he did was appreciated, and the praises lavished upon his professional efforts
were intended as another thorn to be planted in her side, by
building up a reputation for him upon her downfall. His

merit I am fully willing to admit; but I question whether he felt flattered by the approbation he received in the United States. He made his appearance in Philadelphia as Peter Spyke, in "A Loan of a Lover; " Motley, in "He would be an Actor;" and Charles Swiftly, in " One Hour, or the Carnival Ball." Their engagement was a succession of houses—*bad, worse, worst;* and on the 20th of October, they brought it to a close with "The Welsh Girl," "Clatter *versus* Patter," "The Handsome Husband," and the "Carnival Ball." They declined visiting either Baltimore or Boston, and returned forthwith to London, where Madame, no doubt, has recovered the equanimity of her temper, and arrived at the conclusion, that the Yankees are uncivilized brutes, who cannot appreciate good acting. In truth, she has good cause for her spleen.

Celeste followed, as Madeline, in St. Mary's Eve;" and to oppose Forrest's career at the Walnut-street Theatre, played nightly in two pieces, and, on the 3d of November, announced positively her last appearance (until the next time). Her farewells have become truly laughable; but they seem always to answer the purpose of a full house.

Power played on the 5th, Rory O'More; and on the 13th, after his usual success, announced his benefit, Paudheen O'Rafferty, in " Born to Good Luck," and Larry Hoolagan, in " More Blunders than one," when his rich brogue was no longer heard within the walls of Old Drury, but was transferred to the Haymarket, London.

Mrs. H. Cramer played Mrs. Haller, on the 26th of November; a really clever stock actress. And on the 4th of December, Celeste again—Toujour Celeste! another farewell benefit on the 22d of December. Wallack, now the popular manager of the National Theatre, in New York, played the Brigand; Mrs. Walstein, a humble but useful member of the company, took her farewell of the stage, on the 8th of January, to seek retirement in the arms of matrimony—may she be happy. On the 14th of January, 1839, Mr. Seguin and Miss Sheriff opened in "La Somnambula." Of Mr. Wilson, it would be superfluous to say more than that he supported his high reputation as a tenor singer, and warbled himself into the good graces of the audience. Of

Mr. SEGUIN,

I may add, there is a vein of rich, comic humour flowing through every part he undertakes, which would have made him a favourite as a comic actor in the best days of the drama, without the aid of the rich bass voice which reaches your ear in a full tone of melody. He is the buffo par excellence of

P

English opera, a position he will long retain; and strong indeed must he be that rivals pretension to fame, who can wrest the title from him.

Miss SHERIFF,

although the last named, by no means the least of the trio in the list of the songstresses who have visited the New World. She stands second only to Mrs. Wood; and the success of the opera of "Amilie," at New York, has given her fame and reputation throughout the United States superior to any she enjoyed in London. Aided by Wilson and Seguin, she accomplished the usual tour of European Artistes, returning to England with pleasant reminiscences, a purse well filled with dollars, the result of Yankee admiration of her talent; not having been involved in any theatrical *fracas*, so fatal to the popularity of the stars, who frequently permit their tempers to get the better of their common sense, and by one hasty expression of anger mar all their future prospects.

On the 18th of January, "Amilie," the music of which had enchanted the New Yorkers, and held possession of the stage to the exclusion of any other opera, was produced at the Chesnut Street Theatre. I had presented it sufficiently well at the Walnut Street to destroy any great excitement; the airs had become familiar, and, notwithstanding the full force of the chorus from the National Theatre, it failed to draw money. If I am asked for my proof, behold it in the fact, that neither Miss Sheriff, Mr. Wilson, nor Mr. Seguin would venture to take it for a benefit. It was one of those fair (unfair) movements in management, which frequently overthrow well-laid schemes. That the opera was better done at the Chesnut Street Theatre, as a whole, nobody will be fool-hardy enough to deny; but there were detached portions better executed at the Walnut Street, while the scenery was far superior to that presented at Old Drury; and many preferred the counterfeit to the genuine "Amilie."

Herr Cline, Mrs. Watson, and Miss Clarence Wells, filled up the month of February; and the 4th of March astonished us with the presence of my old friends, the Slomans. She opened in "Isabella," he in "Sam Savoury"—attraction gone never to return! While their numerous personal friends rejoiced to see them once more, the public in general cared nothing about them; and even Sloman's ten comic songs failed to produce a house on his benefit night that he would have been willing to pay five hundred dollars for, before the doors opened, as he did to Mr. Warren, for his first benefit in Philadelphia.

CHAPTER XXXVI.

THE late season at the Walnut Street Theatre having in some measure retrieved the losses of the previous one, and my arrangements for the campaign of 1839-40 giving me confidence of a continuation of success, having secured the services of E. Forrest, Burton, Hill, Mr. and Mrs. Seguin, Horncastle, and Latham, Nichols and his horses to commence upon. Mr. Henry G. Freeman, after these engagements were made, gave me notice that the board of agents had come to the conclusion, not to renew my lease unless I agreed to raise the price of admission to the Pit (the support of the house, that nothing but this stupid arrangement could drive away), to thirty-seven and a half cents. Never having previously charged more than twenty-five cents, and having resisted every argument of Forrest, Augusta, and others, to tamper with the prices, I was compelled to yield my judgment to the dictation of gentlemen who, understanding their own business, might, at least have given me credit for understanding mine, after, with care and labour, having raised their theatre to a reputation it had never, since Blake's time, enjoyed. Remonstrance, argument, all was vain—the alternative, leave the theatre. Would to heaven I had done so. But throughout my whole business connection with Mr. H. G. Freeman—(for the other gentlemen of the board were but his satellites: they might oppose his views, but, on the system of freedom of election, if they did, next year they could not retain their seat in the board, his overwhelming vote and interest placing any puppet he chose to nominate in the position of an agent)—the more I yielded, the more he demanded, until at last worn out by the positive injustice of his demands, and the insolent contempt with which a letter addressed to the board of agents was treated, I resolved to give up the theatre. Forced to drive away the staunch support of the house, by levying an advance of fifty per cent. upon the admission, for no other reason than that the Chesnut Street Theatre had advanced their prices; and Mr. H. G. Freeman being also a member of the board of agents of that theatre, sacrificed me. What was the Chesnut Street Theatre, or its arrangement of prices to me, or to my audience? *They* had continually trifled with the prices of admission, I never—maintaining that one fixed price was the way to insure steady patronage. The consequence was, when, as it had always happened, the Chesnut Street managers reduced their prices to the old standard, I was charging seventy-five and thirty-seven and a half cents, the same price, and possessed not the power to reduce to my old prices, without the consent of the board of agents, (that is, Mr. H. G. Freeman). After having ruined the engagement of every star, and played fifty-seven nights under the expenditure of the theatre, fifteen of which yielded only fifty dollars, and in one hundred and fourteen nights having lost six thousand dollars, on the 25th of January, 1840, I graciously received permission to do as I liked, with regard to the prices. I did not lose one night in availing myself of it. Closed for a week, hoping to make the audience forget it—but they were not to be whistled back—my *ruin* was sealed—the doom irrevocable. The board of agents of the Walnut Street Theatre, who should have been my support, the cause, the only cause. During a season of two hundred and sixty-one nights one hundred and fifty-five produced less than half the amount of the nightly expenses required to keep the doors open. The seven worst weeks ran thus: 320 dollars, 284 dollars, 261 dollars, 292 dollars, 339 dollars, 313 dollars, 251 dollars, not the amount of a single good house to pay the expenses of a whole week. Whoever is familiar with the expenditure of a theatre may make a calculation of the losses entailed upon the poor manager, by gentlemen attempting to conduct *his* business according to *their* notions of right and wrong. What a debt of gratitude I owe to the committee of the Walnut Street Theatre stockholders—which I found a barn, with scarcely sufficient scenery to act a plain comedy, tragedy, or farce, and which I left the best stocked theatre for melo-drama, with machinery, &c., in the United States.

Endeavouring, if possible, to stem the tide which I thus early saw must bear me immediately on to ruin, I had prepared appropriate decorations, by Hielge; and although I closed on Saturday, the 14th of September, the longest theatrical season on record, I opened on Monday the 16th, with the theatre renovated, newly painted, seats re-covered, prosenium altered, and kept my curtain down exactly *half an hour* beyond its time. So like magic did this appear, that it was three nights before the audience could be assured that such a thing had been accomplished. On the Wednesday evening, while seated in the greenroom, my ears were assailed by three hearty cheers, which I at first supposed were meant for approbation to Mr. E. Forrest, in Damon, but on walking to the stage, I was told the audience had just discovered the decorations, and were calling for the manager. Upon this effort, so well arranged against time, the press were perfectly silent; a proof what attention their reporters pay to the affairs of a theatre, where the manager does not request a notice. I was anxious to avoid the notice of any change of price in the admission, and leave it to its own course.

Forrest commenced the season with "Virginius," to 398 dollars; played the "Gladiator," "Damon" twice, "Metamora" twice, and "Othello" and "Carwin" for his benefit. On Tuesday, September 24th, 1839, I produced "Richelieu" in a style that surprised everybody. The dresses cost me six hundred dollars, and were made by A. J. Allen. The costume the exact age of Louis XIII of France, the scenery new, the chairs and tables of the same style and date; so perfect was everything, that after the first night Mr. Forrest called me into his room, and after many compliments, concluded thus: "For what you have done for the honour of the profession I will play one night gratuitously for you at the end of this engagement; select any play you think proper." Such a proffer, on such an occasion, from such a man, was a feather in the cap of a manager, which no one has been able to pluck away from me. I never heard of his being equally liberal to any of my contemporaries. The play was cast thus: Richelieu, E. Forrest; De Mauprat, Conner; Banadas, Matthews; De Beringhen, Wemyss; Joseph, Vaché; Francois, J. Smith; Louis XIII., Grierson; Huguèt, Porter: Gaston, Burgess; Clermont, Myers; Captain of Archers; M'Bride; Governor of the Bastile, Kemble; Jailor, Horn; Julie Mortimar, Mrs. Hunt; Marion De L'Orme, Miss Matthews (now Mrs. Eddy). Although the play was thus well acted, the receipts of the first night were only 385 dollars; second, 368 dollars; third, 367 dollars; fourth, 342 dollars; regularly falling off slightly every night. The blight of the prices had fallen upon this whole engagement, and every star engagement that followed throughout a season which promised so much. Forrest's benefit was 852 dollars, but at fifty cents, and twenty-five cents, he had last season 862 dollars, and 851 dollars, instead of 578 dollars, at increased prices. I declined taking "Richlieu," and selected "Metamora," which was acted to 289 dollars. The offer was a liberal one on the part of Forrest, although not so productive as we both anticipated. This first engagement, at the commencement of fifty-six nights during the year, left the treasury a deficiency of about seven hundred dollars, including the expenses of producing the play of "Richelieu." Of Mr. Forrest's performance of this part I can scarcely find words to speak in terms of sufficient praise; it was one of those masterly efforts of genius that sets criticism at defiance, full of beauty, full of faults; but an endeavour to analyze the latter would lead your pen into a strain of panegyric before you had completed half a dozen sentences, by the discovery of a flash of genius so brilliant, as to make you doubt the correctness of your judgment, and pronounce the fault you had determined to expose, a necessary foil to the excellent effect which followed. He evidently devoted no time to the study of character, but committed the words of the part to memory in a hurry; appeared in it before the public in a hurry; before them, to polish his crude ideas of the author as chance might direct; giving full scope to his imagination—an effort no one but a great actor would have dared to attempt. That Richelieu was not in years an old man, even at the time of his death, history informs us, but having been a roué in youth, his impaired constitution became too feeble to support his extraordinary vigour of thought and mind. Forrest represented him as a feeble, tottering old man, thus availing himself of stage trick to give greater effect to his outbreak of passion, and the anathema pronounced on Banadas at the end of the fourth act, was equal to any of Edmund Kean's best efforts, of a similar nature; taking his audience by surprise, and charging onward, until their admiration broke forth into an involuntary acknowledgment of his excellence, continuing several seconds after the fall of the curtain hid the actor from their view. His sudden appearance before the king and the conspirators, who are congratulating themselves upon his death, and the overwhelming agony of his tone and countenance, when refused the pardon of De Mauprat, by his sovereign, was the perfection of art—but his *ha, ha, ha, Count Baradas—ha, ha,* in the last scene was not deserving of the applause it received, and unworthy of Forrest—in my opinion the greatest blemish in the whole play;—but as a whole, Richelieu will never find a better representative. Macready and Vandenhoff both fall infinitely below Forrest, by comparison, in this character. The former gentleman shows the effect of long application and intense study thrown at once into the shade by genius; yet it is strange, that while every body admits Richelieu to be one of Forrest's greatest efforts, the receipts of the treasury when he acts it, fall short of his average houses. The cause of this must be in the play, which is devoid of interest to a common observer, and too classical to suit the taste of that class of society who form the majority of visitors to the theatre.

Burton, on the 5th of October, played "Paul Pry and Billy Lackaday." For six nights his houses averaged only 165 dollars; his benefit was 653 dollars. Hill followed with no better success; two hundred people in the pit, which used to average 600 dollars nightly, was the result of the oppression on the part of the stockholders, and forced submission to it upon mine. On the 4th of November Mr. and Mrs. Seguin and Mr. Horncastle, appeared in " Der Freischutz." I have Mr. Seguin's written testimony, that out of London he had never seen the scenery of this opera so well put upon the stage ; yet the second night produced only 170 dollars. Mr. Seguin's benefit only 247; Mr. Horncastle's 138 dollars ; Mr. Latham's 194 dollars, and Mrs. Seguin's 401 dollars. " Damn all stock-holders and their interference, as Goldfinch damns all dancing masters and their umbrellas, when flung into the ditch." Forrest returned on the 25th of November; his houses worse than on the former occasion. The horses, to whose exertions I was so much indebted last season, commenced on the 11th of December, and although "The Forty Thieves," " Marmion," " The Secret Mine," " The Siege of Tripoli," " Kenilworth," " Blue Beard," and "Billy Button" were offered as attractions, empty benches—and why don't you lower the prices?—what did you raise them for?—were the only objects that met my eyes and ears. The 1st of January, New Year's night, only 259 dollars : instead of an overflowing pit, three hundred and twenty-four tickets were all that I could sell, with two new pieces, in which the horses appeared. Seven benefits, to fire-companies alone, yielded the amount of the nightly expenses, up to the 25th of January, 1840. Never was a bright pros-pect so cruelly killed, murdered, as my arrangements were this season. On the 3d of February, I announced a return to the good old prices, and a new piece, " Sadah and Kalasrade." Mr. Sefton having engaged for me in London, Mr. Macintosh, the stage carpenter of Madame Vestris' Theatre, a complete alteration at my *own* expenses, was again made, and gas intro-duced to light the theatre, from the borders instead of the old plan of wing-ladders. The American Theatre, in Walnut Street, under my direction, was the first to introduce this method, now so universally approved and adopted in the United States. Towards these alterations the Board of Agents liberally contributed *one hundred dollars*, leaving me to pay eight hundred, in making an effort to escape from the slough of despond, in which they had plunged me. All would not do—"Sadah and Kalasrade," with all its beautiful scenery and dresses, failed ; the first night yielding only 277 dollars, 109 dollars, of which was in the pit ; but my pit customers were too justly offended to forgive the past, and left me to ex-tricate myself, if I could, without their aid, although to see Master Diamond and Sanford, they did once honour me with their presence, to the amount of seven hundred and four tickets, in a house of 740 dollars. On the 13th of March, Booth commenced an engagement, and on the 16th, for the first time, in all our engagements, failed to appear as

"Richard the Third," assigning as his reason, that I was neglecting my business, by playing for Mr. Murdoch's benefit, at the Chesnut Street Theatre, and until I came, he would not go upon the stage. This closed our engagement, as I would not permit him to appear on the following night. Burton played twelve nights to more money at the reduced prices, than was received during his previous engagements. E. Forrest, aided by J. R. Scott, commenced his last engagement for the season, on the 22nd of April, in "Damon and Pythias," to a house of 241 dollars—ruinous work; giving him fifty per cent on the gross amount received each night at the doors.

Booth, who promised reformation, and professed penitence, played Hamlet on the 15th of June; and on the 24th, Oronooko, in bare feet. His benefit, on the 27th, Octavian, Shylock, John Lump, and the first act of Richelieu. Throughout this engagement, he had been crazy; and his Richelieu never will be forgotten—imperfect, drunk, and dressed like an English chimney-sweep—on the 1st of May. I found I could no longer place the slightest dependance upon him. He kept faith with me, when he had broken it with almost every manager on the continent; and when taxed with his folly, would say—Ask Wemyss if he believes these stories—he knows I never break engagements. Alas! Mr. Junius, I can no longer, with truth, assert you never did. His twelve nights yielded, including his benefit, 1412 dollars, or 117 dollars per night, for which I paid him, as usual, taking the proceeds of the benefit, 1200 dollars. Quere; how much did I gain by the operation? While ruin stared me in the face, and Burton was converting Cooke's Circus into a theatre in my immediate neighbourhood, on the 1st of July I addressed the Committee thus—

" Philadelphia, July 1st, 1840.

"GENTLEMEN,

" The present position of theatricals in this city, and the very heavy loss of the present season, having placed me in a situation to require some little aid from you, I am induced to lay before you the reasons why I think myself entitled to expect from you some consideration.

" It appears from the books of the theatre, that I have expended in lumber, canvas, paints, cordage, and tin-ware, extra carpenter wages, (not including my regular bill for carpenter-work of 42 dollars per week,) upwards of 7,000 dollars, independent of my rent, which, in six years, has amounted to 20,900 dollars. You have likewise received during the same time, from the bars for rent :—viz., twenty-five weeks for the first seven months, say 50 dollars per week, 1,250 dollars; forty-five weeks for the second year, at 50 dollars, 2,250 dollars; thirty-five weeks for the third year, at 50 dollars, 1,100; thirty-three weeks for the fourth year, at 50 dollars, 1,650 dollars; fifty-two weeks for the fifth year, at 70 dollars, 3,640 dollars; forty-eight weeks for the sixth year, at 70 dollars, 3,360—Total,

15,250 dollars. Thirty thousand two hundred and fifty dollars in addition to the 27,900 dollars, making the gross amount of 41,150 dollars for the five years and seven months, nearly fifteen per cent. per year, reckoning one hundred and seventy-five shares at 275 dollars each.

" The house has been twice decorated by me since it was done by the stockholders in 1834; moreover, half the papering and painting of the lobbies.

" A mistake of my own, not discovered until too late to rectify it, caused me to pay five months' rent before the theatre was ready for performance; and although I can make no complaint upon that subject, it made to me a difference of 1,700 dollars in my expenditure during the first year.

" I now proceed to state what I solicit you to do, and what I trust you will accede to.

" In the first place to require from me no payment in advance for the following year, but to receive the 200 dollars per week from the usual time of opening. Thus making a difference of five weeks in the time for the payment of the whole rent. Second, to paint and paper the lobbies and vestibule, (a new dome if you think proper,) and also the panels of the boxes, according to a design which I will submit for your approval. Thus giving to the house a fresh appearance to enable me to compete with the other theatres.

" Having laboured industriously for five years and seven months, to make the theatre what it is, in point of scenery and machinery, I trust you will not think I have made any unreasonable demand on your courtesy; and by your early answer to this letter, enable me to guide my future movements accordingly.

" There is one subject more to which I would direct your attention—*the police.* It is necessary that at least one half of this burden should be borne by those who receive the emoluments of the bars, from which, (particularly the third tier,) all the disorder in the house arises.

" Yours most respectfully,
(Signed) " F. C. WEMYSS."

This letter remained unanswered. Mr. Freeman met me in the street, and told me a committee would be appointed to wait upon me;—none came. The Arch Street Theatre was pressed upon me by many of my friends, at half the rent I was paying for the Walnut Theatre; and as Mr. H Freeman, Mr. Montelius, Mr. Lagies, Mr. Wickersham, Mr. Peddle and Mr. Donaldson, after blighting my prospects of almost certain success, treated me with contempt, I thought it time to shake off the slavery, which had become too irksome, to the will of these gentlemen, and sent them notice of my intention to resign the theatre on the 31st day of July, when my lease expired. These consistent gentlemen suffered Mr. Dinneford and Mr. Marshall, my successors, to open the pit at twelve-and-a-half cents, and upper boxes twenty-five cents admission; giving them also the rent of the bars, and charging them no more rent than they required of me without them! Thus, in

P 5

fact, making them rent free. Thank you a thousand times, gentlemen, for your kindness. You caught hold of a fool when you got hold of *me*, and having me in your clutches, you made me pay the price of my folly. Not satisfied, like Shylock, to have your pound of flesh, you continually demanded more than your bargain. Your lucky stars, in my insolvency, saved you much inconvenience. Could I have prosecuted the suit commenced, for justice, I have no doubt the result would have been gratifying to me, but mortifying to yourselves; and that I should have received some few thousand dollars as a salvo for all you made myself and family suffer. The rich man always will oppress the poor man; but retribution sometimes, though rarely, overtakes him : powerful friends arise when least expected. I leave you to enjoy the honour of the money obtained for bar rent, and the knowledge that you, and not the manager, should have been indicted for permitting nightly the laws to be set at defiance within those rooms for your exclusive benefit. The theatre closed on Saturday, the 25th of July, for Hadaway's benefit, " The Floating Beacon," and the " Turnpike Gate," never to be opened by me again. In leaving it for the Arch Street Theatre I may have committed an error; but in six years, two only yielded any profit; the other four entailed upon me severe losses. Had I been left to follow my own judgment, without the interference of the stockholders, or rather their committee, I should have contrived to have redeemed all mishaps. Fettered in all my movements, I sank beneath the pressure.

On the 30th of September, Mr. Charles Kean appeared in the Chesnut Street Theatre, as Hamlet. It is fortunate for his reputation he has paid us a second visit, for the Americans did not admit his claims to rank as a first-rate artist when among us a few years ago. He has evidently improved in his style, but there is much room for improvement left. His father's name is a charm around his career which opens all hearts in his favour; the recollection of his excellence must act as the strong inducement to prove himself worthy of his sire's reputation. The best part he acted, during his present engagement, was Claude Melnotte. He looked the part better than any representaive I have yet seen, and that is at least half the battle. On the 15th of October, Miss Inverarity, Miss Poole, Mr. Manvers, and Mr. Martyn, appeared in " Cinderella." Miss Poole was decidedly the favourite; Miss Inverarity is ungainly in person, makes horrible faces when singing, and will never be a favourite in Philadelphia. They produced a new opera, entitled " Fidelio," with some success, On the 4th of November,

Mrs. FITZWILLIAM—

little Fanny Copeland, whom I had seen a child in Dover, whom I remember in London as the Madge Wildfire—alone capable of succeeding Mrs. Egerton, the essence of fun and drollery in female form, made her appearance as Peggy, in the "Country Girl;" therein showing her judgment, making the audience believe she was nothing more than a tolerable actress, until, in Widow Wiggins, she sent them out of the theatre delighted, to talk of nothing else until they could induce a friend or companion to return to the theatre on the following evening. Never did an actress make so great a hit on her first appearance, and nightly she continued to win upon the favour of her audience. In twelve nights she acted Peggy, Widow Wiggins, Albina Mandeville, Widow Brady, Sally Scraggs, Helen Worrett, Madame Manetta, Kitty Skylark, and Louisa Lovetrick. In broad farce she is irresistible; and now and then a little touch of pathos falls beautifully from her lips; but in elegant comedy there is too much of the chamber-maid. Helen Worrett was too much for her; and even Albina Mandeville would have been as well let alone; but it is unjust to find fault or quibble about one or two parts, where so many were acted in a manner to make her audience anxious for her return. Mrs. Fitzwilliam will make more money in the United States than any lady who has ever visited it, with the exception of Miss Fanny Kemble.

On the 30th of December, R. C. Maywood announced his intention of withdrawing from the firm of Maywood & Co., and leaving his partner, Mr. L. T. Pratt, alone in his glory.— Maywood had been becoming daily more and more unpopular, but that need not have forced him to lay down the sceptre he had wielded so long. Every manager is popular or unpopular, according as the breeze of public favour sets in; and if the stock-holders drove him from the helm, at least he had a sweet revenge, for they sent for him to cross the Atlantic and take charge of the Theatre, as the only person capable of stopping its downward course.

Mr. Pratt announced that Mr. W. B. Wood, as his acting manager, Mr. G. F. Jervis, as his stage manager, and reduced the price of admission to seventy-five cents, boxes, and thirty-seven-and-a-half-cents, pit. This, more than all other causes, has ruined the prospects of the theatre, being an acknow-ledgment that talent of a superior order must always be charged for at a higher rate; consequently, when the boxes are seventy-five cents, it is generally admitted there is nothing worth seeing, and the theatre is deserted; when, on the contrary, a dollar is demanded for admission, it is paid unwillingly, with many comments on the rapacious disposition of the manager. In the present instance, what an agreeable situation for me; the Walnut Street Theatre demanding the same price for admission as the Chesnut Street. My boast had been, superior talent at less prices; what chance, with equal attraction, had I for success?—None; yet Mr. Freeman stuck like a leech to the bond, until all the blood was gone, and then allowed a short breathing time before final execution. And this gentleman pretended to be actuated in all these dealings by a friendly disposition towards me.

Charles Kean commenced the career of new management on the 30th of December, 1839, as Hamlet; Celeste, on the 6th of January, as the Child of the Wreck in the "Wept of the Wept-ton-Wish; but horses were drawing better houses now than any two-legged animals. On the 11th January she took a benefit, at which poor Finn acted, for the last time, Monsieur Jaques—left New York for his home after a long absence, on Monday afternoon, in the steamboat Lexington, and was one of one hundred and seventy-five who perished by fire, by ice, and by water on that dreadful night.

Celeste's last benefit, if she does not take another, was fixed for the 18th of January. Miss Elizabeth Wood, a daughter of the veteran, W. B. Wood, made her first essay as Amanthis, in "The Child of Nature." The time was when such an announcement would have filled the Chesnut Street Theatre. The audience, on the present occasion, might be select, but they were not numerous; the success of the young lady, very doubtful. However, on the 4th of February, she appeared as Amelia Wildenhaim, in "Lovers' Vows." On the 8th of February, Miss Poole, Manvers and Guibelei. A benefit was given for the purpose of raising a fund to present to the widow and children of Henry J. Finn, an actor of whom America should have been proud; but like all such attempts, unless taken up voluntarily by the citizens, they but add mortification to grief: Madame Celeste played the Maid of Cashmere, on which occasion I lent the services of Plumer, and would have lent the aid of the whole company, and closed the Walnut Street Theatre on that night, could I have aided the good intentions of both manager and actors towards the family of the deceased.

Celeste took another farewell benefit, playing Vanderdecken, in the "Flying Dutchman," Susanne, and the Frontier Maid. What an indefatigable lady she is—nothing tires—nothing daunts her. She nurses a sick husband all night, and appears as fresh as a lark at rehearsal again in the morning. We are for ever permitting her to say good bye, and always glad to see her return to say good bye again.

Vandenhoff and daughter succeeded Celeste, and Maywood'

benefit took place on the 9th of March, when Mr. Wilson, Mr. Giubelei, and Miss Sheriff lent the retired manager their aid, in "Somnambula," he playing Jock Howieson, written by Lockhart, the son-in-law and biographer of Walter Scott, for Mackay of Edinburgh, to whom the great unknown first revealed himself, at the "Theatrical Fund Dinner," in Edinburgh, as the author of the Waverley Novels.

On the 23rd of March, a novelty was offered for the benefit of Mr. Pratt, in the shape of "Der Freischutz," in the German language, by a company of German actors. On the 20th, Hervio Nano appeared as the "Gnome Fly," to a very good house. On the 15th of April Charles Kean; and on the 26th, Wilson, Giubelei, and Miss Sheriff produced the new opera of the "Postillion of Longjumeau." Mrs. Fitzwilliam, Herr Cline and Balls terminated the list of stars, and the theatre closed for the season, on the 13th of June, with "Laugh when You Can," and "A Good Night's Rest."

On the same night Mrs. Arann's Garden opened with a loud flourish of trumpets, under the direction of Mr. Ward, with an attempted "Eruption of Mount Vesuvius," planned by Macintosh, who evidently did not know what he was about; he was straining to produce an effect of something which he had seen or heard of, but which he knew not how to accomplish. The laugh of derision, at the end of the exhibition, at once annihilated all hope of future success. Unpaid bills, assignment for the benefit of creditors, and a hasty departure from Philadelphia, the result of months of preparation, and a system of puffing carried beyond the usual bounds; a fortunate escape, that the deluded spectators did not demolish the canvas and boards, which constituted the only value of this "Eruption," which was to astonish the city—and it *did* astonish our citizens so much that they have not yet ceased to wonder how they could have been so gulled. This failure was succeeded by a success as extraordinary. On the 17th of June, 1840,

Mademoiselle FANNY ELLSLER,

the divine Fanny! the glorious Fanny! the astonishing Fanny! of the light fantastic toe—who turned the heads of all the ladies and the hearts of all the gentlemen, who produced a perfect mania for dancing, until the citizens of Baltimore danced into the traces of her carriage, proud of the honour of dragging the immortal Fanny from the theatre to her hotel—made her first appearance in Philadelphia as Lauretta, in the ballet of "La Terantule," and afterwards danced the "Cracovienne." She was to the ballet what Mademoiselle Garcia had been to opera, creating a taste which awaits only de-

velopement to make a good corps de ballet a necessary ap-
pendage to every well-regulated theatre. It is not too much
to predict that a theatre appropriated to opera, Italian, as
well as English and French ballet, will be found rising up
among us, annihilating every species of dramatic amusement
which attempts to rival it. Why the press should have assailed
the private character of a young lady whose career had not
been marked by profligacy, black mail editors alone can answer. However their paragraphs may have wounded a delicate
and sensitive mind. they had no effect upon her power to
attract crowded audiences. So brilliant a career, in America,
has never been recorded. Her price, five hundred dollars
per night, prevented the possibility of a manager making
money who had a company of actors to pay at the same time;
but it wound up Mr. Pratt's season with an eclat that promised to benefit his arrangements. Elliot had in New York
played off the admitted attraction of Celeste with good effect
against her all-powerful rival, and made an engagement with
me for her to play on the same nights at the Walnut Street
that Ellsler appeared at the Chesnut. This was the first engagement between us ever concluded, but destined to remain
unfulfilled: in the middle of preparations for her reception, I
received a note from her husband, stating, she had abandoned
him, and it was out of his power to comply with the terms of
his contract. Sick, and deserted, appealing to my forbear-
ance, and asking commisseration, I could not find it in my
heart to oppress a man so stricken. I returned the agreement, cancelled, and never saw poor Elliot but once again.
Deep must have been the provocation that could have induced
a woman so devoted as Celeste appeared to be to him, to cast
him off for ever, and on a bed of sickness—yes, of death, for
he did not long survive the blow. Abandon husband and
child and fortune, to seek protection in a land of strangers!
Many rumours injurious to her reputation were circulated,
but not one received credence from those who knew the parties intimately. She returned to the United States, on his
death, to claim her child, and left America, so long her home,
heart-broken, to think her dearly beloved daughter—whom
to clasp once more to her heart, she had braved the perils of
the ocean—had been taught to harbour thoughts derogatory
to her mother's honour, and refused the protection offered to
her by her father's relatives. Poor Celeste! thy case was indeed a hard one—thy last farewell, a mournful one. May
your future career be happy and prosperous.

CHAPTER XXXVII.

The Season of 1840—'41. W. E. Burton. Charlotte Cushman. Her perseverance. Buckstone. Opening of the Arch Street Theatre. Difficulties upon difficulties. Mr. John Braham. Power's last engagement in Philadelphia. The loss of the steam-ship President. The Manager's last kick. The Opera of "Norma" produced in splendid style. Unjust treatment of Mr. Wood. His letter to the Editor of the "Herald." The Walnut Street Theatre, under the management of Dinneford and Marshall. Hervio Nano. Mitchell in Philadelphia.

THE season of 1840-'41 is one which will never be forgotten. What hopes, what fears, what wishes, what threats did it give rise to—to crush in one short year the whole of the contending powers, each voice of whom, at the commencement, declared for open war—four Richmonds in the field, and all annihilated. Burton had been actively engaged in altering Cooke's circus into a theatre, to be christened The National, with the avowed purpose of ruining the managers of the Chesnut Street Theatre, little dreaming that his own ruin would precede their own downfall. As an actor, Mr. W. E. Burton has no superior on the American stage; but it is not always the best actor who makes the best manager; his faults here are: first—want of nerve to fight a losing battle; in success he is a great general, to be dreaded by all who come in opposition to his interest.

His theatre, on the opening night, Monday, the 31st of August, 1840, presented a scene of splendour never witnessed in America. In decorating a house for the amusement of the public, if any fault could be found, it was of ornament, the gilt moulding on a pure ground of white being too much crowded; the eagles supporting the drapery of the proscenium boxes, were the most chaste and beautiful things I ever saw. Mr. Foster, who came among us with Cooke, and whose experience at the Adelphi Theatre, in London, gave him all the requisite knowledge, seemed to have bent all his energy to this one purpose, and succeeded perfectly. Burton was fortunate, too, in securing the aid of Haviland to superintend the alterations. His opening pieces were the "Rivals," and "A Roland for an Oliver;" his company, Mr. P. Richings stage manager, J. R. Scott, James Thorne, Shaw, Whiting, Graham, Neafie, T. Placide, C. Porter, Becket, Brooke, Quayle, Herbert, Oakey, Stafford, Boulard, Woodbury, Master Reed J. Van Stavoreen, Bright, Ince, and Reed; Misses C. Cushman Melton, S. Cushman, E. Petrie, Porter, Fanny Ince, Jones Wilson, Delamere, Collingbourne, Flannigan, Wilkins: Mesdames Brooke, Becket, and Ferrers; a strong and judiciously selected stock company, to which his own name added a tower of strength ; yet he did not give his company a fair chance. In over anxiety to commence the starring system, he checked their rising popularity. Hacket was the first star—the weakest he could have selected—and Abbot, who followed, was really, as far as attraction was concerned, no star at all. Graham failed, but appears to have had no favourable opportunity to display his powers, and, in returning to England, showed that he, at least, possessed a quality most rare in actors —common sense. Of the actors new to the Philadelphia public, whom Burton introduced,

Miss CHARLOTTE CUSHMAN

deserves more than a passing notice. This young lady is a proof of what perseverance, steadily directed to one object, will accomplish ; more especially where genius, giant-like, proceeds hand-in-hand along with it. She commenced her theatrical career as a singer, announced as a pupil of Mr. Maeder, her voice pronounced to be of a most extraordinary nature, rarely possessed by a female. She failed, whether from loss of voice, or deficiency in her musical education, or both, I cannot record; but nothing daunted her. Repudiated as a singer, I find her grasping at once at the honours of tragedy—attempting the part of Lady Macbeth, (since so admirably sustained by her,) but at this time beyond her powers. Not discouraged by this second failure, if it is not too harsh to term it so, I find her descending from the stilts of the Bowery Theatre, under Hamblin—occupying the humble station of a walking lady at the Park Theatre, in New York, cheerfully performing any part allotted to her by the manager, at the same time closely studying the manners and peculiarities of all the European actors, male or female, with whom her position brought her in contact; and, as subsequently appears, carefully hoarding the knowledge of her art thus acquired for future action, yet not advancing with rapid strides in the favour of the audience, by whom she was tolerated, but not supposed to possess the talent which they afterwards became proud to honour. Her masculine mind at once perceived, that the only means of success was to cultivate the acquaintance of the gentlemen conducting the newspapers ; fugitive pieces of poetry appeared in the papers, and in the popular periodical magazines, under the signature of " Charlotte Cushman." These answered the double purpose of placing her name before the public, as a lady of literary talent, and securing the notice of the publishers to her dramatic career. At length, Nancy Sykes, in " Oliver Twist," gave her an opportunity of proving what she was capable of accomplishing. As a portrait of female depravity, it was painfully correct; and in all her future career, she never surpassed the excellence of that performance. In leaving the Park Theatre, to join Burton in Philadelphia, she at once opened the road to that fame which she rapidly acquired; here she had a field for the prosecution of her abilities, which was at this time filled by older and abler favourites in New York. The success of the "Naiad Queen" carried her name triumphantly along with it; and at the end of the season, she had assumed a position, which enabled her to return to the Park Theatre, as the leading actress of the American stage; and her ambition will not be satisfied, until she can add, the leading actress of the English stage, as she progresses in her future career. The visit of Mr. Macready to the United States, and the high opinion he entertained of her merit as an actress, opened the road to London, where her success will secure not only renown, but fortune, on her return to her native country.

Of late years it has become the fashion to place theatres under the direction of ladies, and Miss Cushman has figured as the manager of the American Theatre, in Walnut Street, under my successor, Mr. Marshall; but even the popularity of her name could not command success in such an undertaking,—hers she proved incompetent. At the end of one season, W. R. Blake was announced as her assistant, (but, in fact, her manager,) to give her an opportunity of retiring, without wounding her feelings, sufficiently mortified by the knowledge, that the reins of power must pass from her hands, or the doors of the theatre be closed for want of patronage. Here is another defeat to be over-mastered; and I risk little in prophesying, if ever a National Theatre is erected in New York, upon purely Amrrican principles, Miss Cushman will be one of the great promoters of the design, and not unlikely the lessee and manager; she is fully impressed with Richelieu's motto—"*There is no such word as fail;*" and in the spirit of good feeling I say to her, go a-head.

The Chesnut Street Theatre was opened under Pratt and Dinmore, (the late treasurer,) on the 29th of August. One night previous to the opening of the National, Murdoch was announced as the stage manager; the performance, the "School for Scandal" and "Popping the Question;" stars announced, Fanny Ellsler, E. Forrest, Power, Mr. and Mrs. Wood, and Buckstone. The last named gentleman made his first appearance on the 7th of September, as Jemmy Wheedle and Selim Pettibone; one of the few authors who have proved themselves also good actors. Buckstone's reputation depends more upon his writing than his acting, yet there is a quaintness of manner and peculiarity of voice, which renders him,

without any claim to greatness, a valuable member of a
theatrical company. As a star, he has no pretensions to
notice, and wisely joined his fortunes to Mrs. Fitzwilliam,
who found in him an able assistant, and thus maintained a
position which alone he never could have held with success.

On the 7th of September, I announced the opening of the
Arch Street Theatre, under my direction. Hielge had re-
decorated the house; the gas had been introduced; scenery
painted for a new piece, entitled the "Provost of Paris;"
Hadaway had been appointed stage manager, and every thing
wore the aspect of a prosperous commencement. Mr. Thomas
Newton marred all my prospects; he had promised me faithfully, if I would permit him to take off the hands employed
at the Arch Street Theatre for two days, to enable Mr.
Burton to open, whose gas fixtures he was also making, he
would bring down all the force from the National Theatre on
the Tuesday, and be ready for me in time. I assented; but
the gas fixtures were so incomplete, on the first night, at the
National, Burton would not permit a single hand to leave his
place until all was finished. In this he was perfectly right;
but the two days lost on my work were attended with most
disagreeable consequences. At six o'clock, on the evening of
the 7th of September, Mr. Nicholson, the Superintendant of
the Philadelphia Gas Company, sent me word that the pipes
had not been proved, and the gas could not be turned on. In
vain I pleaded the ruin which must follow such a disappointment; he replied, the rules that governed him were imperative, and could not be departed from. The crowd, assembled before the doors, waiting for admission, became
clamorous; they were sufficiently numerous to reach across
Arch Street, in front of the theatre. I was compelled to inform them that the gas could not be turned on. While I
addressed them from the piazza, Mr. Hadaway performed the
same kind office on the opposite side of the street. We persuaded them quietly to disperse; and thus, instead of opening
to five or six hundred dollars, which appearances indicated, on
the 7th of September, I opened on the 8th, with Rice, (Jim
Crow,) to 152 dollars. Who can control the uncertain chance
of fate? Had I known or dreamed of the possibility of such an
occurrence at twelve o'clock, I would have ransacked the city
of Philadelphia, and been prepared with oil to light the
house upon this unfortunate night. It was the first time in
my managerial career I had ever appointed a certain night
for any certain event to come off, and failed to accomplish it.
If Mr. Newton had been an actor, such an occurrence would
have been impossible. Why he deceived me, who had obtained for him the contract, in opposition to the opinion of
several of the members of the board of agents—who procured

for him the job from Burton, and also the alteration of the fixtures of the Walnut Street Theatre, it is a problem I have tempted to solve more than once, but it is inexplicable to me. The consequence was ruin. My resources had been crippled by my last season in Walnut Street; the aid of my friends taxed to the utmost, to enable me to prepare for a campaign, which terminated, as far as I was concerned, without a blow. On the following night, the gas was very imperfectly lighted; and it was half an hour after the time of beginning before the lamps in front of the theatre could be lighted, giving to those who presented themselves to purchase tickets, ideas that we could not be ready for performance. The 8th of September yielded 152 dollars, the 9th, 61 dollars, the 10th, 93 dollars, the 11th, 98 dollars, Rice's benefit, on the 12th, 195 dollars—the receipts of the five nights, 601 dollars; out of which, Rice, by contract, was to receive 250 dollars. On the Monday, a new piece, and a very good one, entitled "The Sixes; or the Devil is in the Dice," produced only 90 dollars, Tuesday 43 dollars, Wednesday 30 dollars, Thursday 18 dollars. On Friday morning I assembled the company in the green room, told them that a contest like this must be useless, entailing misery all around; that they had better, before it was too late, provide themselves with situations for the winter; and thus disbanded those who were willing to depend upon my exertions. They deserted me not, even in these apparently desperately circumstances; I deserted them, conscious that distress, starvations and misery alone could attend a further attempt to prosecute such a commencement. The ladies and gentlemen deserve my thanks, which I am proud thus to tender them, for their kind intentions. On Friday, I did not attempt to open the doors; and strolling into Burton's theatre, found myself much amused by a good representation of a piece in which old Time had provided a safe receptacle for all managers. Moyamensing Prison, my friend Burton, it is dangerous to tamper with; true jokes; a few months found you, among others, ready to avail yourself of this same sanctuary. Who would have thought that I, who felt myself strong in the affections of a certain portion of the play-going community, should have been the first to run, before a shot from the enemy had reached me, a victim to the treachery of a friend. I went to Baltimore, where no better fate awaited me. There politics had turned the heads of the whole population, who were themselves nightly engaged as actors in large processions, bearing lanthorns, banners, and soul-inspiring mottos. Harrison and Van Buren night after night engaged the minds of all, either as active partakers in the exciting scene, or as passive spectators, admiring the splendour with which each party strove, in this contest, to outdo the other. Theatres, or any place of public amusement, were superfluous; even those who possessed the right of free admission would not honour us with their presence. Thus it proceeded from bad to worse, until the 30th of November, I returned again to the Arch Street Theatre, and opened with Hill, having reduced my prices to twenty-five cents, boxes, and pit, twelve and a half cents, to contend against a similar movement on the part of Marshall and Dinneford, at the Walnut Street Theatre. I opened this time to an excellent house, although Mr. Newton had not completed his gas fixtures, and I had been obliged to call in another to finish his work. I had 246 dollars; the pieces, "Sudden Thoughts," "The Green Mountain Boy," and "O. K." Booth opened in Richard, on the 12th of December, to 300 dollars. All promised hope of success, when he again placed the thermometer below zero by appearing upon the stage drunk. Down went the houses to 70 dollars, and 80 dollars, then to 24 dollars, and 18 dollars. The theatre continued open until the 30th of January, when I requested the stockholders to release me from all engagements, cancel the lease, and I retired heartily disgusted with every thing connected with the Arch Street Theatre, which to me had been one source of annoyance after another, entailing a loss upon my already crippled resources of three or four thousand dollars.

Rice, Hill, Booth, Sandford, Williams, Wood and his dogs, and Tom Flynn, were the stars. "O. K." "New Notions," "A Wife for a Day," "the Lion of the Sea," "Norman Leslie," "the Serpent Lady," "the Convict's Child," and "the Brazen Drum," the new pieces; the whole season sixty-three nights, ten weeks and a half; the whole receipts, 5630 dollars, of which 1000 dollars were paid to the stars, leaving an average of seventy-three and a half dollars per night. During the last few weeks, arrest for debt followed arrest, execution followed execution, until, to keep my person out of gaol, I was compelled to apply for the benefit of the insolvent laws, a discharge under which I received at the March term of the court in 1841. My large establishments were completely broken up. Philadelphia, Baltimore, and Pittsburgh Theatres, all passed from my hands—my property disposed of under the sheriff's hammer, at a time when real estate would hardly be taken as a gift—ruining me, without aiding my creditors. A theatrical wardrobe, the most extensive in the United States, which ten thousand dollars could not replace, sold for one hundred and thirty-six dollars!!! The Pennsylvania Theatre, which cost me fifteen thousand dollars, exclusive of the mortgage of five thousand dollars, sold, subject to the same mortgage, for sixty-two dollars. The month of April, 1841, found me without one cent, crushed, heart-broken and degraded in my my own estimation, by the white-washing process I had been compelled to undergo. I have never been the same man since. Difficulties which previous to this epoch in my life, I gloried in surmounting, have been suffered to master me. My energy of character, which gave me nerve to face any emergency, seems to have deserted me, and I have lived to be refused an engagement in the Philadelphia theatres at one-fourth of the amount at which 'my services therein were formerly eagerly sought for. In all this, let me not forget my obligations to *my good friend*, Mr. Samuel Hays, the grocer, at the corner of Eleventh and Water St. He was the first as early as June, 1840, to place the sherriff upon my back, in return for the exertions of myself and all the members of the Strembeck family, to recommend him customers, when he first located himself in the neighbourhood of Eleventh and George Street. I had paid him yearly several hundred dollars, and refused to avail myself of the law's delay in discharge of this claim : he was the first to cry mad dog, and loose the officers of the law upon my falling, but not then hopeless fortune. It was a greater satisfaction to me to pay him than it could have been to him to deprive my wife and children of the few comforts which years of untiring industry had placed around them. For the attempt, he has not been, or will he be, forgotten in our many pleasant recollections. Should he ever be placed in a similar situation, may he meet with no such urgent creditor. As a foil to this, thank God, there is one bright spot which cheered me in misfortune. Mr. Wilson, and the carpenters of the Walnut Street Theatre, when they heard of the distress which existed in my family, entered into a subscription from their hard-earned wages (although they were also my creditors to a larger amount than a mechanic ought to lose by his employer,) and tendered it to me. Although I did not accept the offering, the kind feeling which dictated it is imprinted upon my heart ; and to those men I feel grateful for the first really pleasant hour I experienced from the time of my failure; it was a balm which soothed my feelings and turned them once more into their proper sphere of action. Mr. Wilson had been placed in his present position by my recommendation to the stockholders, and thus proved that his heart is in the right place.

Having thus brought my connexion as manager of a Philadelphia Theatre, for the present to a close, let me return to the rivals whose movements now occupied the public attention. Mr. E. Forrest was at the Chesnut Street from the 21st of September until the 3d of October, when Power succeded him, retaining possession until the 24th. On the 27th, Mr. and Mrs. Wood, and Mr. Brough, with Mr. Leffler, commenced

an opera season. No sooner was the name of the Woods seen
on the play bills, then Burton announces in large capitals, the
engagement of Miss Clifton, Mr. and Miss Vandenhoff, Mr.
Buckstone, Mr. Braham, Mrs. Fitzwilliam, Mr. Power, Mr.
Guibelei, Miss Poole, Mr. and Mrs. Seguin, Mr. Hackett, Mr.
Browne, and the promise of an Italian opera. The steam
was evidently rising fast—boilers preparing for expansive
action, to burst with a terrible explosion, scattering dismay
on all around. Either these announcements were a managerial
device to attract attention from Old Drury and the Woods, or
the managers must have fallen into a sleep, or have been guided
by wrong counsel, to loose thus their hold upon these stars,
who alone could enable them to resist the energetic movements of their younger opponent. On the 10th of November,
Fanny Ellsler and Mons. Silvain, followed the Woods. Half
of Fanny's attraction is gone—the houses good, but not great
—the treasury gasping in agony, and the theatre evidently *in
articolo mortis*, playing only four nights a week, not opening
the doors the nights on which the graceful Fanny did not appear. Forrest comes once more to the rescue—a powerful
ally, but unable to command success. Then Le Compte and
a corps de ballet; and, and finally, an announcement that the
theatre will be closed on the 4th of January, to prepare for
Bellini's opera of "Norma." No want of amusement in this
our Quaker City—four theatres open; the Chesnut, the
National, the American, and the Arch Street; Raymond and
Waring's Circus, with Le Fort and Otto Motty; Promenade
Concerts at the Museum *a la Musard*, by Frank Johnson and
and his celebrated band, to usher in the year 1841.

On the 16th of November, Tyrone Power, so long the able
support of the Chesnut Street Theatre, deserted Old Drury,
for the newly erected National, where he appeared as Sir
Patrick O'Plenipo, and Doctor O'Toole. Whether he profited
by the change in a pecuniary point, is not the question if he
lost "caste:" Burton gained credit for indefatigable exertion to
annihilate Pratt and Dinmore, who seem, in Murdoch, inex-
perienced as he was in management, to have placed the reins
of government in hands too weak to compete with such an adversary as Burton. On the 30th of November, 1840, one of
the brightest names in the annals of English Theatres was announced at the National—

Mr. JOHN BRAHAM,

who appeared as Henry Bertram, in "Guy Mannering." In
his best day, he was a miserable actor; but singers—and such
singers, so rarely heard—are not expected to be actors. His
fame as the first tenor singer of the English stage had long

been undisputed: the "little orange boy" was received with acclamation wherever he went—his name sufficient to fill the largest theatre, and no musical festival was considered worth attending where Braham was not. Cathedral, concert-room or theatre, he was the magnet of attraction. Who that heard "Jeptha's Rash Vow" could ever forget the volume of voice which issued from that diminutive frame, or the ecstacy with which "Waft her Angels through the Skies" thrilled every nerve of the attentive listener? He ought to have visited the United States twenty years sooner, or not have risked his reputation by coming at all. Like Incledon, he was only heard by Americans when his powers of voice were so impaired as to leave them to conjecture what he had been, and mourn the wreck that all had once admired. His very fame prepared his condemnation, and he committed a fatal error in selecting a concert-room for his debut in North America; thus dulling the edge of curiosity which would have filled the theatre to overflowing on his first appearance. Then, in visiting the city of Philadelphia, he should have gone to the Chesnut Street, which, like the Park in New York, can alone give an actor lasting reputation. This every star has discovered, who, in their eagerness to secure better terms at any other place of public amusement, dig the grave of their reputation. No failure to attract an audience was ever more apparent than his; while but one opinion—that of disappointment—was heard from every body. Whatever sum Burton promised to give him was intended to be fully paid; but the artist failed to draw the crowds anticipated, and the manager could not fulfil his contract. He took his benefit on the 14th of December, as much displeased at the result of his engagement as any auditor with his efforts to amuse. Braham, as a composer, enjoys a reputation which will survive even the recollection of his American failure. Some of his ballads, for simplicity and beauty, have never been excelled.

On the 19th of December, Burton produced, under the direction of Foster, "the Naiad Queen," the success of which for some time eclipsed all other theatrical attraction; the whole public was directed nightly to the doors of the National Theatre. As a spectacle, it has never been equalled in the United States; but the great charm was "the Fifty Female Warriors," headed by Miss Charlotte Cushman and Eliza Petrie. Such a display of ladies' legs, no mortal man could resist the opportunity of seeing—the theatre was crowded nightly—Mr. Burton in the high road to reap the reward of all his exertions—fortune lay before him. But the dogged spirit of opposition, and a determination not to be content with his own success, unless he could blight all chance of recovery to the Chesnut Street Theatre, induced him to lay it

aside, to produce " Norma," on the 11th of January, for which
he was not prepared either in scenery or dresses.   In offering
Miss Sutton, Mrs. Mardyn, and Miss Inverarity, in opposition
to Mr. and Mrs. Wood, Mrs. Bailey, and Mr. Brough, he only
exposed his own weakness; and, notwithstanding Mrs. Wood's
sickness, after the seventh night, gave him a chance which he
could not have calculated upon, the failure of " Norma" more
than counterbalancing the success of the ' 'Naiad Queen," the
dresses of which were pressed into the service of the former
piece, and gave Mr. Burton a blow from which he never recovered.   The public cried out against this course, and his
popularity as a manager was gone—the charm of his name had
vanished, and with it, all his future exertions—his doom was
fixed.   The splendid theatre he had called into existence was
destined to pass into other hands.   Yet, after all the row,
which closed the opera at old Drury, he produced a capital
piece, in which the hit at failure of " Norma," the supernumeraries, taking the battle chorus for their cue to strike, and
place the theatre in an uproar, caused shouts of laughter and
applause every night.   It was giving him *one* blow, while he
dealt to his adversaries *two*—and very hard, uncharitable
blows they were.

On the 25th of February, 1841, Tyrone Power commenced
the last engagement he was ever doomed to act in Philadelphia.   He proceeded to New York, where, on Tuesday, the 9th
of March, he made his last appearance on the stage of any
country, as Gerald Pepper, in the " White Horse of the Pep-
pers," and Morgan Rattler, in " How to pay the Rent."   On
the following day he sailed from New York in the steamship
President ; his fate, to this hour, a sealed book—not a vestige
of the ship, her crew, or passengers, have either been seen or
heard of.   Farewell, Power : long will it be ere thy memory is
forgotten, and longer ere thy place will be supplied, upon the
stage, which mourns thy loss.

On the 10th of April, Burton produced "Tippoo Saib, or the
Storming of Seringapatam," with thirty horses, which proved
the manager's last kick—who departed for the National Theatre, in New York, bearing me along with him, as his aid-de-
camp, and left Foster to produce the "Seven Champions of
Christendom," on the 10th of May, which closed the first season of W. E. Burton's management in Philadelphia, not much
to his satisfaction.

On the 11th of January, 1841, Messrs. Pratt and Dinmore,
aided by the Messrs. Fry, Mr. and Mrs. Wood, Mrs. Bailey,
and Mr. Brough, produced the opera of " Norma," in a style
so superior as to pluck the feather from the cap of so able a
manager as Mr. Wallack, who, until this day, could boast of
" Amilie" as the only opera which had been presented to the

American public, as an opera should be represented; but Philadelphia now took the lead. The chorus, sixty in number; the orchestra equally full and complete ; the dresses, scenery, properties; and lastly, the principal singers, the best the English stage could boast. "Norma," as produced at the Chesnut Street Theatre, was a dramatic representation to be proud of. What a pity it should have involved all concerned in difficulty. For seven nights the Theatre presented an array of fashion, pleasing to the spectator, as well as profitable to the manager, when Mrs. Wood, from the nightly exertion required, broke down under the effort, and the theatre was closed from the 20th until the 25th of January. On the 4th of February it was played for the last time, for a complimentary benefit to the translator, J. R. Fry : tickets of admission on the occasion, two dollars each. The whole affair exploded in a grand row. It appears the receipts nightly taken were not sufficient to pay the nightly expenditure, and Messrs. Pratt and Dinmore wished to make the Woods the last party to be paid, while they expected, and insisted upon being the first. The theatre closed abruptly, and a tempest in a teapot followed; the managers came out in a printed statement in the *Courier and Inquirer*, from which I quote. They go back to transactions which had previously taken place, admitting that in former engagements there was an unpaid balance of 546 dollars, for which they gave a note; but before it reached maturity, urged upon Mr. Wood the propriety of giving up the note, and taking for it the picture of Mrs. Wood, in the lobby of the Chesnut Street Theatre, which cost 660 dollars—the price it appears they paid Mr. Thomas Sully for the picture and frame. Mr. Wood finally consents to this arrangement, and bore off a picture, which Maywood & Co., when "La Somnambula" was filling their treasury to overflowing, insisted upon having painted, to be placed in the most conspicuous part of the theatre, as a mark of admiration for the talent of Mrs. Wood, and to perpetuate the memory of her great success. Now gentlemen, had you spared yourselves this abject piece of flattery, you would have escaped the mortification which followed, and the proof you gave to Mr. Wood of the high value you placed upon the work of art, you so'anxiously pleaded to Mrs. Wood for the privilege of being allowed to have painted, at your expense.

In order to excite public resentment against Mr. Wood, the managers further stated, in previous engagements, (without mentioning how many,) they had promptly paid him 21,377 dollars—a large sum of money; but, upon mercantile principles, certainly no reason why Mr. Wood should lose by defalcation upon present payments, because he had made money

by previous dealings between the parties. They acknowledge
a balance due to Mr. Wood of 421 dollars, but do not consider
this a sufficient cause for the opera, which on their own statement, it appears, does not pay. The long and short of the
matter is—they agreed to give Mr. Wood for the services of
his wife, and other artists, one half of the receipts each night;
the other half was not sufficient to cover the expenditure of
an opera, produced upon so large a scale, and in so perfect a
manner. They wished Wood to reduce his terms, and if he
refused his assent, they had no objections to reduce them for
him, by an unpaid balance, which he resisted. It appears further, by a card from Mr. J. Reese Fry, that the complimentary
benefit was accepted solely as the means of meeting responsi-
bilities to certain performers, assumed by his brother, in consequence of the unexpected stoppage of the opera, after the first
week's representation. The proceeds of that benefit have all
been disbursed for such purposes. " Neither myself, nor any
one in my interest, (so writes Mr. J. R. Fry,) received any further reward from the production, than the delight shared by
the public in witnessing the proper performance of the work
of a great master."

The newspapers, on an *exparte* representation, attacked
Mr. Wood, who, smarting under former experience, in hand-
ling a gentleman belonging to the press too roughly, wisely
resolved to give up the contest, and sail for England. Here
is the letter he despatched to Mr. Bennett of the *New York
Herald,* on leaving the shores of the United States.

" At sea, ship George Washington,
" February 8, 1841.

" DEAR SIR,

" I cannot leave these shores without expressing the sincere respect
and esteem which Mr. Wood and myself entertain for the American public, while at the same time I make known my sentiments towards those
of my own countrymen, who have been the cause of the principal anxieties
and annoyances which we have suffered in this country. I can assert, and
with the most heartfelt satisfaction I do so, that some of the warmest and
best friends I have on earth, are Americans, and beg that it may be distinctly understood, that had my intercourse and business transactions been
confined to them alone, no difficulty,' I feel assured, would have ever
taken place between myself and any portion of the public. Every per-
plexity in which I have been concerned in this country, has originated
with my own countrymen, and I am sorry to add, with Englishmen belonging to my own profession—a profession unfortunately degraded by
many belonging to it—who, instead of using the honest means which they
possess to dignify and exalt it, find a delight in seeking to bring down to
their degraded level, all who aspire to respectability in its ranks. Permit
me, sir, also to observe, that the *offences* laid to my charge have been of a
strictly private nature, and arising out of my business, with which the
public have assuredly no more right to interfere than with the private

transactions of a merchant. It appears to me that much ill-feeling, and consequent annoyance, might be spared, both to the public and the stage, if those who profess to be friends of the latter, would pay less attention to the stories circulated by the envious and dissatisfied of our profession; and that the press itself would not become less dignified by criticising justly, without fear or favour, the performances of the stage, and by completely discarding from their employ the services of such reporters as entirely neglect, or totally destroy the prosperity of an actor, because he is not inclined to *pay* for extra puffs, or to play gratuitously for the benefit of their favourites, or by any other method to conciliate their good-will. I have lived long enough in the world, to entertain the conviction that a plain, straight-forward course is the best, and will not, on compulsion, be forced into singing gratuitously for every complimentary benefit which a few *disinterested committee-men* think proper to *patronise*, by compelling all performers who may happen to be in the country to "*volunteer*" their services, or suffer their high displeasure.

"With many thanks to all my friends, I respectfully take leave for the present, without ever intending again to attempt to pursue my profession in this country. I hope to return, after a brief period, with Mrs. Wood (whose health is at present too feeble to allow her to exercise her art) and shall bring with me several new operas, with one or more singers of established reputation, to support Mrs. Wood, who have not experienced the displeasure of any one in America, professionally, or otherwise.

"Yours respectfully,
(Signed) "JOSEPH WOOD."*

This may be some consolation to you, Mr. Burton. If Braham proved too strong for *your* pocket, "Norman" and the Woods silenced for a time the batteries of your adversaries altogether. On the 19th of February, the Chesnut Street Theatre opened for the benefit of Miss Alexina Fisher, when W. R. Blake, who had been unceremoniously ejected from the Walnut Street Theatre to make room for Tom Flynn, played a short engagement, Henry Placide appearing on the same nights. What a shame the theatre should be deserted when such an actor plays—all proved useless—and the Chesnut Street Theatre quietly expired, until the first of May, when it once more attempted to raise its head, with Richings as stage manager—a bad doctor in a desperate case; but with the aid of opera, Miss Poole, Mrs. Seguin, Miss Marshall, Messrs. Manvers, Giubelei, and Seguin, Mr. and Miss Wells, he contrived to keep open until the 21st of June, closing with "Norma," (which had revived with Mrs. Seguin, Miss Poole, and Guibelei, with a reduced orchestra and chorus,) and "Faint Heart never won Fair Lady," for his own benefit.

I must now say a word or two about the American Theatre, Walnut Street, which since I resigned the lease, when the exactions of the agents became too onorous, had been taken by Messrs. Dinneford and Marshall, Mr. H. G. Freemen allow-

* Published in the New York Herald, of Thursday, February 11, 1841.

'ing them to open the theatre, with the upper boxes at twenty-five cents, and the pit twelve-and-a-half cents—an importation of low prices from New York, not required by the state of theatricals in Philadelphia, but to which even the Chesnut Street Theatre was reduced in 1845. Rare consistency, forcing a man who had worked hard for six years to improve their property, to increase his admission to thirty-seven and a half cents to the pit, and now permitting it to be reduced two hundred per cent; the income of the bars was also surrendered to the new tenants. Am I to believe, gentlemen, that you designedly forced me to abandon the theatre, or that a feeling of anger now prompted your actions towards me by your liberality to my successor? At least I know, while they have been rent free, you have lost five thousand a year by sacrificing your previous tenant—no consolation to me I assure you; although I think I had a claim to a little more favour than ever was extended to me, and was by no means sorry to get rid of the frivolous complaints, continually uttered by Mr. Freeman upon some subject or another. On the 14th of October, the announcement met my eye, while at Baltimore; thus it ran :—Under the sole direction of W. R. Dinneford; W. R. Blake, stage manager, Fredericks, Charles, Howard, W. H. Williams, J. Barnes, Harrington, Hadaway, N. Porter, Ewing, Curtis, B. Williams, Henry Colvin, Wells; Miss Mitchell, Mrs. Flynn, Miss Rock, Mrs. Charles, Mrs. Kinloch, Mrs. La Forrest, Miss Murray, Miss A. Kinloch, Miss J. Kinloch, Mrs. Brittenham, Mrs. Myers; Collingbourne, Prompter, and eight corps de ballet girls. The play " Honey Moon,' and the farce of " A Roland for an Oliver." Prices of admission—lower boxes 50 cents; second and third tier, 25 cents; the pit 12 and a half cents. *Jubilate.*

A very strong company who continued to play with success many of the old comedies, but managers never can let well enough alone. I have done the same thing often myself; but a looker-on sees more than a gamester; and in stopping the career of the company for Mr. Hervio Nano, the Gnome Fly, the manager committed an error, which the sudden falling off of his houses soon gave him intimation of. On the 24th of December Booth played; and on the 28th, with a long flourish of trumpets, Blake produced his own play of " Norman Leslie," a very badly constructed tedious melo-drama, long enough for three. I never saw Miss Medina's piece upon the same subject; and do not plume myself upon my own; but comparing the two, and the very effective manner in which it was placed upon the stage, I wonder that any body ventured to look at it after the first night. Hard sentence this—but true. Shortly afterwards, Tom Flynn assumed the management, producing " Mazeppa," " Rookwood," and other horse-pieces, and The Old Walnut, as the newly-created rulers of the pit termed it, progressed steadily—now pretty good, now very bad, until the end of June, when Dinneford and Marshall closed their first season, cordially hating each other, and determined to separate, each endeavouring to procure the theatre for the following season, without reference to the other. Now it was I was importuned to make an offer, which my friends assured me would be accepted, to resume the reins of management. I refused steadily to listen to any overture which did not come directly from the Board of Agents; and even then, hinted that I did not think we should agree twelve months. I felt my grievance at their hands, and smarting under it, should have pursued a course so diametrically opposite to my former one, that it is fortunate we did not come together again at this time. We can now maintain an armed neutrality, from which proposals may hereafter issue from either party, with the certainty that they would be respectfully received, and carefully considered. On the 7th of July, for three weeks, I assumed the stage management for Dinneford. Here I met Graham, from Mitchell's Theatre—a very good actor, whom I should be happy to have with me. While here I lost my father-in-law, Mr. Jacob Strembeck, placing my family in mourning, and gladly closed the theatre, under orders, on the 21st of July, for Dinneford's benefit—" Luke the Labourer," " Don Giovanni," and " The Village Lawyer."

On Wednesday the 24th March, 1841, William Jones and W. R. Blake opened the Arch Street Theatre, with " Wives as they Were, and Maids as they Are," and " Of Age To morrow." Mr. Jones had been of age long enough to keep out of such a speculation, even with the powerful aid of Forrest's talent, the chief inducement. He seems to have forgotten one thing, that this talent has at all times to be powerfully paid for. In this, Forrest makes no distinction to friend or foe—if any, he treats his foes in business with more consideration than his friends. Henry Placide, Rice, E. Forrest, Murdoch, Mrs. G. Jones, and even Judge Conrad's new play of " Aylesmere," which should have been acted by agreement during his last engagement with me at the Walnut Street Theatre, and was now played at the Arch Street Theatre on the 14th of June— nothing could save the management from dissolution, which lingered on to the 25th of June, when, in spite of all the care and all the attraction that could be offered, its doors were once more closed.

Mitchell, of New York, resolved to try the National in Philadelphia for a month or six weeks. He injudiciously doubled the price charged at the Olympic Theatre, and gave it up at the very time the citizens of Philadelphia were beginning to

Q 5

appreciate the burlesques so admirably performed by his company. He is an able drill-sergeant, and has reaped a handsome reward for his presevering zeal in the city of Gotham, where his audiences enter into all the fun and glee of his pieces with the *goût* of the most enthusiastic admirers of Hudibras. He commenced his trial here on the 12th of June, 1841, and departed from the city not very favourably impressed with the judgment or taste of our citizens.

CHAPTER XXXVIII.

Discharge in the Insolvent Court. Stage Manager of the National Theatre, New York. Mutiny among the Stage Carpenters. A Dilemma. Mr. Park Benjamin *versus* the Philadelphia Critics. Burning of the National Theatre. The Bowery Theatre closed by Order of the Chancellor. Thomas S. Hamblin's Address to the Public. Hamblin's Generalship.

HAVING received my discharge and my protection from the Judges of the Insovent Court, on the 6th of April, Burton, who had taken the National Theatre from Wilson, in New York, offered me the stage management, which I accepted, and proceeded to New York, on Sunday afternoon, April the 10th. On Wednesday, the 13th, we opened with the "Naiad Queen." Of all the scrapes I ever was placed in, the opening night at the National Theatre was the most difficult and trying. The mechanics seemed to work unwillingly; and among the theatrical carpenters there was a feeling, that Philadelphia managers had better stay at home—they had no business in New York. Every order was obeyed with a grumble; and, finally, while Burton, who had observed this, was speaking to me upon the subject, one of the men replied to him, when he had justly observed, that he had not addressed his conversation to him—that the men had made up their minds not to be humbugged. He told him he could leave the theatre. He said he would, and take all the other hands with him too; on which Burton called for the master-carpenter, and said—" Mr. Johnston, pay these men whatever may be due to them, and turn them every one out of the building." Away he walked into the manager's room, when we both burst out laughing at the pretty predicament we were in. This was Tuesday afternoon—the piece was to be produced on Wednesday. He said, " Was I not right ?" " Decidedly so. The only thing now to be done is, without loss of time to supply their places." Ben Hamilton and little Marks, the property men, were at once set to work. I was despatched for Mr. Hitchens, Niblo's master-carpenter, and Burton went in search of Professor Mapes, to ask his assistance, as to where or how a few carpenters could be obtained. Jake Johnston, who had been with me at the Chesnut Street Theatre, in Philadelphia, was staunch to the interest of his employer. Mr. Hitchens promised his own assistance, and one more hand in the morning, and so we had to abide the result. Mr. Burton's conduct was prompt and judicious; and if we only got through this difficulty, good government and discipline throughout the theatre would be established at once. He drilled all the ladies in the military evolutions; and with a determination that every thing should be done well, we both went to work.

On Wednesday morning the rehearsal was got through tolerably well, although Miss Charlotte Cushman could not find her way to the theatre until I was despatched in a cab to bring her there in style—wishing her, in my heart, any where but bothering me. Here a new difficulty arose: Miss Eliza Petrie, who had been sent for from Philadelphia, had not arrived, and there being now no possibility of seeing her before five or six o'clock, we were compelled to make ourselves as easy as possible with the assurance received, that she would be with us in time. Oh! the horrible confusion of that afternoon. Nothing ready—everybody hurrying everybody. Five o'clock came; down I hurried to the steamboat, and returned with the cheering news that Petrie had arrived, and I had safely left her at Miss Cushman's lodgings to prepare for the theatre. I believe this news spurred us both on; it was now past the time when the doors should open. Not a transparent water for bath hung on a truck either made or mounted. Burton now came to me with a face full of anxiety: "Can we open? —Don't give it up until the last moment. Have a placard painted, stating that some of the machinery has not arrived from Philadelphia. If the worst comes to the worst, dismiss them with a promise for to-morrow evening; we are on the horns of a dilemma. If we play, in all probability we damn the piece; if we do not, we damn the prospect of the season. Now, where is Johnston? Jake, can you get us through this, if we make an act, to set the bath scene? For the honour of old Philadelphia, don't see us beaten this way." "Mr. Wemyss, I will get you through it; all I ask is the act drop before the bath scene. "Burton, he says he will do it; what will you do?" (a pause). Then he said, "Have you nerve to try it? it will prove your stage-managership. It is for you to say, you are the master; I am ready, if you will run the risk." "Go ahead!" In two minutes, the doors were open, and in half an hour the house comfortably filled: and at half-past seven o'clock up went the curtain. I had but one bell that would ring, to give the carpenters warning for all the traps. I had to run below to see every trap ready, and give the cue. Nixen, the prompter, worked well; and never did man aid another as Burton did me on this occasion. The awful bath scene passed, without disapprobation—for a most scandalous affair it was—but that over, I felt assured that all would go right. After Burton had finished his part, with a banner, he headed the procession on the stage, acting as the fugleman. Charlotte Cushman's admirable method of commanding her female warriors, whose dresses and manœuvres made the theatre resound with applause, brought the third act, or, on this occasion, the fourth act, to a close, amid a peal of approbation. The last act took care of itself. I had the pleasure of hearing Burton called for; and black, tired, and begrimed, he took me by the hand, and thanked me. Off we started, in due time, to Windhust's, where, over a hot supper, we laughed at our fears of the morning; and thus ended my first night of management in New York. To those unaccustomed to theatres, it will appear marvellous, but it is not the less true.

On the 29th of April, I made my first bow in New York, at the National Theatre, (since the summer of 1824, when the Chatham Theatre, under Barrere, was in the full tide of success,) as Belmour, in "Is he Jealous?" Miss Charlotte Cushman playing Harriet, and Eliza Petrie, Rose. As this little piece depends entirely on the dialogue, these young ladies amused themselves at my expense; if they ever read their parts, it certainly was not with any intention of committing the words to memory. Before an audience with whom I was familiar, such an occurrence would have been of no consequence, but on this occasion, I not only felt mortified, but expressed my mortification in no very measured terms. My reputation as an actor, having some character to uphold, was placed in jeopardy by way of joke! and it was not until I played Flexible, in "Love, Law and Physic," I had an opportunity of proving my pretensions to histrionic fame were well founded.

The next difficulty in management, was that Burton, always on the look-out for novelty, and as if in defiance of the dearly bought experience of his late season, in Philadelphia, laid aside the "Naiad Queen," to announce Booth, J. R. Scott, and Miss Clarendon, in "Othello," for Monday night. He went to Philadelphia, on Sunday morning, and on Sunday evening, about ten o'clock, Mr. Scott, came into my room, at the American Hotel, to give me personally information he could not act on the following night. In vain I endeavoured to persuade him to remain in New York, as he was here, and if disappointment must accrue, to let it fall on the Philadelphia managers. He said no, he had pledged his word to return, on Monday, and by the first train in the morning he intended to start. Why he took the trouble to show himself in New York, on Sunday evening, to say he could not play on Monday, is a question more easily asked than answered. In management, I used to boast I never suffered myself to be placed in a situation from which, by the exercise of a little ingenuity, I could not extricate myself with credit. Finding arguments useless, I told him to sleep upon the matter, and so would I, and in the morning I trusted he would change his opinion. My first inquiry, on Monday, was for Scott. My messenger returned with the intelligence that he was gone. Burton away—no Othello—and an Iago, of whom I whom I had more doubt and misgiving than the rest. Booth was evidently not himself, and the information I had to impart to him was not calculated to improve his state of mind. I despatched a courier to Mr. Wilson, at his farm, on Long Island, with a request that he would play Othello, to which he assented; and thus prepared, I made my appearance at rehearsal. The audience received the apology for the absence of Mr. Scott with very good humour. Naturally expecting it, Mr. Booth, who was to cause the disappointment, the play went on. Not much to my satisfaction, at the end of it, the audience called for Booth, who refused to go on; imposing upon me the necessity of making a second speech, and giving to Mr. Park Benjamin an opportunity of exercising his wit, by calling me in the newspaper, the tall gentleman in black, mourning the murder of his friend Roderigo; which part I had acted in the play, and the critics of Philadelphia used to say I acted it well. But there is no accounting for difference of taste; and when we are in Rome, we must do as Rome does; and the opinion of the editor of the New World is intitled to ——. Fill that space up to suit yourself, good reader.

This tragedy, which had been heralded as a combination of talent, with Booth, J. R. Scott, Wemyss, Shaw, Miss C. Cushman and Miss Clarendon, was the worst performance presented at the National Theatre, under Burton's management; and his *friends*, on his return from Philadelphia, did not forget to tell him of it. For a metropolitan theatre, it was disgraceful. Wilson's Othello put the audience to sleep; Booth's Iago was almost as bad; and Miss C. Cushman, as Emelia, and Shaw, as Cassio, was the only approach to acting seen upon the stage that evening.

At the close of Booth's engagement, Burton wisely replaced the "Naiad Queen" upon her throne. She fortunately proved again triumphant; but the hiatus in her reign had not been profitably filled, and had nearly overthrown her power, which yielded on the 24th of May, to "Semiramis—The Daughter of Air," a clever alteration of a play, by Burton, in which

Isherwood painted some scenery which entitled him to be placed in the rank of the first artists. Miss Cushman also, took the city by surprise, in a part, which, if it had been written for her peculiar style, would scarcely have hit the mark as well : to this part is she indebted for all the reputation she shortly gained throughout the United States. This was the stepping-stone to the ladder of fame she has rapidly mounted.

On the 28th of May, " Semiramis," and " Love, Law and Physic," was the performance, the last which ever took place within the walls of the ill-fated National Theatre. In the afternoon of that day, as was [my custom when I expected Burton, I walked down to the steamboat landing to await the arrival of the Philadelphia boat. On touching the wharf, I was joined by Burton; we walked up West Broadway, to Leonard Street, and as we entered the theatre, Mr. Oakey called me, and asked, " If that was Burton?" I said " Yes." " Do you know, Mr. Weymss, the theatre has been on fire?" " No; how long ago?" " Not ten minutes since." He pointed my attention to the place, and on examining the prompter's box, I found three distinct marks of fire in as many different positions. While thus engaged, Shiers, the gas man, passed through from the interior of the house, with his torch not lighted; I said, " George, do you know anything about the theatre being on fire?" He treated the matter so lightly, hurrying past without even looking at the spot, which was the object of curiosity to every one else present, that when we discovered fire in more places than one, still burning, my suspicions were directed towards him. Burton, who had been talking to Oakey, now gave orders that all the doors should be shut, and said to me, " The man who did this is in the building now." " You go one way, I'll go the other; with a strict search we may find him." We had neither of us any suspicion of further danger. We met at the painting room, and proceeding to the flies, I stopped suddenly and said, " Burton, I smell fire here;" he replied, " That's nothing : it proceeds from the scorched wood in the prompter's box just below you." " No, it's too strong for that—it comes in the direction of Wilson's rooms." While speaking, the door leading to these apartments was opened by Mr. Russell, who informed us they were on fire. The water closet had been fired; Wilson's desk, and many of his papers were on fire, while the room was littered up with old play bills and newspapers; down stairs fire was discovered under one of the ottomans in the Turkish saloon, with a box of lucifer matches, from which about one-third had been extracted, no doubt for the purpose of igniting waste paper wherever it might be found. The ticket-office belonging to the third tier was the last place where fire was discovered; making in all seven fires, which, in a few minutes longer, would have rendered all aid to the National Theatre vain. Mr. Smith, who kept the refectory under the theatre, brought me some matches, which, he stated had been thrown from a window. This led to another search; and marks of fire which had smouldered and gone out, were found in the room next to Mr. Russell's bed-room. I went by Burton's desire to the police-office, when an officer, on hearing the particulars, questioned Shiers closely, who denied having any key that would open the door leading to Mr. Wilson's rooms; but upon trial, it was found the key he used opened those doors readily. On this Mr. Shiers was taken into custody. The performance went on as if nothing had happened; a double watch was placed upon the premises, and all supposed to be safe. Burton and myself left the theatre together, resolving to return before we went home for the night. We desired the city watchmen, as we passed, to keep a bright look out for any suspicious character that might be seen lurking around. Between one and two o'clock we returned to the theatre, and found the watchmen and Mr. Russell on the alert. They reported all safe, and retired for the night.

Between six and seven o'clock, Mr. Shaw came to my chamber door, and desired me to get up as quick as possible, the National Theatre was in flames. I ordered a cab, while I hurried on my clothes, and arrived at the corner of Leonard Street and Broadway with Shaw, just in time to hear, not see, the roof fall in. The rapidity of the flames had been such, that scarcely an article could be saved. When the watchman left the building, he declares everything was safe; yet he had not proceeded to Broadway, when on looking towards the theatre, he saw flames issuing from the artist's private room, the last window in the upper range. Mr. H. Lewis was the first actor on the spot belonging to the theatre, and on seeking admission at the stage room, he was prevented by Thomas Hurd, or Heard, a man in no way attached to the theatre, from entering; and thus Burton's property and my own, in the manager's room, which might have been saved, was doomed to destruction. On the examination, at the police-office, this Heard, was committed to take his trial. Why these two men, Shiers and Heard, were permitted to escape without trial, is a mystery. Had I been placed in Mr. Burton's situation, the most searching investigation into the cause of the destruction of this theatre, should never have been abandoned by me, until I had lost all power to proceed farther. It now remains enveloped in mystery, and a thousand conjectures, with rumours of all kinds, have assailed the reputation of several of the gentlemen who should, like Cæsar's wife, have stood above suspicion. For my own part, I am fully convinced, if Heard had been tried, whether convicted or not, the truth would have been discovered, and the guilty brought to punishment. A clearer case of incendiarism was never brought to public notice; but who was the incendiary, or incendiaries, if more than one, is now a secret, which will descend with them to the grave.

This fire destroyed for me the few private dresses I yet retained from my whole stock, and made me, as an actor, a beggar indeed. On Sunday morning I started for Philadelphia, there to remain until summoned by Mr. Burton, to whom I was pledged until the 4th of July. How faithfully I redeemed that pledge, refusing every offer made to me, Mr. Dinneford, and others, can bear witness; and with surprise, although not anger, I received the intimation from Burton, that for the following year he intended to attend to the business of the stage himself, and would not make me an offer of the highest salary he should give to any one, as he considered it totally beneath my notice. I told him that was all I wished; I should take the Front Street Theatre, in Baltimore, the stockholders of which were only waiting for my arrangements with him to be brought to a close. " The very thing for you; go, and anything in the way of attraction I have, command freely. I have no doubt you will do well." And so we parted; and so remain the best of friends.

It is somewhat curious to remark that at this period the theatres in New-York were all at their lowest ebb;—the property of Mr. Simpson in the Park, advertised for sale, as under seizure for rent, by Messrs. Astor and Beekman;—his process in all probability intended as a protection, instead of an oppression to Mr. Simpson; the National burnt, and not likely to be re-built again; and the Bowery closed by an injunction for non-payment of license, on which subject Mr. Thomas Hamblin thus addressed his fellow-citizens:—

" Bowery Theatre Closed—By order of the Chancellor, on the complaint, and at the request of the managers of the society for the reformation of Juvenile delinquents.

To my Fellow-Citizens,

" It is with the most painful feelings my duty compels me to announce to you, that the Bowery Theatre is closed, in obedience to a mandate from the Court of Chancery, sued out and issued, at the instigation of the managers of the society, for the reformation of juvenile delinquents. Some nine years since the Legislature of this State inflicted a yearly tax of 500 dollars, on the performance of the Legitimate Drama, represented in the New York Theatres only; and on this law I have already paid upwards of 4000 dollars, which has been applied to the support and maintenance of juvenile thieves and other offenders.

" It will not surprise the public to be informed, that in these times of universal depression, I am unable to meet this demand on the instant, nor that I should solicit the indulgence usually granted in the payment of other taxes. Last week I addressed a respectful letter to the gentlemen above designated, soliciting a delay. To my astonishment, this reasonable request has been answered by a suit at law, and an injunction, commanding me to close my doors. Harsh and hasty as the measure is, I feel it nevertheless my duty to obey it. Like a good citizen, I shall bow to the majesty of the law, although ' I cannot kiss the rod that smites me.'

" I trust without offence, I may be permitted to regret the act, and question the necessity that may be thought to exist, for proceeding to such harsh legal measures, for the recovery of a tax due but on the 1st instant; more particularly when the complainants were aware that their proceedings would deprive most unexpectedly upwards of one hundred persons, employed in this establishment, of all means of obtaining bread in these times of universal distress. Armed for the present, with a little brief authority, the managers of the juvenile delinquents have struck a blow which must be severely felt by the honest and laborious persons in my employ, their wives and families ; a blow which I think every feeling and manly heart will designate as uncalled for, unprovoked, impolitic and oppressive.

(Signed,)   " THOMAS S. HAMBLIN."

" BOWERY TEATRE, May 18, 1841."

My friend Hamblin is a good general, he made capital of closing for one week ; raised the ire (dander) of the Bowery boys, who would not stand their theatre being closed. They determined that Tom Hamblin should go ahead, and they pushed him ahead. He opened on the 24th, and played to better business than he had seen within the walls for two years. The National burning down, removed the dangerous rivalship of Burton, who had compelled him to reduce his prices, and gave him once more a fair field of exertion, which he soon improved, and placed himself again in a position free from pecuniary embarrassment.

In bidding adieu once more to New York, I leave it with a hope to return some day and take up my residence there. My prejudices in favour or Philadelphia have been removed, and I am compelled to admit that New York is the first city in the Union for business of every kind. Different expressions these to those that may be found in the earlier part of this work; but "a wise man corrects error, while a fool perishes in his folly."

On board the boat, which carried me to Philadelphia, I found Miss Cushman ; the burning of the theatre, and the proceedings of the previous day, were of course the topics of conversation. Her suspicions pointed to a party as yet unimpeached, but who could have no motive for such a diabolical act.

On my arrival in Philadelphia, Mr. Blake tendered me the Arch Street Theatre, for a benefit in the name of himself and his partner, Jones. Mr. Lewis Pratt offered me the Ches-

R

nut Street for the same purpose; and lastly, after much prompting, Dinneford offered the Walnut. Here I confess, I would rather have received condolence, and with a better chance of. success. However, I accepted the. first offer, had hosts of volunteers; and on the 10th of June, had the mortification to find that an actor really in want should never be patronized. A few dollars would have been most acceptable, but the citizens of Philadelphia were not disposed at this moment to give them to me; I lost money by the benefit of condolence. On the 17th, Miss Charlotte Cushman, with the aid of a committee of arrangement, at the Chesnut Street Theatre, did not fare much better; and Burton also on the 19th, at his own theatre, was made to feel how little sympathy the misfortunes of managers or actors meet from the great body of our citizens. It would be difficult to find three actors. standing higher with the public in professional reputation.than Miss.C. Cushman, Mr. Burton, and Mr. Wemyss; yet on this occasion all were mortified that they should have been induced to make attempts which proved so abortive. *Vanitas, vanitatis, et omnia vanitas!*

CHAPTER XXXIX.

Opening of the Front Street Theatre, Baltimore. Addam's Engagement. Charles Eaton, another Temperance Man. " The Manager in Distress." A Good Joke. Liberality, characteristic of Sailors. Booth and Addams in the same piece. Buckstone and Mrs. Fitzwilliam. " London Assurance." The Press, its Assumptions, and Treatment of Actors.

I COMMENCED my season at the Front Street Theatre, in Baltimore, on Monday, the 6th of September, 1841. The directors had thought proper to let it to Mr. Ward for a short season, who suffered sad havoc to be made among the scenery and properties; to replace which put me to much trouble and inconvenience, and the stockholders to some expense. The opening pieces were, " Carpenter of Rouen," and " Simpson & Co." —the company, Wemyss, Matthews, Philips, Thorne, Ash, Eddy, Brittenham, Kimber, Newton, Brennan and Bowers, Mrs. Philips, Mrs. D. Anderson, Miss Matthews, Miss Helen Matthews; to whom were afterwards added, Harrison, D'Angelis, Mr. and Mrs. Smith, Weaver, Lyne, Clemens, Williams, Eytinge, Gourlay, and four ballet girls. The first stars were the Hungarian Singers, followed by A. Addams, whom I had not seen for three years. He played an excellent engagement, but in the renewal, his old failing ruined our rising reputation : —would it were death, without benefit of clergy, for an actor

to appear upon the stage drunk. On the 2nd of October I perpetrated a deed of horror, in attempting to alter Sakspeare's
tragedy of Macbeth into a melo-drama, under the title of the
"Three Witches of the Blasted Heath." If it did not succeed,
at least it gave me an idea of what might be done with the play
by the judicious introduction of the pageantry, by which I
shall profit hereafter. On the 7th of October, a new play, entitled "The Black Knight," possessing some merit, and written
by a gentleman belonging to the press, was produced. What
its fate might have been if the citizens of Baltimore had
given it a fair hearing, cannot now be guessed at. So little
curiosity, or so little inclination, to support an American
author, was exhibited on this occasion, the receipts taken
were only forty-four dollars and fifty cents ! damping the
spirits of author, actors, and manager—the worst house of the
season. On the following night the receipts were doubled,
the audience appeared much gratified, and the author's night
might have produced a tolerable house, but the first night
cooled his ardour, and he declined the risk of further mortification. On the 9th of October, Booth and Addams played in
"Othello ;" after which they appeared in "Venice Preserved,"
"Jane Shore," "Pizarro," and "Douglas." Charles Eaton,
another *temperance man*, played a very good engagement
singly, beating the two great tragedians who preceded him.
Eaton was always popular with a certain class. Poor fellow,
he went from Baltimore to Pittsburgh, where he ended his
mortal career, having, in a fit of intoxication, walked over
the ballustrading of the Exchange Hotel, falling eighteen or
twenty feet, and being picked up a mass of bruised and
broken bones ; he breathed and lived a few hours, but never
spoke after the fatal accident.

On the first of November, for my benefit, I produced
"Zanthe," to 369 dollars, with "The Manager in Distress ;"
during the performance of which, many persons, imposed upon
by the seeming reality, vacated their seats, in compliance
with my address, and applied at the box office for the return
of their money, to be laughed at for their credulity, losing
good seats to take their chance of catching a glimpse of the
stage from the dress boxes, as best they might. The joke had
almost ended in earnest ; it was some time before the officers
could restore good humour. It is almost incredible that, in
Baltimore, where theatres have existed for fifty years, the
citizens could have been so prastised upon: the joke must
remain in force for many years : and none enjoyed it more
than the dupes themselves, when the first feeling of anger had
subsided. A celebrated slack-wire dancer, Madame Romanini,
added to the attraction of the Bal Masque, in "Zanthe,"

astonishing the good people of Baltimore by the agility of her movements.

This was a season of wonders, in Baltimore. While playing "Jane Shore," an unsophisticated son of the Ocean was so wrapt up in the play that, as Mrs. Philips lay down to die in the last scene, of want, suddenly sprang over the boxes, and with the activity of a cat, placed himself at her side upon the stage, saying he would be damned if any woman should starve in that manner while he had a shot in the locker; and he actually insisted upon forcing upon her the contents of his purse. An explanation ensued, and he was conducted back to his seat in the boxes, where the audience gave him three cheers; and I shall never forget the honest smile that lighted up his weather-beaten face. He was the magnet of attraction for the remainder of the evening, although he had turned the last act of the tragedy into a farce highly relished by the audience.

On the 18th of November, A. Addams attempted Cardinal Richelieu. The fame acquired by E. Forrest, in this part should have stimulated his pride;—*drink had done its work*—the mind of the actor is gone; he is incapable of committing a new part to memory: there was not even an attempt to produce effect; a school boy who should have read the play as a task, and read so badly, would have been whipped. At the conclusion, the feeling of the audience was not one of pity, but of contempt; a few of those present, hissed; but respect for what he had been, restrained the majority from joining in this insult. I know of but one very slender consolation, his friend Booth, butchered this part more cruelly; he was laughed at—Addams despised. There was 364 dollars in the house; he repeated the part on the following evening to 32 dollars; further comment is useless.

Mr. Buckstone and Mrs. Fitzwilliam played an excellent engagement, terminating on the 10th of December. Reports now reached me, from Philadelphia, that Burton's pecuniary embarrasments increased so fast, it would be impossible for him to keep his theatre open; that his scenery, wardrobe and other property, was under seizure for rent, to be sold by the sheriff. This actually took place; Mr. Newton becoming the purchaser, and Mr. Burton being allowed to proceed, under a new arrangement with Mr. Wharton, the ground landlord, giving him one chance more to recover his losses.

On Monday, the 13th of December, "London Assurance," which Madame Vestris, by the aid of furniture alone, had made successful; and which, for a few nights, revived the drooping fortune of every theatre in which it was acted, was produced at the Front Street Theatre, in Baltimore, in a style which will be remembered as long as comedy is talked about at all. I played it fourteen nights, ten of which were in succession; the weather was very inclement, hail, rain, snow and frost, yet the house was well attended; if the clerk of the weather-office had been my friend, its success would have been equal to my expectations. To my friend Tom Flynn, was I indebted for the copy, although in a few days afterwards I received a marked London Book, from Mr. Meadows, of Covent Garden. Mr. Samuel Butler was the next star, and then the horses in "Rockwood" and "Mazeppa."

Miss Clifton took the Holiday Street Theatre, which had during the winter been without a tenant, and on Monday the 31st of January, announced to open it in conjunction with W. E. Burton! To Mr. Burton the speculation at the Holiday Street was the final act in the drama of his management. I had been open one hundred and twenty-seven nights, on the 31st of January, 1842, when I had contrived to fulfil all my engagements—actors paid in full of all demands—not by signing receipts to that effect, but receiving their money—all the demands of the season, out of doors, discharged, when Mr. Burton, who had promised me every assistance, but refused every request for pieces, &c., that I made to him, appeared in Baltimore to oppose me as manager. In the first week, with the aid of Miss Charlotte Cushman, and Mr. Chippendale, I received only 403 dollars; Chippendale's benefit amounting to 54 dollars, and Miss Charlotte Cushman's to 105 dollars: this was a hard blow, but the week that followed was worse, 166 dollars being the amount of the week, or 47 dollars per night for the two weeks, in which the Holiday Street Theatre had been playing to tolerable houses. Finding I could not support this conflict, I called General Welsh to my aid, and placed the horses in my circus, first giving a Dress Ball in honour of Washington's Birth Day, on the 22nd of February. If Burton had cause for exultation in the commencement, the horses had the power to draw away all his customers but those represented by that curse to all theatres, the stockholders' tickets. He retreated from Baltimore, routed and dismayed, leaving his actors to find their way out of the city in the best manner they could, his own fortunes completely prostrated, only to be relieved by the benefit of the Insolvent Court, or the Bankrupt Act. On the 4th of April, the horses having succeeded in vanquishing the foe, I again opened the theatre. Mr. Proctor, whom I ought never to have announced as a star, fixed the fate of the season. On the night fixed for his benefit he was so intoxicated, I was compelled to dismiss the assembled audience. Even the grand encampment, which commenced on the 16th of May, was, by bad weather, rendered unavailable. Governor Porter and suite of Pennsylvania, and Governor Thomas and suite of Maryland, could not induce the ladies to turn out through torrents of rain, and the encamped soldiers looked like so many half-drowned mud-larks. I closed on the 23d of May, but cannot now say all the bills were paid. Printers, actors, officers, even *musicians*, were in arrear.

Mr. Thomas Wildey, Colonel Myer, Mr. Hyde, and Mr. Sanderson, form a pattern worthy of imitation, as members of a board of agents, always willing to aid instead of crushing their lessee. In any difficulty in which I was placed as the manager of the Front Street Theatre, I never asked for either advice or pecuniary aid, that it was not given, and cheerfully. To those gentlemen, and the other members of their board, I return my grateful thanks, not only for favours received, but for others of greater mangnitude, offered, but declined by me, because I could not see the justice of placing these gentlemen in a position which might have compelled them to assume many of my debts, as a reward for their kindness, and the good opinion they entertain of me both as a man and a manager. It is a proud satisfaction to me, in surrendering the theatre into their hands, to know that they appreciate the motives which guided me in that determination.

I have now arrived at the time when my friend Joe Cowell informs the world he found me in a *"cellar,"* (and a very comfortable basement it was,) selling pills and periodicals, where, could I have commanded a little more money to have continued my system of advertisements, I should have done well enough, but the funds did not come in fast enough, and the moment I ceased to advertise on a large scale, a very small purse would contain all my receipts. This leads me, in a theatrical point of view, to the influence of

THE PRESS.

Generally upon all subjects connected with the daily affairs of life, I know that I here approach a tender subject—one which, like a hornet's nest, the more you ruffle it, the greater number of stings will be inflicted upon you. No man has been more indebted to editors of newspapers for kindness than I have, and few have had more abuse lavished upon them from a similar source, or have been at times more harshly treated. My object, therefore, is to direct the attention of my readers, most of whom I presume are visitors of the theatre, to the manner in which the press is subsidized to deceive them; but let them speak upon this subject for themselves.

This circular bears date, Philadelphia, April 2nd, 1835. Here it is :—

(COPY.)

"With a view to avoid some of the inconveniences which result from a diversity in the charges of advertising in the several newspaper establishments in this city, the publishers of the daily papers have recently adopted a scale of prices by which it is their intention hereafter to be regulated. It has, therefore, been thought due to you, as well as to themselves, to present for your consideration the following item which relates to theatres, circuses, and *other* places of amusement; and we take the liberty of suggesting, that the first of the present month presents a suitable period for commencing this arrangement.

EXTRACT FROM THE REGULATIONS:

"Amusements.—On bills of performance of theatres, circuses, &c., not exceeding one square per night, shall be charged two dollars per week; and no card of any person shall be inserted on any other terms than those of the regular rates. All *puff* communications to be charged the same as advertisements, by the square, at the same prices.

JASPER HARDING,	WM. FRY,
MUFFLIN and PARRY,	EDWARD CONRAD,
N. SARGENT,	Z. POULSON,
JOS. R. CHANDLER,	PETER HAY and Co.

"To Mr. F. C. WEMYSS, Manager."

At this period there was an agreement with those newspapers in which I advertised, to insert the daily advertisement of the Walnut Street Theatre, for sixty dollars per year. But these gentlemen, in the plenitude of their power, fix a day for a new arrangement, one day antecedent to the date of their printed card, Mr. Joseph R. Chandler, being the only one who qualified the notice, so as not to involve any breach of previous contract. Instead of the first of the present month, his notice ran—at the expiration of existing contracts. This was honestly done, and like himself, although he sanctioned by his name and influence the new arrangement.

The continued puffing fostered by this system has had a most malign influence upon the interests of the theatre, and a still worse one upon the private character of the actor; it enabled managers to place before the public a class of persons who in former times would not have been tolerated beyond a first appearance.

There was a time when the opinion of a well-educated man (whose refinement of taste in classic literature rendered him capable of writing a criticism both upon the merits of the author and actor) was received by the latter with deference; his faults judiciously pointed out, induced him to apply a remedy, while praise from the same source urged him on to future exertions. The pit, then frequented by men whose judgment the actor most relied upon—whose censure they dreaded—whose good opinion they courted, and who decided, viva voce, upon their merits, during the performance of a part—these opinions the press echoed, rarely modifying, and from which decision, so confirmed, the actor had no appeal. This power the press has lost over the mind of the actor, who knows that for a few dollars he can have his own opinion of his abilities paraded in the newspapers, to procure fame at a distance from the circle where his merit is known and classed. It is the actor's pocket, not his mind, that is taxed. "How much will it cost to enable me to travel through the United States as a star?" That is the calculation—not, have I the ability to maintain such a position—but have I the money to secure it by the puff preliminary in certain widely-circulated newspapers. The success, like that of all quacks—depends upon the constant iteration of puffs upon merit, which has no existence but in the columns of these purchased newspapers.

Again, how frequently a critique upon the able manner in which an actor has supported a principal character, appears in the newspapers, when no such performance ever took place, some accident causing a change of pieces, the knowledge of which never reached the reporter, whose article was in type, although he had not been at the theatre during the evening—and, when discovered, who thinks of it beyond the momentary laugh raised against the editor, thus caught in a trap, except some minor actor who, having been unceremoniously abused for acting badly a part he never appeared in, is silly enough to seek an explanation or demand an apology which, if given, is couched in such language as to be more offensive than the original paragraph. Who has forgotten a certain gentleman belonging to the Chesnut Street Theatre, who, indignant at being termed "a thing," instead, upon an apology from the editor, which being promised, appeared, the following morning, thus—"Mr. —— called upon us, and requested we would correct the statement of yesterday, wherein, speaking of his merit as an actor, we called him 'a thing.' We sincerely ask his pardon, and thus publicly inform our readers, that Mr. ——, of the Chesnut Street is No Thing." The wit of this is no apology for its baseness; but it is a fair specimen of such redress as actors feel for such offences.

There are found low-minded men in all trades and professions. When a manager meets a low-minded editor, his insolence is intolerable. I can quote an instance in which an editor, having been excluded from the free list for a long course of unprovoked abuse and hostility towards a theatre where he was an invited guest, had the impertinence on the following morning to ask in the column of his own paper, which he termed the medium of the press, by whose authority he was refused : he would show the arbitrary manager, that "the liberty of the press" was not to be controlled by his caprice or pleasure.

The press, politically, should be free as air; it is the safeguard of liberty, defending at the same moment the rights of the governed and governors: but the moment it enters the domicile of a private citizen to destroy the peace of his family, it should be bound with chains of adamant. What right has a man, who, more fortunate in pecuniary circumstances than his neighbour, can command money sufficient to publish a few thousand printed sheets daily, in form of a newspaper, to utter expressions therein as items of news, calculated to provoke a breach of the peace, and which, uttered in the presence of the aggrieved party, would subject this same editor to personal chastisement? I ask, what right has such a man to shield himself from the consequence of such an act, under "the liberty of the press?" Bah! This is the tyranny of the press—a worse tyranny than any despot ever exercised, the fear of which is felt in the jury-box and on the bench. The law of libel is no protection to the citizen from such an assault as I have described. The jury cannot agree, legal prosecutions are expensive; and if, surmounting all these difficulties a citizen obtains a verdict, the judge inflicts the mildest sentence the law permits him to record, to shield himself from columns of abuse, which he has no desire to see launched against him for the discharge of an unpleasant duty. The convicted editor, in the first sheet which follows the sentence, triumphantly records the result, in which he probably states with truth, the character of the prosecutor was valued by the court and jury at *one cent*, which *we* (Lord Byron says, these gentlemen always use *we* for *I*) paid, and wish the gentleman joy of the opinion his fellow-citizens entertain of him. This is the redress the law affords a defenceless man against one armed with a daily press to renew the assault. I ask any one who has been bold enough to tell these self-constituted censors of his morals and all his actions, that they should not assail him with impunity, and appeals to the law to suppress the aggression, whether this be not a true picture of the result? But reverse the case. Let a citizen, goaded by repeated insult, commit an assault and battery upon the sacred person of an editor, he will find the law, which will be resorted to, has the power not only to fine but imprison him, while the judge, in pronouncing sentence, will read him a homily upon the enormity of his offence, and assure him that the court is determined at all hazards to protect the liberty of the press.

As a source of advertising *business*, a newspaper is invaluable to the community, and is now extensively used by all who wish to prosper; but why the proprietor of a popular sheet for this purpose should claim the right, by virtue of *the liberty of the press*, to regulate all places of public amusement to which they demand free admission, under the penalty of refusing to notice them in the reading matter, and sometimes even refusing to insert the paid-for advertisement, unless accompanied by tickets for the editor, is a practice subversive of the correction the press should exercise (if at all) over these very places of amusement, all of which are eulogized until some unfortunate cannot pay his advertising bill; and then his place of amusement, already tottering, is doomed to certain destruction. Now let me show the amount of money which the tickets demanded and given by a theatre would produce, if paid for, as they should be, if the editor charges for his advertisement:

The proprietor, a season ticket, valued at the minimum price, is 15 dollars; the reporter, ditto, 15 dollars; the editor, ditto, 15 dollars; an order to admit four persons every Saturday—this is to treat the devil and the journeymen at the manager's expense. All this has been submitted to, rather than provoke the ire of an editor. And these orders, which in the year amount to 104 dollars, have actually been sold at the doors, stopping the money which would have been paid into the treasury for admission. I must do the proprietors the justice to say, this last arrangement met with their decided disapprobation; but the evil to the theatre remained unabated—the same request for orders was made on the following Saturday. I have now shown that each paper received one hundred and forty-nine dollars in the course of the year, over and above the two hundred and eight dollars for puffs and advertisements, with the extra cards for actors' benefits, amounting to at least fifty dollars more. Now as twelve newspapers, some daily, some weekly, enjoyed these privileges, and four theatres open, it follows, that the enormous sum (excluding the fair business part of the transaction, in paying for the advertisements and puffs) of seven thousand one hundred and fifty-two dollars is annually paid by the theatres of Philadelphia, to purchase the good will of the gentlemen who direct the liberty of the press, which, with the receipts for advertising, &c., amount to nineteen thousand one hundred and fifty-two dollars. A great deal has been said about black mail: this is a private affair, altogether independent of the management; if it exist, the actor or his friends pay that; but, certainly, nobody will doubt the *freedom of the press*, after reading this chapter, in its supervision of public amusements.

The following, written by Leigh Hunt, of the *London Examiner*, nearly fifty years ago, forms so good a glossary for reporters, that I cannot avoid transcribing them :—

A crowded house.—A theatre, on the night of a performance, when all the back seats and upper boxes are empty.

A good actor.—The general term for an actor who gives good dinners.

A fine actor.—One who makes a great noise: a tatterdemallion of passions; a clap-trapper: one intended by nature for a towncrier.

A charming play.—A play of dancing, music, and scenery: a play in which the author has the less to do the better.

Great applause.—Applause, mixed with the hisses of the pit and gallery.

Unbounded and universal applause.—Applause mixed with hisses from the pit only. This phrase is frequently to be found at the bottom of the play-bills, declaring the reception a new piece has met with.

Leigh Hunt must certainly have had before him "the vision" of the present newspaper critics, making allowance for progressive improvement in the art of puffing.

CHAPTER XL.

Opening of the Pittsburgh Theatre, by Dinneford. A failure. Burton. Forrest. Mr. Tasistro in Hamlet. Fanny Elisler. Miss Jane Sloman. Tom Flynn. Risley and Sons. A Wanton Act. End of the Season of 1841-'42.

DINNEFORD, who had become lessee of the Arch Street Theatre, opened the winter campaign of 1841, on the 7th of August, with "Pizarro," and "Simpson and Co." His business for several months very good; but, as usual with the Arch Street property, it was a promise of success, to be succeeded by failure and abandonment. He produced "Rookwood," the "Bronze Horse," &c.; finally departed for Pittsburgh, where the last season had been so disastrous to me, notwithstanding the Slomans, Mr. Jones, Brough, Madame Otto, Miss Lee, (with La Bayadere,) Eaton, H. J. Finn—all put forward claims to the support of the Pittsburghers. The weather was so inclement, that the stars, both from the east and west, met half frozen at the top of the Alleghany mountains, which was the barrier beyond which none could proceed for three weeks. Mr. Jackson, the present proprietor of the Bowery, was the manager. The theatre was open for seventy-two nights, the average receipts sixty-two dollars!! which, deducting the money paid to stars and actors for benefits, would make the treasury receipts about forty dollars. For the first time since the theatre was built, the actors returned to Philadelphia and

Baltimore, with a balance due to them for salary, which was afterwards paid; at least one-half the company were arrested, and bailed by my friend, George Beale, who started them on to me as another batch of *chased actors* from the Pittsburgh Theatre. This was the second losing season at Pittsburgh. The weather, and my own folly in yielding to the wishes of a few, in converting the pit into a parquette, (which the gallery were determined should not be so occupied in peace, jeering every one who took a seat in it, until it was replaced as a pit,) were the chief causes in bidding farewell to the theatre, which I made several attempts again to occupy. I bade farewell to the last link which had any hold upon my regard as a manager. My old Pittsburgh friends condescend to call upon me when business brings them to Philadelphia, and we laugh at the happy times we have passed within the walls of the now smoky palace—the Pittsburgh Theatre, to which, and its proprietor, Mr. E. Simpson, I wish success, most sincerely hoping that it may repay to him all losses he has sustained by others, as well as myself.

Burton opened his National Theatre on Saturday, the 21st of August, disappointing the audience on the first night, Conner being unable to proceed with the play of "Money." I was called upon to act Belmour, which I did cheerfully to oblige Burton. On Monday, the 23rd, E. Forrest commenced an engagement. How he runs from one theatre to the other, like the fox, doubling, until he reaches his starting ground again; more attractive by his temporary absence. It is a dangerous experiment, which his popularity alone enables him to pursue with success.

Burton produced "London Assurance,' on the 15th of November, with Browne, himself, Buckstone, Miss Clifton, and Mrs. Fitzwilliam, five stars, determined to eclipse the Walnut Street, where Flynn had been too quick for him. He added an aviary of living birds, and fountains of real water, to the other attractions of scenery and properties; and thus closed the year 1841.

The Chesnut Street Theatre, still languished under the management of Mr. Pratt, Mr. Dinmore having retired, opened for the season with "Much Ado about Nothing," and "Faint Heart never won Fair Lady," on the 28th of August. On the 31st, Mr. Tasistro, a gentleman well known in the literary world, attempted to act Hamlet. He can handle his pen much better in a newspaper paragraph, than he could guide his tongue upon the stage through such a part. What is there so terrific in those foot-lights, which tongue-tie the most loquacious who appear before them, while those behind them see no difficulty in the player's art? Let them try it,

Mr. Tasistro, and they will be more lenient in their strictures upon you.

On the 3rd of September, the "queen of dance," Mad. Fanny Ellsler, appeared in "La Sylphide," and then La Bayadere;" but all in vain—the novelty was over. The attraction which, could enable a manager to pay such exorbitant terms, had ceased; this last engagement, bringing the Chesnut Street Theatre nearer to the crisis which all could now predict.— Richings attempted to revive several of the very old comedies; but there is now, alas! no audience in Philadelphia to appreciate such plays; and it was a waste of money, for no good purpose. "Barnaby Rudge" was next tried; but melo-drama rarely succeeds at this theatre, and never, as the principal attraction—the scenery, stage, and machinery, want modern improvement, before, in this, any manager can compete with the Walnut Street Theatre, where every thing is perfect for such pieces. On the 5th of October, Miss Jane Sloman appeared as a pianist; she did not produce the sensation expected. A theatre is not the place for such an exhibition, which belongs to the concert-room. Mr. and Mrs. Sloman performed on the same evening, but the house was not worthy of the occasion: her benefit took place on the 9th. On the 21st, the Ravel Family failed to attract even money enough to defray the current expenditure; and on the 27th of October, the theatre closed for the season—a very short, and very unprofitable one —with Richings' benefit. Alas! poor Chesnut, Burton has sealed your doom, dragging himself down in the ruin he has created around him.

On the 31st of August, the Walnut opened under the management of Thomas Flynn, Marshall the lessee, with a new piece—a mixture of "Undine" and the "Naiad Queen"— entitled the "Water Queen." It failed, and merited its fate, the transparent sea being the only redeeming feature in the piece; tiring the audience, until their patience was exhausted; and half of them left the theatre before the great scene was brought before them. If Flynn failed in this, he shortly converted a defeat into a triumph, by producing the "Naiad Queen," and throwing down the gauntlet to Burton,—making a great noise about this piece, when he was quietly preparing "London Assurance;" and took both Burton and the city by surprise, on the 6th of November, by a display of carpets, cushions, pianos, candelabras, chairs, tables, flower-pots, and statues—all real: played the comedy without the assistance of a star, and took the gold off the gingerbread, while the two other houses in Chesnut Strret were dreaming upon the possibility of getting it ready. Had Flynn done nothing more during the season, the tact he displayed in this, proved his capacity to manage the theatre in a manner most likely to ensure success. Burton, with all his energy, could not recover from this blow, the stock company of the Walnut Street returning more money to his treasury, than his five stars, in the same play. As to Mr. Pratt and Mr. Richings, they seem to have gone to sleep; and after both Burton and Marshall had surfeited the city with the name of "London Assurance," they announced the Chesnut Street Theatre to open with this play, throwing away some hundreds of dollars, without the chance of any return to the treasury.

The Arch Street Theatre opened, under the management of Mr. Charles Porter, as *The* American Theatre, in contradistinction to the Walnut, which leaves out the article; but soon tired of such folly, Mr. Porter resumed the old title of Arch Street Theatre. He commenced on the 28th of March, and lingered on till the 4th of July; the season only remarkable for having introduced upon the stage Mr. Risley and his sons, since so well known to fame and Europe. The performance was here merely termed neat—so neat to him, it has produced a fortune *nett.* He has many imitators, but no successful competitor. His performance is both pleasing and elegant; the ease with which the boys accomplish most astonishing feats adds to the pleasure as well as the amusement of the audience.

The National Theatre, under Burton, closed on the 26th of January, 1842, never again to open as "his" theatre. He proceeded to Baltimore, where the last nail was driven into the coffin that was to bury all his ambitious hopes of being alone the director of dramatic taste in the city of Philadelphia. The beautiful scenery was wantonly destroyed; chopped to pieces, to prevent it falling into other hands; and whether done by Burton or Newton, or by both, Mr. Burton's reputation as a man suffered severely, without attaining the object; for Welsh and Mann converted it into a splendid Circus and Amphitheatre, in a short time after the destruction, intended to have been complete, was perpetrated. Welsh and Mann have reaped the harvest which Burton planted; to them his ruin has been the source of emolument. There is also a story, which was made the subject of judicial proceedings, in Baltimore, against Hielge, the artist, of wantonly destroying the newly-painted scenery, at the Holiday Street Theatre, Baltimore, by priming it over with smudge, and also against Mr. Newton, for so carelessly ripping out certain gas fixtures underneath the stage, as to endanger the safety of the house. The artist escaped by pleading orders received to prepare the canvas for repainting in some new piece, which never made its appearance, and the manager's conduct became the subject of discussion. Miss Clifton also, who, it appears, only lent her name for the purpose of obtaining the theatre for Burton, but who was never interested in the proceeds, was summoned, to answer for certain unpaid bills, which it is to be hoped, will teach her prudence for the future. Marshall was persuaded to unite his forces with Pratt at the Chesnut Street, and, by acting in concert, to save both theatres. The amount of money agreed to be furnished by the former gentleman, was speedily swallowed up in the losses sustained; and Marshall, frightened from the course, wisely resolved to devote his attention entirely to the Walnut Street. Dr. Lardner commenced his scientific lectures, with great success; and Pratt announced, on the 2nd of March, 1842, that he had formed a coalition with W. E. Burton, and with a double company, would open Old Drury, with the play of "Money," and the farce of "State Secrets." This alliance offensive and defensive, between the belligerents, *both ruined in the contest*, was made too late. Nothing could save either the managers or the theatres, which were both in the agonies of death. Hackett, E. Forrest, Miss Clifton, Signor de Begnis, all lent their aid in vain. The theatre closed its short season, passing out of the hands of Mr. Pratt, who had been engaged in the management from the commencement of the partnership of Maywood and Co., in 1833; and thus ended the eventful season of 1841-2, in which all the theatres supported themselves longer without the aid of any European star (newly imported) than had happened for twenty years. To this circumstance is to be attributed the downfall of the Chesnut Street Theatre, and the failure of Burton at the National. The Walnut can always do without this foreign aid, and the Arch Street never will do, with or without it, for a longer period than one season, under any one manager.

CHAPTER XLI.

The Era of Petticoat Government. Mr. and Mrs. Brougham. Concerts *a la* MUSARD at the Chesnut Street. Charles Thorne at the Olympic. The Black Raven. The failure of the Lady Manageress. Pills and Periodicals. The author opens the Olympic. Forrest and Macready. Letter of Forrest to the Editor of the LONDON TIMES. The Right to Hiss.

I now record the era of petticoat government; and as the world is now governed, directly or indirectly, let sovereign man say what he pleases in denial, I see no reason why the theatres should not be placed directly under the influence of the fair sex. The Chesnut Street Theatre was opened on the 7th of September, 1842, by Miss Mary Maywood, as lessee;

and as the stockholders had attributed the unpopularity of their theatre to the mismanagement of Mr. Robert Campbell Maywood, it was but a just triumph that they should offer him this lease, as the only person they could think of to redeem their interests. He wisely declined all responsibility, placing his daughter at the head of the establishment, he assuming the acting management only. The first performance under the new arrangement was the "Man of the World," and "State Secrets:" the company — Richings, stage manager; Maywood, acting manager; W. B. Wood, Andrews, Matthews, Thomas Placide, Charles, Stanley, Watson, Eberle, Jervis, Bowers, Godden, Hines, Henrie, Perring, and Kelly, the prompter; Misses Maywood, Ayres, Helen Matthews, Jones, Thompson, Norman, Seale, George; Mesdames J. G. Porter (Miss Duff,) Maywood, Charles, Thoman and Rogers.

To checkmate this move, Mr. Marshall, on the 22nd of September, announced that the Walnut Street Theatre would open, under the direction of Miss Charlotte Cushman, with the "Belle's Stratagem," and "A Nabob for an Hour." I regret I have no list of the company.

The first effort of the rival queens was Dr. Lardner, at the Chesnut Street Theatre, with "Historical Sketches of the Revolution," and "Tableaux Vivants;" and John Sefton with "Sixteen-string Jack," and the "Golden Farmer," at the Walnut Street Theatre. On the 17th of October, Miss Maywood received the powerful aid of Madame Celeste, while Miss Cushman offered, on the same night, in opposition, Mr. E. Forrest, at the Walnut Street Theatre. On the 31st of October, Mr. and Mrs. Brougham made their first appearance, the lady as Lady Teazle in the "School for Scandal," and Mrs. Fitzgig in the "Irish Lion." She was a very beautiful woman, but, as an actress, inferior to any one I call to mind as a leading stock actress in any of our large theatres. Her success was greater than her pretensions entitled her to, but most unsatisfactory to herself—but vanity must sometimes meet with rebuke. Of her husband I am prepared to speak in a far different strain. Mr. Brougham is the best representative of Irish characters who has ventured to appear since the loss of poor Power; and even in Tim Moore, which Power rendered so irresistible, he made a most favourable impression on the audience, retaining to this moment their good will whenever he appeared before them. He was the original Dazzle in the play of "London Assurance," and as a light comedian he possesses the first great requisite—he looks and moves like a gentleman upon the stage, a quality in which most of our actors are very deficient; he has, likewise, all the spirit necessary to support the sprightly dialogue of a comedy. I do not think his starring engagements have aided his purse, but they have given him popularity, which will for ever render him a most valuable member of a good stock company—while in Irishmen, he may occasionally indulge, as a star, with success.

On the 5th of December, Mr. and Mrs. Seguin, and Mr. Shrivall, commenced the longest opera season ever continued by an English company, during which they produced " The Israelites in Egypt," and only suspended their performances for a few nights, on account of the domestic calamity of the Seguins, in the deaths of two children, by scarlet fever ; until the 17th of February, when a complimental benefit was given to Mrs. Seguin, whose worth as a woman, no less than her talent as a singer, deserved, under the circumstances, such an expression of feeling by the ladies of Philadelphia. The performances were " Norma," and " Zampa," two of the best operas which the troupe acted, and the receipts were worthy of the occasion. I must not forget to mention, that on the 27th of January, 1843, the " Stabat Mater" was produced at the Chesnut Street Theatre; first and second parts supported by Mr. Seguin, Mr. Shrivall, Mr. Richings, Mr. Archer, Mrs. Seguin, Mrs. Bailey, and Miss Coad. The Chesnut Street Theatre closed for the season with Mrs. Seguin's benefit. The receipts of this opera season, which must have paid the stars, does not appear to have satisfied the fair manageress, whose unpaid bills and actors' salaries became, thus early, a scource of annoyance. She published a very foolish card in the newspapers stating the sum received by the opera troupe, and the amount lost by the theatre. If the object was to excite sympathy or commiseration, it failed to produce either. Could she have done better, she would not have pursued the engagement, and few stars, (Booth and Jim Crow only can I call to recollection,) ever abate one cent of their demand, in favour of the theatre they may ruin, but to which, when the engagements are formed, they are expected to attract not only money enough to pay their engagement, but to yield a handsome surplus to the treasury. If they fail to do this, the public will only laugh at the manager for any complaint he may be foolish enough to utter, either in the play-bills or the newspapers, both famous for the *truth of their assertions !*

On the 13th of May, Miss Maywood attempted to retrieve lost ground, by fitting up the Chesnut Street Theatre as a grand Promenade, and giving Concerts *a la Musard.*. The statues, the shrubbery, and the fountain were all in good taste; but the orchestra, placed in the centre of the stage, destroyed all the effect. It broke the charm of the scene on the very threshold ; and, in attempting to promenade, a lady and gentleman could scarcely pass abreast of this ill-shaped lumbering contrivance. The band was under the direction of Mr. Watson, Bellini Smith, Mrs. Watson, Miss Clarence Wells, Mr.

Clirehugh, the Misses Cummins, and last not least, the lion pianist, Mr. Wallace. All proved failures; the fashionables made their appearance on the first night, and, to speak technically, the thing did not take. Miss Maywood kept it open thirty-three nights, the band diminishing every week; and finally closed, to resign the theatre, on the 31st of July, into such hands as he stockholders should dictate.

On the 9th of January, 1843, Mr. Charles Thorne, of the Chatham Theatre, in New York, opened Welsh's Olympic Theatre, (late Burton's National,) with " Boots at the Swan," " Hell Upon Earth," and " Kill or Cure." The very title of the second piece was enough to startle the citizens, and raise a hue and cry about the morality of the drama. However clever the piece might be, it was an injudicious selection for an opening night. Burton appeared here as a star. Right—*that* my friend is the proper way to redeem your fortune. Your talent as an actor is appreciated and sought after; abandon all thoughts of management, and five years will find you in a better condition than when you commenced your alteration of Cooke's Circus. Whether the atmosphere of this house rendered him petulant, or Mr. Thorne did not yield that courtesy which every manager should show to a brother manager, in distressed and broken circumstances, or Burton really neglected his rehearsals, as alleged, he refused to go on with his engagement, and on the 18th of January, I find him announced at the Walnut Street, with Booth and Hill, in " Town and Country." Thorne, in one week, abandoned the city, leaving actors, carpenters, &c., to shift for themselves.

Miss Charlotte Cushman, like Miss Mary Maywood, discovered that they were out of their proper sphere of action; that the energy of a Madame Vestris, the only female who ever successfully conducted a theatre, did not belong to either of them. W. R. Blake relieved Miss Cushman, at the Walnut, the following season; and, divested of the cares and annoyance of management, she surprised Mr. Macready, by the vigour of her performance in the Queen, in " Hamlet," Lady Macbeth, &c., which opened to her present good fortune and high reputation.

What has become of the Arch Street all this time, is scarcely worthy of notice, but for the fact that Mr. Porter associated Mr. Pratt, so ungenerously ousted by his former friend and partner, Maywood, from all participation in the management of Old Drury. But it required longer heads and stronger purses than P. &. P. possess, to make any thing of such a hopeless property. Pratt retired, and the doors were as usual closed long before the period a season should be brought to its regular conclusion. A Mr. Russel was the next lessee, who strange to say, is reported to have made money—if he

did, he is the wisest man who ever entered the doors for——
he kept it, refusing to pay his actors. One lady honoured his
shoulders by the application of a cowhide, for the deficiency,
but I did not hear that this castigation produced the desired
effect. The money he retained as liquidating damages for
the assault upon his person.

During this time, I was quietly occupied behind my counter,
selling my pills and periodicals, furnishing my friends with a
capital cigar, and refusing offers of the most advantageous
kind to assume the management of various theatres; one
from my friend Simpson, of Pittsburgh, so liberal that I fear
to record it, not only because my veracity might be called in
question, but that every body would exclaim—what a fool!
if he refused such an offer, he deserves every evil that may
hereafter fall upon his head. But I was determined never
again to place my foot upon the stage, while there remained
a possibility of obtaining a living by any other method. Day
by day, I saw the amount of my sales decrease, for want of
means to maintain the system of advertising I had commenced, and which proved so successful; yet I despaired not,
until I found that the profits, so far from supporting my
family, were so small, that we were eating up the goods belonging to other people. Then I came to a full stop, while
the deficiency was within the power of control.

My old partner, Lewis T. Pratt, now made a proposal to me
to unite with him, and make application for the Chesnut Street
Theatre, which, after the failing season, under Miss Maywood,
was advertised to let. Macready, and other stars of name and
talent were known to be engaged for the Park Theatre, New
York, and with such aid, Old Drury generally had been successful; *without it*, for the last twenty years—*never*. We made
the application, which was favourably received; but before
we forwarded the signatures of those gentlemen we had proposed as security for the payment of the rent, Mr. Marshall,
of the Walnut Street Theatre, made an offer, which by the
payment of a few hundred dollars in advance, secured the
lease. So ended that; but as I never suffered myself to be
defeated in any project my mind was bent upon, when perseverance could secure the object of my wishes, I at once determined to obtain the National Olympic; and turning over in
my mind the best means of obtaining possession of a theatre,
which, as such, had failed under Burton, Thorne, Amherst,
and Richings, Mr. John H. Oxley presented himself suddenly
before me, to ask my advice upon the subject of business. I
told him I had made up my mind to take the National. He
proposed joining me in the speculation, and in three days from
our first conversation, the lease was signed, and possession obtained. The difficulty was, to obtain a company at so late a

period; in this we succeeded beyond our expectations. We had Wemyss, Oxley, Matthews, Shaw, Mossop, Lewis, Winans, Faulkner, Flemming, Becket, Jervis, Collingbourne, F. Myers, Edwards, Colvin, Brown, Bowers, Horn and Neal; Mrs. A. Knight, Madison, Abbott, Cantor; Misses Thompson, Wheeler, Norman, E. Moore, Downs, Porter and Smith—a very good array of names. We opened on the 23rd September, 1843, with the Honeymoon," and "Perfection." Receipts 66 dollars; not a very flattering prospect of success. Oxley was anxious to obtain the aid of James Wallack, who had just returned from England. Although I agreed perfectly with him, that the name in our announce bill would add strength, I cautioned him against expecting much in the way of attraction from Mr. Wallack; yet I supposed, after an absence of two years, we might calculate upon engaging him without loss. His first night was only 117 dollars; his whole engagement, second night, 62; third, 79; fourth, 60; fifth, 60; his first benefit 108 ! ! ! then, 48; 64; 34; 43; 52; his second benefit and last night, 80; whole amount, 677 dollars. Paid Mr. Wallack 276 dollars, for twelve nights. The disastrous commencement, although it disarranged our plans, did not frighten me, knowing that E. Forrest, with whom we ought to have commenced our season, and who was engaged expressly to oppose Macready, at the Chesnut, was to follow. The plan was, not to act on the same night the same play, but to follow each performance; if Macready played "Hamlet" to-night, we acted it the following night, &c. By these means, we succeeded in creating an excitement to witness the different style of two actors, at the head of their profession, in the same parts. We had the best of the contest, until the petulance of Mr. Forrest's temper upon trifles, induced him to leave hastily for New York, and gave him the appearance of running away from a contest in which he was really the victor. If regret could have availed, he expressed himself freely upon the subject, repenting at leisure the hurried action of a moment. "Ira furor brevis est," used to be a copy at school for Latin beginners; Mr. Forrest would do well to translate and consider it; it would have saved him from the very ridiculous position he occupied in the mind of every thinking man, for the petty malevolence which, for injuries, real or supposed, he exhibited in hissing Mr. Macready, in the Edinburgh Theatre. Let me ask my American readers what would have been the fate of Mr. Macready, if he had dared to hiss Mr. E. Forrest in any theatre in the United States? He would have been turned out, if not otherwise maltreated; certainly never have been allowed to act again in America, notwithstanding the undoubted right he might claim as an auditor to express his disapprobation. Lucky it was for Mr. E. Forrest that John Bull rarely troubles himself about these

trifling matters. The quarrel of *two buffoons* is of no consequence in Great Britain to any but themselves; and he was
not even able to make capital out of it for his native America
—which, in charity, I am compelled to suppose, must have
been his motive. His own-good sense assures him he is wrong,
and having failed to produce even a newspaper excitement
beyond a passing paragraph, he is ashamed of the littleness of
his conduct. What a pity great men should thus expose their
weakness.

I copy the following letter from the New York Spirit of the
Times, of the 9th of May, 1846:

FORREST AND MACREADY.

"TO THE EDITOR OF THE LONDON TIMES,—SIR,—Having seen in your
journal of the 12th instant, an article headed "Professional Jealousy," a
part of which originally appeared in *The Scotsman* published in Edin-
burg, I beg leave, through the medium of your columns, to state that at
the time of its publication, I addressed a letter to the Editor of *The Scotsman* upon the subject, which, as I then was in Dumfries, I sent to a friend
in Edinburgh, requesting him to obtain its insertion; but as I was informed
The Scotsman refused to receive any communication upon the subject, I
need say nothing of the injustice of this refusal. Here then I was disposed
to let the matter rest, as upon more mature reflection, I did not deem it
worth further attention; but now, as the matter has assumed a questionable shape by the appearance of the article in your journal, I feel called
upon, although reluctantly, to answer it.

"There are two legitimate modes of evincing approbation and disapprobation in the theatre—one expressive of approbation, by clapping of
hands, and the other by hisses to mark dissent; and as well-timed and
hearty applause, is the just meed of the actor who deserves well, so also
is hissing, a salutary and wholesome corrective of the abuses of the
stage; and it was against one of these abuses that *my* dissent was expressed, and not, as was stated; 'with a view of expressing his (my)
disapproval of the manner in which Mr. Macready gave effect to a particular passage.' The truth is, Mr. Macready thought to introduce a
fancy dance into his performance of 'Hamlet,' which I thought, and
still think, a desecration of the scene, and at which I evinced that disapprobation, for which the pseudo-critic is pleased to term me an ' offender,' and this was the only time during the performance that I did so,
although the writer evidently seeks, in the article alluded to, to convey a
different impression. It must be observed also, that I was by no means
' solitary' in this expression of opinion.

"That a man may manifest his pleasure or displeasure after the recognized mode, according to the best of his judgment, actuated by proper
motives, and for justifiable ends, is a right, which, until now, I have
never once heard questioned, and I contend, that right extends equally
to an actor, in his capacity as a spectator, as to any other man, besides
from the nature of his studies, he is much more competent to judge of a
theatrical performance than any *set-dissent* critic, who has never himself
been an actor. The writer of the article in *The Scotsman*, who has most

unwarrantably singled me out for public animadversion, has carefully
omitted to notice the fact, that I warmly applauded several points of Mr.
Macready's perfomance; and more than once I regretted that the audience did not second me in so doing. As to the pitiful charge of professional jealousy preferred against me, I dismiss it with the contempt it
merits, confidently relying upon all those of the profession with whom I
have been associated, for a refutation of this slander."

"Yours, respectfully,

"March, 1846.   "EDWIN FORREST."
—Times, 4th of April.

Did ever man occupying the position of Mr. E. Forrest,
pen so many lines of bombast and egotism, as are here paraded for publication.   The audience of the Edinburgh
Theatre are fully able to appreciate the talent of Mr.
Macready, without taking their cue from Mr. E. Forrest; nor
can his opinion of Mr. Macready's acting, alter the position
he now holds of the first Tragedian belonging to the English
stage, any more than could Mr. Macready's opinion of him
wrest from Mr. E. Forrest the proud distinction he justly
wears of being the first Tragedian of the American stage—a
title sufficiently honourable to gratify the pride and ambition
of any man. Let him gain "bays" in a foreign land, if he
can, but he can win no prouder station than he holds, among
his own countrymen. Mr. E. Forrest is evidently smarting
under the hisses directed towards him at the Princess' Theatre,
on his first appearance there. His vanity forbids him to place
these to the account of want of talent in himself, or error in
judgment of those who exercised a right (a very doubtful one)
so to express their opinion. But Mr. Macready was accused
in the newspapers of having paid persons to insult Mr. E.
Forrest. Mr. Forrest believes no such nonsense, but appears
to have been over-anxious to repay Macready a supposed debt
of this kind. As a stage director few possess the tact and
judgment of Macready; and if he *did* introduce a fancy
dance in "Hamlet," (in what scene we are left in the dark,)
his mature judgment no doubt could give a sufficient reason
for the introduction. If it was on the stage where the tragedy is enacted before the Court of Denmark, I can, as a stage
manager, see no objection to such a dance, as the prelude to
the performance which follows, rather tending to remove suspicion of the trap he (Hamlet) has designed to "catch the
conscience of the king." Be it as it may, Mr. Forrest, as an
actor, was wrong in the theatre to express an opinion at all.
He is too old an artist not to have witnessed more than once
an auditor or several auditors, turned out by the mandate of
the pit for interrupting the performance, by hisses to the
annoyance of the majority assembled to witness a play, although they were only exercising a right, "which until now,

he has never once heard questioned." Why, in the Chesnut Street Theatre, in 1826, during the performance of Kean in "Othello"—"Mr. Wood told the audience he had despatched officers to expel such as disturbed the audience, and that they should be prosecuted to the utmost rigour of the law. The officers did their duty, and the play went off without the slightest noise. It is generally believed that the disturbance was occasioned by some apprentice boys, who were hired to express that dislike to Mr. Kean, their employer was fearful of exhibiting himself."—*United States Gazette.*

If this proceeding was correct, what becomes of *the right to hiss?*

I think it was pretty strongly questioned, although I agree with Mr. E. Forrest, that it is the best corrective of the abuses of the stage, and judiciously exercised, of service to the actor. It is the only censure he dreads, and is most sensitive upon; but should never be exercised by *one actor* towards *another.*

"We have received the following note from our fellow-citizen, Mr. Hackett," says the *Courier* and *Enquirer* of May 9th, 1646, "to which we give place with pleasure :—

"To the Editors of the Courier and Enquirer,—Will you afford me the medium of replying to various inquirers, who are desirous to learn whether either of my old editions of Shakspeare's 'Hamlet' contains any authority for Mr. Macready's having introduced a 'fancy dance' before the play-scene in that tragedy.

"Imprimis—I presume curiosity upon the subject to have grown out of the republication here of the following paragraph from a British journal : —

"'Mr. Macready and Mr. Forrest :—Mr. Edwin Forrest, the American Tradegian, has written to the London *Times,* justifying his conduct in hissing Mr. Macready during his performance of 'Hamlet,' at the Edinburgh Theatre. He states, he frequently applauded parts of which he approved, and had an equal right to hiss at passages which he thought erroneous. The truth is, says Forrest, Mr. Macready thought fit to introduce a fancy dance into his performance of 'Hamlet,' which I thought, and still think, a desecration of the scene.'

"I will venture to explain, what I suppose, Forrest meant by a "*fancy dance.*"

"Hamlet, after his instructions to the players, and his confidential remarks to his friend, Horatio, just before the play-scene commences, observes to him—' They are coming to the play—I must be idle—get you a place.' Consequently, I have always understood Hamlet to mean by the word *idle,* in this situation, that he must seem to have no fixed motive or industrious object, during the performance of the play about to be represented, policy dictating the expediency of his appearing listless and unoccupied, in order that his guilty uncle, the king, might disregard his presence, attend closely to the play, and become entrapped into some exhibitions of compunction and remose.

" Mr. Macready, however, when I saw him act ' Hamlet' at the Park Theatre, in 1843, appeared to construe the word *idle* very differently ; for the reason that he immediately assumed the manner of a silly youth, tossed his head right and left, and skipped back and forth, across the stage, five or six times before the footlights, at the same time switching his handkerchief, held by a corner over his right and left shoulder alternately; indeed, making gyrations not unlike those fire-ribbons, which I have seen idle and thoughtless urchins cut in the air, with a stick burnt to a live coal at one end, until the whole court have had sufficient time to parade, and be seated, until Hamlet finds himself addressed by the king, who enquires after his health.

" I therefore submit whether this manner of Mr. Macready's rendering the scene upon the stage, is not what was only *comparatively* referred to as ' *a fancy dance*,' by Mr. Forrest, being elsewhere, also, alluded to as ' *a pas de mouchoir*.' At all events, I beg to state, that in no edition of Shakspeare which I own, or have ever seen, is there any pretext for the introduction of *a dance* before the play-scene, or upon the stage erected for the performance before the king and court of Denmark.

" The public's obedient servant,
" JAS. H. HACKETT.

" Astor House, April 29th, 1846."

Who made Mr. Hackett " *sole judge and umpire*" of an- other's thoughts? He has no pretension to be admitted as a tragedian. His attempt to act a few characters written by Shakspeare, always give rise to a sneer and a smile by the actors; while contempt would be a better word to ex- press the feelings of the audience, who are rarely, numerous upon such occasions. In his own sphere, Hackett is an actor above mediocrity; but as a tragedian—good lack! good lack! —yet he writes as if he would say with the immortal bard—

" —— I am Sir Oracle,
When I ope my lips, led no dog bark."

He knows enough of the business of the stage, to know that two actors rarely play the same part in exactly the same way —surely, nobody will think of hissing Mr. Charles Kean for the great improvement he has presented to the public, in the display introduced into the tragedy of " Richard the Third ;" yet Mr. Hackett will look in vain at his two old editions of Shakspeare, or his twenty-two modern ones, if he possesses them, for the authority for such melo-dramatic display. Every actor, occupying the high station claimed by Mr. E. Forrest or Mr. Macready, has always been allowed to regulate the stage business of those scenes in which they are engaged; and unless, while all around is progressing, we are prepared to let the stage stand still, every effort of a master mind, although it may not be successful, is worthy of a fair trial, and should be protected from all assaults from the profession, jealous as they

always have been of the success each obtains over the other.
Forrest's calculation no doubt was, that, as in America, at
Boston and Baltimore, they drove Mr. Kean from their stage,
for an impertinence they would not brook, so the Edinburgh
people would chastise his insolence as a foreign artist. If they
had driven him from the stage in Great Britain, the excitement
and sympathy of the citizens of the United States would have
secured such a succession of triumphant engagements in the
theatres in America, as never could be dreamed of by an actor,
and he would have closed his professional career, (if such really
be his purpose, as he stated in Dublin,) in a perfect blaze of
glory.

Let me now leave England, and return to the National
Theatre in Philadelphia where after Forrest's departure, the
"Mysteries of Paris," dramatised by John Sefton, F. C.
Wemyss, and James Gann, was placed upon the stage with a
celerity which astonished every body. "The King of the
Mist," scenery by Russel Smith, kept up the attraction, until,
on the 28th of December, we had recovered lost ground, and
appeared to have the tide of success full in our favour, with
Silsbie, the Ellsler Brothers, the Virginia Minstrels, &c.
Booth offered to play, but I confess I was afraid of him; he
had been playing his usual antics in Boston and New York.
I was decidedly opposed to making an attempt, which, if followed by a failure, would have again ruined all chance of the
success which now seemed within our grasp; unfortunately,
Mr. Oxley yielded to my opinion. Had I permitted him on
this occasion to exercise his own judgment, Booth's triumphant
engagement at the Walnut Street, which turned the tide of
popular favour back to that theatre, would have been ours.
Never did Booth act better, behave more steadily, or draw
more money than during this engagement in Philadelphia,
(which I had thrown away). A singular piece, under the
title of "Blud-a-Nouns," in which the actors were all frogs,
possessing much merit, was produced, from the pen of Dunn
English. Several scenes were much applauded; but it was
too long, and became tiresome—the curtain fell, not to rounds
of applause, but to a shower of groans and hisses. "Oseola,"
a play by Col. Sherborne, "Handy Andy," "The Enchanted
Lake," "Yara," "Linda," "The Imp," "Rookwood," "Mazeppa," "Robert Emmet, "Tom and Jerry in Philadelphia,"
and another drama by Dunn English, entitled the "Doom of
the Drinker," failed to produce money. Our hard fought
and dearly gained battle, was snatched from our grasp in the
very hour of victory and triumph, by one false move. We
closed on the 27th of April, after a season of 185 nights,
which the lessees, Welsh and Mann, were the only parties

Q

who derived any benefit. Oxley retired from the management, and I made preparations to re-open on the 11th of May.
I sent for Landers from New York, and with the aid of John
Wiser, the artist, produced "Fortunio" in a style which,
under any other circumstances, must have succeeded. The
unfortunate riots in May, 1844, when bloodshed and murder
roamed throughout certain portions of the districts, placed
the city under matial law. The proclamation to that effect,
was issued on the very day I purposed opening—the consequence—nobody could attend the theatre for thirteen nights.
I struggled on, to close without a hope of future effort. The
theatre was surrendered to General Welsh, who determined
to establish an amphitheatre upon the scale of Astley's in
London. He has succeeded, and with the enterprise and capital he possesses, must succeed. Welsh and Mann's amphitheatre in the city of Philadelphia, is destined to become a
conspicuous place of public amusement, whose fame will resound through every city in the Union.

CHAPTER XLII.

The Chesnut and Walnut United. Miss Cushman Resigns. J. M. Field.
G. Vandenhoff. Wallack. Macready. Burton opens the Arch Street.
Mr. Anderson. Pratt and Wemyss again together. The "Monks of
Monk Hall." Fear of a Row. Mr. Crisp. Mrs. Mowatt. The
Ethiopian Opera Company. Mr. Fry's Opera of "Leonora." Con-
clusion. *Finis Coronat Opus.*

THE Chesnut and Walnut Street Theatres being once more
united under the same management, Marshall opened the
Old Drury on the 7th of September; W. R. Blake announced
as *exclusive* stage manager; C. Cushman acting manager—thus
giving the lady an opportunity of resigning her dignity without wounding her professional reputation. "Man and Wife,"
and a "Lover by Proxy," in which J. M. Field, an actor
whose reputation depends more upon the skill with which he
writes for a newspaper—(belonging to the corps editorial,
we must support him)—than dramatic tact or genius, played
Charles Austencourt and Harry Lawless. He appeared among
us, and departed again without an enquiry made. On the
14th of September, the Walnut opened with "Laugh when
you Can," and "Woman's Life"—here the error committed
by Maywood & Co., of charging seventy-five cents and fifty
cents at the Chesnut Street Theatre, to see the same company
who, in removing from the corner of Ninth and Walnut
Street, were only worth fifty cents for the boxes and twenty-

five cents for the pit, was committed. G. Vandenhoff was the only star. The Chesnut Street was occupied by the French Opera company until the 23rd of October, when Macready opened as Macbeth. On the 13th of November, the Italian Company, under Vattellini, played Bellini's "Norma" in the original language ; produced "Bellisario," "Il Puritani," "Lucia di Lammermoor," and "Gemma di Vergy." Wallack played on the 29th of November, followed by Hackett on the 7th of December. Ole Bull astonished the audience by the wonderful execution of his bow. On the 18th, Macready returned, playing "The Bridal," and the theatre closed for the season on the 26th ; minus, how many dollars, Mr. Marshall ? This is the first taste you have had of the bitters of management; your actors unpaid; your credit out of doors for the first time sullied; your legitimate sphere of action, the Walnut Street Theatre, occupied by Howes as a circus; and the folly demonstrated of one man attempting to conduct two theatres in the same city at the same time.

Mr. Burton, not contented with the success which crowned his efforts as an actor everywhere, again grasps the truncheon which had fallen from the hands of Russell and Deverna, and assumes the management of the Arch Street Theatre, on the 3d of June, 1844. Chance threw into his hands some excellent actors : George Barrett, Burke and wife, and others returning from the south and west, enabled him, after the first week or two, to carry on a war with some prospect of success; and where success attends him, he is always indefatigable in his exertions. Finally, he obtains the theatre from Mr. Lovatt, and opens for the fall season, on the 9th September, with Mr. Macready as Hamlet ; E. Forrest playing on the same night, at the Walnut Street, whose season he commenced on Saturday, the 7th, as Damon, determined to have one night to himself before commencing the contest a second time, in which he was so successful before—the chance had fled. Macready, at the Arch Street Theatre too, had the best of the battle, it being announced as his farewell engagement in Philadelphia. Throughout his tour of the United States, he encountered M. E. Forrest, either on the same night, or immediately preceding him, or announced in the bills to follow him. Mr. Macready uttered no complaints upon this determined dogging of his track, which proved detrimental to his purse, if not his reputation. Then why should Mr. E. Forrest or his friends charge Mr. Macready with unfairness of conduct to him, in England ? I do not believe Mr. Macready suffered the movements of Mr. E. Forrest, in London, to engage his attention for an instant, although the course of conduct Mr. Forrest pursued towards him, in the United States, might lead

Forrest to expect some retaliation, where the tables were changed, and the American tragedian was the foreign artist.

The season 1843–44, was noted for the number of musicians of talent who visited America, Ole Bull, Vieux Temps, Wallace, Nagel, &c., &c. Ole Bull was the only fortunate one; wherever he played, the enthusiasm of the *dilettanti* filled his pockets, while the Concerts of all the other were but thinly attended.

Mr. ANDERSON,

A young man unknown to fame, of the Macready school, without servile imitation, appeared as Hamlet, in the Arch Street Theatre: his engagement was not profitable to Manager Burton, who terminated it rather abruptly, to produce "Putnam;" but on a second visit to the Chesnut Street Theatre, under Pratt and Wemyss, and a third one with Burton, his talent had been more justly appreciated. The attempt made to hiss him off the stage, in retaliation for Forrest's reception in London, was frowned down; and what might have proved an unpleasant termination to his career in Philadelphia, became the means of fixing him firmly in the estimation of the play going public. His greatest merit as an actor is the earnest manner with which he enters heart and soul into the assumption of character, and never flags from the commencement to the termination—thus carrying his audience, once enlisted in his favour, with irresistible force along with him. There is something too much of vehemence in his Claude Melnotte; and it is only the earnest manner in which he performs his task that covers the glaring absurdity of the termination to the fourth act. His impersonation of the Stranger is the best I can call to recollection, since Edmund Kean, who was in this character unapproached by any artist of his day. Mr. Anderson's future career in the United States will be similar to that of Mr. James Wallack at the same age —triumph upon triumph awaits him—his reward, a fortune in a brief space. But, to return to his first engagment, by which, having reaped neither fame or money, he was so loud in his denunciation of Burton's treatment, as to publicly declare nothing could induce him to act in any theatre over which Burton had the slightest control. Burton's *good luck* overcame this obstacle, when Anderson was a card worth contending for. Mr. Rodney engaged him to act at the Holiday Street Theatre in Baltimore, but could procure no actors; his first two nights gave promise of such a brilliant engagement, that when Rodney was unable to keep his theatre open, he was induced to bury the hatchet, and act with Burton, at the Front Street Theatre, where, once reconciled, he induced

him to return to the Arch Street Theatre, very much to our
regret. There is now a strong desire to see him again; and
his next engagement in the Quaker City will be a great one,
act at which Theatre he may—the Arch, the Chesnut, or the
Walnut.

My old partner, Pratt, having obtained the lease of the
Chesnut Street Theatre, after delays which rendered success
all but hopeless, made me the proposition to try our fortunes
once more together—and on the — day of October we opened
with "Simpson and Co.," "Love in Humble Life," and "The
Blue Domino." John Sefton, stage manager; the company—
W. Chapman, Jamieson, Charles Howard, Wemyss, C. Smith,
Jordan, Byrne, Mossop, Forrest. Stafford, Dawes, Matthews,
Brunton, Anderson, Grierson, Kemble, Solomon, Sullivan;
Miss H. Matthews, Mrs. A. Knight, Mrs. Jordan, Mrs. Kemble,
Mrs. Smith, Miss M'Bride, Mrs. Forrest, Mrs. Hautonville
the Misses Wagstaff, Miss Archer, Miss Sinclair, the dancer
Petite Gertrude, and Madame Celeste. In the commencement
we were doomed to disappointment; Miss Nelson, who was
engaged to open the theatre, did not arrive; the Saturday
night was lost, and the bill announced for Monday, which we
determined, Miss Nelson or no Miss Nelson, should commence
the season, was changed from "La Sylphide" to the three
farces named; and on Wednesday, when the lady did appear,
she played to a beggarly account of empty boxes—yet insisted
on playing the six nights, which yielded her nothing and kept
the people out of the theatre. Jim Crow Rice was the next
star, and the admirable manner in which he acted the burlesque opera of "Otello," made his engagement profitable to
himself, and of course acceptable to the managers. His re-
engagement was not so successful; but thus far, despite of all
opposition, we were successful in the main point—that is, in
paying the actors regularly. A Mr. Lippard was publishing a
book entitled "The Monks of Monk Hall," in which he exposed, right and left, the profligacy both of the rich and powerful, and the poor and worthless of the city of Philadelphia.
By the advice of my worthy friend, Ashbell Green, at that
time one of the Deputy Attorney Generals, I procured an interview, and he drew up a contract, for which, under certain
considerations, Mr. Lippard agreed to dramatise his own work
for the Chesnut Street Theatre, and to furnish me with a
copy of the play in fourteen days from the date of our agreement. The scenery was painted, the properties arranged, and
the piece announced for representation. No sooner had the
bill been placarded, than young Mercer, tried and acquitted
for the murder of Peberton, assaulted the bill-poster, some one
having told him that he figured conspicuously in it. Judge

Conrad, my old and good friend, came up to my house in a state of great excitement, to say that somebody had told him he figured in the play. I told him that he ought to know me better than to suppose I would tolerate such a thing against a friend, and handed him the sheet to which he alluded, his name having been struck out by my own hand from the play. This completely satisfied him, and he departed with his good opinion of me, I am sure, not lessened by our interview. Down I went to the theatre—here there was excitement upon excitement—everybody was of belief that there must be a fling at them—some laughed—others swore—while some threatened,—and Mr. Singleton Mercer actually applied for two hundred pit tickets, to give away, for the purpose of a grand row, which my treasurer was fool enough to refuse to sell him : he afterwards purchased *twenty-five !* and when the play was withdrawn he actually had the impudence to request the return of this money. My friend Green, now with me, looked over the play, and on Saturday night gave me his opinion that there was nothing that could reasonably be objected to in it—he and those connected with the theatre alone had only seen the manuscript. Threats of tearing down the theatre, sacking it, &c., were now openly heard ; and to all applications my answer was—this play will certainly be acted on Monday night. So closed the Saturday performance ; at least an assurance to the manager of a full house on Monday, let the result be what it might. The play bills, on Sunday, were the magnets of universal attraction ; wherever one was posted, there was a crowd perusing it. At two o'clock, I received a note from Mr. M'Call, the mayor of the city, desiring to see me at his house, at four o'clock, upon a subject that would not brook delay. I presumed it was the "Monks of Monk Hall," and repaired with a play bill, at the time stated. His honour met me with bland courtesy, and informed me that my play-bill was libellous—directed me to see Mr. Green, (deputy attorney-general,) with whom he had a conversation on the subject, and to see him again at his office at nine o'clock on Monday morning. Away I hied to my friend Green. What could we do? We both laughed. "Well," said he "this is a pretty affair—I approved your suggestion—I advised you to try this affair ; and now as a public officer, I may be called upon to try you for acting it. I tell you there is no power to prevent you doing so ; bu I would rather that you should see your friend, Constant Guellou ; his head is cooler upon this subject than mine, and you know you can rely upon the advice he will give you being both sound and legal, and, moreover, guided by good feeling for your welfare. Do nothing in this business rashly : I will meet you at the mayor's office on Monday morning." My friend Guellou had caught the excitement, and he had been to my friend A. Godey, to request he would see me upon the subject—the excitement increasing every hour. Godey would not advise me one way nor the other, after hearing my story, but left the matter to a night's reflection and the interview with the mayor in the morning.

I met the mayor, according to appointment, and offered him the play to read; this he declined. I then proposed that he should walk up to the theatre and see the rehearsal, that he might judge whether there was any thing objectionable; this too was declined. He said he did not doubt that every thing was as I had represented it; but that we had just escaped from riot and bloodshed—were in the height of a popular election—the blood of all parties warm—(the news was just coming in of the defeat of the whigs in New York, on the other side of Cayuga Bridge, in the presidential election)—that he appealed to me as a good citizen and the father of a family, not to commit an act which might cause me regret during my natural life, should riot and bloodshed flow from it—that if I persisted, he could afford me no protection from the police of the city. My partner, Mr. Pratt, being out of town, I told him, in such a case, I was unwilling to take the responsibility of withdrawing the play, upon my own shoulders—that in all probability Mr. Pratt would arrive in the city by two o'clock—to let matters rest as they were until then, and I would see him again. In the meantime, the rehearsal went on—message upon message, threat upon threat, was communicated to me upon the stage. At twelve o'clock, a note came from Mr. Evans, the president of the board of directors, advising the withdrawal of the play. My friend Guellou's opinion was, I had an undoubted right to act it; but were he in my place, he would not, under the circumstances, run the risk. This opinion (as his opinions always have weight with me) did more towards the final determination than all the rest. Indeed, to Mr. Guellou belongs the credit, if any be due, of having prevented the performance; he knows I always follow his advice when asked; and I did not dare to let my own opinion weigh as a straw in the the balance, after his decision both as a lawyer and a friend. At one o'clock, General Cadwallader, one of the board of agents, who had been sent for by the mayor, made his appearance at the theatre, to request the play might not be acted. In half an hour afterwards, I received the following letter from his honour the mayor :—

(COPY.)

"Mayor's Office, November 11th, 1844.

"MESSRS. WEMYSS AND PRATT—

"Gentlemen, as mayor of the city, I have to request that the exhibition of the piece called the 'Quaker City,' advertised for this evening, at the

Chesnut Street Theatre, may not take place, for reasons I have verbally communicated to Mr. Wemyss.

" Respectfully your obedient,
" P. M'CALL."

" NOTICE.—In obedience to this request, the public is respectfully informed that the performance will *not* take place.   The entertainment for the evening will be ' Grandfather Whitehead,' the ' President Incog.,' and ' He is not a-Miss.'   " PRATT AND WEMYSS."
   Chesnut Street Theatre, Nov. 11, 1844.

I once more repaired to his office. I proposed to him that the curtain should rise, and the performance be suffered to proceed, scene by scene ; that on the slightest opposition being manifested by the audience to stop the play, the curtain should instantly fall, and some other piece be substituted.— He replied, that would be just as bad as acting the whole play ; the mischief, if any was really intended, would by that time be fully accomplished. He stated, that this young man, Mercer, had purchased tickets, he was informed, for the avowed purpose of putting down the play. "Then," said I, "why not arrest him, and bind him over to keep the peace ?" "Because, Mr. Wemyss, I really think you have struck the first blow in your play-bill." Ere we parted, 1 yielded the point, and consented to withdraw the play, on the condition that he would give a statement to the public, which should exonerate the managers from all blame. "Grandfather Whitehead" was substituted for "The Monks of Monk Hall ;" and now the difficulty was to prevent a row, because the piece was *not* performed. An excited populace filled the whole square from Sixth to Seventh Street ; all the police of the city could scarcely keep order. The play-bills on the boards, in front of the building, had to be torn off before any thing like quiet was obtained ; the doors of the theatre were closed by eleven o'clock, and not till then did the crowd gradually disperse.

My opinion has never been changed upon this subject. Had the play been acted, no row, or at least no more than takes place when any favourite actor disappoints an audience, would have occurred. The play was really a good one ; once heard, it would have secured a run. Had its satire been aimed at the low and vulgar, it would not have been assailed ; but it struck at judges, members of Congress, editors, as well as thieves and murderers. I saw a mass of filth and obscenity played at the Chatham Garden as the prohibited play ; I could not recognise a line. It is sufficient to say, my play was in five acts, this in two ; that is proof enough they were not the same, although Mr. Lippard furnished the MS. portion of it. He so far forgot himself as to assault Mr. Asbell Green, the only real friend he had in the whole transaction, as the author of the suppression : no opinion was ever more falsely adopted.

Having complied with the request of the city authorities, at a sacrifice of pecuniary interest, at least the managers should have been protected from the slime and filth of the press, which, from Maine to Florida, harped upon the fiddle string offered to them by the *Spirit of the Times* in Philadelphia, of obscenity. The mayor never read nor saw the play ; no such reason was ever given for the request to withdraw it. I yielded a point of right to a request from the authorities of the city, and what was my recompense?—abuse and slander.

I have laid the whole of the affair before my readers, yet newspaper after newspaper reiterated the libellous falsehoods, and, in future ages, as reference, will be received, as truth of holy writ, in deep damnation of the managers of the Chesnut Street Theatre, who deserved the thanks of the whole community. That Mr. M'Call did not, under his signature, as Mayor of the city of Philadelphia, protect us from this injustice, I have ever felt the hardest part of this altogether hard business. The idea of prohibiting a play, without even reading it, is new indeed ! The most intolerant censor of the public press reads an article before condemnation.

The effect of this upon the interest of the theatre, was a loss of seven hundred dollars in two weeks, for until Mr. Anderson appeared, no one visited the theatre at all. We owed the actors one week's salary, and this they made a plea not only for neglect of duty, but to leave the theatre when they pleased, and how they pleased. To Mr. Anderson an apology was due; it was not until his two last nights that he found we had really a good company, when they chose to work. As the attraction of the evening, on the 22nd of December, we produced the "Bohemian Girl," with Mr. Fraser, Mr. and Mrs. Seguin, Monsieur Martin, and Julia Turnbull. Marshall produced a melo-drama of the same name at the Walnut, concocted by Burton and Foster; he went still further : he impudently announced Balfe's opera, with scarcely a note of the music. These were good advertisements for our theatre, and the "Bohemian Girl" was played thirteen nights out of an engagement of eighteen, and afterwards revived in the spring. The bitter hostility of the *Spirit of the Times,* and the succession of libels, day after day, which appeared in its columns against the Chesnut Street Theatre, induced Pratt and Wemyss to prosecute for libel,—the first time in my theatrical career I ever troubled myself to notice legally the slang of a newspaper. Mr. Hill followed the opera, but with no attraction. In order to induce the fashionable circles to continue their visits, we made an arrangement to produce the

comedy of "Old Heads and Young Hearts" with the Park
company of New York. Mr. Chippendale, Mr. John Fisher,
Mr. John Povey, Mr. Dyott, Mr. Crocker, Mr. Gallott, Miss
Clara Ellis, Mrs. Henry Knight, Mrs. Duvenal, Mrs. Dyott,
and Mr. Lewis, the prompter, were added to our own com-
pany; and it will be scarcely believed, they could not play to
an average of a hundred dollars per night, benefits included.
It therefore became obvious, that the best plan would be to
close the doors, first trying Mrs. Shaw, and a portion of the
Bowery company: Mr. Clarke, Mr. Milnor, Mr. Dyott, Mr.
John Fisher, and Mr. Crocker,—all would not do; and the
Chesnut Street closed its doors, minus two thousand dollars.
The Park company, united with the Chesnut Street, were
worth one hundred dollars per night; but the Bowery, the
• Park, and Chesnut Street—all these, with the aid of Mrs.
Shaw, the best actress of the American stage, were worth
only fifty dollars per night; the stockholders, as usual, loud
in their denunciation of the management, and Dr. Lehman
complaining that they had no amusement.

Young Murphy, who had been my call-boy, and who commenced his theatrical career with me, called to know if I
would make an arrangement with Palmo's Ethiopian Opera
Company. We proposed terms, which they accepted, and
commenced with "La Sonnam-bu-ola," to 326 dollars. This
success continued for a month, the only profitable one during
the management of Pratt and Wemyss: so that negro-singing
and dancing, after all, is the amusement best suited to the
audience of the Chesnut Street Theatre, Philadelphia. While
we were making arrangements to produce a piece called the
"Fall of Kisichack," by General Harlan, the news of the
burning of the Bowery Theatre, on the night of the 15th of
April, reached us. I at once offered to place the Chesnut
Street Theatre at the disposal of Hamblin, if nothing better
offered. Mr. Jackson, whose individual enterprise has erected
the present Bowery Theatre, and brought successfully to its
present condition, answered this letter, declining for the present. Hamblin issued proposals for a large Theatre in Broadway, but failed in bringing his project to bear. This last
misfortune seemed to have paralysed all his energy, and he
wisely resigned to younger hands the task of future toil. That
Mr. Jackson has proved himself worthy to succeed Hamblin,
his spirited career bears witness, in the face of all difficulties:
he has placed the new Theatre, which he opened on the 25th
of August, 1845, as firmly in the affections of the audience, as
it ever was in its palmiest days. Long may he continue to
enjoy his good fortune.

On the 4th of June, 1845, an opera, by Mr. Fry, was placed
before the public, in a style of which Messrs. Pratt and

Wemyss have reason to be proud : every scene, every dress, every property, was perfect ; sixty choristers, and forty-two musicians ; the principal characters supported by Mr. Fraser, Mr. and Mrs. Seguin, Mr. Richings, Mrs. Breenton, and Miss Ince ; the subject of the libretto, the " Lady of Lyons,' the title of the opera, " Leonora." A great deal has been written and said about plagiarism, and want of originality of thought and execution : but I appeal to any musician, whether such an opera be not a creditable performance to a composer. Had Mr. Fry selected New York, instead of Philadelphia, for the first field of his operations, the whole United States would have teemed with praises—praises, long and loud, would have greeted the eye of the composer from all quarters. The sin he committed was daring to present the first lyrical drama ever composed in America to the citizens of Philadelphia for judgment, before the New Yorkers had an opportunity of passing upon its merits. Should it be played with success in Europe, how altered will be public opinion in its favour here ! Mr. Fry may plume upon it as a work of art, to be proudly cherished. I know no greater gratification, as a manager, than having been the means of placing it before his countrymen. It was acted sixteen nights, although the expense attending such a production, rendered it unproductive both to the author and the managers, the Seguins reaped both money and fame.

Of Mrs. Seguin's performance of Leonora, I can only say it was the most perfect thing I have ever seen, since Miss M. Tree's Zaidé, in Coleman's play of the " Law of Java," and I can hardly magnify such unqualified praise. On the last night, she was presented with a silver pitcher, bearing a suitable inscription—a well deserved compliment ; a similar one should have been made to Mr. Chubb, the leader of the orchestra of the Park Theatre, to whose aid much of its success was due.

The theatre closed on the 6th of July, never to open again, under Pratt and Wemyss. Our application for a renewal of the lease received no answer from the *gentlemen*, Mr. Evans, Gen. Cadwallader, Dr. Lehman, and Mr. Philips. We walked out, and Burton walked in, but to this moment we have not been informed by the gentlemen of the board, whether Mr. Burton was or was not their tenant.

Gentlemen are not bound by the common courtesies of life in their dealings with *vagabond play actors* —and why should they be ? They don't object to receive the player's money to swell their fortunes, by way of dividend, but treat him in all other respects like an outcast from society. Neither Mr. Pratt nor myself would have occupied the theatre at all, had we not expected the lease to have been renewed for the following year. It was a hopeless attempt for 1844-45, which we trusted 1845-46 would enable us to work upon. The stockholders had ample security for their rent, which, having received from our friends, justice to them, if not to us, required, at least, an answer to an application, and I may be permitted to add, the renewal at least for another year.

The Chestnut Street Theatre now changes hands every season. Better convert it, gentlemen, into stores, or into an hotel, it will pay you better ; while it stands, it will always be the theatre for foreign artists, without whose aid its doors must remain, as at present, *closed*. Burton says he lost there all he made by the Arch Street Theatre, and abandoned it at the end of the season. Marshall burnt his fingers with it. It might be made to pay as an Opera House, open, only for that purpose, a few weeks at a time ; but as a regular Temple of the Drama, its fate is sealed for ever.

The last act of kindness I received at the hands of my Philadelphia friends was a complimental benefit on the 19th of March, the proceeds of which were most serviceable. To that public to whom I am indebted for many acts of kindness, the last by no means the least,) which I still hope to enjoy, I submit the foregoing pages, and if a single individual has derived an hour's amusement from their perusal, I am repaid for the length of my task, and have but to add with pleasure,

Finis Coronat Opus.

H. L. M'Lane, Printer, Glasgow

WS - #0039 - 071123 - C0 - 229/152/18 - PB - 9780282008970 - Gloss Lamination